EC COMPETITION LAW IN THE TRANSPORT SECTOR

EC Competition Law in the Transport Sector

LUIS ORTIZ BLANCO
BEN VAN HOUTTE

CLARENDON PRESS · OXFORD
1996

Oxford University Press, Great Clarendon Street, Oxford OX2 6DP

Oxford New York
Athens Auckland Bangkok Bogota Bombay
Buenos Aires Calcutta Cape Town Dar es Salaam
Delhi Florence Hong Kong Istanbul Karachi
Kuala Lumpur Madras Madrid Melbourne
Mexico City Nairobi Paris Singapore
Taipei Tokyo Toronto
and associated companies in
Berlin Ibadan

Oxford is a trade mark of Oxford University Press

Published in the United States
by Oxford University Press Inc., New York

British Library Cataloguing in Publication Data
Data available

Library of Congress Cataloging in Publication Data
Ortiz Blanco, Luis.
EC Competition law in the transport sector / Luis Ortiz Blanco,
Ben van Houtte.
p.   cm.
Includes bibliographical references and index.
1. Transportation—Law and legislation—European Economic
Community countries.   2. Antitrust law—European Economic Community
countries. I. Houtte, Ben van, 1956-   . II. Title.
KJE6868.O78 1996   341.7'56'094—dc20 96-29006

ISBN 0-19-826089—X

1 3 5 7 9 10 8 6 4 2

Typeset by Hope Services (Abingdon) Ltd.
Printed in Great Britain
on acid-free paper by
Biddles Ltd.,
Guildford & King's Lynn

To Marta and Odette

Foreword

As commissioner responsible, first in the years 1989–93 for transport policy, and now for competition policy, I have had to devote much of my time to the subject matter of this book. It is an area where the European Commission's policy has really only taken off about ten years ago, and I have been fortunate to see it through to a stage approaching maturity. The emergence of competition in the transport industry is, I believe, one of the successes of the Delors era. The Commission's role in this process has been instrumental, from starting the debate by means of extensive consultations of industry and users, through many years of sometimes difficult political discussions, to the eventual adoption and application of legislation.

Luis Ortiz Blanco and Ben Van Houtte are well placed to describe this process. As two of the officials of the Commission's competition department, they were closely involved in the development of policy—the former in shipping, the second in aviation—and in the application of legislation in the years following its adoption. They combine exposure to the policy debate with experience of enforcement of the competition rules in this sector, and this background helps to make this book go beyond a simple legal analysis of the rules and decisions by injecting a wider perspective into this area and setting out an assessment of progress made.

The picture which emerges from this book is not always, I must add, a pretty one. It is clear that in the early days there was little political commitment outside the Commission to submit the transport sector to the discipline of competition. Member States and industry have resisted, at times fiercely, the development of a Community policy in this sector. As in some other sensitive areas, courageous decisions by the Court of Justice have helped to change this attitude. The Commission has had to proceed carefully, leave room for gradual implementation of competition rules and sometimes compromise the orthodoxy of the resulting legal framework. With the benefit of hindsight, however, these now look as almost minor blemishes. The application of the competition rules in transport cases is increasingly perceived as a routine matter which is not fundamentally different or more difficult than in other industries.

The authors have set out to draw a candid picture of the situation. They have not hidden the difficulties encountered while a competition policy for the sector developed, they make no secret of inconsistencies or gaps in the resulting legal framework. At the same time they provide a wealth of information on the interpretation of the substantive as well as procedural rules and on the relationship between the various legislative texts which apply to the different transport modes. The Commission's enforcement policy is extensively documented, and this will no doubt help practitioners and students understand the complexities of legislation and decision-making.

Karel Van Miert *Brussels, April 1996*

Foreword to the Spanish Edition

This book deals with a subject of great importance and one full of difficulties.

It is clear that the regulation of transport is an essential element in the effective establishment of a single market. It is also clear that free competition, as a fundamental principle of the single market in the European Union, must, with the necessary adaptations, constitute the abiding principle in the transport sector.

The ascendance of competition principles in transport has met and continues to meet with serious resistance in the European Union. Indeed, the transport sector has always been one of the most heavily regulated sectors in the Member States where regulation has ranged from restrictions on access to the market to the regulation of tariffs themselves. It goes without saying that invariably behind this regulation lies the wish to protect some important interests.

Possibly, however, it is not so much the protection of the interests of certain business concerns but more particularly the protection of the State's very own interests (interests represented by the public undertakings directly involved in the sector) which has caused the EU Member States' reluctance to apply fully the competition rules to transport.

These factors explain the slow and tortuous evolution which the application of competition rules has experienced in the EU transport sector.

This process of evolution of the competition rules can only adequately be analysed from the basis of a complete knowledge both of the EU common transport policy and of the competition rules flowing from the Treaty of Rome; and it should be recognised that both subjects, transport law and competition law, are sufficiently complex and significant to merit separate specific studies.

This book is therefore of great value and, moreover, extremely useful dealing, as it does, with both normative aspects of the application of EU competition rules in the transport sector.

However, the merit of this work does not lie merely in the difficulties or importance of the subject. It also lies in the way in which the analysis has been carried out. The authors, Luis Ortiz Blanco and Ben Van Houtte, are officials of the European Commission who have worked specifically in the Transport Division of DG IV on the application of competition rules in the transport sector. They, therefore, have a thorough knowledge of this subject, not only from a theoretical perspective but also in relation to the practical application of the rules.

One might be forgiven for thinking that it is simply this knowledge gained from their official responsibilites of applying the competition rules which the authors have brought to this work. That would be incorrect. A glance at the footnotes and the bibliography is enough to confirm the extensive and sound knowledge the authors have of the relevant doctrine in this area.

This profound doctrinal and practical knowledge not only makes for a complete analysis but also enables the authors to advance a critical appraisal of undoubted worth.

With all this, this book is destined to become a reference text, of absolute necessity for anyone concerned either with transport law or with the EU competition rules.

The conclusions drawn by the authors will certainly need to be taken into account in the evolution of Community law in this sector; an evolution which, moreover, will have to take place fairly quickly.

While it remains more expensive to travel by aeroplane between European capitals than between Europe and the United States, it will be difficult for the individual citizen to believe that the competition rules have been applied to transport in the European Union.

Alberto Bercovitz   *Madrid, November 1995*
Professor of Commercial law

Preface

This book has its origins in a series of notes which the authors drew up in English some time ago and which now, corrected, expanded and, above all, updated (in order to cover the period up until 1 March 1996) has gone to press. Chapters 1, 2, 3, 4 and 6 were written by Luis Ortiz Blanco. Ben Van Houtte wrote Chapter 5. Chapter 7 was co-written by the authors, each bringing together his conclusions on his corresponding section of the main text. The book is to a large extent the fruit of the authors' experience in handling cases within the Transport Unit of the Competition Directorate-General of the European Commission, DG IV.

Chapters 1, 4 and, in part, 7 were originally written in Spanish and translated by Adrian Melman. Francisco López, Kieron Beal and Chris Hutchins helped in the preparation of the English version of the book. Paul Hitchings and Trevor Soames took charge of the final version of the manuscript.

Alberto Bercovitz, John Temple Lang, Richard Lyal, Cora Zapico and Trevor Soames made valuable comments on various sections of the book. Helmuth Schröter, Eric Van Ginderachter and Berndt Langeheine will recognise some of their ideas in the text. Alain Alexis, as Joe Hennon, contributed not only his ideas but an abundant source of information. Hans Witt from DG IV, Sabine Klein and Pepa Michel, of the Commission Office in Madrid and the staff at the library for International Legal Studies (ILS) at Harvard Law School helped in the search for bibliographical material.

To all these people, the authors extend their most sincere thanks. The authors remain uniquely responsible for any errors or omissions that may be contained in this book and the opinions expressed are purely personal.

Brussels, March 1996.

Table of Contents

Abbreviations

ACE	Auto Car Europe
ACI	Allied Continental Intermodal Services Ltd
ANTIB	*Association Nationale des Travailleurs Indépendants de la Batellerie*
BAT	British American Tobacco
BIFFEX	Baltic International Freight Futures Exchange
BR	British Railways
CAI	Community of Automobile Interests
CCI	*Chambre de Commerce et d'Industrie*
CEWAL	Associated Central West Africa Lines
CFI	Court of First Instance
CMB	*Compagnie Maritime Belge*
CRS	computer reservation systems
CTP	common transport policy
DB	*Deutsche Bahn* (German Railways)
DSB	*Danske Statsbaner* (Danish national railway company)
DSVK	*Deutsche Seeverladerkomitees* (German Shippers' Council)
EAC	East African Conference
EATA	East Asia Trades Agreement
EATE	*Entreprise Artisanale de Transport par Eau*
ECAC	European Civil Aviation Conference
ECJ	European Court of Justice
EEA	European Economic Area
EFTA	European Free Trade Association
ENS	European Night Services
ERTA	European Agreement on Road Transport
FAS	free alongside ship
FEDER	European Development Fund
FEFC	Far Eastern Freight Conference
FETTSCA	Far East Trade Tariff Charges and Surcharges Agreement
FOB	free-on-board
GATS	General Agreement on Trade Services
GATT	General Agreement on Tariffs and Trade
GDP	gross domestic product
HOV-SVZ	*Havenondernemersvereniging SVZ*
IATA	International Air Transport Association
ICAO	International Civil Aviation Organization
ICG	Irish Continental Group
IMO	International Maritime Organization
ITU	intra-modal transport units
MCN	Maritime Container Network

MMC	Monopolies and Mergers Commission
NVO	Non-Vessel-Operating Carrier
OECD	Organization for Ecomomic Cooperation and Development
OEM	original equipment manufacturer
SFL	Scandinavian Ferry Lines
SNAT	*Société nouvelle d'armement transmanche*
SNCF	*Société Nationale des Chemins de Fer* (French Railways)
TAA	Trans-Atlantic Agreement
TACA	Trans-Atlantic Conference Agreement
TEU	Treaty on European Union
TOA	tolerated outsider agreement
TRIPS	Trade-Related Aspects of Intellectual Property Rights
TSA	Trans-Pacific Stabilization Agreement
UIC	*Union internationale des chemins de fer*
UIMP	*Universidad Menéndez Pelayo*
UIRR	*Union internationale rail-route*
UNCTAD	United Nations Conference on Trade and Development
WTO	World Trade Organization

Table of Cases

TABLE OF CASES BEFORE THE EUROPEAN COURT OF JUSTICE
AND THE COURT OF FIRST INSTANCE

(Alphabetical)

TABLE OF CASES BEFORE THE EUROPEAN COURT OF JUSTICE
AND THE COURT OF FIRST INSTANCE

(Numerical)

European Community Decisions and Communications

DECISIONS

COMMUNICATIONS

Table of EC Legislation

Treaties

Secondary Legislation

DECISIONS

DIRECTIVES

NOTICES

Table of Conventions and Agreements

Table of National Legislation

1

Transport and Transport Policy

1.1. THE TRANSPORT INDUSTRY[1]

Since the entry into force of the Treaty of Rome in 1958, the transport industry, faithful servant that it is, has undergone significant change in order to adapt to the growth and needs of international trade. The industry has, however, experienced only minor change since the start of the 1980s.

Perhaps the most striking change in Europe since the 1970s has been the spectacular increase in road transport, both of passengers—particularly in private vehicles—and of goods, and the parallel increase in infrastructure investments made necessary by this development. As a result, infrastructure policy, typical of post-war Europe, has seen a resurgence in recent years. Such a policy is justified now as it once was not only by the need to rely on better modes of transport, but also by the need to boost the economy during times of economic crisis. Recent manifestations of policy include the Channel Tunnel and the planned creation of trans-European networks (of motorways, seaways, combined transport, and others).

With regard to passenger transport, European railway investment has concentrated on developing fundamental new techniques and infrastructures, for example high-speed trains (TGV, Eurostar, AVE, etc.), to compete with other modes of transport. There has been a huge increase in air transport capacity for long-haul journeys and, consequently, maritime transport has been relegated to the short-haul ferry market.

In transportation of goods, road haulage has unleashed fierce competition to rail transport. The latter has not proved sufficiently versatile in adapting to the needs of industrial users, due in part perhaps to administrative burdens. Liner shipping has undergone a revolution comparable to the one occasioned by the introduction of steam engines in the middle of the last century, with the massive employment, since 1970, of containers in world trade.

In the European Union (EU), the transport industry currently represents around 4 per cent of the gross national product. If personal and private transport is also included, this figure lies between 7 per cent and 8 per cent. In 1991, employees in the transport sector constituted between 4 per cent and 5 per cent

[1] See the Commission's Communication to the Council entitled 'The future development of the common transport policy. A global approach to the construction of a Community framework for sustainable mobility'. Document COM (92) 494 of 2 Dec. 1992. This is published also as Supp. 3/93 of the *Bulletin of the European Communities*. See in particular paras 10–34.

of waged labour. In absolute terms this amounted to 5.6 million people: 2,509,000 of whom were employed in road haulage, 897,000 in rail transport, 24,000 in inland waterway transport, 217,000 in maritime transport, 349,000 in air transport and 1,569,000 in related activities.

The transport equipment industry—which directly employs 2.6 million people—is one of the main EU industrial sectors. Its volume of sales is surpassed only by the food industry. Its largest section is the motor vehicles industry (over 75 per cent)[2] followed by the aerospace industry (14 per cent) and—further behind—shipbuilding and the rail materials industry. Its rôle as one of the catalysts of economic growth in Europe is further reinforced by the fact that the transport equipment industry is one of the main customers of other basic industrial sectors, such as the iron and steel industry, mechanical engineering and electrical and chemical industries.

The transport sector is a growth industry in the EU. The demand in the industry is generally proportionate to gross domestic product (GDP). Taking the average annual economic growth in the EU since 1970 as 2.6 per cent, the growth in goods transport services has been 2.3 per cent and passenger transport services 3.1 per cent. It should be noted, however, that the increase has not been uniform for the different modes of transport, or with respect to passengers and goods.

Freight transport activities have increased over the last twenty years by more than 50 per cent. This has been above all by road, the growth of which has more than doubled in absolute terms and amounts at the present time to around 70 per cent of the overall sector's activity. Rail transport has decreased by 15 per cent in absolute terms, and its share of the total of goods transport activities has dropped from 28 per cent to 15 per cent. Inland waterway transport, despite slight growth, has seen its relative weight in the freight transport sector reduced by one third and stands at 9 per cent. Following a pattern similar to inland waterway transport, transport by oil pipelines has grown marginally in absolute terms, but decreased in relative terms to 6 per cent of the total activity in the sector.

Maritime transport is of paramount importance in terms of tonnage for the longest, fundamentally international routes. At present, approximately 95 per cent of international trade in goods is carried by sea. From 1975 to 1985, the volume of transported goods grew by approximately 35 per cent. Since 1985, there has been stagnation in the market, but it has been estimated that ocean-going trade will increase again at a rate of 2.1 per cent per annum to the year 2000.[3]

---

[2] It has been calculated that one out of 10 jobs in the EU depends, directly or indirectly, on the motor vehicles sector.

[3] Figures taken from *EEC Maritime Industries*, Report of Moore Stephens, Accountants, 1989. Cited in *New challenges for maritime industries*, Commission Communication to the Council, European Parliament and Economic and Social Committee. Document COM (91) 335 of 14 Oct. 1991, p. 4.

The Union's substantial participation in international trade depends almost entirely on maritime transport services: around 90 per cent of foreign trade and 33 per cent of trade between Member States is shipped by sea.[4] The proportion is far smaller in the case of Member States' domestic trade. It is calculated that only between 2 per cent and 3 per cent of goods originating from and destined to consignor and consignee in the same Member State are shipped by sea.[5]

In respect of passenger transport, travel expenses account for 15 per cent of private consumers' expenditure and an average of 2 per cent of the expenditure of undertakings and governments.[6] Transport activity has increased by more than 85 per cent over the last twenty years, due chiefly to the increased use of private motor cars, which has doubled in absolute terms, accounting now for 79 per cent of the total. Rail transport has increased by approximately 25 per cent in absolute terms, but its relative importance has diminished, from approximately 10 per cent to between 6 per cent and 7 per cent of the total passenger transport. Similarly, coach transport increased in absolute terms by 45 per cent, but the proportion it represents within passenger transport fell 3 per cent to below 9 per cent.

Air transport currently accounts for 6 per cent of passenger transport, even though it has quadrupled in the last twenty years, and continues to spiral upwards. Air passenger transport is expected to continue growing at a rate above the rate of growth of GDP. This is a result of the ever-increasing commercial links between the various EU countries, and between the latter and non-member countries: a change in holiday habits: a higher level of available income: and the high elasticity of demand in these tourist services.

Nevertheless, the industrial importance of transport is much less than its importance as a basic factor of production in other industrial sectors and, above all, as an indispensable auxiliary activity which sustains the whole of international trade. Transport constitutes a very sizeable part of the costs of manufacturing industries and the price of end-products. An up-to-date, efficient and competitive system of transport is the best guarantee that all types of products reach their markets at the most suitable price and with the highest service quality conditions. Transport is, therefore, the essential link which ties the EU to the world economy.

However, the importance of transport services goes beyond the purely economic. Transport is the binding link which brings together people and products from all European regions, above all the remoter regions.

---

[4] Erdmenger, J., 'Developments and prospects of the maritime transport law of the European Communities', *European Transport Law*, Vol. 23, No. 5. 1988, pp. 543–555, at p. 543.

[5] European Commission, *The future development of the common transport policy*, above n. 1, at para. 14.

[6] Ehlermann, C.D., 'Liberalization and EC competition policy in the transport sector'. A paper presented by C.D. Ehlermann, former Dir. Gen. for competition in the Commission, to the Universidad Menéndez Pelayo (UIMP) Seminar on 'Transport and communications: market or regulation?' Santander, 13 July 1992.

The integration of Member States' transport systems has been developing along with their economic integration, and technical and regulatory barriers have been gradually abolished, albeit more slowly than a climate of greater political co-operation within the EU would have permitted.

1.2. THE COMMON TRANSPORT POLICY AND THE EC TREATY

When the Treaty of Rome entered into force in 1958, the Europe of the Six was a continental block which contained at least four national markets (if one takes the Benelux market as one). The focus of attention was on modes of inland transport: rail, road, and inland waterway transport. Title IV of Part Two of the Treaty was devoted to transport. There were eleven articles in total (from Article 74 to Article 84) and only one paragraph in one of those articles for maritime and air transport (Article 84(2)).[7]

The successive enlargements of the Community changed this situation dramatically. The advent of nine, ten, twelve, and, finally, fifteen Member States meant, first, new national markets had to be integrated into a single market; secondly, in the new Community geography, maritime, and air transport held places of equivalent importance to the three modes of inland transport; thirdly, and particularly with the accession of new southern Member States, transport infrastructures became a key element for economic growth in those areas.[8]

Transport policy is one of the three original common policies of the Community. Because of its central importance for the integration of all the peoples and national economies of the EU,[9] its importance is comparable to the Customs Union. The transport provisions of the Treaty, however, do not establish common principles upon which a transport policy for the Community may be implemented. They only provide for a procedure whereby the Council has to adopt the guidelines for such a common transport policy. It has been said that the reason for this was that when the European Communities were formed, there was little or no consensus on the direction or content of a transport policy. Consequently, no common position could be formulated. This is probably due to the specificities of the transport sector. These specifics are more administrative than economic.[10]

---

[7] Following the entry into force of the TEU the amended Arts 74–84 are to be found in Title IV of Part Three of the EC Treaty.

[8] The way in which the last of these enlargements will influence the future common transport policy is hard to anticipate. In its formative phase, and in the last years of its emergence (which are the phases being reviewed here), only the countries of the Europe of the Twelve have had a decisive influence.

[9] For the Community transport policy in general, see the bibliography at the end of this work.

[10] See Kapteyn, P.J.G., and Verloren Van Themaat, P., *Introduction to the Law of the European Communities*, edition produced by L.W. Gormley (Graham & Trotman, London, 1991) Ch. X.3. See also *Butterworths Competition Law* (Butterworths, London, 1992), pp. IX/169 *et seq.*

1.3. DIFFERENT APPROACHES TO THE COMMON TRANSPORT POLICY

Transport in the EU was—and to a large extent still is—characterized by a great measure of governmental intervention and a confused network of bilateral and multilateral inter-state agreements in which the Member States used to and still do participate.[11] One of the elements of national transport policy was for Member States to support their own carriers and protect them from international competition.

The transport sector is one of the few sectors in which the majority of the fundamental principles of the Community have not been implemented or, at least, have only been applied after enormous delay. Amongst them figures most significantly the freedom to provide services. The basic reason for the delay in the principle being applied in transport was the apparent direct inapplicability of Article 59 of the Treaty in transport matters. As the Court held for the first time in its judgment in the *French Seamen* case, Article 61(1) of the EEC Treaty established a special exemption from the general rules of the Treaty relating to the freedom to provide services in transport matters.[12] Article 75 of the Treaty, in turn, provided that, within the framework of the common transport policy, the Council would have to establish 'the conditions under which non-resident carriers may operate transport services within a Member State'.[13] By virtue of Article 84(1), this provision is only applicable to transport by rail, road, or inland waterways. With reference to maritime and air transport, Article 84(2) of the Treaty conferred upon the Council the power to 'decide whether, to what extent, and by what procedure appropriate provisions may be laid down for sea and air transport'. From the whole of these provisions one could interpret, as the Court expressly did after 1986, that the principle of freedom to provide services was not directly applicable to maritime and air transport—nor to inland transport—except if, and on such terms as the Council decides.[14] [15] Advances

[11] See Kapteyn and Verloren Van Themaat cited in *Butterworths Competition Law*, above n. 10, at para. 287.

[12] See judgment of the ECJ in Case 167/73, *Commission* v. *France*, [1974] ECR 359. For a commentary on this, see *infra* Ch. 2. According to Art. 61(1) of the Treaty: 'Freedom to provide services in the field of transport shall be governed by the provisions of the Title relating to transport'.

[13] Art. 75(1)(b) of the Treaty.

[14] See, in particular, the Judgments of the ECJ in Joined Cases 209–213/84, *Ministère Public* v. *Lucas Asjès ('Nouvelles Frontières')*, [1986] ECR 1425 at p. 1457, at para. 37; in Case 4/88, *Lambregts* v. *Belgium*, [1989] E.C.R. 2583, at paras 8 and 9; and in Case C–49/89, *Corsica Ferries France* v. *Direction Générale des Douanes Françaises*, [1989] ECR 4441, at paras 10–13.

[15] Although it might also have been interpreted that, specifically in matters of maritime and air transport, and given the inapplicability of the transport Title to these two methods, Art. 61(1) of the EEC Treaty referred not to Art. 75 (applicable exclusively to inland transport) but to the general rules of the Treaty (in this case, Art. 59), as the ECJ then explicitly ruled in respect of the competition rules. See Kuyper, P. J., 'Legal problems of a Community transport policy with special reference to air transport', *Legal Issues of European Integration*, No. 2, 1985, pp. 65–85, especially pp. 72–5. The Court's pre-emptive decision in the *French seamen* case, virtually in the form of an *obiter dictum*,

in freedom of transport services were thus left subject to the will of the Council which, even now in early 1996, maintains specific restrictions on the full and unconditional application of this basic principle of the EC in most forms of transport.[16]

The absence of interest in creating a single transport market and the differences of opinion between the Member States have their roots in history and geography.[17] The Benelux countries, due to their small size, have developed transport by road or inland waterway for bulkier goods to a greater extent, while in France and Germany, where the distances are greater, rail has been given priority, and measures have been taken to limit the long-distance transport of goods by road. Italy has also made great railway investments to foster the development of their southern regions. The remainder of the Community countries have developed road transport as a priority. These differences in the structure of the national transport systems have meant that, in order to reach a common policy, the conflicts of interest between Member States have had to be overcome.

Therefore, transport policy has had a slow start. The debate between the Member States has centred on whether harmonization of the conditions of competition should precede liberalization or vice versa and on whether the adoption of measures in the various sectors of interest would have to be made on a case-by-case basis or as part of an overall plan.

With respect to transport by road, rail, and inland waterways, Benelux adopted a favourable stance to the freedom to provide services within the single market, whilst Germany and Italy laid stress on the need to harmonize the conditions of competition, before opening up national markets to foreign competition, in order to protect their own transport undertakings.

In maritime transport, the United Kingdom, Denmark, and Greece have been the most ardent defenders of freedom of navigation. In the case of Greece, its generally liberal stance has not prevented it maintaining protectionist points of view with respect to cabotage traffic to and from its numerous islands, on grounds of national security. France, Germany, Belgium, and Italy, with far smaller fleets, have adopted a generally more protectionist stance. Spain and Portugal further reinforced this tendency when they joined the Communities. The accession of Austria, Finland and Sweden has won over followers to the liberal faction.[18]

had fundamental consequences on the development—or, rather, the paralysis—of EC transport policy in all sectors. One could have imagined that, if upon the completion of the single market at the end of 1992 the Member States had failed to agree on a reasonable timetable for the application of the principle of freedom to provide services in the maritime and air transport sectors, the ECJ could have rectified its earlier jurisprudence and ruled the principle applicable in those sectors.

[16] As will be seen, the timetables agreed for the liberalization of maritime cabotage and certain forms of inland transport on some occasions go far beyond the year 2000.

[17] See Erdmenger, J., *Vers une politique des transports pour l'Europe*, (RTL Editions, Brussels, 1984).

[18] This very brief summary undoubtedly is apt to be simplistic. Each Member State maintains a particular stance for each particular matter, and thus a generally protectionist country may be tremendously liberal at times and vice versa.

The differences between the Member States' points of view in relation to air transport have been minor since the majority of them were in favour of reserving one half of air traffic for their own companies and not allowing access to their national markets by companies from other Member States. The only exceptions to this rule are in the United Kingdom, where there are no public companies in the sector and, to a lesser extent, the Netherlands and the Nordic and Scandinavian Community countries.

Only the years and the gradual assumption of national competences by Community policy have contributed to reducing the differences between the more liberal and the more regulatory and restrictive countries.

1.4. THREE PHASES OF THE COMMON TRANSPORT POLICY

1.4.1. First phase (1958–1973/74)

The first phase of Community transport policy runs from the entry into force of the Treaty of Rome to 1973/74. During this phase, the EC, guided by the Commission, concentrated almost exclusively on attempting to create a common market for transport by road, rail, and inland waterways, opening up national markets to competition between carriers from all the Member States. The Commission formulated its ideas in a 1961 Memorandum[19] and in a 1962 Action Programme,[20] which got a cool reception in the Member States.

Given that the provisions of the Treaty were not explicit as to what it should contain, and that the Member States did not appear very disposed to create a common transport services market, the first phase of the common transport policy (CTP) evolved amidst discussions between the Commission and the Member States over the interpretation of the Treaty.[21]

1.4.2. Second phase (1973/74–1983/85)

In 1973, at the end of the first phase, the accession of Denmark, Ireland, and the United Kingdom to the EC introduced more liberal, and less land-centred, views into a stagnating transport policy.

In October 1973, the Commission re-defined its strategy with regard to the Member States in a Communication to the Council on the development of the CTP.[22] The Commission stopped putting forward an overall liberalizing policy

---

[19] *Mémorandum sur l'orientation à donner à la politique commune des transports.* Document VII/COM (61) 50 final, of 10 Apr. 1961.

[20] *Programme d'action en matière de politique commune des transports.* For the first steps of the Common Transport Policy, see Pinay, P., 'Règles de concurrence et transports dans le cadre de la C.E.E.', *Annuaire Français de Droit International,* Vol. 8, 1962, pp. 781–805, at pp. 783–786.

[21] See below, Chs 2 and 3, Section I.

[22] Commission Communication to the Council on the development of the common transport policy, Document COM (73) 1725 final, of 24 Oct. 1973, and Supp. 16/73 of the *Bulletin CE.*

through the rapid dismantling of barriers on entry to the national transport markets. Instead, and despite continuing to emphasize the need to apply the principle of free provision of services in the sector, it adopted the more cautious stance of accepting what was on offer from the Member States, on a case-by-case basis, and centred its efforts on the harmonization of conditions of competition.

On the other hand, in 1974, two fundamental events took place for the development of the CTP in the maritime and air transport sectors: the Court gave judgment in the *French Seamen* case,[23] and, under the auspices of the United Nations, the United Nations conference on Trade and Development (UNCTAD) Code of Conduct for Liner Conferences was adopted.[24]

Despite the Court's support for its arguments and the ways opened up for the development of a transport policy for all modes of transport, the Commission continued channelling its efforts into inland transport. It secured the adoption by the Council of a series of technical regulations which did not really encompass the CTP's true objective: namely, to obtain the creation of a single market by applying the principle of freedom to provide transport services in the Member States.

1.4.3. Third phase (1983/85–1993)

From 1983 onwards, the Commission presented various proposals for a structured development of the CTP, in several memoranda concerning the inland (1983), air (1984)[25] and maritime (1985) sectors.[26]

Subsequently, the fact that the Council had not adopted minimum measures to ensure freedom to provide inland transport services between Member States, nor adopted conditions in which a Community carrier would be allowed to carry out inland cabotage operations in countries other than his own, induced the European Parliament to bring proceedings for failure to act against the Council, pursuant to Article 175 of the Treaty.[27] Although this ruling concerned inland transport only, its consequences were also felt in the other modes of transport.[28]

A second crucial event in this period was the adoption and entry into force of the Single European Act in July 1986.[29] The Act represented the Member

---

[23] See above n. 12.   [24] On these two events, see below, Ch. 2.

[25] Back in 1979, the Commission prepared an air memorandum, but with little success. See below.

[26] See below for these memoranda.

[27] See the judgment of the ECJ in Case 13/83, *European Parliament* v. *Council of the European Communities*, [1985] ECR 1513.

[28] It took some time for the Council to react adequately to this judgment. In Case C–17/90, *Pindud Wieger* v. *Bundesanstalt für den Güterfernverkehr*, [1991] ECR I–5253, the plaintiff argued that the reasonable period of time for liberalizing transport services referred to by the ECJ in Case 13/83 had lapsed. The Council narrowly escaped a decision that it had failed to comply with the Court's first judgment. For discussion on this case-law see the Comment of Slot, P.J., in *Common Market Law Review*, Vol. 29, No. 4, Aug. 1992, pp. 807–813.

[29] The main modification introduced by the Single European Act was the introduction of qualified majority voting instead of unanimity in many matters. It also established that the procedure for

States' political agreement to complete the internal market by no later than 1 January 1993. Many of the advances which occurred in maritime and air transport in 1986 and 1987, and the 1988 agreement to liberalize the inland transport market then followed. Beforehand, none of the Commission's proposals had been received with the slightest enthusiasm by the Member States.

The Community then embarked on a process of liberalization which, guided by the Commission, sought to create greater opportunities for commercial initiatives in transport within the Community. The years since 1985 have witnessed a phenomenal proliferation of EC legislation. This has been pre-eminently directed to unleashing competitive forces and to winning, sector by sector, transport markets over to competition.

1.5. DEVELOPMENT OF THE INLAND COMMON TRANSPORT POLICY[30]

It has taken thirty years to reach the first agreements on the liberalization of the transport market on a Community scale, and some agreements still have to be reached before the Single Market becomes a reality in some specific sectors.[31] Such immobility in such a dynamic sector is surprising.[32] The lack of the CTP's thrust in transport is due both to the great differences between the governing legislation of the Member States and to the importance of the interests at stake. The first attempt to create an overall policy for inland transport goes back to 1983 when the Commission presented to the Council its Memorandum on inland transport, the first of a series of three relating to the different modes of transport.[33]

1.5.1. Road transport

The fundamentally national nature of road transport in the early days of its development meant that the majority of Member States adopted measures without giving thought to their neighbours. Generally, public restrictions on transport activity were implemented by limiting access to the market, fixing tariffs, imposing tax charges to recover infrastructure expenses, and requiring the

the adoption of measures in the sea and air transport sectors would be the procedure in Art. 75 of the Treaty. (This is the procedure for the adoption of measures in inland transport). In this way, the Single European Act put an end to the procedural vagueness of the first version of Art. 84(2) of the Treaty.

[30] See Degli Abbati, C., *Transport and European Integration*, Office for Official Publications of the EC. Luxembourg, 1987.

[31] In particular in cabotage and passenger transport. See below.

[32] See Dawson, R., and Renaux, G., (Eds), *EEC Transport Policy*, (study written by the Club de Bruxelles under the direction of Reginald Dawson and Geneviève Renaux) (Club de Bruxelles. Brussels, 1989) at p. 12.

[33] The Memorandum on inland transport was published as Document COM (83) 58 final, of 9 Feb. 1983.

satisfaction of certain technical requirements (for vehicles) and professional requirements (for drivers). All of these factors are to be found nowadays in the inland CTP.

Originally, these measures were intended to limit the effects of road transport competition on rail transport and served as protection to national carriers already established who, until the 1960s, did not generally have to face competition from carriers from other countries.

With the creation of the European Communities, exposure to external competition became a worrying risk and the national carriers' protectionist interests manifested themselves in a distinct lack of progress in the CTP. The differences between Member States with regard to the treatment of the weights and dimensions of vehicles, technical controls, social regulations, qualifications for joining the profession and tax treatment surfaced clearly and served to block any form of integration.

The number of Community measures in these areas has increased dramatically. Once the illusion that a rapid liberalization would be achieved was lost and in the absence of areas in which the Member States would have been more receptive to its proposals, the Commission moved the emphasis of transport policy—which until the mid-80s focused almost purely on inland transport—to the harmonization of conditions of competition. Harmonization has now been largely accomplished for conditions of access to the carrier's profession[34] and for technical issues[35] and social matters.[36]

Tax harmonization has been far harder to achieve and remains limited. In 1991, an initial agreement was reached to harmonize the level of taxation on road diesel oil but it was only in 1993 that the first measures were adopted to harmonize taxes on vehicles and the toll system on motorways. Thus, a system for charging non-resident carriers the cost of using the infrastructures was devised.[37]

Beyond harmonization, even in areas of great commercial significance, the task of achieving a still incomplete common market, has also been arduous.

Council Regulation 11 of 1960[38] was the first measure of any relevance adopted in the sphere of inland transport.[39] It derives directly from Article 79

---

[34] See Council Reg. (EEC) 3572/90, OJ 1990 L 353, p. 12, which consolidates and amends in some respects the provisions in force on the matter, in particular Council Dirs 74/561/EEC and 74/562/EEC, regarding admission to the occupation of road haulier and to the occupation of road transport operator in national and international transport operations.

[35] Relating, *inter alia*, to tyres, suspension, brakes, weights and dimensions of international transport vehicles, technical control of vehicles, road safety (safety belts, speed limiters, transport of hazardous goods, etc.) and to environmental protection (exhaust emissions).

[36] Such as, e.g., the age and qualifications of drivers of industrial vehicles and periods of driving and rest.

[37] Council Dir. 93/89/EEC, OJ 1993 L 279, p. 32.

[38] OJ 1962, 52, p. 1121, Spec. Ed. Series I (1959–1962), p. 60.

[39] Despite being treated here in the context of road transport, Reg. 11 applies to inland transport in its entirety.

of the Treaty of Rome. Both the Treaty and the regulation prohibit discrimination in tariffs and conditions of transport on the basis of the country of origin or destination of the goods. The original intention of both was also to bring an end to the tariffs supporting national carriers. These are prohibited by Article 80 of the Treaty. Member States could use direct subsidies to transport undertakings instead; a substitute which is more effective, less discriminatory, and more susceptible to direct control by the Commission.

Another key measure during the first stage of the common inland transport policy was Council Regulation 1017/68.[40] This was the first of the competition regulations derived from Regulation 141, (the regulation which excluded transport services from the application of Regulation 17).[41]

Together with this regulation, the regulations which best illustrate the development of the inland CTP towards liberalization and unification of the Community market are the ones relating, on the one hand, to non-resident carriers' access to national markets in international transport and cabotage and, on the other, to the system of pricing in transport.

With reference to access to the goods transport market, 'Community quotas' for permits were established with effect from 1968. These gave their holders the right to provide transport services between any pair of Community countries. Cabotage, in other words the provision of transport services within a single Member State by a carrier from another Member State was prohibited, or subject to numerous restrictions, in almost all of the Member States.

Community quotas for international transport were small to start with,[42] but they became bigger with time. In 1988,[43] it was decided to abolish the quota system for transport between Member States and for traffic in transit to non-Member States as from 1 January 1993. In their place, a system of Community licences granted on the basis of qualitative criteria was to be instituted.[44]

Finally, with regard to cabotage within a single Member State, the Council also introduced in 1989, by way of an initial and limited measure of liberalization, a system of Community quotas.[45] In October 1993, the original number of permits was raised to 30,000 for 1994, and it was agreed that this number would increase every year by 30 per cent as from 1995, until all-round liberalization of the market in 1998.[46] Several aspects deserve comment. First, this belated agreement came after 1 January 1993 and its effect is delayed until 1998. Secondly, it will not achieve creation of the Single Market in road transport.

---

[40] OJ 1968 L 175, p. 1, Spec. Ed. Series I (1968[I], p. 302. Reg. 1017/68, like Reg. 11, is applicable not only to road transport, but also to rail and maritime transport.

[41] On all these regulations, see below, Ch. 2.

[42] Initially 1,200 permits, pursuant to Council Reg. (EEC) 1018/68, OJ 1968 L 175, p. 13.

[43] Council Reg. (EEC) 1841/88 (OJ 1988 L 163, p. 1), amending Council Reg. (EEC) 3164/76 (OJ 1976 L 357, p. 1).

[44] This was done by means of Council Reg. (EEC) 881/92, OJ 1992 L 95, p. 1.

[45] Council Reg. (EEC) 4059/89, OJ 1989 L 390, p. 3.

[46] Council Reg. (EEC) 3118/93, OJ 1993 L 279, p. 1.

Finally, it was only possible due to the aforementioned agreement between the Member States on the various excise and duties which non-national Community carriers could be charged for the use of their infrastructures.[47] The agreement also sought to harmonize the operating costs borne by the carriers from the various Member States so as to avoid unfair competition (thereby satisfying Germany's repeated request).

As far as the pricing system on the transport market is concerned, tariff bands (*tarifs à fourchette*, or bracket tariffs) were commonplace from 1968 until very recently. They dictated the maximum and minimum levels between which tariffs for international goods transport had to be fixed. The tariffs would be negotiated between Member States and the Commission would arbitrate in case of dispute.[48] This system was abolished in January 1990, when pricing was liberalized.[49]

The first steps towards the creation of a Community market in passenger transport were taken in March and July 1992.[50] In fact only non-scheduled services in international traffic and certain services with accommodation included have been liberalized. Scheduled services have not been liberalized. The opening-up of national markets is even more restricted for types of cabotage. As can be appreciated, advances towards liberalization in passenger markets have occurred very belatedly and cautiously. True liberalization has been considerably delayed.[51]

1.5.2. Rail transport[52]

Railways did not appear to provide a solid foundation for integration and liberalization at a Community level since a real international rail transport market did not *de facto* exist, there being merely a juxtaposition of national markets in which the railway companies exercised a *de jure* monopoly. European railways, with their governments' international support, and with their own private mechanisms of co-ordination (such as the International Railway Union, UIC, or the Community of European Railways) appeared impermeable to Community initiatives. Intervention nevertheless became necessary eleven years after the entry into force of the Treaty. With the object of curbing the enormous deficit accumulated by railway companies, in 1969 the Council adopted certain common

[47] See *supra*, n. 37.

[48] Council Reg. (EEC) 1174/68, OJ 1968 L 194, p. 1. Prices could vary within a band of 23 per cent below the maximum tariff, with certain exceptions.

[49] Council Reg. (EEC) 4058/89, OJ 1989 L 390, p. 1.

[50] Council Reg. (EEC) 684/92, OJ 1992 L 74, p. 1, on international passenger transport, and Council Reg. (EEC) 2454/92, OJ 1992 L 251, p. 1, on the conditions under which non-resident carriers may operate road passenger transport services within a Member State.

[51] The two regulations just cited provide that before the end of 1995, the Commission shall report to the Council on the implementation of this regulation, and may propose new liberalizing measures.

[52] See Bauchet, P., and Rathery, A., 'La politique communautaire des transports', *Problèmes Politiques et Sociaux*, Paris, No. 712, 8 Oct. 1993, pp. 1–67, pp. 25 *et seq.*

rules for the normalization of the accounts of railway undertakings[53] and provisions relating to Member State action with regard to public service obligations.[54] These texts and others[55] aim to improve the transparency of economic benefits granted by Member States to their railways by creating clear accounting procedures and to ensure that the railways receive an equitable reward for public service contributions.

The most important advance in the EC railway policy took place in 1991 with the adoption of Council Directive 91/440/EEC, on the development of European railways.[56] The objective of the Directive is to help EC railway companies adapt to the Single Market and increase their efficiency, by granting them management independent of the State; separating management of railway operation and infrastructure from the provision of transport services; improving the economic structure of undertakings and permitting access to the Member States' national networks by international groups of railway undertakings and by railway undertakings engaged in combined international transport.

The promotion of the combined transport of goods[57] is precisely one of the CTP's objectives in the inland sector. Various Community measures have been targeted at the promotion of combined transport since 1975 when it was agreed to free it from the quota system, on condition that maximum use was made of rail, and that transport units (containers, trailers, semi-trailers) were loaded and unloaded at the railway stations closest to the points of origin and destination.[58]

Another of the Community priorities in the railway sector is the creation of a high-speed railway network, with the aim of uniting the main European capitals in the 21st century. This calls for the co-ordinated effort of all the Member States to meet the substantial investments in the infrastructures required.

1.5.3. Inland Waterway Transport[59]

The main inland waterway transport market problems in the Community relate to the excess and fragmentation of supply. Community policy has been to try to

---

[53] Council Reg. (EEC) 1192/69, OJ 1969 L 156, p. 8, Spec. Ed. Series I (1969[I]), p. 283.

[54] Council Reg. (EEC) 1191/69, OJ 1969 L 156 p. 1, Spec. Ed. Series I (1969[I]), p. 276, as amended by Council Reg. (EEC) 1893/91, OJ 1991 L 169, p. 1.

[55] In subsequent years, the Council adopted one decision and three regulations relating to State aid, re-organization of undertakings and the harmonization of regulations governing their relations with Member States, accounting and annual accounts, and calculation of railway companies' costs.

[56] OJ 1991 L 237, p. 25. On this see the important article by Alexis, A., 'Transports ferroviaires et concurrence. Les principaux apports de la Directive 91/440' *European Transport Law*, Vol. 28, No. 4, 1993, pp. 499–516.

[57] In the Community context, combined transport means transport which is carried out by using two or more means of inland transport, e.g. rail and road transport, or inland waterway transport and road transport. Multimodal transport refers to transport in which various modes of transport are connected, e.g. air and inland, or maritime and inland transport. The latter (maritime/inland) is multimodal transport (or, in North American terminology 'intermodal') *simpliciter*.

[58] Dir. 75/130/EEC, OJ 1975 L 48, p. 31. This Directive has been amended on many occasions to date. [59] See Bauchet and Rathery, above n. 52, p. 30.

eliminate capacity surpluses, and to carry through the re-conversion of the sector which involves numerous independent waterway carriers and small-business
undertakings. Community action has been restricted by the existence of the
Mannheim Convention which, since 1868, has regulated navigation conditions
on the Rhine. The Convention introduced total freedom of navigation on this
North European trade artery, in whose waters two-thirds of the total
Community inland waterway traffic is carried. Another obstacle to the development of an inland waterway CTP has been the opposition of the Netherlands to
Community initiatives. This country did not want to change the organization of
a market which has been highly favourable to the interests of the Port of
Rotterdam and Dutch carriers, undoubtedly the most powerful in Europe.

In 1989, the Commission managed to persuade the Council to address structural reform and the liberalization of the inland waterway transport market. In
April 1989, the Council decided to adopt measures for the restructuring of the
sector with an eye to reducing the surplus capacity by means of a scrapping
process co-ordinated at a Community level. This was done through the establishment of specific bonuses and an 'old-for-new' replacement system which
makes the commissioning of new barges contingent on the scrapping of an
equivalent cargo capacity or on the payment of a special fee. The object is to
deter carriers from increasing their capacity.[60]

In December 1991, the Council finally agreed on a regulation fixing the conditions of non-resident carriers' access to national inland waterway markets in
the Community and resolved the outstanding issue of the right of cabotage for
Community carriers in any Community country. This system entered into force
in January 1993, with certain exceptions in place until 1995.[61]

1.5.4. Infrastructures and Trans-European Networks[62]

In terms of infrastructure, the bulk of Community efforts logically concentrate
on the infrastructures of inland transport in its various forms. The attention paid
to seaports and airports has also been significant and important but, in economic
terms, the investments made in them represent a far lower percentage than that
devoted to inland transport infrastructures.

In the 1980s, and despite increasing demand for transport, investments in
transport infrastructures in Europe, expressed as a percentage of the GDP, fell
to the present figure of 1 per cent. In 1989, investments in infrastructures for
road transport accounted for around 66 per cent of the total, investments for rail
transport 23 per cent, investments relating to inland waterways 1.5 per cent, sea
ports 3.5 per cent and airports 5.6 per cent.

---

[60] Council Reg. (EEC) 1101/89, OJ 1991 L 116, p. 25.
[61] Council Reg. (EEC) 3921/91, OJ 1991 L 373, p. 1.
[62] See Commission communication 'The future development of the common transport policy
. . .', above n. 1, paras 18 and 19, Dawson and Renaud, above n. 32, pp. 34–35 and 134 *et seq.*,
and Bauchet and Rathery, above n. 52, pp. 34–37.

The increase in the demand for transport and the relative fall in investment in infrastructure has put major pressure on the capacity of road and railway networks, which have at some levels reached saturation point. Not even increases in investment in airports (from 2.9 per cent of the total in 1980 to 5.6 per cent in 1989) have been sufficient to put an end to airport congestion; however, this is also due in part to the rather unsatisfactory air control mechanisms in Europe.

The Commission's interest in infrastructures dates from its 1961 Memorandum on the general tack of transport policy. Following a difficult initial period, during which Member States showed little enthusiasm to collaborate in a co-ordination procedure which had been set up in 1969, the Council accepted in 1978 the Commission's 1976 proposal for the creation of an Infrastructures Committee.[63] Even before this, the Commission had presented proposals to the Council for the Community-wide adoption of measures for the planning, financing and charging of utilization costs of infrastructures.

The first Community action regarding infrastructure planning took shape belatedly. First, at the end of 1990, a rail network for high-speed trains was devised. Subsequently—pursuant to Articles 129B and 129C of the EC Treaty[64]—a regulation[65] and three decisions relating to the establishment of trans-European networks for combined transport,[66] motorways,[67] and inland waterways[68] were adopted.

The Commission has always been in favour of granting economic support to projects with Community interest and of creating a specific permanent instrument for this purpose. Since the mid-1970s, the Commission has presented various proposals to the Council resulting in several programmes for the financing of short-term and medium-term infrastructures. Additionally, in November 1990, the Council established an action programme for the transport infrastructure.[69] Aside from this specific programme, the Cohesion Funds—created for Greece, Spain, Ireland, and Portugal under Article 130D of the EC Treaty, as a result of the entry into force of the Treaty on European Union (TEU)—and the European Development Fund (FEDER) will also be used to finance infrastructure projects.

The thorniest problem for the liberalization of road transport, charging for the costs of using infrastructures, has only been resolved recently,[70] and then only partially. The Commission continues to gear its proposals towards resolution of this problem.

---

[63] Council Decision 78/174/EEC, OJ 1978 L 54, p. 16.
[64] These articles were added to the original text of the EEC Treaty by the TEU.
[65] Council Reg. (EEC) 1738/93, OJ 1993 L 161, p. 4.
[66] Dec. 93/628/EEC, OJ 1993 L 305, p. 1.
[67] Dec. 93/629/EEC, OJ 1993 L 305, p. 11.
[68] Dec. 93/630/EEC, OJ 1993 L 305, p. 39.
[69] Council Reg. (EEC) 3359/90, OJ 1990 L 326, p. 1.
[70] See above the section relating to tax harmonization and Council Dir. 93/89/EEC.

1.6. DEVELOPMENT OF THE MARITIME COMMON TRANSPORT POLICY

Until well into the 70s, in the absence of a common policy, the Member States—all members of the OECD—adopted the Code of Liberalization of Current Invisible Operations as the basis of their maritime policy. This helped lessen the gravity of types of discrimination by Member States against each other's shipping companies.[71]

Until 1977, the Community institutions did not adopt a single formal act in the maritime transport sector.[72] A few years before, in 1973 and 1974, there were three crucial events to which reference has already been made, which laid the foundations for Community maritime policy and ultimately drove it forward:

(1) The enlargement of the Community with the entry of Denmark, Ireland the United Kingdom in 1973. In the new Community geography, maritime and air transport would henceforth have the same importance as inland transport.

(2) The clarification by the European Court that the general rules of the Treaty were applicable to transport as a whole—and, more specifically, to maritime transport—even in the absence of a common transport policy having been developed.[73]

(3) The adoption in Geneva, two days after the Court's ruling, of the Code of Conduct for Liner Conferences,[74] around which the first initiatives of Community maritime policy, until that time non-existent, were forged.

The Community's maritime policy therefore started to develop as from 1974, and did so around three main objectives: the promotion of safety-at-sea, the protection of Community fleets against unfair practices by shipping companies from non-member countries and, above all, the acceptance of the conference system in liner shipping as a form of organization of the market.[75] The first important advances took place, however, many years after, in 1986, one year after the

---

[71] See the Commission Memorandum of 1985 on the common maritime transport policy entitled 'Progress towards a common transport policy. Maritime transport (Communication and proposals by the Commission to the Council)'. Document COM (85) 90 final, of 14 Mar. 1985, to which detailed reference will be made below.

[72] The first was the Council Decision of 13 Sept. 1977, setting up a consultation procedure on relations between Member States and third countries in the shipping matters and on action relating to such matters within international organizations, OJ 1977 L 239, p. 23.

[73] Judgment of the ECJ in the *French Seamen* case, see above, n. 12. For this judgment, see below, Ch. 2.

[74] For this UN convention, see *infra*, Ch. 4.

[75] On these lines, see Vermote, Lieven, 'Le Code de Conduite des conférences maritimes et le compromis de Bruxelles, une analyse du contenu et de la portée du règlement CEE n° 954/79 du Conseil des ministres des Communautés européennes', *European Transport Law*, Vol. 21, No. 1, 1986, pp. 3–36, p. 3.

Court found against the Council for failing to establish a common transport policy in the inland sector.[76]

The true catalyst of Community maritime policy was the UNCTAD Code of Conduct for Liner Conferences. It led to the adoption of the first Community maritime policy instrument, Regulation 954/79, or the 'Brussels Package'.[77] This regulation, which had its origins in the discussions between the Commission and Member States on the incompatibility of the UNCTAD Code with the EEC Treaty, turned into an instrument of external maritime policy for the Member States and the EC. It formed the first important element of a Community policy which until then was barely drafted. The Code of Conduct was the ideal pretext to the policy and was quickly established as the core around which the EC's maritime policy was initially shaped.

The 'Brussels Package' was an important milestone in Community maritime policy. However, the policy then remained, as before, in a state of more or less complete hibernation until 1986. Until 1979, the list of achievements of Community maritime policy was short. An initial decision establishing a consultation procedure,[78] a recommendation relating to the ratification of certain international maritime conventions on safety-at-sea:[79] a decision relating to the maritime activities of certain third countries:[80] and a package of technical measures were adopted. After the 'Brussels Package' and until 1986, the few measures adopted were also technical in nature, aimed at the ratification of certain international conventions or the amendment or implementation of previous measures.

The advances made in transport policy in 1986 were prepared in 1985 and were made possible by the effective, if belated, impetus of the Commission and the decisive support of the European Parliament.

The Commission considered in 1985 that the time had come—almost thirty years after the signing of the Treaty of Rome—to develop a more coherent overall framework for Community maritime transport policy. The Maritime Memorandum was prepared by the Commission in 1985. Its task was to formulate a series of principles for maritime policy and it proposed on the basis of these a new—and first ever—framework for Community policy.[81] The memorandum acknowledged the significance of the major recession in the Community maritime industry during the 1970s. It revised past Community actions and proposed new measures which, in view of third countries' attitudes and the maritime relations between Member States, the Commission considered necessary to promote the Community's maritime and commercial interests.

---

[76] Judgment of the ECJ in the case between the European Parliament and the Council of Ministers concerning the common inland transport policy, see above n. 27.

[77] Council Reg. (EEC) 954/79, on the ratification by the Member States of the UNCTAD Code of Conduct of Liner Conferences, OJ 1979 L 121, p. 1.

[78] See above n. 72.   [79] OJ 1978 L 194, p. 17.

[80] OJ 1978 L 258, p. 35, as amended by OJ 1989 L 97, p. 47.

[81] The 1985 memorandum was cited at n. 71.

As a general principle, the Commission maintained that the defence of the Community maritime industry's interests should not be conducted through the adoption of protectionist measures to curb third countries' protectionism. Instead it sought a commercially-oriented policy of a multilateral nature. This was important in view of the Community's dependence on international trade and its interests in the international shipping market. This policy was considered also to be the most beneficial to the European industries using maritime transport and the most coherent one for attaining the Treaty's objectives.

In the Commission's opinion, the actions proposed in relation to third countries would also have to be accompanied by measures guaranteeing the equality of treatment of all Community shipping companies by the Member States. Within the Community sphere, therefore, the Commission made clear that it was necessary to abolish flag discrimination and move towards the creation of a single market in maritime transport. Whilst in other areas of business the single market was already, more or less, a reality, in maritime transport the creation of an economic area without internal borders and open to economic operators from all the Member States had been enormously delayed, and there still existed numerous restrictions on the access of Community shipping companies to the various national markets of the Member States.

OECD countries have generally endorsed a liberal economic philosophy. But the developed countries were not—nor are—always exemplary at putting into practice free trade principles, even though they have often tried to export such ideas to other countries, *inter alia*, to developing countries. In maritime terms, the theoretical promotion on an international scale of the values of free trade and multilateralism as opposed to protectionism, unilateralism and bilateralism, stands in stark contrast to the common practice of numerous developed countries who protect their own merchant fleets by unilateral and bilateral measures. Indeed, the OECD countries continue to maintain numerous restrictions on the freedom of access of foreign shipping companies to the cargoes generated by their trade. This is with the avowed or at least disguised aim, (at times with a variety of strategic considerations) of protecting their own national shipping companies from foreign competition.

The Community countries were not, nor are, an exception in this respect. In the Community maritime transport arena, major restrictions still persist in the free provision of services by shipping companies of other countries, including those of other Member States.

In the international field, many of the Member States had concluded bilateral interstate agreements which provided for the distribution of traffic between the national shipping companies of individual Member States and those of third countries, with the exclusion of other Community shipping companies. In the national sphere, certain Member States had unilaterally imposed restrictions on the free provision of services between their own ports. Maritime cabotage services in many cases were, and still are, the exclusive preserve of the national shipping companies of each of the Member States. Finally, various community countries have also unilaterally directed by means of legislation that certain cargoes (for example, liquid hydrocarbons, or cereals, or other types of cargo), or proportions of certain cargoes (for example, 30 per cent of oil products imported by the country in question) had to be carried exclusively by shipping companies which flew their own national flag.

With the aim of starting gradually to apply the principle of freedom to provide services in maritime transport, the Commission proposed to the Council in 1985 that they adopt a draft regulation which, without completely liberalizing the provision of maritime services within the EC, opened up new possibilities to Community shipping companies in categories of traffic reserved by the Member States to their own national shipping companies. These were chiefly traffic in certain goods, bilateral trade between Member States and third countries and—with certain exceptions—cabotage services within a single Member State.[82]

As a whole, the Memorandum formulated a Community policy fundamentally centred on the international aspects of Community maritime transport policy. It placed far greater emphasis on this than on the intra-Community policy aspects. The maritime relations between the EC and third countries were deemed to take priority over the maritime relations between Member States within the Community. The Commission justified this choice by the distinctly international character of the sector. In its opinion, even the intra-community aspects of maritime policy had to take into account the international context.[83]

The debates on the draft legislation contained in the Memorandum got under way but only four of the measures proposed by the Commission were finally approved by the Council. Some of these—like the one relating to the freedom to provide services—contested major amendments. The draft Directive on the common definition of 'national shipping company', and the draft amendments to the Council decision on consultations with third countries were rejected. The regulations on freedom to provide services, application of Articles 85 and 86 of the Treaty, unfair pricing practices and freedom of access to trans-oceanic trades were adopted on 22 December 1986. The first of these measures entered into force on 1 January 1987 and the remainder on 1 July 1987, thereby opening up a new age in Community maritime policy.

Council Regulation 4055/86,[84] unlike the Commission's draft, applies the principle of freedom to provide services exclusively to international maritime transport, excluding transport between ports of a single Member State. The application of the principle of freedom of provision to the types of traffic defined by the regulation involves the abolition of all restrictions on the carriage of certain goods and of restrictions derived from the cargo-sharing clauses in the bilateral agreements made between some Member States and third countries.

[82] 1985 Memorandum, above n. 71, Annexe II.2.
[83] See the 1985 Memorandum, above n. 71, Introduction, pp. 1 and 2.
[84] OJ 1986 L 378, p. 1.

Regulation 4056/86[85] permitted the application of the competition rules with control mechanisms similar to those existing in other economic areas under Regulation 17, to international maritime transport, excluding cabotage. It also authorized traditional liner conferences (as defined in the UNCTAD Code) with a generous block exemption [86].

The precedent for Regulation 4057/86[87] is the system of information established by the Council in 1978 to supervise the activities of shipping companies of certain third countries—in particular, those of the Socialist Block—in zones of operation in which the foreign carriers directly competed with Community shipping companies.[88] [89] The regulation is, to a large extent, a logical consequence of this system.

The regulation establishes the procedure under which the Community can, in certain circumstances, impose redressive (or countervailing) duties on the rates offered by third States' shipping companies which operate in Community trades. The regulation follows the lead initiated by various OECD countries which had exercised control over the tariff practices of specific States' shipping companies suspected of offering artificially low rates made possible by the financial support of their countries of registration.[90]

The last of the four 1986 Council Regulations, 4058/86,[91] is the successor of a 1983 Decision relating to counter-measures in the field of international merchant shipping.[92] It allows the Community to take co-ordinated action when any measure taken by a third country, or its agents, limits, or threatens to limit, freedom of access of Community shipping companies or vessels registered in the Community to that country's maritime trade. The co-ordinated action may take the form of complaints through diplomatic channels or measures directed against the shipping companies which are the beneficiaries of a third country's action ('counter-measures'). Complaints through diplomatic channels have to precede the counter-measures.

After this first package of maritime measures in 1986, the Commission in 1989 proposed the adoption of further measures. In its Communication to the Council of August 1989,[93] the Commission proposed the adoption of various legislative instruments, some of which the Council had previously declined to

---

[85] OJ 1986 L 378, p. 4.   [86] On this regulation, see below, Ch. 4.

[87] OJ 1986 L 378, p. 14.

[88] Council Dec. 78/774/EEC, of 19 Sept. 1978, see above n. 80.

[89] Oddly, the only time regulation 4057/86 has been used was not against a shipping company of a socialist country, but against a Korean shipping company. See Council Reg. (EEC) 15/89 of 4 Jan. 1989 introducing a redressive duty on containerized liner cargo carried between the Community and Australia by Hyundai Merchant Marine Company Ltd of Seoul, Republic of Korea, OJ 1989 L 4, p. 1.

[90] E.g. the US Shipping Act 1984 establishes in its Section 9, 46 USC app. 1708, the procedures for monitoring the activities of 'controlled carriers' of third countries which operate on US shipping routes.

[91] OJ 1986 L 378, p. 21.   [92] Dec. 83/573/EEC, OJ 1983 L 332, p. 37.

[93] Commission of the EC, 'A future for the Community shipping industry. Measures to improve the operating conditions of Community shipping'. Document COM (89) 266 final, of 3 Aug. 1989.

approve in 1986. Thus, for example, it tried again, and again without success, to win approval for a common definition of Community shipowner, and the creation of a Community ship register.

Only one relative success resulted from the proposed cabotage regulation. The cabotage reserves of some Member States were maintained even after the adoption of the first maritime regulation on the freedom to provide services because such reserves were not abolished by the regulation. The agreement on their gradual abolition was implemented by Regulation 3577/92. The regulation allowed for transitional periods for its application beyond the year 2000.[94]

More recently, the maritime CTP has evolved towards the adoption of measures to supervise the technical adaptation of vessels to common EC safety requirements. Such supervision is conducted by the State authorities of the port with the object of avoiding hazards to safety, in particular risks to the environment, from non-standard vessels.

Perhaps the measure of greatest commercial importance recently adopted in the EC is the regulation on liner consortia. In 1986, by adopting the first package of four maritime regulations, the Commission pledged to the Council to study the state of co-operation agreements between shipping companies, the objective of which is the establishment of containerized joint services. In 1989, the Commission proposed that the Council grant it powers to adopt a block exemption regulation authorizing such powers. The Council delegated such powers by regulation in February 1992,[95] and in April 1995, the Commission finally adopted Regulation 870/95, authorizing liner consortia subject to specific conditions and obligations.[96]

1.7. DEVELOPMENT OF THE AIR COMMON TRANSPORT POLICY[97]

In the thirty years which followed the entry into force of the Treaty of Rome, air transport was organized, in a similar way to inland transport, on the basis of the public regulation of conditions of competition, rather than on the free market. The Governments controlled, unilaterally or bilaterally, access to the market (authorizing or otherwise new air carriers to operate at their airports), the available transport capacity on the routes (determining the frequency of flights and even the type of aircraft), the distribution of such capacity between the airlines (typically, by halves for national carriers on each route) and tariffs (fixing the prices which the users would have to pay). Also, certain international organizations such as the International Air Transport Association (IATA) set about

---

[94] Council Reg. (EEC) 3577/92, OJ 1992 L 364, p. 7, as amended by OJ 1993 L 173, p. 33.
[95] Council Reg. (EEC) 479/92, OJ 1992 L 55, p. 3.
[96] OJ 1995 L 89, p. 7. On this Reg., see below, Ch. 4, Section II.
[97] See Dawson and Renaud, above n. 32, pp. 9–11, Bauchet and Rathery, above n. 52, pp. 51 and 52.

introducing even more restrictions on the commercial freedom of air transport undertakings.

As a consequence, Community air transport has been characterized by the existence of virtual national monopolies, market sharing and very high tariffs. This system has not produced advantages for consumers and perhaps not even for the airlines themselves, the economic efficiency of which is likely to have been affected by so many years of regulation.

Compared with the United States system, the European air system is characterized, like the rail system, by the dearth of private companies and the proliferation of public corporations which receive considerable sums of money as State subsidies to support their commercial viability.

1.7.1. The initial phase

Until the *French Seamen* judgment,[98] the Member States objected to the Community intervening in the maritime and air sectors. Since 1974, the Commission's interventions have been very cautious and piecemeal. As a result, the European model of liberalization of the air market has not followed the United States example of opening the markets up in one go to free competition in matters touching upon the right of access, capacity, and tariffs. Instead it has tried to accommodate elements of free competition and state intervention in a more flexible way.

In 1978, and on the Commission's proposal, the Council adopted the first programme of priorities in air transport, and in July 1979 the Commission published its first Memorandum on the Community's contribution to the development of air transport services in which the Commission stressed that a European regional framework for air transport would have to be designed as a subdivision of the international air system, from which it could not be separated.[99]

In December 1979, using as a legal base Article 84(2) of the Treaty, the Council adopted a decision setting up a consultation procedure on relations between Member States and third countries in the field of air transport and on action relating to such matters within international organizations.[100] The Community thereby equipped itself with the first instrument with which to exercise joint action in external relations in air transport matters. Here it is also worth mentioning the agreement between the Community and the European Civil Aviation Conference (ECAC), which seeks to avoid the two organizations duplicating work and enables the Community to make the most of the ECAC's experience.

Other subjects which the Council undertook to study in 1980 were the limitation of the noise of subsonic aircraft, accident investigation and rescue

---

[98] See above n. 12.   [99] Doc. COM (79) 311 final, of 6 July 1979.
[100] Dec. 80/50/EEC, OJ 1980 L 18, p. 24.

measures, technical harmonization and harmonization of conditions of work in the sector.

In June 1983, about three years after the Commission made its proposal, the Council adopted a Directive which constituted the first tangible step to improving international air transport between the different regions of the EC.[101] The objective of the Directive was to establish a transport network between the Member States which would not be based on bilateral agreements but on the private initiative of air transport undertakings and which suggested the desirability of Community policies and procedures being established to protect traffic rights and supervise tariffs.

The Commission prepared a second Memorandum on air transport in March 1984 in which it developed the ideas which it had suggested in 1979[102] and which would culminate in the adoption of the first package of measures of liberalization of the Community air transport market, in December 1987.

1.7.2. The first package of liberalizing measures (1987)

The first package involved a modest step towards the internal market and free competition, and was made up of four legislative instruments.

First, Council Regulation 3975/87[103] establishes the procedure to be followed for implementing the rules of competition in air transport, and is the twin of Regulations 1017/68 for inland transport and 4056/86 for maritime transport, and a first cousin of Regulation 17.[104] With various amendments, this regulation continues to be the legal basis for the Commission's actions in air transport competition matters.

Secondly, Council Regulation 3976/87[105] empowered the Commission to grant block exemptions in the sector. As a consequence, the Commission adopted in 1988 three exemptions of its own stamp, the first relating to the joint planning and co-ordination of capacities, the sharing of revenue, consultations on tariffs on scheduled air services and the allocation of slots at airports:[106] the second, to computer reservation systems:[107] and the third, to ground handling services at airports.[108] Regulation 3976/87 has also survived to the present day, although it has been amended on two occasions, dovetailing with the phases of

---

[101] Council Dir. 83/416/EEC, OJ 1983 L 237, p. 19, as amended in 1986 by Dir. 86/216/EEC, OJ 1986 L 152, p. 47.

[102] Commission of the EC, 'Progress towards a common transport policy. Air transport (Communication and proposals by the Commission to the Council)'. Doc. COM (84) 72 final, of 15 Mar. 1984.

[103] OJ 1987 L 374, p. 1.

[104] The relationship between these regulations will be examined throughout this book, especially in Chs 3, Section II, and 6.

[105] OJ 1987 L 374, p. 9.   [106] Comm. Reg. (EEC) 2671/88, OJ 1988 L 239, p. 9.

[107] Comm. Reg. (EEC) 2672/88, OJ 1988 L 239, p. 13.

[108] Comm. Reg. (EEC) 2673/88, OJ 1988 L 239, p. 17.

liberalization, to allow the Commission to adopt new exemptions on the expiration of the first and second exemptions.[109]

Thirdly, Council Directive 87/601/EEC[110] put into operation a new system for the approval of scheduled flight tariffs on international intra-community routes. Before being valid, the tariffs had to be approved by the aviation authorities of the countries at both ends of the routes. This system is known as 'dual approval'.

Fourthly, by means of its Decision 87/602/EEC, on air carriers' access to scheduled routes and services, and on the sharing of capacities,[111] the Council adopted a new system of sharing capacities between Member States' companies, on each route. Before 1987, the share-out was almost always done 50/50, with the result that the number of seats offered by an airline on a route could be no greater than that of the airline of the country to which it was flying. Decision 87/602 allowed the market shares to vary between 40 per cent and 60 per cent in types of bilateral traffic. The decision also established multiple designation on routes between certain very busy airports: compared with the traditional designation of a single carrier by each State on one route, the Decision authorized the States to nominate more than one national airline to operate on the same route.

1.7.3. The second package of liberalizing measures (1990)

The second package was adopted in June 1990, and established a transitional and provisional system allowing Community air carriers to continue adapting to a more competitive future environment, which would come about with the third package. The second package of liberalization measures consists of three regulations.

Council Regulation (EEC) 2342/90,[112] on tariffs of scheduled flights, established a 'dual disapproval' system: for the tariff proposed by an air carrier on routes between Member States to be rejected, it was necessary for the two States to refuse to authorize it. However, this system did not apply to very low tariffs, below 30 per cent of the reference tariff.

Council Regulation (EEC) 2343/90,[113] on air carriers' access to scheduled routes and services, provided that the air carriers' market shares on intra-Community routes could vary between 75 per cent and 25 per cent, and that multiple designation was already possible on routes on which there were over 140,000 passengers or 800 return trips a year.

Lastly, Council Regulation (EEC) 2344/90[114] amended Regulation 3976/87, so that the Commission would be able to grant new exemptions to the agreements authorized in 1988.[115] In 1991, the Commission adopted new stricter

---

[109] See below.   [110] OJ 1987 L 374, p. 12.   [111] OJ 1987 L 374, p. 19.
[112] OJ 1990 L 217, p. 1.   [113] OJ 1990 L 217, p. 8.   [114] OJ 1990 L 217, p. 15.
[115] See above.

regulations for the same categories of agreements, in particular Regulations 82/91 (on ground handling services),[116] 83/91 (on computer reservation systems)[117] and 84/91 (on joint planning and co-ordination of capacities, tariff consultations and slot allocation at airports).[118]

The most important step towards the liberalization of air transport in the Community took place in July 1992, namely, the third package of liberalizing measures, after the 1987 and 1990 packages.

1.7.4. The third package of liberalizing measures (1992)

The third package consists of three regulations of the Council of Ministers relating to operating licences, access to the market and tariffs. Alongside these three regulations, another two relating to certain amendments of the competition rules applicable to air transport undertakings have been adopted and certain harmonization measures have been proposed which, in the near future, will supplement the legislative panorama in Community air transport in the Single Market.

As a technical requirement preliminary to access to an air route, Council Regulation (EEC) 2407/92[119] establishes new criteria and objective methods for granting operating licences.

Secondly, in relation to access to the market and sharing of capacity between air carriers, Council Regulation (EEC) 2408/92[120] establishes freedom to provide air transport services between Community countries, without restrictions,[121] and abolishes once and for all on international intra-community flights the sharing of capacity between airlines. Moreover, it also allows without restrictions the multiple designation on the Community's internal international routes.

Air cabotage is authorized until April 1997, only in the case of flights connected with an intra-Community route, with a maximum available capacity for these purposes of 50 per cent of the total aircraft capacity and, as from such date, without restrictions.

The only restrictions on the freedom of access to intra-Community routes are clearly defined by reference to public service requirements, airport congestion and air traffic control, and environmental issues.

Thirdly, Council Regulation (EEC) 2409/92[122] establishes with respect to the tariffs, be they for passengers or cargo, that airlines will be at liberty to fix their own tariffs without intervention, in principle, by the public authorities. However,

---

[116] OJ 1991 L 10, p. 7.   [117] OJ 1991 L 10, p. 9.   [118] OJ 1991 L 10, p. 14.
[119] Council Reg. (EEC) 2407/92, OJ 1992 L 240, p. 1.
[120] Council Reg. (EEC) 2408/92, OJ 1992 L 240, p. 8.
[121] Which enables the possibility of a carrier from country A flying between airports located in countries B and C. If Community countries, belonging to the same supra-national political entity, are not involved, this particular right of intra-Community cabotage could be dubbed, in traditional terminology, *the fifth freedom*. This terminology, as commonly used as it is, appears to be obsolete in intra-Community air transport. On the 'freedoms' in air transport, see below, Ch. 5.
[122] Council Reg. (EEC) 2409/92, OJ 1992 L 240, p. 15.

certain tariffs which the aviation authorities consider excessively high or low may be suspended. On the other hand, the Commission has accepted for the time being that airlines continue consulting on their respective tariffs, within IATA.

Finally, in tandem with the main block of the third package, the Community regulations implementing the competition rules have been amended.[123] As a direct result of amending Regulation 3976/87[124] for the second time, the Commission adopted Community Regulation (EEC) 1617/93 (on joint planning and co-ordination of capacities, tariff consultations and slot allocation)[125] and Commission Regulation (EEC) 3652/93[126] (on computer reservation systems), which amended Commission Regulation 83/91.[127]

Unlike the rules adopted under the first and second package, the competition rules adopted with the third package do not include a block exemption for agreements relating to ground handling at airports. The Commission has recently proposed a draft Council directive on this type of service.[128]

Other measures of harmonization relating to safety on aircraft, reservation of tickets, pilot licences, limits on pilots' flying hours, the noise produced by aircraft and carriers' public liability were also proposed, all with the aim of avoiding unfair competition, improving safety and protecting consumers.

The third package of liberalization comes from the hand that created the Single Market and the need to enable every Community air carrier the opportunity of offering his services between any Community airports. Its future achievements may, however, be frustrated by the unavailability of time slots at airports due to airport congestion, and to the limited capacity of the—also congested—air space.

1.8. RELATIONS WITH NON-MEMBER COUNTRIES AND EXTERNAL COMPETENCES[129]

The Commission has always considered it unacceptable that the Member States have developed over many years a system of bilateral agreements with third countries to regulate their relations in the transport sector, particularly as con-

---

[123] Council Reg. (EEC) 2410/92, amending Reg. 3975/87 (quoted in n. 103), OJ 1992 L 240, p. 18, and Council Reg. (EEC) 2411/92, amending Reg. 3976/87 (also quoted in n. 105), OJ 1992 L 240, p. 19. Reg. 3975/87 was previously amended by Council Reg. (EEC) 1284/91, OJ 1991 L 122, p. 2, with the aim of establishing a special shortened procedure for the adoption of interim measures in certain circumstances.

[124] See above.   [125] OJ 1993 L 155, p. 18.   [126] OJ 1993 L 333, p. 37.

[127] The validity of Comm. Reg. 83/91 had been previously extended by means of Comm. Reg. 1618/93, OJ 1993 L 155, p. 23.

[128] See *Press Release IP (94) 1206*. The new draft is not now based on Art. 90 of the Treaty, like the Commission's previous proposal for a Commission Directive(Doc. SEC (93) 1896 final), but on Art. 84(2) of the Treaty. The directive is not yet adopted at the time of writing (Mar. 1996). See below, Ch. 5.

[129] See Commission of the EC, 'The future development of the common transport policy . . .', above n. 1, paras 291 *et seq.*

cerns access to the market (including the access of carriers from third countries to the national market). For the Commission, many of the bilateral agreements may be incompatible with Community law—in particular with the principle of non-discrimination on the grounds of nationality and with the competition rules—and would, under the control of the Community institutions, have to be amended or rescinded.

The Member States, however, have resisted the exercise of Community powers in this area, and have continued negotiating new agreements or amending the old ones. This has happened in particular in inland waterway transport and aviation, where the isolated unilateral interventions by some Member States have not only prejudiced the Community's greater power of negotiation but have also opened breaches between the Community countries.[130] They have furthermore obstructed the Community's action in some international organizations, such as the International Maritime Organization (IMO) and the International Civil Aviation Organization (ICAO). As a consequence, the full effect of the CTP's instruments has been limited by the absence of a parallel and coherent development of the external dimension of the Community's internal liberalization policy.

Faced with the Member States' resistance, the Commission held until very recently that the Treaty of Rome implicitly provided for the external dimension of the CTP. Despite the fact that the Community had started to exercise its external powers based on Articles 61, 75 and 84(2) of the Treaty, the Commission had never waived the applicability of Article 113 in matters of trade in transport services. It based its claim to external competence both on the international nature of transport and on the decided cases of the European Court.

The first aspect was especially the case for maritime transport, where the huge majority of instruments adopted by Community institutions are pre-eminently international in nature,[131] but was no less so in inland waterways and air transport.[132] The entry into force of the Agreement on the European Economic Area (EEA) would guarantee the implementation of Community legislation in a geographical area which covered not only Community countries but also non-member countries.[133] Finally, the Community's role on international organizations

---

[130] In its Report on 'The future development of the common transport policy . . .', above n. 1, para. 301 and Annex II, the Commission illustrates its annoyance with an example: the extensive network of routes which US air carriers have been able to create in Europe thanks to the division in Community ranks, faced with the virtual absence of connecting routes for European air carriers in the US.

[131] See *supra*, para. 1.6.

[132] With reference to inland transport, the Community and its Member States concluded agreements with Yugoslavia in 1991, and with Austria and Switzerland in 1992. In civil aviation in 1988, a consultation procedure was approved on the external relations of the Member States and on action on international organizations. On the other hand, the 1992 agreement with Sweden and Norway extended to these countries the internal community system.

[133] Ch. 6 of Pt Three (Arts 47 to 52) and Annex XIII of the EEA Agreement contain specific provisions on all forms of transport which refer with very few variations to the Community texts on almost all occasions although, in respect of some of them, the Contracting Parties only 'take note'.

and in multilateral agreements on transport had been expanding progressively. In particular, and pre-eminently in the context of the General Agreement on Tariffs and Trade [GATT], the Commission found itself negotiating on behalf of the Community and its Member States the possible liberalization of services, of which transport is a vital part.

The Commission also believed that it had clear backing for its aspirations in the European Court's decisions since the 1970s. In 1971, in the context of a case relating to road transport, the Court had established that, since the Community is developing common internal rules, it also acquires powers on external negotiations likely to affect those common rules.[134] In 1976, in a case relating to inland waterway transport, the Court had held that, if the Community has internal competence to attain a specific objective, it implicitly commands exclusive external competence in the matter, in so far as the exercise of that external competence is necessary to attain such objective.[135] In 1978, in a case relating to an international agreement on the trade in goods, the Court had also held that the commercial policy mentioned in Article 113 of the Treaty constitutes a dynamic notion which follows the development of international trade.[136] Subsequently, the Commission wanted to regard further judgments of the Court as vindicating, subject to certain nuances, its interpretation of the Treaty.[137]

Consequently, the Commission concluded that the Community had exclusive authority to conclude bilateral or multi-lateral commercial agreements on services, especially agreements on transport, including those regulating capacity and market access, traffic rights and tariffs.[138]

Such was its certainty that, by virtue of Article 228(6) of the EC Treaty, it asked the Court to clarify whether the Community had exclusive authority or not to conclude the General Agreement on Trade Services (GATS) and the Agreement on Trade-Related Aspects of Intellectual Property Rights, including trade in counterfeit goods (TRIPs), annexed to the Agreement setting up the

[134] Case 22/70, *Commission* v. *Council* (European Agreement on Road Transport, ERTA), [1971] ECR 263.

[135] Opinion 1/76 on the case relating to the agreement establishing an European Fund for the lay-up of inland waterway transport capacity, [1977] ECR 741.

[136] Opinion 1/78 relating to the international agreement on natural rubber, [1979] ECR 2871.

[137] See, in particular, the judgments of the ECJ in Case 41/76, *S. Donckerwolcke and another* v. *Procureur de la Republique*, [1976] ECR 1921; in Case 174/84, *Bulk Oil* v. *Sun International*, [1986] ECR 559; and in Cases 59/84, *Tezi Textiel* v. *Commission*, [1986] ECR 887, and 242/84 *Tezi Textiel* v. *Minister van Ekonomische Zaken*, [1986] ECR 933.

[138] Art. 113 of the Treaty had been interpreted up to now in three main ways: for some, the external powers in matters of common commercial policy extended both to goods and to services; for others, they were limited to goods; an intermediate position contended that Art. 113 applied only to services closely linked to the international sale of goods. In this context, the CTP was considered almost separately, as external authority in this sphere appeared to derive implicitly from the Transport Title of the Treaty, as the Court appeared to have confirmed in its ERTA Judgment and in the Opinion on the European inland waterway Fund. See Timmermans, Christiaan W.A., 'Common commercial policy (Art. 113 EEC) and international trade in services'. In F. Capotorti and others (Eds.) *Du droit international au droit de l'intégration. Liber Amicorum Pierre Pescatore*, (Nomos. Baden-Baden, 1987), pp. 675–689, at p. 677.

World Trade Organization (WTO). In its Opinion,[139] contrary to the Commission's expectations and diverging from the line of argument which it had maintained in the 1970s,[140] the Court concluded that, although in matters relating to trade in goods, the Community has exclusive external competence, the competence in matters of trade in services is shared with its Member States. The Court has confirmed this case-law subsequently in another Opinion relating to a decision of the Council of the OECD.[141]

It is still too early to know what will be the consequences of this jurisprudence. *Prima facie*, the sector in which the Community initiatives might suffer most appears to be air transport, where the Commission had asked the Council to enlarge the scope of application of Community regulations to international air transport with third countries, on the basis of Article 84(2) of the Treaty.[142] In the current circumstances, the Member States may be disinclined to concede powers even on the basis of this provision and who knows whether any of them will not even regret having given up too many powers to the Community in the context of establishing the CTP.

Historically, the CTP's external advances by virtue of the Title on transport of the Treaty—especially Articles 75 and 84(2)—which might appear excessively unambitious when the Court was expected to support the Community's external powers in matters of trade in services by virtue of Article 113 of the Treaty, amount to a considerable advance with respect to the situation ten years ago. It should not be ignored that one of the reasons why the Member States have been more flexible in the field of transport has been the risk of an adverse verdict on the question of external powers over services.

Looked at from another perspective, the Opinion on the GATS and the WTO does not leave complete liberty to the Member States to negotiate bilaterally international agreements on services, but, in establishing the shared competence of the Community, may force the Member States and Community institutions to reach an understanding, on pain of causing the external paralysis both of the Community and of the Member States. On that basis, and provided the Commission enforces the part of external competence which does accrue to the Community, the consequences of the Opinion might be less important than might first appear.[143]

---

[139] Opinion 1/94, [1994] ECR I–5267.

[140] Timmermans, above n. 138, p. 689, considered the first decisions of the ECJ on the common commercial policy 'daring', and noted the Court's ever-increasing caution on the matter, as time has confirmed.

[141] Opinion 2/92, [1995] ECR I–521, relating to the competence of the Community or of one of its institutions to participate in the third revised decision of the Council of the OECD relating to national treatment.

[142] See below, Ch. 5.

[143] Perhaps the complete opposite of the apparently innocuous reference to Art. 61 of the Treaty in the *French Seamen* judgment. See above n. 14.

2

The Background to the Application of Competition Rules in the Transport Sector[1]

2.1. SPECIFICITY AND UNIVERSALITY

The treatment of transport services under the competition rules of the EEC Treaty (now EC) was problematic from the outset. Immediately after the entry into force of the Treaty, the question was raised whether its general rules, and in particular the competition rules, applied to the transport sector. None of the eleven Articles of Title IV in Part Two of the EEC Treaty (now Part Three of the EC Treaty) refers to competition issues except Article 77, which deals with State aids in the inland transport sector. On this basis, the Council came to the conclusion that Articles 74 to 84 constituted a separate legal regime for the transport sector within the Treaty, and that, with few exceptions (for example, State aids, because of the explicit reference in Article 77) most of the provisions of the Treaty did not apply to transport. In line with this interpretation, only the Council through specific legislation could introduce competition rules in transport pursuant to Article 84(2) for sea and air transport and Article 75 for inland transport. This interpretation was defended by France, Germany, Luxembourg, and, to a lesser degree, by Belgium.[2]

The opposite interpretation, based on the so-called 'universality principle', was supported by the Commission along with Italy and the Netherlands. It proposed that the general provisions of the Treaty also applied to transport. The transport provisions contained in Articles 74 to 84 of the Treaty only amended or replaced the general rules, where necessary, to take into account the special nature of transport. Their view was that, taking into account where necessary the specific nature of transport, all of the provisions of the Treaty were applicable to transport.[3]

Article 84 of the Treaty had also given rise to a heated discussion between the Commission and the Council about whether the authors of the Treaty intended air and sea transport to be regulated more specifically in every aspect

---

[1] On this subject, see in particular Schröter, H., in Groeben, H. von der, Thiesing, J. and Ehlerman, C.-D., Kommentar zum EWG-Vertrag, 4th Edn., Vol. 2, Articles 85–109. (Nomos. Baden-Baden), 1991, pp. 2023–61.

[2] See Blonk, W. A. G. 'Regulation (EEC) No. 1017/68 of the Council of July 19, 1968 Applying Rules of Competition to Transport by Rail, Road and Inland Waterway,' *Common Market Law Review*, Vol. 6, No. 4, Oct. 1969, pp. 451–65, at 452.

[3] *Ibid.*

by the Council or whether the general rules of the Treaty outside the transport Title and Chapter, such as the right of establishment, the competition rules, and the rules on State aids were applicable to the sea and air transport sectors.[4]

Article 84 of the Treaty, before the modifications introduced by the Single European Act,[5] read as follows :

Article 84
1. The provisions of this title shall apply to transport by rail, road and inland waterway.
2. The Council may, acting unanimously, decide whether, to what extent and by what procedure, appropriate provisions may be laid down for sea and air transport.

Article 84(2) was interpreted by the Council as comprehensively withdrawing the sea and air transport sectors from the general rules of the Treaty.

The Commission had supported the universality of the Treaty openly since 1960. On 12 November 1960, the Commission transmitted to the Council a memorandum the title of which was *Applicabilité aux transports des règles de concurrence énoncées dans le Traité de la Communauté économique européenne et interprétation de l'application du Traité en ce qui concerne la navigation maritime et aérienne.*[6] In this document, the Commission informed the Council that the preparatory work necessary for the elaboration of a common transport policy had led it to study more closely the relationship between the general rules of the Treaty (and in particular competition rules) and the special rules concerning transport. The Commission indicated the results of such examination and summarized briefly the thesis it had adopted, defending the 'universality' of the Treaty.

The Commission reaffirmed its initial interpretation as expressed in the first memorandum on several occasions. The two more important documents in this respect are the *Memorandum sur l'orientation à donner à la politique commune des transports*, of 10 April 1961,[7] and the *Programme d'action en matière de politique commune des transports*, of 16 April 1962.[8]

Those who advocated the 'specificity' of the transport Title against the 'universality' of the Treaty maintained that from both the position of Article 84(2) in the Treaty and the wording of this provision in isolation, it could be argued that there were no provisions in the Treaty of Rome applicable to sea and air transport. Along these lines, it was argued that if the Council felt so strongly that

[4] See Bredimas, A. E., 'The Common Shipping Policy of the EEC', *Common Market Law Review*, Vol. 18, No. 1, Feb. 1981, pp. 9–32, at 9–10.

[5] As stated, the main modification introduced by the Single European Act was the introduction of qualified majority voting instead of unanimity. It also established that the procedure for the adoption of measures in the sea and air transport sectors would be the procedure in Art. 75 of the Treaty. (This is the procedure for the adoption of measures in inland transport). In this way, the Single European Act put an end to the procedural vagueness of the first version of Art. 84(2) of the Treaty.

[6] COM Doc. VII/S/05230 fin., of 12 Nov. 1960.

[7] VII/COM(61)50 final, of 10 Apr. 1961.

[8] For the first steps of the CTP, see Pinay, P., 'Règles de concurrence et transports dans le cadre de la C.E.E.', *Annuaire Français de Droit International*, Vol. 8, 1962, pp. 781–805, at 783–6.

sea and air transport had to be subject to the Treaty, the Council could simply have taken a unanimous decision to that effect. If the Council did not in fact take such a unanimous decision (and it is noteworthy that, since the Single European Act, unanimity is no longer the rule here), all debate on universality of the Treaty versus specificity of the transport sector, would be foreclosed.[9]

Against this objection, it was argued the rules of the Treaty cannot be replaced by the discretion of Member States sitting in the Council. Furthermore, the role of interpreting the Treaty is attributed by the Treaty itself to the European Court, not to the Council.

Put in a different way, the Council of Ministers for transport cannot alter the sovereign decision of Member States to form a common market with common rules for all of them and for all the economic sectors which have not received different special rules from the Treaty. The role of the Commission is to propose any appropriate measures and to take the necessary steps to ensure that the Treaty is respected, including challenging Member States and the Council itself before the European Court.

For that reason, it is most surprising that in the first memorandum of the Commission of November 1960 the specificity of sea and air transport and the world context in which these modes have to be placed made the Commission conclude that: 'il faudrait examiner si, en attendant qu'une réglementation d'ensemble adaptant les règles du Traité à la navigation maritime et aérienne puisse être établie, il y aurait lieu de suspendre, par une décision du Conseil, prise en conformité de l'article 84 § 2, l'application des articles 85 à 94 à l'égard de ces deux modes de transport.'[10]

It is evident that at the time the Commission believed that the proper means for excluding competition rules from the transport sector, at least from the maritime and air transport sector, was through the use of Article 84(2). From today's perspective, this might seem to go directly against the system of the Treaty, because no rule explicitly empowers the Council to disapply competition rules in the field of transport, not even Article 87 of the Treaty.[11]

For these reasons, it has been said that the universality and the specificity theories lead in practice to more or less the same result: a Regulation on sea and air transport that would adapt the rules of the Treaty to the particularities of these sectors. The only difference in practice was that the Council and the Commission could not agree on whether it was legally necessary, before such a Regulation was adopted, to suspend, by means of a decision taken under Article 84, certain rules of the Treaty (the approach of the Commission) or whether such a suspension decision was unnecessary, based on the 'specificity of the transport Title' (the Council's approach).[12]

[9] See Bird, J., 'Further Debate on the Treaty of Rome, Art. 84, para. 2 as it may affect Maritime Transport', *European Transport Law*, Vol. 2, No. 1, pp. 24–47, at 30–2.

[10] Memorandum of 12 Nov. 1960, above n. 6, last para.

[11] See below, Ch. 3, on the interpretation of Art. 87 of the Treaty.

[12] In this sense, see Pinay, above n. 8, at pp. 800–1.

2.2. REGULATION 17 AND REGULATION 141[13]

The controversy surrounding the theory of the applicability of the competition rules to transport arose in more practical terms after the adoption in 1962 of Regulation 17, the first regulation vesting enforcement and investigation powers in the Commission in the field of competition law. The Council adopted this regulation without excluding any economic sector from its provisions. According to the universality principle, this could have enabled the Commission to apply Articles 85 and 86 of the Treaty in the transport sector using Regulation 17.

However, transport undertakings were well aware that as long as the interpretation of the Commission concerning the universality of the Treaty and the applicability of competition rules to transport was contested by certain Member States, it was very unlikely that any action would be taken against them by the Community institutions, for concluding restrictive agreements or entering into restrictive practices. As long as the Community was unable to give them precise instructions, transport undertakings could feel safe.

In effect, after the publication of Regulation 17, even Member States which supported the universality of the Treaty and the applicability of Regulation 17 to the transport sector, tried to find a compromise which would allow clarification of the situation for transport undertakings *vis-à-vis* the competition rules contained in the Treaty. Member States and the Commission agreed that the competition rules contained in Articles 85 and 86 of the Treaty should only be applied after efforts for the realization of a common transport policy had achieved concrete results. The Commission then began to draft a separate regulation which would have the effect of exempting transport undertakings from the application of Regulation 17, at least provisionally.

Accordingly, in a certain sense the adoption of Regulation 17 provided the opportunity for the Council to ask the Commission to surrender any potential powers over transport, in return for the specific powers it had received to deal with restrictive agreements and abuses of dominant positions in general. Once Regulation 17 was adopted, an arrangement was found. The Commission agreed to propose Regulation 141,[14] a regulation which rendered Regulation 17 inapplicable to the transport sector.[15] In so doing the Commission ceded real powers already granted it by the Council, and the Council for its part committed itself

[13] On this point, see Pinay, above n. 8, 8, at pp. 784–5.

[14] Council Reg. 141/62 of 26 Nov. 1962, exempting transport from the application of Council Reg. 17, OJ 1962 124, p. 2753 (Special Ed. 1959–1962) p. 291. Amended by Reg. 165/65/EEC, OJ 1965 210, p. 314, and by Reg. 1002/67/EEC, OJ 1967 306, p. 1.

[15] Six months before, in April 1962, the Council had adopted Reg. 26, applying certain rules on competition to the production and trade in agricultural products, OJ 1962 30, p. 993, Special Ed. 1959–62 p. 129, as amended by Council Reg. 49/62, OJ 1962 53, p. 1571. Unlike transport, which has been characterised as 'special sector' but in reality is not, the agricultural sector is genuinely 'special' under the Treaty, because the possible application of competition rules different from the common ones was expressly provided for in Art. 42. See below, section 2.5.

to adopting a Regulation in the field of inland transport immediately after Regulation 141 was approved, (remembering that transport has not been excluded from Regulation 17). In arriving at this solution, none of the institutions involved renamed their own views on the issue of whether competition rules should be applied in transport, whether they should not be applied at all or whether competition rules for transport should be different. The prospective regulation applying competition rules to the inland transport sector was at that time a mystery. Only when the negotiations began was it apparent that the Council was not ready to accept that standard or common competition rules were applicable to transport in general and to sea and air transport in particular.

It is interesting to note that in the preamble (*exposé des motifs*) to the report accompanying the draft of Regulation 17, it was stated that the scope of Articles 85 and 86 could be made more precise for certain economic sectors. In transport the Commission had forwarded to the Council a report on the application of competition rules as well as on the interpretation of Article 84(2) and on the position of air and maritime transport within the Treaty. The Commision noted that depending on the solutions to be adopted on the subject, the scope of Articles 85 and 86 might eventually be defined in the transport sector pursuant to Article 87 2(c).[16]

From this, it is apparent that the Commission had not ruled out the possibility of adopting special provisions in favour of transport undertakings, in as much as these exceptional rules would be justified by the need to cater for the special aspects of transport, as foreseen in Article 75 of the Treaty for inland transport. However, on the basis that Regulation 17 contained no exclusion of transport, the Commission thought that it applied fully to transport undertakings.[17]

A report with a draft of Regulation 141 was submitted by the Commission to the Council on 27 September 1962. The proposal of the Commission was entitled '(Draft) Regulation No . . . on the non-applicability to transport by rail, road and inland waterway of Article 85 of the Treaty, as well as of the provisions which are based upon this Article'.[18]

Nothing was said in the draft concerning sea and air transport.[19] The text

[16] 'Enfin, en fonction d'une expérience plus étendue, le champ d'application des dispositions des articles 85 et 86 pourrait être précisé pour certaines branches économiques. Pour le transport, par exemple, la Commission a décidé de saisir le Conseil d'un mémoire sur l'applicabilité des règles de concurrence ainsi que sur l'interprétation de l'Article 84 § 2 concernant la position de la navigation maritime et aérienne par rapport au Traité. Selon les solutions qui seront adoptées en cette matière, il y aura éventuellement lieu de préciser à l'égard de ce secteur les champs d'application des articles 85 et 86, conformément à l'article 87 § 2 (c)'. Quoted from Pinay, above n. 8, at p. 784, n. 7.

[17] See Pinay, above n. 8, at pp. 784–5.

[18] 'Règlement No. . . . visant à suspendre, dans le domaine des transports par chemin de fer, par route et par voies naviguables, l'application de l'Article 85 (CEE), ainsi que des dispositions prises ou à prendre en vue de son application'. Document VII/IV/COM(62) 259 final, of 27 Sept. 1962.

[19] In the introduction (*exposé de motifs*), point 1, reference is made to the Nov. 1960 Memorandum on the applicability of Arts 85 and 86 of the Treaty to sea and air transport (see above, n. 6), and the 'universality' theory is reaffirmed for *all* modes of transport. It is not apparent why the draft Regulation dealt *only* with inland transport.

contained three versions of the draft regulation, one by Commissioner von der Groeben, one by Commissioner L. Schaus and a consolidated one. The one proposed by Commissioner Schaus also included in the Regulation the suspension of Article 86 of the Treaty.

From the title of the main draft, it seems that, at the time, the Commission considered that secondary legislation might derogate or exclude specific sectors of the economy from the Treaty or competition rules. The legal base for the draft regulation were Articles 74 and 75 together with Article 87(2)(c). The Commission may have felt that the last of these provisions indeed allowed for the exclusion of the transport sector from the EEC Treaty.

The intention of the Commission seemed to be to avoid not only the use of Regulation 17 to enforce Articles 85 and 86, but also to prevent the direct application of these provisions by national courts and authorities to transport undertakings. Subsequent case-law shows that Article 85(1) is directly applicable, subject to the provisional validity of agreements for which no individual exemption procedures are provided[20] and that Article 86 is directly applicable, unconditionally before national courts and competition authorities.[21]

In the end, whilst adopting Regulation 141, the Council took Article 87 as the exclusive legal basis, without reference to specific paragraphs and made no mention of Articles 85 and 86 of the Treaty. This was done not for substantive legal reasons, that is, not because the Council rejected the idea that secondary legislation could derogate from the Treaty, but because it wanted to avoid giving an opinion on the universality of the Treaty and on the applicability of Articles 85 and 86 to transport. In effect, if the Council had agreed to the inclusion of Articles 85 and 86 in the title of Regulation 141, it would have implicitly accepted that Articles 85 and 86 did in fact apply to transport before Regulation 141 was adopted. Indeed, in spite of the Council's attempts not to prejudge the issue of the applicability of the general rules of the Treaty to transport, the use of Article 87 as the legal basis for Regulation 141 could point to the same conclusion.[22]

Finally, the draft of Regulation 141 anticipated a limited derogation from Article 85 and Regulation 17 for inland transport and foresaw that after two years Regulation 17 was to apply in this sector, if no specific provisions (*modalités particulières*) running counter to Regulation 17 were adopted before 31 December 1964. The future Regulation was justified on the basis of the need provisionally to suspend the applicability of Article 85 and Regulation 17 as long as the Community had not worked out whether the specific characteristics of the transport sector made it appropriate to adopt specific provisions applicable to

---

[20] Regarding the doctrine of provisional validity in general, see below Ch. 6, para. 6.4.1.2.

[21] This point has been confirmed for air transport in the judgment of the ECJ in Case 66/86, *Ahmed Saeed* v. *Zentrale*, [1989] ECR 803.

[22] In this sense, see the Opinion of Adv. Gen. Reischl in the *French Seamen* Case, below at n. 35, at p. 380.

transport. In this draft, the regulation would appear to have been a form of stop-gap measure.

On 26 November 1962, the Council adopted Regulation 141. It established that Regulation 17 did not apply to transport in general, thereby enlarging the scope of the draft regulation to sea and air transport. Until 31 December 1965 the competition rules would not apply to transport by rail, road and inland waterway, and thereafter they would. For sea and air transport, no date was set after which the Competition rules were to apply.

No mention was ultimately made of Article 85 and the regulation did not prejudge the question whether the transport Title in Part Two of the Treaty set forth a specific regime for transport outside the general rules of the Treaty, or whether the rules of the Treaty, including competition rules, applied to transport. The adoption of a final choice between the theory of specificity and the theory of universality was avoided.[23]

In Regulation 141, the Council deviated considerably from the views of the Commission. In particular the Council considered it of paramount importance to adopt a Regulation which did not determine the controversial and fundamental point of whether or not the general rules of competition applied to transport. Although Articles 85 and 86 were finally removed from it, Regulation 141 could not avoid reference to Regulation 17. If Regulation 141 exempted transport from the application of Council Regulation 17, it is logical to conclude that before Regulation 141, Regulation 17 applied in the transport sector. Regulation 17 could not have a wider scope than Articles 85 and 86, in respect of which it is simply an implementing provision adopted pursuant to Article 87 of the Treaty. It should therefore follow that Articles 85 and 86 were equally applicable to transport and that the efforts of the Council not to prejudge the question of the universality of the Treaty and the applicability of competition rules to transport had been in vain.

In order to disassociate itself from this obvious interpretation, upon the adoption of Regulation 141 the Council issued a press statement which explicitly reserved the question, in the following terms : 'les Ministres avaient adopté ce texte en précisant dans une déclaration au procès-verbal que la solution juridique adoptée dans ce cas d'espèce ne préjuge en rien la position des Etats membres sur le problème de l'applicabilité au transport des règles générales du Traité.'[24] This regulation was consequently further tainted with the spirit of compromise.

In conclusion, Regulation 141 can be viewed as an element in a package deal, which served to counterbalance Regulation 17 and as a compromise between two different options which were defended by Member States and by the insti-

---

[23] See Pinay, above n. 8, at pp. 794 and 800–1.
[24] Agence Europe du 26 novembre 1962, *Bulletin Quotidien* no. 1420. Cited from Pinay, above n. 8, at p. 782.

tutions of the Community. It was clearly intended not to prejudge the universality/specificity debate.[25]

2.3. REGULATION 1017/68

Regulation 141 provided for rules to be adopted in relation to rail, road, and inland waterway by 31 December 1965. Article 2 of the regulation foresaw that the Council should adopt appropriate provisions in order to apply rules on competition to transport by rail, road, and inland waterway and, to this end, the Commission was to submit proposals to the Council before 30 June 1964. Under Article 3 of Regulation 141, Article 1—which provided for the non-applicability of Regulation 17 to transport—would remain in force with regard to transport by rail, road, and inland waterway until 31 December 1965. This meant that the Council was obliged fairly quickly to act on the Commission proposal.

The Council did not commit itself to any timetable for the sea and air transport sectors. While Regulation 141 established a deadline for appropriate provisions to be adopted for inland transport, the question for sea and air transport was delayed *sine die*, as already explained.

Following the adoption of Regulation 141 and pursuant to its Article 2, the Commission submitted to the Council a draft regulation on the rules of competition applicable in the inland transport sector on 5 June 1964.[26] The Commission proposed that, while adding certain particular provisions for inland transport, Regulation 17 should be reinstated as the procedural regime for the application of competition rules by the Commission to transport, as in other sectors of the economy. This proposal was not accepted by the Council. A new draft was submitted to the Council on 13 March 1968[27] which, apart from a few alterations in its wording and numbering, was adopted by the Council on 19 July 1968.[28] The Council finally adopted a new set of competition rules, including substantive and procedural provisions, implicitly denying the applicability of Articles 85 and 86 of the Treaty to inland transport and rejecting the universality of the Treaty. In the meantime, it had twice proved necessary to prolong Regulation 141, once until 31 December 1967, and again until 1 July 1968. Rather curiously, and probably for reasons of legal security, it was decided that Regulation 1017/68 would come into force retroactively on 1 July 1968.[29]

Regulation 1017/68 can be seen as a forerunner in the application of competition law to the services sector. At the time of the approval of Regulation

---

[25] In this sense, see Pinay, *ibid*.

[26] Document VII/IV/ COM (64) 184 Final of 5 Jun. 64, Suppl. of *EC Bulletin* 7/64.

[27] Document COM (68)142 final of 13 Mar. 1968.

[28] Council Reg. (EEC) 1017/68 of 19 July 1968, OJ 1968 L175, 13 Mar. 1968, p. 1. Spec. Ed. 1968, I, p. 302.

[29] See Blonk, above n. 2, pp. 453–4.

1017/68 in 1968, it was clear to the Commission that, regardless of the fact that services were not explicitly referred to in Articles 85 and 86, competition rules applied not only to trade in goods, but to trade in services as well. However, this matter had not yet been decided by the Court.[30] Regulation 141, specifying that a major service sector like transport would not be subject to Regulation 17, and Regulation 1017/68, applying competition rules to inland transport, meant modest progress in this respect, although in many other respects they represented a step back for competition policy.

2.4. THE EUROPEAN COMMISSION AND REGULATIONS 141 AND 1017/68

The attitude of the Commission in 1962, when it accepted Regulation 141, and in 1968, when it accepted Regulation 1017/68, can be explained by the historical background to the approval of both regulations.

First, Regulation 17 was the desired tool to begin enforcing EEC competition law. The controversy surrounding the universality of the Treaty had not been settled, and the Commission sympathized, more or less, with the 'specificity' of the transport sector (although not with the specificity of the transport Title of the Treaty, which it felt ran counter to the principle of universality underpinning the Treaty). Hence, the Commission was ready to give up a part of the economy, which in any event it could not from the outset manage properly, in order to obtain wide and non-controversial powers in all other sectors of the economy. Like any emerging administration, the Commission took time to develop the confidence, experience and legitimacy needed for it fully to discharge its functions.[31] The embryonic competition policy was sufficiently removed from transport concerns and the Commission did not worry unduly about leaving this sector aside for the time being.[32]

Second, Regulation 1017/68 was adopted at a time when the newly born Communities had just gone through one of their major crises, the 'empty chair' crisis, when the French ministers boycotted the meetings of the Council. The

---

[30] A clear statement in respect of the applicability of competition rules to services is contained in the ECJ Judgment in Case 172/80, *Züchner* v. *Bayerische Vereinsbank*.

[31] For commentary on the evolution of the European Commission's competition policy and on the history of DG IV, see Wilks, Stephen, 'The Metamorphosis of European Competition Policy', *Russell Working Papers No. 9* (University of Exeter, Exeter, 1992) at pp. 5 *et seq*.

[32] As Wilks, *ibid*, points out, citing, *inter alia*, the second edition of Goyder, D.G., *EEC Competition Law*, (Oxford European Community Law Series, Clarendon Press, Oxford, 1988), pp. 45–6, during the first decade of its existence, following the approval of Reg. 17, DG IV paid more attention to vertical agreements between undertakings at different points of production (e.g. exclusive distribution or patent licence agreements) than to the large horizontal cartels between direct competitors, which were as common as ever in transport. The Commission's hand was largely forced in this direction by the avalanche of notifications of agreements of this type which followed the entry into force of Reg. 17 and of the consequential huge backlog of cases.

crisis was eventually resolved by the 'Luxembourg Compromise'.[33] With one of the major promoters of the Communities considering whether to withdraw and disassociate from any commitment to further economic and political integration, the Commission might have felt that it was not in a position to press the Council and push things further, and that it would have to content itself with the inland transport Regulation as approved in 1968; particularly given that the differences between the primary sources of law, (principally Articles 85 and 86 of the Treaty), and the secondary legislation adopted by the Council (particularly Articles 2,5,7 and 8 of Regulation 1017/68) seemed minor.

Regulation 1017/68 clearly identified itself as the source of competition law in the inland transport sector, establishing legislative form, as it did, in the Council's rejection of the universality principle which had been touted by the Commission. However, contrary to what the Council might have thought, Regulation 1017/68 could not create a new and distinct competition law for inland transport, different from the standard competition rules contained in Articles 85 and 86 of the Treaty. Subsequent case law made clear that the Treaty rules on competition apply to all economic sectors, including transport. Thus the application of EC competition rules in the transport sector must not be regarded as a branch of transport policy but of competition law.[34]

2.5. THE *FRENCH SEAMEN* CASE

The controversy concerning the 'universality' of the Treaty was finally resolved in 1974, in favour of the interpretation that had been advanced by the Commission since 1960. In a very important judgment under Article 169 of the Treaty—the *French Seamen* case[35]—the Commission attacked several French legal provisions which, in its view, inhibited the free movement of workers within the Community. The Commission argued that they contravened Article 48 of the Treaty and its implementing legislation (which prohibits any discrimination between EU citizens on the grounds of nationality).[36]

Under French law at the time, a certain proportion of the crew of French

---

[33] France abstained from taking part in the Council's meetings for seven months, with effect from the Council meeting on 30 June 1965. The 'Luxembourg Accord' was reached on the 28 and 29 Jan. 1966. Literature on this phase in the history of the Communities is too numerous to mention.

[34] See *Halsbury's Laws of England*, 4th Edn, Vol. 52 (Butterworths) para. 18.63.

[35] ECJ judgment in Case 167/73, [1974] ECR 359. For a comment on this judgment, see Close, George L., 'Article 84(2) EEC : The development of transport policy in the sea and air transport sectors', *European Law Review*, Vol. 5, No. 3, June 1980, pp. 188–207, at 190–1; see also Bredimas, above n. 4, 4, pp. 14–16.

[36] Under Art. 4 of Reg. 1612/68 (OJ 1968 L 257) 'Legislative, regulatory or administrative provisions of the Member States limiting, in number or percentage, by enterprise, by branch of activity, by region or at the national level, the offer of foreigners are not applicable on citizens of other Member States'.

merchant ships were required to be French nationals.[37] The Commission considered that the French legislative provisions were in breach of Community law, and brought an action against France for failure to fulfil its obligations under the Treaty. The case raised directly, for the first time before the ECJ, the question whether the general rules of the Treaty applied to transport (in particular, maritime transport) or whether the transport sector was outside the scope of the Treaty and was intended to be regulated entirely by the Council on the basis of Article 84(2) for sea and air transport. If outside the Treaty, it would represent a *tabula rasa* as far as the application of Community law was concerned.

The Commission argued that it was not possible to conclude from the existence of Title IV of the Treaty, dedicated to transport, that the rules of the Treaty did not apply. The structure of the Treaty implied that it was applicable to all branches of the economy, save where express provision is made to the contrary. Examples of the latter included Article 61(1), which exempts the field of transport from the general rules on freedom to provide services,[38] and Article 77, which partially limits the application of the rules on State aids to transport. The Commission also referred to the judgment of the Court of 31 March 1971,[39] in which the application of the general rules of the Treaty had been implicitly accepted by the Court, and argued on the grounds of legal certainty that Article 84(2) could not serve to support a different interpretation in respect of sea and air transport.

In its defence, the French Government advanced a twofold argument. Firstly, it argued that the incriminating provision did not in fact apply to Community seamen because administrative instructions were given that Community seamen had to be employed on the same footing as the French. Secondly, it argued that in any event France was under no obligation to comply with Article 48 of the EEC Treaty, especially with regard to seamen, since the Council had not taken measures in accordance with Article 84(2) of the EEC Treaty.

In his submissions to the Court, Advocate-General Reischl argued contrary to the French interpretation that, within the Treaty system as a whole Article 84(2) was an exception within an exception, which therefore must be interpreted narrowly. In addition he considered that Article 84 had to be looked at as a whole. The fact that under Article 84(1) the Treaty rules on transport did not apply to sea transport did not imply the inapplicability of the general provisions of the Treaty. Moreover, the fact that the list in Annex III to the EEC Treaty

---

[37] Art. 3, para. 2 of the French *Code du Travail Maritime* of 1926, and *arrêtés* of 21 Nov. 1960 and 12 June 1969.

[38] This declaration adopted by the ECJ in para. 28 would be rich in consequences for the application of the principle of freedom of services in transport. See Ch. 1, para. 1.3, n. 15. See also the judgments of the ECJ in Joined Cases 209 to 213/84 *Ministère Public* v. *Lucas Asjès*, [1986] ECR 1425 at p. 1457; Case 4/88 *Lambregts* v. *Belgium*, [1989] ECR 2583 at paras 8 and 9; Case C–49/89 *Corsica Ferries France* v. *Direcion Générale des Douanes Françaises*, [1989] ECR 4441, para. 7 *et seq.*

[39] Judgment of the ECJ in Case 22/70, *Commission* v. *Council (ERTA)*, [1971] ECR 263.

(invisible transactions) related to Article 106 (payments between Member States[40]) did not exclude sea transport supported the proposition that the Treaty did apply to the sector.

For its part, the Court examined the place of Article 84(2) in the system of the Treaty and concluded that the Treaty rules having been conceived as applicable to the totality of economic activities, could only be dissipated by express Treaty provision. An example might be Article 38(2) of the Treaty, under which the rules laid down for the establishment of the common market apply to agricultural products to the extent provided for in other parts of the Treaty.[41] The Court also stated that 'when Article 74 refers to the objectives of the Treaty, it means the provisions of Articles 2 and 3, the attainment of which the fundamental provisions applicable to the whole complex of economic activities seek to ensure . . . Far from involving a departure from these fundamental rules, the object of the rules relating to the common transport policy is to implement and complement them by means of common action . . . Consequently, the said general rules must be applied in so far as they can achieve these objectives'.[42]

Finally, the Court ruled that in spite of the fact that the rules in Title IV of Part II of the Treaty were not applicable to maritime transport until the Council had decided otherwise, the general rules of the EEC Treaty applied to shipping, as well as to any other means of transport.[43] As a consequence of the application of the general rules of the Treaty to transport (in this case to maritime transport), the Court declared that the application of Articles 48 to 51 was not optional, but compulsory for the Member States.[44] This implied that the Council, in the exercise of its powers derived from Article 84(2), could not adopt special provisions in maritime transport incompatible with the general provisions of the Treaty and that the special provisions should not vitiate the substance of the general ones.[45]

The Court later confirmed that the transport sector is subject to the general rules of the Treaty with reference to State aids in inland transport. In particular, it was held that Article 77, which at the time was found within Part Two, Title IV, on transport and concerned with State aids to inland transport, was not exempt from the general system of the EEC Treaty on State aids.[46]

Despite the Court's unequivocal pronouncements, the controversy did not end with these rulings. The question shifted, for some Member States, to the interpretation of 'fundamental and general rules of the Treaty', which the *French Seamen* ruling did not define in detail. Some confined the definition to provisions found in Part Two. Others included Part Three of the Treaty, as well as Parts Four, Five and Six. Competition rules—which are in Part Three—would only

---

[40] Following the TEU, the text of the old Art. 106 was transferred to Art. 73H of the EC Treaty, to which Annex III now refers. The provisions were applicable until 1 Jan. 1994.

[41] Judgment above n. 35 at paras 21 and 22. [42] *Ibid.* at paras 24 to 26.

[43] *Ibid.* at paras 32 and 33. [44] Para. 33 of the judgment.

[45] See Bredimas, above n. 4, and Close, above n. 35.

[46] ECJ judgment in Case 156/77, *Commission* v. *Belgium*, [1978] ECR 1881.

be applicable to transport if they could be categorized as 'fundamental and general rules'.

This additional question was answered by the Court in 1986 in the *Nouvelles Frontières* case.[47] The Court held, again against the French Government, that competition rules formed part of the general rules of the Treaty, and were fully applicable to air transport. The French Government argued that the *French Seamen* case was limited to stating that Part Two of the EC Treaty applied to the transport sector, but did not extend to include the competition rules as they were found in Part Three.

The Court rejected this argument, and referred to Article 61(1) as the only Treaty provision whose operation was subject to the adoption by the Council of appropriate rules.[48] The Court noted that Article 77 was clearly based on the supposition that the competition rules, which include rules on State aids, were applicable to transport even though the common transport policy had not yet been defined. The Court stressed that economic sectors could be excluded from the competition rules only by express provision in the Treaty. So, for example, under Article 42, the competition rules apply to the agricultural sector 'only to the extent determined by the Council within the framework of Article 43(2) and (3) and in accordance with the procedure laid down therein, account being taken of the objectives set out in Article 39'. Unlike agriculture, the Treaty's transport rules did not provide for special legislation to determine how Articles 85 and 86 were to apply. It was clear from the Treaty that transport had not been granted the same status as agriculture because no such article similar to Article 42 of the Treaty existed in respect of transport. Accordingly, the competition rules (Articles 85 and 86) were construed to apply without recourse to any implementing provisions based on Articles 75 or 84 of the Treaty.[49]

2.6. SEA AND AIR TRANSPORT

Like the development of the common transport policy itself, the establishment of instruments applying competition rules to the transport sector has been difficult and has taken place on a piecemeal rather than on a global basis. In contrast to all other economic sectors, the adoption of the competition rules and content of those rules have in the various transport sectors been viewed by Member States and by the Council as mainly a facet of the common transport

[47] Joined Cases 209–213/84 *Ministère Public* v. *Lucas Asjès*, above n. 38. For a comment on this judgment, see *Butterworths Competition Law* (looseleaf, Butterworths, London 1992), at p. IX/171, 301.

[48] This interpretation was proposed again by the Commission in its suit against the French Government in the *Nouvelles Frontières* case, and has been confirmed on various occasions by the ECJ, e.g., in its judgment in Case 49/89 *France* v. *Direction Générale des Douanes Françaises (Corsica Ferries)*, above n. 45.

[49] See Ritter, Braun, and Rawlinson, *EEC Competition Law. A practitioners' Guide*, (Kluwer, Deventer, 1991), pp. 562 *et seq.*

policy, and less part of competition policy. This has provoked some difficulties in the drafting, interpretation, and implementation of the competition rules in the transport sector.

Following the adoption of Regulation 1017/68, Regulation 4056/86 was the next measure to be adopted in 1986. The regulation relates to maritime transport.[50] Next in 1987, Regulation 3975/87 was adopted in 1987 in relation to international air transport between Member States.[51] Both measures were part of two packages of legislation directed specifically at those sectors. [52]

The background to Regulation 1017/68 has already been discussed.[53] In a nutshell, Member States did not accept in 1962 and 1968 that Articles 85 and 86 were applicable to the transport sector and, faced with the Commission's weakness or lack of interest, adopted—or more exactly—reinvented specific competition rules for various forms of inland transport.

The *French Seamen* judgment was crucial to the future, long-term application of competition rules to transport. Nonetheless its effect was not felt immediately. In its wake, firm opposition from some Member States and the economic recession of the 1970s permitted only slow and modest advances in competition policy in general and in transport in particular.[54] In addition it was at this time that the Commission decision taken by cartels received the Court's definitive backing and the Commission was able to continue its gradual refinement of tools to be applied to horizontal restrictive agreements and practices—tools so assiduously employed in the 1980s.

The main impetus for reaching the agreement on the application of competition rules to maritime transport, which ultimately resulted in Regulation 4056/86, came from outside the EC. In addition to the *French Seamen* judgment, another major development took place in 1974, this time in Geneva, which is at the root of the application of competition rules to maritime transport. The United Nations Convention on a Code of Conduct for Liner Conferences, the so-called UNCTAD Liner Code, was approved on 6 April 1974.[55] Member States, including the recently joined United Kingdom, Ireland, and Denmark, did not reach a common position during the negotiations prior to the adoption

---

[50] Council Reg. (EEC) 4056/86, OJ L378, 31.12.1986, p. 4.

[51] Council Reg. (EEC) 3975/87, OJ L374, 31.12.1987, p. 1.

[52] For the legislation accompanying the sea and air transport regulations, see Chs 4 and 5 below.

[53] See above at Ch. 2.3. *et seq.*

[54] As related by Wilks, above n. 38, in its second decade community competition policy had to contend with a European industry in full crisis. The Member States tried to overcome this with State subsidies and the undertakings themselves formed 'crisis cartels', something which the Commission had always opposed. To paraphrase Wilks, the pressure from Governments and industry for a more pragmatic interpretation of competition policy to be adopted, to moderate it, in other words, with an industrial policy, made the 1972–82 decade difficult for DG IV.

[55] United Nations Conference on Trade and Development, Geneva, *Conference of plenipotentiaries of the United Nations on a Code of Conduct for Liner Conferences. Held at Geneva from 12.11. to 15.12.1973 (Part One) and from 11.3 to 6.4.1974 (Part Two).* Vol. II, Final Act (including the Convention and Resolutions and tonnage requirements). United Nations, New York, 1975. [Document TD/CODE/13/Add. 1]. For the UNCTAD Liner Code, see below, Ch. 4.

of the Code. For its part, the Commission considered that the UN Convention was contrary to the Treaty on several grounds: first, the basic discrimination on the basis of nationality inherent in the Code: and second, the inconsistency of the Code with competition rules. The Commission initially commenced proceedings under Article 169 of the Treaty against Member States which had signed the UN Convention, but later it agreed with the Member States which had signed the Code not to proceed against them provided they did not ratify the Convention without its prior approval. Once negotiations were under way between the Commission and the Member States and following lengthy discussions, a consensus was reached on the conditions for ratification of the Code of Conduct by the Member States.

Council Regulation 954/79, known as the 'Brussels package', was accordingly adopted in 1979, allowing Member States to ratify the UN Convention provided they introduced certain specific reservations to it.[56] As early as 1979, the last recital of the preamble to the 'Package' envisaged that a regulation would need to be drawn up permitting the existence of traditional shipping conference cartels under European law so that such shipping conferences would not constitute a breach of the competition rules.

Indeed, after the adoption of the 'Brussels package', the Council's emphasis was centred on the question of how to authorize liner conferences under European competition law (conceiving this as a transport policy measure), rather than on the development of competition policy in the shipping sector. The immediate reason for the approval of Regulation 4056/86 was the exemption of liner conferences, not any desire to apply competition rules to the shipping sector. Nevertheless, aside from the privileged status of liner conferences, the Commission was then able to deal with the shipping sector in a similar way to its treatment under Regulation 17 of all other economic sectors. Accordingly, Regulation 4056/86 became the second competition regulation to enjoy a double legal nature, that is, to incorporate both substantive and procedural matters.[57] It authorized certain categories of agreements (substantive nature) and provided for detailed rules akin to the rules in Regulation 17 for the application of Articles 85 and 86 of the Treaty in maritime transport (procedural nature).

The background to air transport was somewhat different. In the maritime sector Government intervention had been scarce and everything had been left to the initiative of commercial parties. This included the conditions under which competition should operate, namely under a system of 'self-regulation'. In contrast, in both the air transport and inland transport sectors Government involvement had been extensive.

---

[56] Council Reg. (EEC) 954/79, concerning the ratification by Member States of, or their accession to, the United Nations Convention on a Code of Conduct for Liner Conferences. OJ 1979 L121, p. 1.

[57] As will be seen later in Ch. 3, the first regulation of this kind was Reg. 1017/68.

The third transport-related implementing modal Regulation was adopted one year after the maritime regulation. The passage of Regulation 3975/87, like Regulation 4056/86, was helped through firstly by the Court's judgements in the case between the European Parliament and the Council (1985)[58] and in the *Nouvelles Frontières* case (1986)[58a] and secondly by the subsequent implementation of Article 89 procedures against the major European airlines.

The third element behind the adoption of the air transport regulation was the Single European Act. The spirit of the Act was crucial for two reasons. First, it would permit—when implemented—free access to previously closed EC national markets for any EC carrier. Second, competition rules would have to be applied to prevent limitations on competition being reintroduced into the sector, this time by private parties as opposed to public bodies, by means of agreements and restrictive practices.

Twenty-five years elapsed between Regulation 141 and Regulation 3975/87. This latter regulation represents the last, for the time being, of the cycle of competition regulations in the transport sector. It has not, however, set in stone the Commission's powers in specific areas of the maritime and air sectors.[59]

The reasons for the period of delay are manifold. In the first place, the Council took six years to adopt legislation on inland transport, instead of three. Furthermore, the Commission took six more years to react to its defeat in Regulation 1017/68 (where the universality of the Treaty had been formally rejected), and only after the *French Seamen* case did it have the courage to announce proposals to obtain from the Council effective powers for the application of Articles 85 and 86 to the sea and air transport sectors.

The first time the Commission announced procedural regulations for maritime and air transport was in 1975 in its *Fifth Report on Competition Policy*.[60] One year later, in the *Sixth Competition Policy Report*, a preliminary draft competition regulation for air transport was announced. The sea transport draft regulation was, in the meantime, put on the back burner due to the negotiations over the United Nations Code of Conduct for liner conferences.[61] In the *Seventh Report*, the Commission announced a draft regulation for air transport for mid-1978. With the Commission and Member States final acceptance (subject to certain reservations) of the UNCTAD Code, and the ongoing negotiations over the 'Brussels package' (seeking to put the Code in line with the Treaty), the Commission announced that the first draft of a regulation for maritime transport would be delayed. Nevertheless it made it known in this latter Report that the work had already commenced.[62] In the *Eighth Report*, the Commission was

---

[58] See above, Ch. 1.4.3.   [58a] See above, n. 38.

[59] See text immediately below. See also below Ch. 4, for a description of sectors still subject to the transitional procedural regime under Arts 88 and 89 of the Treaty.

[60] V Rep. Comp. 1975, paras 14–15.

[61] VI Rep. Comp. 1976, paras 16–18. On the influence of this UN Convention on the adoption of Reg. 4056/86 see below Ch. 4.

[62] VII Rep. Comp. 1977, paras 47–8.

reluctant to propose a regulation for air transport and undertook with Member States a structural study of the competitive conditions in the air transport market. This restored the maritime regulation to first priority in the Commission's regulatory work in the transport field. The Commission reported that the drafting process continued.[63] In 1980, in the *Ninth Report*, the Commission indicated that an air transport draft had been submitted. It also announced that in so far as maritime transport was concerned, the adoption of the 'Brussels package' meant that a draft maritime Regulation could be expected in 1980.[64]

The first maritime draft was finally submitted in 1981. The Council discussed the Commission's proposal for more than five years. A maritime competition regulation was eventually adopted in 1986, to enter into force on 1 July 1987. The air transport regulation was adopted at the end of 1987 and entered into force in 1988, a full nine years after the first Commission proposals in this area.

The acquisition by the Commission of powers of control and sanction in maritime and air transport in the 1980s was part of a dual process of expansion of competition policy. On the one hand, expansion took place into sectors not previously subject to competition rules. This movement started cautiously at the end of the 1970s in the service sectors and yielded its first fruit in the mid-1980s with the first decisions in the banking and insurance sectors.[65] At the same time, the Commission's predominant focus shifted from vertical to horizontal agreements, in other words to traditional price-fixing, supply-control and market-sharing cartels.[66] Both because this had been seen until then as unfurrowed ground and because of the high frequency of horizontal agreements in this sector, transport was destined to receive priority attention from the Commission in the final years of the 1980s and the beginning of the 1990s.

The granting by the Council to the Commission of effective powers to apply competition rules was neither complete nor without a price. It was incomplete because the transport competition regulations do not cover all the sub-sectors of transport. Regulation 4056/86 does not apply to cabotage shipping nor to 'tramp' shipping as defined by the regulation. Regulation 3975/87 applies only to national and international flights between airports situated in Community countries, that is, it covers exclusively intra-Community and cabotage air transport, the latter having been made subject to detailed enforcement rules only very recently.[67] It does not apply to international transport between Community air-

[63] VIII Rep. Comp. 1978, paras 38–40.   [64] IX Rep. Comp. 1979, paras 12–15.

[65] Other sectors of expansion of community competition policy during the third decade from 1982–92 have been in the control of mergers of businesses and public undertakings, especially in the telecommunications and energy sectors. See Wilks, above n. 38, pp. 11 and ff.

[66] Wilks, *ibid.*, at p.12. The Commission's most successful measures occurred in the chemical industry.

[67] As an accompanying measure of the 'Third Package' of liberalizing measures, in which Art. 1(2) of Reg. 3975/87 was modified in this sense, by removing the word 'international'. See below Ch. 5.

ports and airports situated in third countries. These types of transport are, pursuant to Regulation 141, still subject to the provisional rules of Articles 88 and 89 of the Treaty and as far as Article 85 is concerned, restriction agreements remain provisionally valid as long as neither the competent national authority nor the Commission have acted under such provisions.[68]

In comparison with the scope of application of Regulation 1017/68, the provisions of Regulations 4056/86 and 3975/87 are more limited.[69] In the case of the maritime regulation, a limitation on the type of maritime services—irregular or 'tramp' services are excluded—confines the application of Regulation 4056/86 to other than these minutely defined services.[70] In the case of air transport, the limitation is purely geographical: only intra-community air transport—in spite of the Commission's proposals in the framework of the last packages of liberalization measures—may be dealt with under Regulation 3975/87.

It is worth noting a couple of points on the relative applicability of the transport regulations and Articles 85 and 86 of the Treaty. Because of the limited scope of the application of the regulations, not every type of behaviour incurring the prohibition of the Treaty articles is challengeable under the procedural rules of the competition regulations in transport. At the same time the opposite is true: not every form of conduct which falls within the scope of one of the transport regulations can be rendered subject to Articles 85 and 86 of the Treaty. This will only be possible if the conditions of application of these last two provisions are complied with.[71] [72]

The price for the powers given to the Commission was that Regulation 4056/86 granted the most generous block exemption ever to liner conference agreements and practices. Similarly, Regulation 3975/87 was accompanied by the *quid pro quo* of Regulation 3976/87. The latter enabled the Commission (which had undertaken to act accordingly) to adopt block exemption regulations for a series of traditionally restrictive agreements which existed under the regulated system and in particular, for horizontal price-fixing by means of tariff consultation between airlines, normally under the aegis of IATA. 'Exceptions' for 'technical agreements' were provided by both regulations.

[68] For the effects of Reg. 141, see below Ch. 3, Section I.

[69] See Art. 1(2) of Reg. 1017/68, Art. 1(2) of Reg. 4056/86 and Art. 1(2) of Reg. 3975/87.

[70] This exclusion may have, however, few practical repercussions. See below Ch. 4.

[71] In particular, the agreements have to be restrictive and substantially affect trade between Member States. Some authors have doubted that this generally occurs with agreements in international maritime transport. See Forwood, N. 'Jurisdictional limits to the application of EC competition rules to international maritime transport', in Barry Hawk (ed.), (1992) *Annual Proceedings of the Fordham Corporate Law Institute. International Antitrust Law and Policy.* (Trans-national Juris Publications / Kluwer. New York / Deventer, 1993), pp. 907–924.

[72] The scope of application of each regulation (which is limited in maritime and air) and of Arts 85 and 86 of the Treaty are different from each other and similar to two excentric circles of similar size in a venn diagram. Some types of conduct may fall within the scope of application of one regulation and yet not fall within the scope of application of the rules of the Treaty and vice versa. Only the types of conduct which fall within both circles will be challengeable under the transport regulations.

2.7. THE LEGAL FRAMEWORK

We have seen that Regulation 141 excluded all forms of transport from Regulation 17. At the same time, the regulation provided for competition rules to be adopted for inland transport within a specified period. No deadline was stipulated for the application of competition rules to shipping and to air transport.

After Regulation 141, a series of three regulations—one for each mode of transport—were adopted. Regulation 1017/68 was the first to take up the role of a Regulation 17 in inland transport. Regulations 4056/86 and 3975/87 followed, many years later and only partially fortified the weak power to implement competition rules in maritime and air transport which had existed until then.

The significance of the 'modal approach' set forth in Articles 1 and 2 of Regulation 141 was threefold. First, given the fragmentary nature of subsequent legislation, it meant that, whenever Articles 85 and 86 of the Treaty were infringed in areas not covered by the modal regulations, Articles 88 and 89 would be applicable. Concerning activities not directly related to the provision of transport services, these should be treated under Regulation 17.[73] Second, it meant that according to the Commission's interpretation carriers' non-transport activities should be dealt with under Regulation 17. Third, it assumed that carriers' activities in transport sectors different to their own (for example, inland transport activities of shipping companies) would have to be addressed under the transport regulation applicable to each activity. The latter point is extremely important within the debate on multi-modal transport price-fixing on the part of liner shipping conferences.[74]

Competition rules in transport are thus characterized by a scattered legal regime which provides for different rules depending on the modes of transport, the type of services and the agreements involved. In practice, anyone having to deal with competition issues in transport may find themselves subject to five different procedural regimes and rules which can potentially be applied at the same time: the transitional rules of the Treaty, Regulation 17, and the three modal Regulations.

The Commission has developed procedural provisions for the three different modal Regulations in a series of separate regulations. Each essentially recasts the relevant provisions of Regulation 17 and its ancillary regulations, which apply to all other economic sectors subject to Articles 85 and 86:

(1) The implementing provisions relating to the form, content and other requirements of complaints under Article 10, and to applications and notifications under Articles 12 and 14(1) of Regulation 1017/68 have been adopted by

---

[73] See below, Ch. 3, Section I.   [74] See below, Ch. 4.

the Commission by means of Regulation 1629/69.[75] Provisions relating to the right to be heard of undertakings and interested third parties (Article 26(1) and (2) of Regulation 1017/68) have been adopted by means of Regulation 1630/69.[76]

(2)   The implementing provisions relating to the scope of the obligation to notify conciliators' recommendations and arbitration awards (Article 5[5]) and to the form, content and other details of complaints (Article 10), notifications (Article 12) and the right to be heard of undertakings and interested third parties (Article 23[1] and [2]) provided for in Regulation 4056/86 have been adopted by the Commission by means of Regulation 4260/88.[77]

(3)   The implementing provisions relating to the form, content, and other requirements of complaints (Article 3), applications and notifications (Articles 3[2] and 5) and the hearings of undertakings and interested third parties (Articles 16[1] and [2]) provided for in Regulation 3975/87 have been adopted by the Commission by means of Regulation 4261/88.[78]

These regulations reproduce virtually without variation the implementing regulations of Council Regulation 17 as applied in 1969 and 1988. These are, Commission Regulation 27 (on applications and notifications)[79] and Commission Regulation 99/63/EEC (on the right to be heard). Regulations 1629/68, 4260/88 and 4261/88 were amended with a view to developing the competition rules of the Agreement on the European Economic Area (EEA),[80] but have not been updated to conform with Regulation 3385/94, which has replaced Regulation 27 outside the transport sector.[81]

The system of procedural rules for competition in the transport sector is complicated, as you can see. The system also poses some, but fewer problems of a substantive nature:

(1)   All the modal regulations contain an exemption for technical agreements.[82]
(2)   In inland transport, Article 4 of Regulation 1017/68 grants a block exemption to certain groups of small and medium size undertakings.
(3)   In maritime transport, Articles 3 and 6 of Regulation 4056/86 grant a block exemption to certain agreements of members of liner conferences and, in certain circumstances, their customers. On the other hand, the Commission has

---

[75] Comm. Reg. (EEC) 1629/69, OJ 1969 L209, p. 1, Spec. Ed. 1969 II, p. 381.
[76] Comm. Reg. (EEC) 1630/69 containing forms I, II and III. OJ 1969 L 209, p. 11, Spec. Ed. 1969 II, p. 381.
[77] Comm. Reg. (EEC) 4260/88, OJ 1988 L 376, p.1, containing form MAR.
[78] Comm. Reg. (EEC) 4261/88, OJ 1988 L 376, p. 10, containing form AER.
[79] Comm. Reg. (EEC) 27, OJ 1962 35, p. 1118 (Spec. Ed. 1959–1962, p. 132).
[80] Comm. Reg. (EEC) 3666/93, OJ 1993 L 336, p. 1.
[81] Comm. Reg. (EC) 3385/94, OJ 1994 L 377, p. 28.
[82] Art. 3 of Reg. 1017/68. Art. 2 of Reg. 4056/86 and Art. 2 of Reg. 3975/87.
[83] Comm. Reg. (EC) 870/95, OJ 1995 L 89, p. 7.

recently adopted block exemption Regulation 870/95 for liner consortia.[83]

(4) In air transport, unlike inland and maritime transport, the substantive exempting provisions are to be found in separate Commission Regulations, all of them derived from Council Regulation 3976/87, which delegate powers to the Commission for the adoption of certain exemptions.[84] At the present time, the following Commission Regulations are in force:

(a) Regulation 1617/93[85], exempting the following categories of agreements:

• Joint planning and co-ordination of schedules (Article 2).
• Joint operations (Article 3).
• Consultations on tariffs for passengers and cargo (Article 4).
• Slot allocation and airport scheduling (Article 5).

(b) Regulation 3652/93, granting a block exemption for certain agreements between undertakings on computer reservation systems (CRS).[86] This regulation has to be read in conjunction with Council Regulation 2299/89, on a code of conduct for CRS.[87]

At the present time, a block exemption for agreements relating to ground handling services no longer exists.[88] The Council is considering a Directive to resolve the problems raised by these services at airports.[89]

On the other hand, and in parallel with the Community competition rules in transport, the rules of the EEA Agreement have to be taken into account. Despite their more than reduced importance following the accession of Austria, Sweden and Finland as full members of the EU, the EEA Agreement continues to be applicable in relations with Norway—the only non-Community participating country of some size—Iceland and Liechtenstein. The competition rules applicable to undertakings are to be found in Chapter 1 of Part Four, in Articles 53 to 60, in Protocol 21 and in Annex XIV of the Agreement.[90]

Articles 53 and 54 of the EEA Agreement correspond to Articles 85 and 86

---

[84] Council Reg. (EEC) 3976/87, OJ 1987 L 374, p. 9, as amended by Council Reg. (EEC) 2344/90, OJ 1990 L 217, p. 15, and by Council Reg. (EEC) 2411/92, OJ 1992 L 240, p. 19.

[85] Comm. Reg. (EEC) 1617/93, OJ 1993 L 155, p. 18. This Reg. has replaced Comm. Reg. (EEC) 84/91, OJ 1991 L 10, p. 14, which in its turn replaced Comm. Reg. (EEC) 2671/88, OJ 1988 L 239, p. 9.

[86] Comm. Reg. (EC) 3652/93, OJ 1993 L 333, p. 37. This Reg. has replaced Comm. Reg. (EEC) 83/91, OJ 1991 L 10, p. 9 which—in its turn—replaced Comm. Reg. (EEC) 2672/88, OJ 1988 L 239, p. 13.

[87] Council Reg. (EEC) 2299/89, OJ 1989 L 220, p. 1, as amended by Council Reg. (EC) 3089/93, OJ 1993 L 278, p. 1.

[88] Comm. Reg. (EEC) 82/91, OJ 1991 L 10, p. 7, which replaced Comm. Reg. (EEC) 2673/88, OJ 1988 L 239, p. 17, granted a block exemption for agreements on handling Reg. 82/91 has neither been extended nor replaced by another similar one.

[89] See *Press Release IP (94) 1206*, of 13 Dec. 1994. See also below, Ch. 5.

[90] It should be noted that, otherwise, the EEA Agreement also contains specific provisions on transport in Ch. 6 of Pt Three (Arts 47 to 52) and in its Annexe XIII. See above, Ch. 1.

of the EC Treaty. Article 57 of the EEA Agreement refers to Regulation 4064/89 on merger control.[91] Article 59 of the EEA Agreement reproduces with minor variations Article 90 of the EC Treaty. Protocol 21 refers to general and specific procedural rules for the application of competition rules.[92] Finally, Annex XIV introduces certain adaptations to Regulations 1017/68 and 4056/86, for their application in relations with non-Community member countries of the EEA Agreement.[93]

Chapters 3, 4 and 5 try to describe the substantive competition rules which apply to transport. Chapter 6 deals with the procedural rules. Chapter 7 draws some conclusions. Reference will be made throughout the book to the changes introduced by the EEA Agreement wherever they have any substantive nuance which needs to be emphasised.

[91] Council Reg. (EEC) 4064/89, OJ 1989 L 395, p. 1, corrected version in OJ 1990 L 257, p. 13.

[92] In particular, Art. 3(1), paras 6 to 14 of Protocol 21, refers to Regs 141, 1017/68, 1629/69, 1630/69, 2988/74 (on time-barring of proceedings and penalties; see below, Ch. 6), 4056/86, 4260/88, 3975/87 and 4261/88.

[93] Annex XIV, Section G of the EEA Agreement.

3

The First EC Competition Regulations for Transport

Section I: Regulation 141

3.1. SCOPE[1]

Pursuant to Article 1 of Regulation 141:

Regulation 17 shall not apply to agreements, decisions or concerted practices in the transport sector which have as their object or effect the fixing of transport rates and conditions, the limitation or control of the supply of transport or the sharing of transport markets; nor shall it apply to the abuse of a dominant position, within the meaning of Article 86 of the Treaty, within the transport market.

It is not clear how far Article 1 of Regulation 141 should be interpreted as extending the exception to the applicability of Regulation 17 in the transport sector.

The first problem is to identify the scope of the non-applicability of the procedural rules of Regulation 17 to transport activities. Article 1 of the regulation clearly has limited scope. However, this article gives conflicting signals. While the first recital of the preamble to Regulation 141 refers to the 'transport sector' in general, the third and last recital refers to 'agreements, decisions and concerted practices directly relating to the provision of transport services'. While the words 'transport sector' give the impression that transport should be understood as the transport market, encompassing both supply and demand for transport services, the wording in the third and last recital may be construed as referring only to agreements relating to the direct supply (provision) of transport services.

On the latter interpretation, the procedural rules of Regulation 17 would apply only to agreements between carriers or, at most, between carriers and users if and when their subject is the provision of transport services. It does not apply to agreements between transport users. This interpretation has never been explicitly supported by the Commission. If it was correct the procedural rules resulting from Regulation 141 (the three modal procedural regulations) would

---

[1] For a full discussion on the implications of Reg. 141 in general, and its Art. 1 in particular, see Pinay, P., 'Règles de concurrence et transports dans le cadre de la C.E.E.', *Annuaire Français de Droit International*, Vol. 8, 1962, pp. 781–805 at pp. 781 *et seq*.

not govern the whole transport market (including the supply and demand sides) but only a part of such market, namely the supply side.

The limited scope of Regulation 141 is restated in the draft regulation submitted by the Commission to the Council on 27 September 1962.[2] In the second and last recitals in the preamble to the draft, it is clearly stated that only transport undertakings, not the transport market as a whole, benefit from the non-application of the rules contained in Regulation 17. Regulation 141 accordingly separates carriers' restrictive agreements (which are subject to specific procedural regimes) from restrictive agreements between transport users which are subject to the general rules of Regulation 17. Demand-side cartels and dominant positions (monopsonies and buying power) have to be dealt with under Regulation 17, although their effects are still felt in the transport market.

This interpretation, based on the wording of the regulation and on the need to interpret exceptions to the general rules restrictively, leads to a duplication of procedural regimes in each modal transport market. This is in addition to the threefold regime stemming from the various procedural rules in transport and to the various transitional regimes. It is difficult to imagine a more cumbersome system of law.

In spite of addressing mainly carriers, Regulation 141 does not provide for a special regime for carriers operating in markets distinct from transport. The procedural and substantive benefits granted to carriers are not granted on an *ad personam* basis. Agreements entered into by a carrier acting in a different capacity or in a market different from its own are subject to Regulation 17 or to other special transport regulations. An example of this can be seen in the agreements between IATA members concerning their agreements on passenger and cargo agencies[3] which fell to be considered by the Commission under Regulation 17.[4] In a similar vein, agreements between air carriers relating to, for example, inland transport, are subject to Regulation 1017/68 and not to Regulation 3975/87, according to the Commission. This is particularly relevant in the case of inland price-fixing by liner conference members, which has been made subject to Regulation 1017/68.[5]

The second problem stems from the laconic wording of this provision. Article 1 of Regulation 141 reproduces sub-paragraphs a) to c) of Article 85(1) of the Treaty. Letters d) and e) are not reproduced in the text of Article 1. Neither is any other activity which could possibly fall within the scope of Article 85(1); the list of restrictive agreements and practices given from a) to e) is non-exhaustive.

---

[2] 'Règlement n° . . . visant à suspendre, dans le domaine des transports par chemin de fer, par route et par voies navigables, l'application de l'article 85(CEE), ainsi que des dispositions prises ou à prendre en vue de son application'. Document VII/IV/COM(62) 259 final, of 27 Sept. 1962.

[3] See the Comm. Dec. in *IATA Passenger Agency Programme* OJ 1991 L258, p. 18, and in the case *IATA Cargo Agency Programme* (OJ 1991 L258, p. 29.

[4] However, a recent judgment of the CFI may have called into question the legal basis of these two decisions. See judgment of the CFI of 6 June 1995 in Case T–14/93, *Union internationale des chemins de fer (UIC)* v. *Commission*, (not yet reported).　　　　　[5] See below, Ch. 4.

It might therefore be thought that Regulation 141 has exclusively precluded the application of Regulation 17 to rate-fixing, capacity agreements and market-sharing in the transport sector, but not to any other restrictive activity. This argument is reinforced by the fact that exceptions to competition rules must themselves be construed restrictively.

The argument in favour of a limited scope for Regulation 141 (and, simultaneously, for a wider scope for Regulation 17) could be defended in the following way :

(1) Derogations from the Treaty (Articles 85 and 86) and from general rules (Regulation 17) must be construed narrowly;
(2) The Council could have employed a wider formula if it had desired to extend the scope of Regulation 141 to the restrictions listed in sub-paragraphs d) and e) of Article 85(1) and to other possible restrictions of competition, pursuant to Article 85(1) (a mistake or drafting error would not have occurred);
(3) 'Directly relating to the provision of transport services' correctly addresses sub-paragraphs a) to c) of Article 85(1) exclusively. Sub-paragraphs d) and e) and unspecified agreements would not be, in the Council's mind, directly related to the provision of transport services.

However, there has been no legal confirmation of this interpretation. Whilst it is true that on a literal interpretation Regulation 141 would apply exclusively to three categories of agreements out of the illustrative list in Article 85(1) of the Treaty, this interpretation might not be in line with :

(1) The recitals of the regulation;
(2) The intention of the Commission and the Council that Regulation 17 not apply to transport;
(3) The fact that Article 2 of Regulation 1017/68 repeats Article 85(1) in its entirety. It reproduces almost exactly the wording of the Treaty and not just the first three sub-paragraphs referred to.

Furthermore, if the interpretation developed above was correct, it would establish a dual regime for each mode of transport: one based on Regulation 17 for the fourth, the fifth and the non-listed types of restrictive agreements and practices; the other based on the applicable transport regulations for the restrictive agreements and practices included in sub-paragraphs a) to c) of Article 85(1). This interpretation would permit the Commission to act under Regulation 17 to put an end to agreements and restrictive practices not directly referred to in Regulation 141, without the limitations imposed by the sea and air transport Regulations.[6]

[6] Maritime cabotage, tramp shipping as defined in Reg. 4056/86 and international air transport between the EC and third countries are still subject to the transitional rules of Arts 88 and 89.

Taking into account the historical background to Regulation 141, which was adopted at the beginning of the debate on the universality principle and the interpretation of the transport Title in Part Two of the Treaty, it would be surprising if the Council intended to preclude the enforcement of Regulation 17 only with regard to those three specific types of restrictive agreements. It is true, however, that they are the restrictive agreements more directly connected with the provision of transport services. Furthermore, given that the last recital of Regulation 141 specifies that the exemption from the application of Regulation 17 applies only to agreements, decisions, and concerted practices directly relating to the provision of transport services, it might be thought that it was not the intention of the Council to oust less directly related restrictive agreements and practices from the ambit of Regulation 17.

But whenever a transport case has been addressed by the Court, it has not raised this question. This would seem to indicate that in the Court's mind Regulation 141 excludes the application of Regulation 17 to all kinds of restrictive agreements and practices.[7] For its part, the Commission has never questioned whether Regulation 141 rendered inapplicable Regulation 17 to all restrictive agreements in the provision of transport services. Most probably, the reason for this particular drafting is simply an oversight, poor legislative drafting or an error, not an uncommon occurrence in competition regulations in the transport sector.

The third interpretative problem with regard to Article 1 of Regulation 141 is that its scope has not been respected by the subsequent procedural transport regulations. For that reason, the scope of the latter coincides partially with the general procedure rules of Regulation 17. The scope of transport regulations has extended beyond inland, maritime, and air carriage, to other types of services, to general sectors of the economy and to parts of the transport market which were not removed from Regulation 17 by Regulation 141. With this, the scope of Regulation 17 has been encroached on by the transport regulations. Consequently, in order to ascertain the applicable procedural rules, the Commission has considered it necessary to take into account not only the self-attributed scope of the regulations adopted for the various transport modes, but also Article 1 of Regulation 141 in the light of its third recital.

The first example which goes beyond the scope of Regulation 141 (and thus falls within Regulation 17) is Article 1(2) of Regulation 1017/68, which extends the applicability of the Regulation to ancillary services. These are by definition not directly related to the provision of transport services, as arguably required by Regulation 141.[8] [9] A second example is contained in Regulation 4056/86

---

[7] See in particular the judgment of the CFI in the *UIC* case, above n. 4, which is addressed further in Section II below.

[8] Art. 1(2) of Reg. 1017/68 is designed to encroach on Reg. 17 sectors more or less related with transport and allow the exception in Art. 3 and the exemption in Art. 4 to cover, at least in part, activities subject to Reg. 17. See below, Section II.

[9] But see the CFI judgment in *UIC*, above n. 4.

and concerns agreements between transport users (shippers, consignees, and freight forwarders) to enter into agreements with liner conferences, which are subject to a block exemption contained in Article 6 of the above Regulation.[10] A third case in which the frontier between Regulation 17 and the modal regulations is blurred concerns the provisions on technical agreements in the transport regulations.[11]

A further case in which a part of the economy formerly subject to the procedural rules in Regulation 17 has been assumed by the procedures of the transport regulations concerns certain air transport-related services. Regulation 3975/87 regulates air carriers, but according to the Commission it is not in principle applicable to agreements which are not directly related to the provision of air transport services. All other agreements and practices by air carriers are subject to Regulation 17 or to the other transport regulations. Nonetheless, this distinction has not always been respected by the Council, because in fact agreements, decisions and practices not directly related to the provision of transport have been made subject to the special rules on competition in transport.

In the past, the Commission considered that some services carried out in connection with air transport operations were not directly related to the provision of such services and could not be regarded as transport services and Regulation 17 should be applied. In its decision in the *Olympic Airways* case,[12] the Commission decided, for example, that handling services for commercial aircraft and passengers at airports did not form part of the transport market for the purposes of Regulation 141, and Regulation 17 was the appropriate instrument.[13] In the *London European/Sabena* case,[14] the Commission imposed a fine on Sabena, the Belgian airline, for having abused its dominant position in the Belgian market for air travel reservations by impeding the access of London European to its computer reservation system. The Commission used Regulation 17 in this case, too. In the *IATA Passenger and Cargo Agencies* decisions[15] the Commission exempted certain agreements between air carriers regarding the appointment of travel agents and the distribution of air tickets on the basis of Regulation 17.[16]

---

[10] According to the proposed interpretation of Reg. 141, which excludes the demand side of the transport market from the procedural rules set forth in Reg. 4056/86, the applicable regulation for the individual exemption of such agreements should be Reg. 17. It is true, however, that in this particular case Art. 87 seems to be a sufficient legal basis for exempting agreements between transport users, and that in this respect Reg. 4056/86 might not be inconsistent with Reg. 141. In this regard, see below Ch. 4.

[11] For these provisions, see the paragraphs dealing with technical agreements in Section II of Ch. 3, Chs 4 and 5.

[12] OJ 1985 L 46, p. 51.

[13] However, in *Press Release IP (94) 1206*, of 13 Dec. 1994, regarding a draft Council Directive on ground handling services, the Commission seems to have put forward the opposite view.

[14] OJ 1988 L 317, p. 47.

[15] See above n. 3.

[16] As stated, the judgment of the CFI in the *UIC* case, above n. 90, seems to go directly against the Commission's interpretation. For a more thorough discussion of the implications of the *UIC* judgment, see below Section II of this Chapter.

It is worth noting that under Article 7 of Regulation 3976/87, following the individual withdrawal of the block exemptions, the applicable provisions are those of Regulation 3975/87, not those of Regulation 17. This is the case not only for joint planning, tariff consultations and slot allocation at airports (which are directly related to the provision of air transport services) but also for agreements and practices concerning ground handling services and computer reservation systems (CRSs).[17] In spite of this, ground handling and CRS services are different from the provision of air transport services, and thus according to the Commission, Regulation 141 should not apply, i.e. Regulation 17 should apply.

The incoherence of Regulation 3976/87 is further demonstrated by the fact that Regulation 3975/87 does not formally extend its scope to air transport-related services or markets, as Regulation 1017/68 does.[18] In light of its scope, Regulation 3975/87 appears not to be directly relevant or applicable to ground handling services and CRSs. Despite the fact that block exemptions are subject to Regulation 3976/87, infringement procedures and individual exemptions in these areas should have been dealt with pursuant to Regulation 17.

The fourth problem in the interpretation of Article 1 of Regulation 141 is that it is not entirely clear whether transport by means of pipelines and other fixed installations is covered by Regulation 141. It appears from the second recital of the preamble to the Regulation that it surely intended to create exceptions for transport by rail, road and inland waterway, by sea and by air. Consequently, other forms of transport—such as pipelines—remain caught by Regulations No. 17.[19]

3.2. GENERAL BLOCK EXEMPTIONS

A further difficulty concerning Regulation 141 relates to its applicability to general block exemption regulations. In other words, can exclusive dealing, patent licensing, specialization, research and development, franchising and know-how agreements in the transport sector be deemed exempted pursuant to the various block exemption regulations granted by the Commission? The question might seem academic, because these exemptions relate largely to trade in goods. However, they do not relate exclusively to goods. There may be cases in which agreements on services are included within these block exemptions[20] and this matter merits further comment.

---

[17] Agreements relating to ground handling services were authorized until 1992, but the Commission and the Council did not consider it appropriate to extend the exemption in the third air transport liberalization package.

[18] See below, Section II.

[19] See Close, George L., 'Article 84(2) EEC: The development of transport policy in the sea and air transport sectors. *European Law Review*, Vol. 5, No 3, June 1980, pp. 188–207, at p. 189.

[20] See, e.g., Art. 2 of Comm. Reg. (EEC) 2349/84 on patent licensing, OJ 1985 L219, p. 15; corrigendum OJ L280, 22.10.1985, p. 32.

The enabling regulations adopted by the Council with a view to allowing the Commission to grant exemption to certain categories of agreements, cast some light over this issue.

The preamble to Regulation 19/65, adopted less than three years after Regulation 141, stated that 'in view of the high number of notifications submitted in pursuance of Regulation 17 . . .' it was desirable to grant exemption to certain categories of agreements, in order to facilitate the task of the Commission;[21] and that for certain types of agreements 'there can be no easing of the procedures prescribed by Regulation 17 . . .'.[22] Later on, Regulation 2821/71, the second Council enabling regulation, also referred in its preamble on three occasions to Regulation 17.[23]

Therefore, the Commission regulations based on Council Regulations 19/65 and 2821/71 (adopted without any reference to transport several years after Regulation 141) and the subsequent Commission regulations are premised on the procedural regime instituted by Regulation 17. Since transport is expressly excluded from the application of Regulation 17 by Article 1 of Regulation 141, logic dictates that none of the Commission block exemption regulations can apply to agreements directly related to the provision of transport services.

3.3. ARTICLES 88 AND 89 OF THE EC TREATY

One consequence of Regulation 141 was that, until the Council adopted special procedural rules for transport under Article 87 of the Treaty, Articles 86 and 85 could only be enforced by means of the transitional rules in Articles 88 and 89 of the Treaty (although, in fact, they were not). The possibilities of effective enforcement under these provisions were much more limited than under Regulation 17, as the Commission found out, for example, in the *Sterling Airways/SAS* case.[24]

First, the Commission's powers under Article 89 are narrowly defined. Secondly, Member States' authorities have never exercised their powers under Article 88, possibly because of the lack of compulsory powers to investigate infringements of European competition law under national law. Thirdly, the Court had held in the *Bosch*, *Haecht II* and *De Bloos/Bouyer* judgments,[25] later confirmed with specific reference to transport in the *Nouvelles Frontières*[26] and *Ahmed*

---

[21] Council Reg. 19/65/EEC, OJ 1965 L 36, p. 533 (Spec. Ed. 1965–1966, p. 35), 3rd Recital.
[22] Reg. 19/65, 5th Recital.
[23] See Council Reg. (EEC) 2821/71, OJ 1971 L 285, p. 46 (Spec. Ed. 1971–III, p. 1032), 7th, 8th and 9th Recitals.
[24] *Sterling Airways/SAS*, X Rep. Comp. 1980 at para. 136 and Bull. EC 12–1980, para 2.1.33.
[25] Judgments of the ECJ in Case 13/61, *De Geus* v. *Bosch*, [1962] ECR 45, Case 48/72, *Haecht II*, [1973] ECR 77, and Case 59/77, *De Bloos* v. *Bouyer II*, [1977] ECR 2359.
[26] Joined Cases 209–213/84, *Ministère public* v. *Lucas Asjes et al.*, [1986] ECR 1425.

Saeed[27] cases, that national courts could not hold anti-competitive agreements in transport to be automatically void under Article 85(2) in the absence of a formal ruling by the Commission or the national authority under Articles 89 or 88, respectively.[28] The Court's reasoning was that until procedural regulations had been issued, the procedure and scope for exemptions under Article 85(3) would be unclear, and as exemptions could be given retroactive effect, it would cause legal uncertainty for courts to declare agreements null and void under Article 85(2). The *Ahmed Saeed* judgment clarified, however, that the absence of a procedural regulation did not prevent courts holding agreements contrary to Article 86 since there is no possibility of exemption from Article 86.[29]

The present effect of Regulation 141 is to maintain procedurally under the transitional regime the application of Articles 85 and 86 to transport activities not covered by Regulations of the Regulation 17 type. Tramp and cabotage shipping and international air transport between the EU and third countries are subject to Articles 88 and 89 procedures because of Regulation 141. Otherwise, they would be treated under the sea and air transport regulations, or under Regulation 17, in conjunction with other parts of the economy.[30]

Section II: Regulation 1017/68[31]

3.4. TITLE

From the beginning, Regulation 1017/68 demonstrates some notable features. Its title, 'Council Regulation applying rules of competition to transport by rail, road and inland waterway', contrasts with the titles of Regulation 17, Regulation 4056/86 and Regulation 3975/87. These three are cited as 'implementing Articles 85 and 86 of the Treaty', or otherwise 'laying down detailed rules for the application of Articles 85 and 86 of the Treaty to maritime (or air)

---

[27] Case 66/86, *Ahmed Saeed and another* v. *ZBUW*, [1989] ECR 803.

[28] This is one aspect of the doctrine of the so-called 'provisional validity', see below, Ch. 6.

[29] On this point, see Ritter, L., Braun, W. D., and Rawlinson, F., *EEC competition law: a practitioner's guide* (Kluwer, Deventer, 1991), at pp. 570–1, notes 63 and 64.

[30] Given that Reg. 141 is no longer applicable in inland transport (see Arts 3 and 1 of Reg. 141) as pointed out by the CFI in its *UIC* judgment, above n. 4, at para. 43, if Reg. 1017/68 were ever derogated from, the applicable procedural regime in inland transport would be Reg. No 17 whereas if Reg. 4056/86 or Reg. 3975/87 were derogated from, Reg. 141 would apply. Thus Reg. 17 would not apply and the Commission would be obliged to use the transitional procedural rules of Arts 88 and 89 of the Treaty in these two sectors.

[31] On this subject, see the contribution of Helmuth Schröter in Groeben, H., Thiesing, J., and Ehlermann, C. D., *Kommentar zum EWG-Vertrag*, 4th Edn, Vol. 2, Arts 85–109, (Nomos, Baden-Baden 1991), pp. 2023–61.

transport'; titles which, unlike the title of Regulation 1017/68, take for granted the applicability of Articles 85 and 86 of the Treaty.

The Council's unwillingness to recognize that competition rules *already* applied in transport made it necessary to reinvent competition rules for road, rail, and inland waterway, as if Articles 85 and 86 were not applicable to these forms of transport. The Council did not in Regulation 1017/68 follow the technique employed in Regulation 17 (which had been adopted six years before) of making reference to the competition rules of the Treaty. Articles 85 and 86 were themselves transposed and tailored for the inland transport sector. The result was the creation of a new set of competition rules, the originality of which derived more from the fact of having (allegedly) been created by Council Regulation than from any fundamental divergence from Articles 85 and 86 of the Treaty. The regulation reproduced those provisions with only minor variations.

It was only many years later that the *status quo ante* Regulation 1017/68 was restored with the adoption of Regulation 4056/86 and Regulation 3975/87. This occurred only once the Court had clarified that transport was unconditionally subject to Articles 85 and 86 of the Treaty, in the same way as any other economic sectors not specifically dealt with by the Treaty (such as agriculture under Article 42 of the Treaty).

3.5. A DOUBLE LEGAL BASIS

This regulation has often been considered something of a curiosity in comparison with Regulation 17.[32] A further surprising feature is that the regulation presents a double legal basis, namely Articles 75 and 87 of the Treaty.

As already explained,[33] the controversy around the universality of the Treaty and the applicability of Articles 85 and 86 to transport highly influenced the adoption of Regulation 1017/68, which, like Regulation 141, reflects its fundamental nature of compromise. This is also reflected in its dual legal basis. The inclusion of both Articles 75 and 87 permitted the representatives of Member States to maintain that a competition regulation in transport could only be introduced within the framework of a common transport policy.

Article 75 serves to classify the regulation as an instrument of common inland transport policy. The recitals and the Articles of the regulation itself testify to the fact that the Council disregarded other considerations (particularly competition law considerations) and aimed at creating a new system of competition rules in inland transport.

Although the use of Article 75 is fully in accordance with the basic philosophy of Regulation 1017/68 (a regulation intended to develop a common transport policy in the inland sector), Article 87 is inconsistent with the Council's clear

[32] See *Butterworths Competition Law*, (Butterworths, London, 1992), p. IX/172, § 305.
[33] See above, Ch. 2.

denial that Articles 85 and 86 applied to inland transport. Regulation 1017/68 rejects the applicability of those provisions for the inland transport sector. In spite of this, the regulation cites as its legal basis Article 87 of the Treaty, which is directly related to Articles 85 and 86.

3.6. ARTICLE 87[34]

Article 87(1) provides that 'the Council shall . . . adopt any appropriate regulations or directives to give effect to the principles set out in Articles 85 and 86'. It is quite paradoxical that Regulation 1017/68 cites, as a legal basis, the Article which relates to the implementation of the competition rules. It is all the more surprising when the regulation continues, in the third and fifth recitals of its preamble, to state that 'the establishing of rules of competition for transport by rail, road and inland waterway is part of the common transport policy and of general economic policy' and that 'the rules of competition for transport derogate from the general rules of competition'.

The substantive provisions of Regulation 1017/68 also questionably remain within the scope of Article 87(1). A regulation based upon Article 87 should, in theory, lay out only implementing provisions for Articles 85 and 86, without restating, even less amending, them. The provisions of the regulation defy this principle not only in the case of the prohibition on cartels and abuses of a dominant position, and the provisions on public undertakings, but also in the case of the exception for technical agreements. The latter provision apparently attempts to alter the prohibition/exemption system provided for in the Treaty and in Regulation 17 introducing in its place a new hybrid category.[35]

It could be argued that, by including Article 87 as a legal base, the Council intended, pursuant in particular to Article 87(2)(c), to redefine for the inland transport sector the scope of the provisions of Articles 85 and 86.

Whether the Council is entitled on the basis of Article 87 to derogate or ignore Articles 85 and 86 is a question that has been debated ever since the Communities came into being. This Article, interpreted as a *carte blanche* for the Council to disapply Articles 85 and 86, would permit the exclusion of the application of competition rules from the transport sector as a whole. On this interpretation Article 87 would allow the Council to alter the essence of competition rules in any sector of the economy and the controversy over the universality of the Treaty and the applicability of competition rules to transport would be

---

[34] For an interpretation of Art. 87 of the Treaty, similar to that proposed here, see Gleiss, Alfred and Hirsch, Martin, *Kommentar zum EWG Kartellrecht*, (Verlag Recht und Wirtschaft. Heidelberg, 1978), p. 386; Deringer, Arved, *The competition law of the EEC*, (Commerce Clearing House. New York, 1968), paras 627–9; Sharpe, T. 'Crisis Cartels', *European Law Review*, Vol. 3, pp. 222–4; and by the same author 'The Commission's proposals on crisis cartels', *Common Market Law Review*, Vol. 17, no. 1, pp. 75–90.

[35] See below 3.10.

irrelevant. The reference in Article 87(2)(c) to the 'scope of application of Articles 85 and 86' would entitle the Council to take certain agreements or even entire sectors out of the scope of Articles 85 and 86 and even to create new substantive rules not envisaged in the Treaty itself.[36] Article 87(2)(c), or even other provisions of the Treaty like Article 103, could be used for reasons of economic policy to derogate from Articles 85 and 86. Articles 85 and 86 would thus have a lower legal 'value' than Article 87 and possibly other provisions of the Treaty. Council regulations, not the Treaty, would take priority in respect of competition and the Treaty would be a source of competition rules only in those sectors where the Council would not have established special rules. In practice, Article 87 would prevail over Articles 85 and 86 and, in a very real sense, such an interpretation would render the competition rules of the Treaty subsidiary, if not redundant.

Most commentators consider, however, that no regulation based on Article 87(2) should be contrary to the substance of Articles 85 and 86.[37] The Council, using its powers under Article 87(2), may implement competition rules in a given area, but may not in so doing eliminate the competitive character of any one economic sector. Moreover, under Article 87(1) the provisions under Article 87(2) must be designed to give effect to the principles set forth in Articles 85 and 86. Accordingly, disapplying Articles 85 and 86 of the Treaty cannot be within the terms of Article 87(2): 'defining the scope' cannot be taken to include 'impeding the application of' Articles 85 and 86 of the Treaty. Only special sectoral rules, like Article 42 of the Treaty, allow the Council to mitigate the full force of Articles 85 and 86.

It is important to note that the fact that it is the Council which adopts the regulations or directives pursuant to Article 87 does not mean that the Council can derogate from or ignore the Treaty. The Treaty has been approved, adopted, and ratified not by the Council but by Member States following a complicated procedure of public international law. In addition, in the internal Community legal order, the Treaty fulfils a constitutional role and ranks far higher in the legal hierarchy than any act the Council might adopt. It is for this reason that only a modification of the Treaty, either along the lines of Article 42 or in some other way, would allow for Articles 85 and 86 not to be applied in a uniform way to all sectors of the economy with the exception of agriculture, the only genuinely special sector for the application of EC competition rules.[38]

[36] The implementing regulations of competition rules in the transport sector would testify to this, for they have created (with the exceptions for technical agreements) what may be seen as a new way to authorize practices and agreements which differs from Art. 85(3).

[37] See Gleiss and Hirsch, at p. 386; Sharpe, T., 'Crisis Cartels', at p. 22 *et seq.*, and 'Commission's proposals on crisis cartels' at pp. 75 *et seq.*, above n. 34, note 120. All are also cited in Van Houtte, Ben, *L'exemption dans le droit européen de la concurrence. Analyse et commentaire de l'article 85(3) CEE*; (unpublished doctoral thesis, University of Cologne, 1983), pp. 70–1.

[38] Agreements concerning agricultural products are exempted from Art. 85(1) in certain narrowly defined circumstances under Council Reg. 26/62, OJ 1962 30, p. 62 (Spec. Ed. 1959–62, p. 129). See in this respect Ritter *et al*, above n. 29, p. 562.

Consequently, it seems clear that Article 87 cannot serve to breach, escape or avoid the application of Articles 85 and 86 of the Treaty. There must be complete consistency between Council measures adopted pursuant to Article 87 and Articles 85 and 86. For these reasons, some provisions in Regulation 1017/68 risk being *ultra vires* the Treaty and, therefore, illegal. In particular, Articles 3, 4 and 6 of the regulation present cause for concern.[39]

Article 87 may also have been cited as a legal base for Regulation 1017/68 in order to permit the inclusion within its scope of certain activities previously falling under Regulation 17 and to grant those activities a more generous regime. However, it seems doubtful that Article 87 could be used for these purposes.

A further possible reason for Article 87's inclusion might have been a desire for 'institutional balance'. Given the Council's stance on competition rules in transport, Article 87 might have been a concessionary gesture from the Council to the Commission when the regulation was negotiated. The inclusion of a typical 'competition' legal basis might have been motivated by the Commission's insistence on the general application of competition policy in all sectors of the economy, subject only to those exceptions specified in the Treaty. Although undoubtedly this aim was not ultimately achieved, the Council may have granted this minor satisfaction to the Commission as part of a compromise solution.

A less convoluted explanation for the inclusion of Article 87 in the regulation might be that the first draft of Regulation 1017/68 included it. This must necessarily have been the case since the first Commission draft proposed that Articles 85 and 86, and Regulation 17 would apply to inland transport. Possibly, from that moment on, it remained inadvertently, even after the Council had rejected the Commission's first proposals in the final version of the regulation.

3.7. SCOPE

Article 1, whose title is 'Basic Provision', sets out the scope of Regulation 1017/68. According to Article 1, the provisions of the regulation shall apply, in the fields of transport by rail, road and inland waterway, to

(1) 'agreements, decisions and concerted practices which have as their object or effect the fixing of transport rates and conditions, the limitation or control of the supply of transport and the sharing of transport markets';
(2) 'the application of technical improvements or technical cooperation or the joint financing or acquisition of transport equipment or supplies where such operations are directly related to the provision of transport services and are

---

[39] See the comments on these provisions in this Section.

necessary for the joint operation of services by grouping within the meaning of Article 4 of road or inland waterway transport undertakings';
(3) 'the abuse of a dominant position on the inland transport market'; and
(4) 'operations of providers of services ancillary to transport which have any of the objects or effects listed above' (points 1 to 3).

The first part of Article 1 of Regulation 1017/68 reiterates Article 1 of Regulation 141. The scope of Regulation 1017/68 covers the three types of restrictive agreements and practices referred to both in Article 1 of Regulation 141 and in Article 85(1)(a) to (c) of the Treaty. Both articles avoid reference to agreements and practices enumerated in Article 85(1)(d) and (e), or to any other possible agreement or practice unspecified in Article 85(1). Article 2 of the regulation in contrast repeats word for word the restrictive agreements and practices referred to in Article 85(1) as a whole. Article 2 broadens the literal scope of Regulation 141 and sheds more light on the intentions of the Council to exclude the application of Regulation 17 to all kinds of restrictive practices and agreements in the transport sector.[40]

The second set of activities incorporated within the inland transport regulation under the second part of Article 1 seem to extend beyond those excluded by Regulation 141 from the application of Regulation 17. The application of technical improvements or technical cooperation and the joint financing or acquisition of transport equipment arguably are not related directly to the provision of transport services, a condition that the Commission has construed to be indispensable for Regulation 141 to apply.[41]

The intention behind the second part of Article 1 may have been to include certain activities within the scope of Regulation 1017/68 which would otherwise have fallen under Regulation 17. This could be the case for some activities specified in Articles 3 and 4 of the regulation, whose direct relation to the provision of transport services is dubious. Some of them at least would normally fall within the realms of Regulation 17.

In respect of technical agreements, agreements and practices under Article 3(1)(a) of Regulation 1017/68 relative to standardization (or harmonization) seem to bear little relation to the provision of transport services. The same can be said of agreements on joint financing or acquisition of transport equipment or supplies (Article 4). Such agreements should have been treated under Regulation 17.

The question arises whether the inclusion of these activities within Regulation 1017/68 (possibly with a view to allowing the Council to authorize them, thereby exceeding the limits of application of Regulation 141) impedes the appli-

---

[40] On the interpretation of Art. 1 of Reg. 141, see above, Section I. On Art. 2 of Reg. 1017/68, see below 3.8.

[41] In the judgment in the *UIC* case, above n. 4, the Court has used this fact as an argument against the Commission's interpretation of the scope of Reg. 1017/68. See text immediately below.

cation of Regulation 17 or suggests the application to these types of activity of criteria different from the normal competition law rules. At present, following the judgment of the Court in the *French Seamen* case, the answer is a clear 'no'.

The inclusion in Article 1 of services ancillary to the provision of transport services is also surprising. Such services, because they are by their very definition ancillary are clearly not directly related to the provision of transport services, a characteristic which the Commission regards as a condition for Regulation 1017/68 to apply.

The inclusion of ancillary services here was prompted by the wish of the Council to make even more clear that *auxiliaires de transport* are subject to the rules of competition applicable to transport undertakings whenever they act as transport principals, that is, as carriers *vis-à-vis* their clients regardless of whether they are transport operators or not.[42]

The reference to ancillary services poses two problems. First, the concept of ancillary services is not defined by the regulation. Secondly, this is a domain in which Regulation 1017/68 partially but clearly overlaps with Regulation 17.[43]

It is clear that forwarding activities are ancillary services because one of the agreements to which the technical exception applies, and for whose very inclusion the scope was widened, is 'consolidation of individual consignments', a typical activity of freight forwarders excepted under Article 3(1)(f) of the regulation.[44]

There may be doubts whether other activities can be considered to be ancillary and, therefore, fall within the provisions of Regulation 1017/68.[45] As we have seen, the Commission interpreted Regulation 141 to exclude from the scope of Regulation 17 only agreements directly related to the provision of transport services. Regulation 17 applied to ancillary operations in the field of inland transport before Regulation 1017/68. The question arises, therefore, whether Regulation 17 and Regulation 1017/68 can apply simultaneously to the same type of activities.

One solution, as there is no reason to give special treatment to services ancil-

---

[42] This flows from the minutes of the Council meeting of 26 Nov. 1962 in Paris, (Document 1631/62 [OJ/CONS 27]) in which Reg. 141 was adopted. Although the Commission did not propose to refer expressly to '*auxiliaires de transport*' in the draft Reg. 141, the Commission and the Council considered that whenever these undertakings carried out transport activities proper, they could be deemed to be included in the regulation. A modification of the text of the draft regulation was not considered necessary for this purpose, since their transport activities were covered by the notion of 'transport undertakings' anyway.

[43] The problems raised by this specific provision will be broached while dealing with technical agreements. See below, 3.10. See also Blonk, W. A. G. 'Regulation 1017/68 of the Council of July 19, 1968 Applying Rules of Competition to Transport by Rail, Road and Inland Waterway', *Common Market Law Review*, Vol. 6, No. 4, Oct. 1969, pp. 451–65, at pp. 455–6.

[44] In this sense, see the conclusions of Adv. Gen. Dutheillet de Lamothe, in Case 10/71, *Port de Mertert*, [1971] ECR 732, at 736–7 (judgment of 14 July 1971).

[45] In the case of port activities, for example, Adv. Gen. Dutheillet concludes that Reg. 1017/68 does not apply.

lary to inland (and not sea and air) transport,[46] and as Regulation 1017/68 goes beyond Regulation 141, is to regard Regulation 1017/68 as being *ultra vires* in respect of ancillary services. A second and milder solution would be to view Regulation 1017/68 as applicable only to specified ancillary operations, Regulation 17 governing any other conceivable ancillary operation. This would allow agreements for the consolidation of individual consignments to be dealt with under the inland transport regulation, which, as just stated, is most probably the reason why the scope of Regulation 1017/68 was enlarged to cover ancillary operations in the first place. The scope of Regulations 17 and 141 would thereby be respected.

Finally, Article 1 of Regulation 1017/68 includes within its scope the abuse of a dominant position on the transport market. Article 8 defines in a manner very similar to Article 86 what an abuse of a dominant position is for the purposes of this regulation.

3.8. THE *UIC* JUDGMENT

Until recently, the Commission had relied heavily on the third recital of Regulation 141 to draw the line between transport and non-transport services and between the transport regulations and Regulation 17. The Court of First Instance in its *UIC* judgment,[47] has interpreted Regulation 1017/68 and Regulation 141 differently. Historically, transport related services which were not directly related to the provision of transport services proper have been treated under Regulation 17. This has been done on many occasions, beginning with ground-handling at airports (*Olympic Airways*) continuing with travel agencies and air freight forwarders (*IATA Passenger and Cargo Agency Programmes*) and ending with computer-reservation systems (*London-European/Sabena*)[48]. In *UIC* the CFI has minimised the importance of the third recital of Regulation 141[49] and has interpreted the scope of Regulation 1017/68 more widely than the Commission had previously.[50]

The consequences of this judgment for the application of competition rules in

---

[46] Conclusions of Adv. Gen. Dutheillet, *ibid.* at p. 737.   [47] See above n. 4.
[48] For these decisions, see Ch. 5.   [49] See the *UIC* judgment, *ibid.*, at para. 43.
[50] *Ibid.* at paras 45–6. Here the CFI relied on the text of Art. 2 of Reg. 1017/68 (which reproduces Art. 85(1)) to maintain that this regulation also applies to agreements which indirectly fix transport prices or other trading conditions. It has ruled that transport-related services which are indispensable for the provision of transport services are subject to the transport regulations. For Art. 2 of Reg. 1017/68, see immediately below.

The CFI at paras 36–9 has also refuted the relevance of the judgment of the ECJ in Case 311/85 *VVR* v. *Sociale Dienst*, [1987] ECR 3801, [1989] 4 CMLR 213, CCH ¶ 14–499, in order to determine whether the services provided by travel agents are to be considered ancillary to transport and to define the procedural rules applicable to travel agents. The Commission had referred to this judgment to argue that travel agents are independent intermediaries performing an independent non-transport activity.

transport are as yet uncertain. The Commission has lodged an appeal against the CFI's ruling but, in the meantime, it has adapted to the judgment. Currently, it is dealing with borderline cases both under the (possibly) applicable transport regulation and Regulation 17, granting the participants the procedural rights of both regulations, in order to avoid the criticism of the CFI in *UIC*.[51] For the immediate future, this may be a provisionally valid solution despite the lack of legal certainty created by applying two procedural regulations at once. As for the past, if the Court upholds the judgment of the CFI, the Commission may be obliged to review and, where appropriate, revise decisions applying Regulation 17 to service sectors neighbouring transport wherever those decisions are still in force and have not been challenged by their addressees.[52]

Restrictive as it is, the Commission's interpretation had the advantage of being clear and widely known by transport-related undertakings. The *UIC* judgment undoubtedly paves the way to litigation in an area in which the doctrine of the Commission seemed to be settled and will further complicate transport competition proceedings before the Commission.

3.9. PROHIBITION OF RESTRICTIVE AGREEMENTS AND PRACTICES

The prohibition of restrictive agreements and practices under Article 85(1) of the Treaty is the starting point for the exemption system, although given that exemption presupposes prohibition the two are not dissociable.[53] Article 85(3) is the channel—indeed, the only channel—through which restrictive agreements can be authorized. Article 85(3) is itself implemented by secondary legislation whether by means of individual decisions or general block exemption regulations which must be consistent with it.

Article 2 of Regulation 1017/68 reproduces with little variation the text of Article 85(1), but it lacks the primacy over secondary legislation which is characteristic of the Treaty. The same applies to Article 5 of the regulation in respect of Article 85(3) of the Treaty.

The position of the prohibition of restrictive agreements *vis-à-vis* its derogations within Regulation 1017/68 shows that the Council did not feel itself bound by the provisions of Article 85(3) of the Treaty—even less by those of Article 5 of the regulation—in particular while adopting Articles 3 and 4 of the regulation.

Moreover, it gives the impression that the Council wanted the standard prohibition/exemption scheme reversed for inland transport. The Council seemed to want the prohibition to apply only in those areas where an authorization had not been granted. In other words, Article 85(1) (or Article 2 of the regulation) was to prohibit only those arrangements which the Council had not decided to

---

[51] See paras 58–65.
[52] This may be the case in particular in the *IATA Agency Programmes* decisions, above n. 3.
[53] See the ECJ judgment in the *Bosch* case, above, n. 25.

permit through authorizations which did not necessarily comply with the competition rules.

While the structure of Regulation 1017/68 remains the same since 1968, its interpretation must adapt to the judgment of the Court in the *French Seamen* case.[54] At the time of that judgment (1974) the argument that the rules of Regulation 1017/68 were independent of the competition rules and legally acceptable even if they failed to comply with Article 85, became untenable.

There is another modification of Article 85(1) of the Treaty in the text of Article 2 of Regulation 1017/68. Under Article 2 of Regulation 1017/68 restrictive agreements and practices are prohibited when they are 'liable to affect' trade between Member States. Under Article 85(1) of the Treaty they are prohibited when they 'may affect' trade between Member States. 'Liable to affect' might not be quite the same as 'may affect'. The term may well connote the need for a higher probability of some effect being produced. '[L]iable' could be understood to mean 'necessarily bound' or 'obliged to'. If it were interpreted in this way, an agreement or practice with only a potential restrictive effect might not fall within the prohibition in the inland transport sector.

Other linguistic versions, however, use—correctly—the same wording adopted by the Treaty. There is no justification for the difference between the recitals of the regulation in the English version and the Treaty wording. Although the intention of Council was precisely to establish a system which was different from standard competition law this particular feature of Regulation 1017/68 in its English version seems simply to have been the result of bad translation. It does not have any effect on the interpretation of the prohibition of restrictive agreements in the inland transport sector. In any event, no such effect would be permissible following the *French Seamen* judgment.

Article 2 of Regulation 1017/68 also adopts a different wording from Article 85(1) of the Treaty when it omits reference in its sub-paragraph a) to 'purchase' and in its sub-paragraph c) to 'sources of supply'. Some have interpreted this to indicate, consistent with Regulation 141, that only the supply of transport services, but not demand, is covered by Regulation 141 and the subsequent modal regulations.[55] However, although the procedural rules of Regulation 1017/68 may not apply to the demand side of the transport market, Article 85(1) and the procedural rules of Regulation 17 do apply.

Finally, the legal weight of Article 2 within Regulation 1017/68 is also reflected by its Article 30(3). Article 30(3) provides that '[t]he prohibition in Article 2 shall apply from 1 January 1969 to all agreements, decisions and concerted practices falling within Article 2 which were in existence at the date of entry into force of this Regulation or which came into being between that date at the date of publication of this Regulation in the Official Journal of the European Communities'.

---

[54] See above, Ch. 2.　　　　[55] E.g., Schröter, above n. 31.

It is surprising and interesting that the prohibition contained in Article 85(1) of the Treaty seems not to have been applicable before 1 January 1969. This makes no sense in the light of the *French Seamen* ruling, where the Court explained that Article 85(1) applied to all sectors of the economy, not specifically excluded by the Treaty, as of 1 January 1958. This provision merely illustrates, once again therefore, the Council's restrictive views concerning the Treaty of Rome's applicability to transport.

In conclusion, it is not possible to interpret Article 2 in isolation from Article 85(1). Any divergence in the interpretation of the provisions would be contratry to the *French Seamen* ruling.

3.10. PROCEEDINGS AGAINST RESTRICTIVE AGREEMENTS

One of the most remarkable features of Regulation 1017/68 is that the prohibition of restrictive agreements and practices provided for in Article 2 is mitigated by several exceptions and exemptions unknown to other areas of competition law. This particularly favourable regime evidences the intention of the Council to pay close attention to the special characteristics of the transport industry;[56] a traditionally protected and regulated sector of the economy. Regulation 1017/68, contrary to standard competition law, provided for new and different ways of declaring inapplicable the prohibition of restrictive agreements, and which may be inconsistent with the general rules of the Treaty regarding exemption from the prohibition of restrictive agreements, i.e., Article 85(3), which is the exclusive—and at the same time superior—provision for permitting derogation from the prohibition of Article 85(1).

Under the inland transport regulation, as under Regulation 17, two broad types of proceedings may be initiated against restrictive agreements and practices. One is of a negative nature: infringement procedures to enforce the prohibition in Articles 85(1) and/or 86; the other of a positive nature: exemption procedures to declare the prohibition inapplicable once it is found that the conditions for an exemption under the Treaty are fulfilled.

Infringement procedures under Regulation 1017/68 do not differ greatly from those applicable in other sectors of the economy under Regulation 17.[57] However, the exemption regime under Regulation 1017/68 is quite different, demonstrating original features which merit some comment.

Under the regulation, there are two means by which the prohibition against restrictive agreements can be disapplied.

First, the regulation contains an 'exception', described by some as a 'legal

---

[56] In this sense, see Wägenbaur, R., 'Wettbewerbsregeln für den Verkehr in der EWG'. *Aussenwirtschaftsdienst des Betriebsberaters*, 1968, pp. 415 *et seq.* (French Ed.: 'Les règles de concurrence applicables aux transports', *Cahiers de Droit Européen*, 1970, pp. 645–62, at 651).

[57] For competition procedures in transport, see Ch. 6.

exception'.[58] Under Article 3, some agreements seem simply and automatically to be released from the prohibition of Article 85(1) without needing to meet the conditions of Article 85(3). As already indicated, not only the legal nature of this exception, but also its content, that is, the list of activities supposedly excepted, are extremely dubious.

Secondly, the regulation allows agreements to benefit from two types of exemptions. The regulation contains a block exemption in Article 4. Unquestionably, it is within the powers of the Council, under Article 87 of the Treaty, to issue block exemptions. However, Article 4 is insufficiently reasoned to establish both that Article 2 (or Article 85(1) of the Treaty) applies and that the conditions for an exemption are fulfilled. Indeed, this provision could well be contrary to Article 190 of the Treaty.

Regardless of Article 85(3), under current practice it may occasionally prove difficult to determine whether agreements exempted under Article 4 are in fact restrictive in the sense of Article 2 of the regulation. Such a situation would obviate the need for the block exemption in the first place.[59]

The second type of exemption is of an individual character. This second type of exemption is itself divided into two forms. The first falls under the conditions in Article 5 of the regulation, which reproduces with slight variations the conditions of Article 85(3). The second, which does not exist in any other competition regulation, is contained in Article 6 of Regulation 1017/68. Under Article 6, crisis cartels must only fulfil two conditions (namely the third and the fourth conditions in Article 85(3) of the Treaty) to merit exemption from the prohibition of restrictive practices.[60]

3.11. THE EXCEPTION FOR TECHNICAL AGREEMENTS

Article 3 of the regulation deals with technical agreements. According to Article 3(1), '[t]he prohibition laid down in Article 2 shall not apply to agreements, decisions or concerted practices the object and effect of which is to apply technical improvements or to achieve technical cooperation . . .'. This paragraph lists seven types of activities, from a) to g), which are deemed to constitute technical agreements.

Article 3(2) provides that '(t)he Commission shall, where appropriate, submit proposals to the Council with a view to extending or reducing the list in paragraph 1'. The list has never been extended or reduced since its inception in 1968.[61]

---

[58] See below, 3.11 and 3.12.
[59] For a more detailed comment on Art. 4, see below, 3.12.
[60] It will be argued that this espouses a dubious legality. See below, 3.14.
[61] In accordance with Annexe XIV, Section G.10 (b) of the Agreement on the European Economic Area (EEA), Art. 3(2) of Reg. 1017/68 is not applicable in relation to non-Community countries participating in the EEA. The reasons for this adaptation are unclear, above all

The English version of Article 3(1) talks about 'agreements . . . the object and effect of which is to apply technical improvements . . .'. Other linguistic versions include the terms '*seulement*', '*solamente*' or words to the same effect, which places this provision in line with the texts of the exception for technical agreements in Regulation 4056/86 and Regulation 3975/87 (Article 2 in both texts). These regulations state that such agreements should have as their 'sole object and effect . . .' the achievement of technical improvements or cooperation, etc. The text in Article 3(1) seems to be a poor translation which could cause confusion.[62] The text should be interpreted as including the word 'sole' in the English version of Regulation 1017/68 as well.

The legal justification for Article 3 is contained in the eighth recital of the regulation. According to the first part of that recital, 'certain types of agreement, decision and concerted practice in the transport sector the object and effect of which is merely to apply technical improvements or to achieve technical cooperation may be exempted from the prohibition of restrictive agreements since they contribute to improving productivity'. This may be regarded as embryonic Article 85(3) reasoning, albeit involving just the first of its four conditions.

Notice that the word 'merely' in the recital is the translation of the French '*seulement*', which was not included in the English text of Article 3(1), as explained above.

The English text states that these agreements may be 'exempted' from the prohibition of restrictive agreements, rather than 'excepted'. The French text says '*soustraits*' which confirms one's impression that Council's intention was probably not to grant an exemption, which it did for Article 4-type agreements, but to go much further and simply disapply the prohibition of restrictive agreements and practices to 'technical agreements' altogether.

Under the system of Regulation 1017/68, Article 3 is conceived as an exception of equivalent effect to Article 2, so that the prohibition of restrictive agreements and practices is simply not applicable in Article 3 cases.

As some authors have stated, for Council ministers the only significant purpose of Article 3 was to permit otherwise illegal agreements under Article 2(2) to exist without disturbance.[63] Article 3 was intended primarily to impede the applicability of Article 2, and this was precisely what it did.[64] Prior to the *French Seamen* ruling, the exception in Article 3 was interpreted as a legal exception which was supposed and designed to be fully applicable without further consideration. The Commission would not retain any right to monitor such agreements, provided that they fulfilled the terms of Article 3, no matter whether they

bearing in mind that no similar reservation is made in respect of the air equivalent of this provision (Art. 2(2) of Reg. 3975/87) although it is made in respect of the maritime equivalent (Art. 2(2) of Reg. 4056/86).

[62] See, e.g., *Butterworths Competition Law*, above n. 32, at p. IX/174, § 308.
[63] See Wägenbaur, above n. 56, at pp. 651–2.   [64] *Ibid.*

fell within the prohibition of Article 2 or not. This interpretation had to be reviewed after the Court pronounced in favour of the universality of the Treaty in 1974.[65] [66]

The eighth recital of the regulation appears to take for granted that the agreements listed from a) to g) are not covered by the prohibition on restrictive agreements. The recital could be interpreted as giving *de facto* recognition of the exclusively technical nature of such agreements. However, strangely the recital goes on to refer to the contribution of these agreements to the improvement of productivity. Such comments are logically more relevant to a discussion of the justification for an exemption than for an 'exception'.

Regardless of the eighth recital and of the Council's possible intentions, it would be very difficult, in practice, to satisfy the Article 3 conditions necessary for Article 2 not to apply. The object and effect of the agreements listed must be solely or exclusively to achieve technical co-operation or technical improvements. In fact, in most cases, the exclusively technical nature of the types of agreements listed seems, to say the least, doubtful. For example, Article 3(1)(c) refers to 'the organization and execution of successive, complementary, substitute or combined transport operations, and the fixing and application of exclusive rates and conditions for such operations, including special competitive rates'. Article 3(1)(g) talks about agreements for 'the establishment of uniform rules as to the structure of tariffs and their conditions of application, provided such rules do not lay down transport rates and conditions'.[67] One might also wonder whether a significant portion of the activities does not in fact have a commercial object or at least a commercial effect.

If the activities listed took place between non-competitors in different markets, the agreements might not be restrictive. This is, indeed, the Commission's general philosophy as expressed in its 1968 Notice on Co-operation Agreements between Undertakings.[68] In principle, the Commission would consider co-operation to be restrictive if the agreements have effects on the conduct of the undertakings involved. The Commission generally aims to ensure that the undertakings involved are not competitors. Indeed, unless the arrangements listed in Article 3 of Regulation 1017/68 are between non-competitors they probably would fall under the prohibition of restrictive agreements.

[65] See above, Ch. 2.

[66] Although it cannot be stated with absolute certainty that it was the Council's intention to impede the application of the Treaty competition rules, it seems that the only way to achieve a similar result without actually ousting the competition rules would have been to exclude such agreements from the scope of the regulation, keeping them under the transitional regime of Arts 88 and 89 of the Treaty. This would not have impeded the application of Arts 85 and 86 but in practice the enforcement of competition rules would have been very difficult. For the problems for the application of Arts 85 and 86 by means of Arts 88 and 89 of the Treaty, see below, Ch. 6.

[67] In a recent decision, the Commission has granted an individual exemption to agreements of this kind in the railway transport sector, denying them the coverage of Art. 3. See the Commission Decision in the case relating *Tariff Structures for combined Transport*, OJ 1993 L73, p. 38.

[68] OJ 1968 C 75, p. 3, corrected by OJ 1968 C84, p. 14.

Furthermore, it is interesting to note that standardization, one of the activities listed in Article 3(1) (under sub-paragraph [a]), is dealt with specifically for other sectors of the economy in Article 1(1)(a) of Regulation 2821/71, which enables the Commission to grant block exemptions in certain areas.[69] Standardization is also included in Article 4(2)(3)(a) of Regulation 17, as amended by Regulation 2822/71.[70] This means that identical conduct is deemed by the same institution (the Council) sometimes to be exempted from notification, sometimes block exempted and sometimes 'excepted'. Given the more conventional approach adopted by the Council in other fields and in light of the limitations imposed by the 'sole object and effect of a technical nature' test, it seems clear that the exception must be construed narrowly and cannot apply when the activities listed are restrictive of competition to any appreciable degree.

Turning to Article 3(1)(c), given the limited scope of application of Regulation 1017/68, Article 3 can be considered applicable to 'the organization and execution of successive, complementary, substitute or combined transport operations' (Article 3[1][c]) only when such transport activities concern the three inland modes to which the regulation refers. This point has important implications for the controversy over the inland rate-fixing activities of liner conferences,[71] which the Commission contends cannot be covered by Article 3(1)(c). The scope of the regulation being limited to inland transport, it does not seem feasible for the exception (or the exemption) contained in the regulation to go beyond the scope foreseen in Article 1.

3.12. TECHNICAL AGREEMENTS UNDER ARTICLE 85(1)

Since the *French Seamen* judgment, Article 2 of Regulation 1017/68 must be understood in terms of a more or less complete representation of Article 85(1). That provision of the Treaty applies to transport and Community secondary legislation must comply with it. This we have already seen.[72] Since that judgment, Article 3 of Regulation 1017/68 must similarly be considered subject to and lower in the hierarchy of legal norms than Article 85(1). Under the EC Treaty, the only possible way to disapply Article 85(1) is through Article 85(3), that is, by granting an exemption to prohibited agreements. This is achieved in a transport context under Article 5 of Regulation 1017/68 which reproduces Article 85(3) of the Treaty in the regulation.

Article 3 of Regulation 1017/68 cannot be regarded as a block exemption. The recitals point out that technical cooperation contributes to the improvement of productivity; an economic advantage, certainly. However, they are silent on the other three conditions for exemption required by Article 5 of the regulation

---

[69] OJ 1971 L 285, p. 46 (Spec. Ed. 1971–III, p. 1032).
[70] OJ 1971 L 285, p. 49 (Spec. Ed. 1971–III, p. 1035).
[71] See below, Ch. 4.   [72] See above, para. 3.9.

and by Article 85(3) itself. Clearly, in 1968, the Council did not consider to be bound by the Treaty competition rules. Today, if Article 3 was seriously intended as a block exemption, the regulation should have argued and established with sufficient reasoning that the conditions for exemption were fulfilled since, otherwise, on account of the Article 190 requirements of legal reasoning, such an exemption would run the considerable risk of being declared null and void.

For Article 3 to be interpreted in accordance with the Treaty it should instead be seen to denote certain agreements and practices as non-restrictive. This interpretation would ensure the legality of Article 3. Despite the Council's probable intention to limit the scope of the Article 2 prohibition (that is, Article 85[1]), we have seen that secondary legislation cannot derogate from the Treaty. Accordingly, if a different interpretation of Article 3 were invoked its validity may be placed in doubt. There is no possible justification for another interpretation of Article 3 on the basis of Article 87 of the Treaty.[73] Article 87(2)(c) permits the Council to define the scope of the provisions of Articles 85 and 86. '[D]efining' is not the same as amending them.[74]

Article 3 should be read as stating that 'the prohibition of Article 85(1) of the Treaty does not apply when the conditions for the application of Article 85(1) of the Treaty are not fulfilled, that is, when the activities of the undertakings are not restrictive in their object or effect'. It should not be deemed to be a 'legal exception' withdrawing 'technical agreements' from the scope of Article 85. Although, as the recitals seem to indicate, this was probably the precise intention of the Council, such a reading is not permitted by the Treaty. At most, Article 3 could be viewed as a 'block negative clearance' for specific arguments, provided they are not restrictive.

No second category of relief from the prohibition of restrictive practices in the EC Treaty exists. There is no hybrid category between the prohibition contained in the first part of Article 85 and the exemption provided for in the third part of the same provision. Exceptions to the applicability of Article 85(1) do not exist. The agreements, decisions, and concerted practices envisaged by Article 3 are forbidden and consequently null and void pursuant to Articles 2 and 7 of Regulation 1017/68 whenever they fall within the scope of Article 2 and they do not demonstrate that they can benefit from an individual or a block exemption.

Regulation 4056/86[75] advances a notably different justification for technical agreements from that in Regulation 1017/68. Indeed, the justification in the former adds weight to the interpretation proposed of Article 3 of the latter. The seventh recital of Regulation 4056/86 states that '*certain types* of technical agreements, decisions and concerted practices *may* be excluded from the prohibition on restrictive practices on the ground that they do not, *as a general rule*, restrict competition' (emphasis added).

---

[73] For the interpretation of Art. 87, see above, para. 3.6 in relation to Art. 2.
[74] See Ritter *et al.*, above, n. 29, p. 571.   [75] See Ch. 4.

The wording of this recital may seem somewhat paradoxical. However, it is clear on two points: first, that only certain technical agreements may be considered excluded from the prohibition of restrictive practices and, second, that such exclusion is based in the non-restrictive nature of those agreements (i.e., they are not caught by the prohibition). Technical agreements in the transport field which restrict competition within the meaning of Article 85(1) cannot escape that prohibition under any of the various modal exceptions.[76]

The Commission wanted to please the Council maintaining the technical exceptions contained in the inland Regulation in the maritime and air transport regulations. The only way to justify the exception of technical agreements after the *French Seamen* case was to invoke the arguments that were in fact invoked in the maritime Regulation. However, although Regulation 4056/86 states that as a rule the specified technical agreements are not restrictive, in fact, they frequently are.

The inclusion of the exception for technical agreements in the sea and air transport regulations following the Regulation 1017/68 precedent can be criticized. After 1974, such provisions could do more harm than good to undertakings. This conclusion is reinforced when one compares exceptions with standard block exemptions. Exceptions are not equivalent to block exemptions. They do not assure legal security. They do not serve to exclude activities normally falling under Article 85(1) from its application. They therefore mislead, provoke misinterpretations and raise false expectations.

In the future it may be necessary to consider the deletion of Article 3 from Regulation 1017/68, Article 2 from Regulation 4056/86 and Article 2 from Regulation 3975/87 so as to clarify the status of technical agreements under the transport regulations.

3.13. THE BLOCK EXEMPTION

The first part of Article 4(1) of Regulation 1017/68 reads as follows :

The agreements, decisions and concerted practices referred to in Article 2 shall be exempt from the prohibition in that Article where their purpose is :

the constitution and operation of groupings of road or inland waterway transport undertakings with a view to carrying on transport activities;

---

[76] The justification of the exception for technical agreements in the air transport sector is, for its part, included in the eighth recital of Reg. 3975/87, according to which 'it is appropriate to except certain agreements, decisions and concerted practices from the prohibition laid down in Art. 85(1) of the Treaty, in so far as their sole object and effect is to achieve technical improvements or cooperation'. This text contains no justification and is a mere repetition of the provision. It does not point out, as Reg. 4056/86 does, that the 'exception' is in reality a simple clarification of the non-applicability of Art. 85(1) of the Treaty in certain cases, under certain conditions.

the joint financing or acquisition of transport equipment or supplies, where these operations are directly related to the provision of transport services and are necessary for the joint operations of the aforesaid groupings; . . .

Railway transport groupings are not included. Given the size of the national EC railways, which in 1968 as today are the only railway transport undertakings in existence, they could not be included.

The first indent of Article 4(1) delimits the scope of the exemption while at the same time serving as a condition for the exemption.[77] All the activities which follow can only be covered by the exemption on condition that an inland transport grouping is formed.

The second indent, which refers to the joint financing or acquisition of transport equipment or supplies, broadens the initial scope of the exemption but does not constitute a condition of exemption. Joint financing may or may not be a feature of these groupings which benefit from the exemption. Joint financing is not in itself exempted but only where directly related to inland transport groupings of small and medium-sized undertakings.

The justification for this block exemption is set out in the ninth recital of the Regulation. It states that:

in order that an improvement may be fostered in the sometimes too dispersed structure of the industry in the road and inland waterway sectors there should also be exempted[78] from the prohibition on restrictive agreements those agreements, decisions and concerted practices providing for the creation and operation of groupings of undertakings in these two transport sectors.

From the ninth recital, the block exemption for inland transport groupings of small and medium-sized undertakings seems to be more of a common inland transport policy measure than a standard block exemption. In addition, the regulation contains no explanation of how the conditions of Article 5 (Article 85[3]) are satisfied. However, it may well not be difficult to justify an exemption for these groupings if ever they fell under Article 85(1).[79]

The block exemption in Article 4 is conditional on two quantitative thresholds :

(1)   the total joint capacity of the undertakings involved must not exceed 10,000 tons in the case of road transport and 500,000 tons in the case of transport by inland waterway;

---

[77] In a very similar fashion, Art. 3 of Reg. 4056/86 sets out the conditions for the exemption and the scope of the block exemption for liner conferences. See below, Ch. 4.

[78] The words 'should also be exempted' refer back to the exception for technical agreements considered in the 8th recital. They indicate that both the exception and the exemption, despite the different description employed, had a similar purpose for the Council, namely to exclude the application of the prohibition of restrictive agreements and practices.

[79] See below on the '*De minimis*' notice, n. 83.

(2) the individual members' capacity shall not exceed 1,000 tons in the case of road transport or 50,000 tons in the case of transport by inland waterway.

The ninth recital clarifies the second individual threshold by establishing that the limits fixed are intended 'to ensure that no one undertaking can hold a dominant position within the grouping'.

It has been argued that few of these groupings would fail to be covered by the block exemption. In view of the high capacity thresholds, most individual companies would fulfil the tonnage requirements and few groupings would exceed the Article 4 thresholds.[80] It is true that the thresholds or tonnage limits foreseen in Article 4(1) of Regulation 1017/68 may be more fictitious than realistic—there seem to be extremely few inland transport undertakings and inland waterway transport undertakings whose individual loading capacity goes beyond the limits of the regulation.[81] Despite what is indicated by the title to Article 4 (which refers to small and medium size undertakings), it might be more accurate to talk about all kinds of undertakings in road and inland waterway transport. It is interesting to note that the Commission's 1968 draft proposal for a competition Regulation in inland transport envisaged much lower limits for the individual loading capacity of grouping members: 100 tons for road transport and 5,000 tons for inland waterway transport.[82]

It is worth noting the role of market power. Depending on the market in which they are involved, the groupings' market power could be either negligible or substantial. If it is negligible, Article 2 (Article 85[1]) would not apply (pursuant to the Commission's Notice on agreements of minor importance).[83] If market power is substantial, the condition in Article 5 (Article 85[3]) would not be fulfilled because the market share would be too high.

It is wrong to think that the relevant market is the Community market for inland waterway transport and road haulage as a whole. The size of the Community market compared to the capacity of these groupings is enormous. In 1968, the maximum capacity of these groupings corresponded to only 0.2 or 0.25 per cent of total Community transport capacity by inland waterway and road haulage. It would be even less today.[84]

If the thresholds prevent the application of the block exemption, groupings may still benefit from an individual exemption. The last part of the ninth recital of the regulation states that:

---

[80] Cf. Blonk, above, n. 43, pp. 458–9, and Wägenbaur, above, n. 56, pp. 652–3.

[81] *Ibid.*

[82] See Art. 3(1)(2) of the draft reg., Document COM(68)142 final, of 13 Mar. 1968.

[83] OJ 1986 C231, p. 2, modified by OJ 1994 C 368, p. 20. In this notice, the Commission holds that agreements between undertakings do not fall under the prohibition of Art. 85(1) when their market share does not exceed 5% of the relevant market and the aggregate annual turnover of the participating undertakings does not exceed ECU 300 million.

[84] See Blonk, above, n. 43, p. 459.

the fact that a grouping has a total carrying capacity greater than the fixed maximum, or cannot claim the overall exemption because of the individual capacity of the undertakings belonging to the grouping, does not in itself prevent such a grouping from constituting a lawful agreement, decision or concerted practice if it satisfies the conditions therefore laid down in this Regulation.

The last words make unequivocal reference to the conditions contained in Article 5.

Finally, Article 4(2) of the regulation states that :

If the implementation of any agreement, decision or concerted practice covered by paragraph 1 has, in a given case, effects which are incompatible with the requirements of Article 5 and which constitute an abuse of the exemption from the provisions of Article 2, undertakings or associations of undertakings may be required to make such effects cease.

It is not clear whether Article 4(2) requires that one or two conditions be satisfied before the Commission may act against an exempted agreement.

One interpretation has it that the provisions of Article 5 must be taken into account while assessing the existence of what the regulation calls 'an abuse of the exemption'. The abuse would be dependent on the Article 5 conditions not being met.

A second interpretation requires an abuse of the exemption to be proved in addition to the non-fulfilment of the conditions in Article 5, before the Commission might act. This interpretation is inconsistent with the system of the Treaty since it would allow restrictive agreements not fulfilling the conditions for exemption to continue to enjoy exemption.

A more complex question is whether 'abusing the exemption', if this means something different from the breach of the conditions in Article 5, could justify action by the Commission. A systematic interpretation of Article 5 in line with other competition provisions would permit this possibility.[85]

The block exemption contained in Article 4 of Regulation 1017/68 was the first granted directly by the Council of Ministers for an unlimited period. The list of block exemptions of this kind is short. Only in maritime transport has the Council of Ministers granted an unlimited block exemption in favour of liner conferences and some of their practices (Articles 3 and 6 of Regulation 4056/86).[86] The block exemption for liner conferences is not unique in this respect therefore because it was preceded by Article 4 of Regulation 1017/68. The block exemptions share other general similarities, in fact, since they are

---

[85] Under Art. 8(3)(d) of Reg. 17, 'where the parties abuse the exemption from the provisions of Art. 85(1) of the Treaty granted to them by decision', the Commission may 'revoke or amend its decision or prohibit specified acts by the parties'.

[86] See below, Ch. 4.

both pure policy measures rather than standard competition legislation implementing Article 85(3) of the Treaty.[87]

In one respect Article 4 of Regulation 1017/68 is even more surprising than Article 3 of Regulation 4056/86. Article 4(2) provided that the block exemption for small and medium sized undertakings' groupings cannot be withdrawn (even though the general procedure for withdrawing block exemptions was already established before 1968 when Regulation 1017/68 was published).

Article 7 of Regulation 19/65[88] contained withdrawal provisions but Regulation 1017 did not follow its lead. For their part, the sea and air transport regulations did not follow the inland regulation but are closer to Regulation 19/65.[89]

Under Article 4(2) the only action to be taken if effects incompatible with the requirements of Article 5 arise, is for the Council—not the Commission—to require the grouping to bring an end to the offending behaviour. There are no powers to withdraw the block exemption or to prohibit the agreement. This illustrates a low-key and lenient approach to enforcement of the regulation. It also goes against the usual distribution of competences between the Commission and the Council under EC competition law.

3.14. INDIVIDUAL EXEMPTIONS: GENERAL

Article 5 of Regulation 1017/68 mirrors Article 85(3) of the Treaty. Its title, 'non-applicability of the prohibition', might suggest that it goes beyond what is normally understood for an individual exemption but the title is in fact a paraphrase of the text of Article 85(3) which states that 'the provisions of paragraph 1 [of Article 85] may, however, be declared inapplicable' in the event that the conditions contained in paragraph 3 are met.

Nevertheless, Article 5 deviates, sometimes substantially, from Article 85(3). Some differences are clear, such as those in the first and second conditions for exemption. The third and fourth conditions in Article 85(3) are adapted almost literally for Article 5. The reason for Article 5 is provided by the tenth recital of the regulation. However, the recital provides no guidance on the interpretation of the first and second conditions or on the differences, albeit small, which exist with the Treaty text.

Article 5 stipulates that the first condition for an individual exemption (i.e., a declaration of inapplicability of the prohibition of restrictive agreements) is that the agreements, decisions, or concerted practices contribute towards:

---

[87] See below, Ch. 4, for the political character of the block exemption for liner conferences.
[88] OJ 1965, 36, p. 533 (Spec. Ed. 1965–6, p. 35).
[89] See Art. 7 of Reg. 4056/86 and Art. 7 of Reg. 3976/87. For a comment on these provisions, see below, Chs 4 and 5.

(1) improving the quality of transport services; or
(2) promoting greater continuity and stability in the satisfaction of transport needs on markets where supply and demand are subject to considerable temporal fluctuation; or
(3) increasing the productivity of undertakings; or
(4) furthering technical or economic progress.

The first condition for an individual exemption under Article 85(3) of the Treaty is simpler and more general requiring that agreements, decisions, or concerted practices 'contribute to improving the production or distribution of goods or to promoting technical or economic progress'.

The alternatives offered by Article 5 for the fulfilment of the first condition for an exemption are apparently more numerous than in Article 85(3). The Article 85(3) condition is more or less expressed in the last two indents of the first condition under Regulation 1017/68 (only 'increasing the productivity of undertakings' replaces 'improving the production or distribution of goods').

Article 5 establishes two further advantages which agreements in the inland transport sector may contribute, thereby meriting exemption. However, neither is more than an explicit expression of the first condition in Article 85(3), tailored specifically for the inland transport sector and they do not add exemption possibilities beyond the scope of the Treaty condition. This fits with the dictates of the *French Seamen* judgment. Since both objectives seem to be reasonable and advantageous and to be compatible with Article 85(3) there does not seem to be a clash between this provision and the rules of the Treaty.

This might not be the case for the second condition of Article 5 of Regulation 1017/68. That provision stipulates that restrictive agreements which promote some kind of economic or technical advantage must also 'take fair account of the interests of transport users'. Article 85(3) provides that a 'fair share of the resulting benefit' must be allowed to consumers.

The obligations towards users might, therefore, seem to have been relaxed by the Council in the inland transport regulation. In particular, it is one thing to 'take fair account' of 'interests' and another to 'allow a fair share' of 'benefits'.

However, it is submitted that, in spite of these divergences and for the same reasons given in relation to the first condition, this provision should also be interpreted in conformity with Article 85(3). The Court's jurisprudence and the Commission's precedents on the form of consumers benefit, therefore, apply fully in the field of inland transport.[90]

In relation to the fourth condition for an exemption under Article 5—which, for the rest, does not deviate from the Treaty—it is worth noting that the tenth recital advances a market definition element for the purposes of the condition which is the equivalent of Article 85(3)(b) of the Treaty. The regulation states

[90] For the interpretation of the second condition of Art. 85(3), see among others Ritter *et al.*, above, n. 29, pp. 90 *et seq.*

that regard should be had to 'competition from alternative modes of transport'. This point is not reproduced in the text of the Article. The idea of the drafters in 1968 might have been to be generous to restrictive agreements in inland transport. At present it is acknowledged that in defining a market, substitute products or services have always to be taken into account.[91]

Finally, Article 5 has a procedural feature which is absent from Article 85(3) and which differs from Regulation 17. Article 5 states that the prohibition in Article 2 may be declared inapplicable with retroactive effect. Under the general system of competition law, this is a matter to be solved by the procedural regulation, i.e., Regulation 17. Regulation 17 grants the availability of retroactive application only to the less prejudicial and less restrictive agreements referred to in its Article 4(2). Like agreements in the transport sector these types of agreement are relieved the requirement to notify in order to obtain an individual exemption from the Commission.[92]

3.15. INDIVIDUAL EXEMPTIONS: CRISIS CARTELS

Crisis cartels in inland transport receive special treatment in Regulation 1017/68. Article 6(1) defines crisis cartels for the purpose of this provision as 'any agreement, decision or concerted practice which tends to reduce disturbances on the market in question'. Agreements of this kind may receive exemption on an individual basis, under certain conditions and following the procedures set forth in Articles 6 and 14 of the regulation.

It is notable that neither the conditions nor the procedure for individual exemption are the same as in Article 85(3) of the Treaty and Regulation 17. Nor do they match Article 5 or the other procedural provisions in Regulation 1017/68. In this particular case, the Council has introduced another substantial test for individual exemption and another procedure for granting it.

As already explained, Article 5 basically mirrors Article 85(3) of the Treaty. Likewise, its application is, with some exceptions, similar to Regulation 17. The individual exemption conditions and procedures for crisis cartels deviate substantially from standard EC competition rules and practice and from the normal distribution of competences between the Council and the Commission.[93]

The availability of exemption for crisis cartels under Article 6 is in principle limited in time. It can only be used 'until such time as the Council, acting in

---

[91] The ECJ's decided cases have clarified repeatedly that substitutional products or services must be taken into accout when defining the market. See, *inter alia,* Case 85/76, *Hoffmann—La Roche* v. *Commission* [1976] ECR 461. Case 6/72, *Continental Can* v. *Commission* [1973] ECR 77. Case 31/80, *L'Oréal* v. *De Nieuwe AMCK* [1980] ECR 3775.

[92] For the notification of restrictive agreements and practices in the transport sector, see below, Ch. 6.

[93] For an additional comment on the procedural rules regarding crisis cartels, see below, Ch. 6.

pursuance of the common transport policy, introduces appropriate measures to ensure a stable transport market'. However, the temporal scope of Article 6 is undefined and the terms of the provision are vague and probably unenforceable. Indeed, whenever an applicant submits a request for exemption, the Commission will probably be forced to accept that a stable market has not yet been achieved and the time for the introduction of such a request seems consequently to be open-ended.

Exemption depends on a state of crisis having been declared by the Council and on the third and the fourth conditions in Article 85(3), or in this case in Article 5 of Regulation 1017/68, indispensability of the restrictions and the non-elimination of competition, being fulfilled.[94] Declaration of a state of crisis by the Council apparently substitutes the Article 85(3) requirements relating to technical or economic progress and consumer benefits. No mention is made of these requirements.

The point of departure for the exemption of crisis cartels is the general presumption that structural crises in transport markets can be solved by means of restrictive agreements and that such cartels by their mere existence fulfil the first and the second conditions for an individual exemption. The economic advantages of solving the state of crisis would be globally sufficient to counterbalance the inconveniences following the restriction of competition. Equally, the handling of the crisis is assumed to provide automatically for consumer benefits.

Article 6 of Regulation 1017/68 could infringe the Treaty since the Treaty does not specifically foresee this particular situation. The adoption of crisis measures might be framed within Article 103 (economic policy) or Article 226 ('regional' economic crises during the transitional period) or other exceptional provisions. In inland transport, Article 75(3) seems to be insufficient to derogate from competition rules in this area. Nor does Article 87 permit derogation from Article 85(3). Accordingly, the '*vires*' of the Council in adopting this provision must be questioned.

The regulation does not explain why it deviates from the general rules, no doubt because it was not accepted that the general rules applied to transport. The eleventh recital to the regulation, which is the basis for Article 6, simply reproduces in summary form, the text of the substantive provision in Article 6(1).

In conclusion, Article 6 may be seen simply to have disregarded the Treaty provisions on exemption of restrictive agreements. In allowing the benefit of exemption in this case, the Community legislator may have gone beyond its powers and infringed Articles 75, 85 and 87 of the Treaty. For the rest, it is clear that the principles of Articles 85 and 86 must be respected by implementing legislation issued by the Council pursuant to Article 87 and that Article 75 cannot be used to breach other provisions of the Treaty.

These difficulties may have been the reason why Article 6 was excluded from

----

[94] Art. 6(3) of Reg. 1017/68.

the '*acquis communautaire*' adapted for application in relations with non-Community countries participating in the EEA Agreement.[95] The reasons for this adaptation are, however, not wholly clear.

The crisis cartel procedure is initiated by interested parties lodging a notification with the Commission under Article 14(1) of Regulation 1017/68. The Commission investigates and submits a report—not a proposal—to the Council. However, it cannot then instigate the exemption procedure proper without prior authorization from the Council. Under Article 6(2) of Regulation 1017/68, the Council must make a prior finding, on the basis of the Commission's report, 'that a state of crisis exists in all or part of a transport market'. In order to do so, the Council must decide by a qualified majority or, where any Member State considers that the conditions set out in Article 75(3) of the Treaty are satisfied,[96] by unanimity.

The regulation does not specify whether the Council's finding of a state of crisis has to be preceded by a notification or whether it can be iniated by the Commission. Both possibilities appear to be open. As a result neither is it necessary for the undertakings to wait for a declaration of state of crisis before notifying, nor is it necessary for the institutions to wait for a notification to happen before exercising their powers.[97]

The Commission does not appear to be obliged to complete an Article 6 report every time undertakings seek a crisis cartel exemption. Neither is the Council obliged to declare formally the non-existence of the crisis. If the Commission considers that there is no basis for declaring a state of crisis, it would be able, without preparing a report for the Council, to deal with the notification by following the general rules for the exemption of agreements in inland transport, contained in Articles 5 and 12 of Regulation 1017/68.[98]

Once the Commission receives the green light from the Council, i.e., the Council declares a state of crisis, it may adopt a decision. The general procedural rules in Regulation 1017/68 then apply.

However, it must be noted that :

(1) decisions applying Article 6(1) do not have retroactive effect;

[95] In accordance with Annexe XIV, Section G.10(c) of the EEA Agreement.

[96] The situation to which Art. 75(3) refers is where the implementation of a common inland transport policy along the lines set forth in Art. 75(1) 'would be liable to have a serious effect on the standard of living and on employment in certain areas and on the operation of transport facilities . . .'.

[97] The truth is that, if the Commission and Council were automatically to do whatever is necessary to declare this state of crisis, they would clearly be opening up the possibility of authorization of these cartels, and somehow encouraging them.

[98] In this case, by application of the principles established in other procedural regulations for transport, (in particular Art. 4(8) of Reg. (EEC) 4260/88 and Art. 3(8) of Reg. 4261/88, OJ 1988 L 376, pp. 1 and 10 respectively). The Commission would probably have to inform the undertakings of its reasons for using the Arts 5 and 12 procedure, giving them an opportunity to comment. For the procedure for exemption of agreements and restrictive practices in the transport sector in general, see below Ch. 6.

(2)   decisions may be granted for a maximum period of three years from the
       finding of a state of crisis by the Council, under Article 6(2);
(3)   under Article 14(5) of the regulation, 'the decision of the Commission shall
       cease to have effect not later than six months from the coming into opera-
       tion of the measures referred to in Article 6(1)'.[99]

This procedure is unique in competition law. It is extremely cumbersome and
necessitates the intervention of two major EC institutions for its enforcement. Its
time limits are extremely vague. It is not currently clear whether the procedure
can actually be used, even twenty-five years after its introduction and Article 6(1)
does not help in solving the question. As to the duration of the effect of the decisions, according to Article 14(5) this depends on Article 6(1). It is therefore as
vague as Article 6(1) itself.

3.16. THE ABSENCE OF NEGATIVE CLEARANCE[100]

Under Regulation 1017/68, there is no provision for the Commission to grant
negative clearance. There is no Article similar to Article 2 of Regulation 17 in
Regulation 1017/68.

The reasons for this are not clear. One reason might be that, once again, the
Council intended to give undertakings in inland transport preferential treatment
by not including this procedure in the regulation. The intention might be that
they need notify to the Commission only the agreements considered by carriers
themselves to be restrictive. However, it might also be a simple mistake, as the
second draft of Regulation 1017/68 was prepared and adopted in a relatively
short time.[101]

It is worth noting that what Regulation 1017/68 terms 'applications' under
Article 5 would be normally called 'notifications' under Article 85(3), pursuant
to Articles 4 and 5 of Regulation 17. The term 'application' used in Article 2 of
Regulation 17 relates to negative clearance, which is not present in the scheme
of Regulation 1017/68. The term 'notification' under Regulation 1017/68 is
used for the notification of crisis cartels. This is a confusing and unfortunate use
of terminology which might produce mistakes if used in the wrong context.[102]

---

[99] The measures to which this provision refers are those introduced by the Council acting in
pursuance of the common transport policy to ensure a stable transport market. As already stated,
one might well wonder whether measures of this kind have ever been taken by the Council. In any
event, this procedure has never been used. See below, 3.21.4.

[100] For a more thorough discussion on this feature of Regs 1017/68 and 4056/86, see below,
Ch. 6.

[101] See Blonk, above n. 43, p. 454. The first draft (Document VII/IV/COM(64) 184 final of 5
June 1964, Art. 2) attempted to apply the rules of Reg. 17, so no lengthy discussion was possible
once this approach was rejected by the Council.

[102] For a critique of this terminology, see below, Ch. 6.

3.17. CONSEQUENCES OF BREACH

As regards the consequences under civil law of the breach of the provisions of the regulation, Article 7 is in line with the Treaty in stating that agreements, decisions, and concerted practices prohibited under the regulation are automatically void.[103]

It is interesting to note that Article 7 is not placed immediately after the prohibition of restrictive agreements, but fifth after Articles 3, 4, 5 and 6 of the regulation, which lay out four different ways of escaping from the prohibition of restrictive agreements and practices. Indeed, Article 7 states that 'any agreement or decision prohibited under the foregoing provisions (not only Article 2) shall be automatically void'.[104]

3.18. THE PROHIBITION OF ABUSE OF A DOMINANT POSITION

Article 8 of the regulation reproduces Article 86 of the Treaty. No comment is to be made in this respect, except that Article 8 and Article 86 of the Treaty must be interpreted, as in other parts of the economy, in the light of case-law of the European Court and current practice of the Commission. As a matter of interest, within the final provisions of Regulation 1017/68, governing its entry into force, Article 30(2) provides that the prohibition of abuses of a dominant position in the inland transport sector was to be applicable only on the day following the publication of the regulation in the *Official Journal of the European Communities*. This was equivalent to an express declaration that Article 86 was not applicable to inland transport prior to 24 July 1968.

3.19. PUBLIC UNDERTAKINGS IN THE INLAND TRANSPORT SECTOR

Article 9 of Regulation 1017/68 is almost identical to Article 90 of the Treaty. However, Regulation 1017/68 was intended to be self-contained and independent from the rules of the Treaty and referred in Article 9(1), to 'the foregoing Articles', while Article 90(1) of the Treaty refers to 'the rules contained in this Treaty, in particular to those rules provided for in Article 6 and Articles 85 to 94'.

If Regulation 1017/68 were genuinely self-contained, Articles 92 to 94 of the Treaty should have been transposed as well. In spite of this, nothing is said about

---

[103] Concerning the abuse of a dominant position, the civil law consequences of the breach of Art. 8 of Reg. 1017/68 or Art. 86 of the Treaty are to be determined by national courts, which are implicitly empowered to fix civil liabilities in this case. See Wägenbaur, above n. 56, p. 651.

[104] This may support the suggestion that the Council wanted to place the prohibition of restrictive agreements and its consequences second to the derogations from this principle. It also illustrates unusual competition law principles applied by the EC legislators to inland transport.

State aids in the regulation. The reason is most probably that it was already evident that the rules of the Treaty were applicable to State aids in the inland transport sector. Indeed, Article 77 of the Treaty provides that 'aids shall be compatible with this Treaty if they meet the needs of coordination of transport or if they represent reimbursement for the discharge of certain obligations inherent in the concept of a public service'. Denying that the Treaty envisages standard State aids rules also applying in the inland transport sector would have been far more untenable than maintaining that competition rules did not apply to transport.

Article 9 of Regulation 1017/68 shows once more that Member States considered, at the time of the approval of the regulation, that competition rules could only be introduced in transport by means of legislative action by the Council.

The truth is that the transport competition rules cannot alter what the Treaty itself established in Articles 85 to 94. Only a Treaty provision would suffice to modify Article 90 of the Treaty. Accordingly, Article 9 has a purely declaratory value and the shortened transposition of Article 90(1) has no practical consequence. Regulation 1017/68 should not be interpreted as excluding the applicability of Article 90 in the inland transport sector. Member States' measures concerning public undertakings in the inland transport sector must in any event be in line not only with Regulation 1017/68 but also with Article 90 of the Treaty. Article 9 is applicable only in as much as it is identical to Article 90. In so far as it does not coincide, Article 90 will cover the loophole.[105]

It cannot be otherwise, as the exclusive application of Article 9 in the inland transport sector would be tantamount to admitting that Member States, regardless of Article 90, could act *vis-à-vis* public undertakings in a manner contrary to the provisions of the Treaty—at least those not reproduced in Regulation 1017/68. Such provisions would include in particular Article 6 of the Treaty on non-discrimination. This conclusion is absurd and must be rejected.[106]

In conclusion, Article 9 adds nothing to Article 90 nor does it deviate substantially from it. It must be interpreted in conformity with Article 90. Article 90 is also applicable in the inland transport sector when Member States contravene provisions not specifically covered by Article 9 (i.e., Articles 6, 91 and 92 to 94 of the Treaty).

Finally, by way of a postscript, Article 9(3) of the regulation has been adapted by the EEA Agreement[107] so that in relations with non-Community participating countries reference to 'appropriate directives and decisions' (which the Commission may address to the Member States to remedy infringements of this requirement) must now be read as 'appropriate measures'. Article 59 of the EEA Agreement, which reproduces with minor variations Article 90 of the EC Treaty, also refers to 'measures'.

---

[105] See Wägenbaur, above n. 56, p. 651.　　　　[106] *Ibid.*
[107] See Annex XIV, Section G.10(g).

3.20. THE INTERVENTION OF THE COUNCIL

Later on, we shall deal with the procedural rules applicable to the three main modes of transport. We shall review similarities and differences between the transport regulations and Regulation 17, and between the different transport regulations themselves.[108] In particular, with regard to the intervention of national authorities (but not of the Council) in Commission proceedings, we shall see that such intervention is limited to their participation in the meetings of the various Advisory Committees. This type of co-operation between Member States and the Commission—most usually in competition proceedings—also occurs under Regulation 1017/68 although forming only one part of the institutional relationships possible there.

Article 17 of the regulation, entitled 'Consideration by the Council of questions of principle concerning the common transport policy raised in connection with specific cases' states:

1. The Commission shall not give a decision in respect of which consultation [of the Advisory Committee] is compulsory until after the expiry of 20 days from the date on which the Advisory committee has delivered its Opinion.
2. Before the expiry of the period specified in paragraph 1, any Member State may request that the Council be convened to examine with the Commission any question of principle concerning the common transport policy which such Member State considers to be involved in the particular case for decision.
3. Further, the Council may at any time at the request of a Member State or of the Commission, consider general questions raised by the implementation of the competition policy in the transport sector.

    . . .

This is an unusual mechanism for control by the Council over Commission decisions. It means that after the standard consultation of the Advisory Committee under Article 16 of the regulation, it is possible for the Council to convene a meeting to consider general questions or questions of principle concerning common transport policy and so prevent the Commission from adopting a decision on any specific case without having first consulted the Member States again, this time within the Council.

The 20-day period after the Advisory Committee meeting leads, first, to a delay in the adoption of Commission decisions, and secondly, to possible additional delay where a Member State decides to request a meeting with the Commission to deal with such questions. The Council shall meet within 30 days from the request. No decision can be adopted by the Commission until the Council meeting has taken place.[109]

---

[108] See below, Ch. 6.

[109] Taking into account the period of time which the Commission takes, as a general rule, before adopting its decisions (often several years), these delays are likely to appear insignificant: 50 days in

Even more anomalous (in light of current distribution of competences in competition law enforcement) is the provision in Article 17(4), according to which in all cases where the Council is asked to meet to consider questions of principle or general questions, the Commission shall for the purposes of this regulation 'take into account the policy guidelines which emerge from that meeting'.

It is more than apparent that the intention of the Council with this provision was to intrude into the Commission's competences under the Regulation 17 regime, placing at the same time competition policy under the control of national transport authorities. However, the text is sufficiently flexible for the Commission, whilst considering and taking into account transport policy guidelines emerging from the Council, to avoid deviating from current competition policy. The Commission and, indeed, the Council itself are bound by the rules of the Treaty. The Council, in any event, cannot avoid the case-law of the European Court or Commission precedent and dictate the adoption or non-adoption, or the thrust, of Commission decisions.

Regardless of the practicalities of this additional consultation procedure (which, in fact, has never been used), the regulation shows once more the attitude of Member States in the Council on the way competition rules should be applied to transport. Once again, the rules are different to the general competition rules in order to water down the application of competition rules in a sector traditionally protected and regulated at national level.

3.21. ENFORCEMENT AND ACTION

Regulation 1017/68 has been applied on only a few occasions, most of them fairly recent. Since Regulation 1017/68 entered into force in 1968 all Commission decisions have been adopted post-1988. There are, however, two exceptions: the *Tankschiffahrtskonvention* and *EATE* cases. The *EATE* decision is the bridge between two periods, one of virtually total absence of application of competition rules in inland transport and the other of normal application of the rules as in other sectors.

3.21.1. First cases under Regulation 1017/68

The first time the Commission applied the regulation was in 1972, when it launched an investigation on its own initiative into the Rhine Navigation Pools and Conventions.[110] The Commission staff examined, from the perspective of

total. However, they are not, precisely for the reasons which make it difficult for the Commission to adopt its decisions with more speed: the formalities which, on paper, appear to be the simplest involve an enormous amount of work for the Commission's and the Council's officials, and days easily turn into weeks in EU bureaucracy.

[110] *Second Report on Competition Policy*, 1972, para. 73. 'Pool' means the agreement to distribute tonnage, revenues or profits concluded between several carriers.

the competition rules established by Regulation 1017/68 and on the basis of information provided by the pools and conventions concerned, the working of five of them: the Duisburg Freight Convention, the French Rhine Traffic Convention, the Kettwig Pool, the Rhine Container-Linie, and the Rhine Grain Shipping Convention.

The vertical agreements binding certain conventions to certain shippers or forwarding agents were also examined: the Duisburg Freight Convention with the chemicals and iron and steel industries, the French Rhine Traffic Convention with French forwarding agents. Under these agreements, the shippers or forwarding agents made loyalty arrangements in respect of all the merchandise covered by the agreement, binding themselves to the pool or convention in question, should merchandise be transported by inland waterway.

As the pools and conventions and their agreements with agents restricted competition within the terms of Article 2 of the regulation, the Commission examined whether the conditions for an individual exemption under Article 5 were fulfilled. Ultimately, the Commission did not formally open proceedings to terminate the infringement or to grant an individual exemption, and it closed the file.

In 1976, following an application under Article 12 of Regulation 1017/68, the Commission published a notice concerning the agreement known as *Tankschiffahrtskonvention* (Tanker Transport Convention).[111] The agreement concerned the laying up of a percentage (between 0 and 30 per cent) of the parties' tanker capacity.

The notice did not contain any arguments on the applicability of the conditions in Articles 2 and 5 of the regulation, either by the parties or the Commission. The Commission did not raise objections to the agreement within 90 days of its publication, and, perhaps mistakenly, an individual exemption was automatically granted for a period of three years, under Article 12 (3) of the regulation.

The Commission has also acted on several occasions in transport-related markets, but using the common procedural rules of Regulation 17. This was the case for the *Eurofima*[112] and *Cauliflowers II*[113] affairs, which were finally settled.[114]

3.21.2. The *EATE* Case and the *Antib* Judgment

The first and only infringement decision adopted pursuant to Regulation 1017/68, between 1968 and 1994, and then only seventeen years after the entry

---

[111] OJ 1978 C 82, p. 3.

[112] In *Eurofima (Railway rolling stock)*, *Third Report on Competition Policy*, 1973, paras 68–9, a consortium of national railway companies was forced to give up their claim to the industrial property rights in new designs of railway rolling stock ordered from a manufacturer.

[113] In *Cauliflowers II*, *Ninth Report on Competition Policy*, 1979, para. 84, the Commission obtained the removal of an obligation on Breton exporters of cauliflowers to use rail transport rather than road haulage.

[114] See Ritter *et al.*, above n. 29, at p. 572.

into force of the Regulation, is in the *EATE* case.[115] In spite of the *French Seamen* ruling, the Commission made no reference to the applicability of the general rules of competition to inland transport.

This case concerned an agreement between two French associations of owner-boatmen and freight-forwarding agents operating on French inland waterways. The agreement was held to be illegal and was refused exemption because it put inland waterway carriers not party to the agreement, who were mainly non-French operators, at a competitive disadvantage. The agreement obliged the freight forwarders to charge a 10 per cent levy on all cargo destined to leave France, regardless of whether the carriage was to be undertaken by French or foreign carriers. The money collected through the levy went into a fund which was administered by a co-operative of French owner-boatmen, EATE (*Entreprise Artisanale de Transport par Eau*), to promote inland waterway traffic, from which non-French carriers were practically excluded, and was refunded only to EATE members, all of them French. Accordingly, the agreement was discriminatory against non-French carriers and infringed Article 2 of Regulation 1017/68.[116]

The Association's regulation was declared to constitute a breach of Article 2 of Regulation 1017/68, pursuant to Article 11(1). The agreement was at the same time refused exemption under Article 5 of the regulation.

One of the parties involved in the EATE levy case, the *Association Nationale des Travailleurs Indépendants de la Batellerie* (ANTIB) appealed against the decision of the Commission to the European Court.[117] They claimed *inter alia* that the EATE levy was not discriminatory as all boatmen were obliged to pay it; the fact that foreign carriers did not have access to inland transport and so could not benefit from the application of the fund was a consequence of French legislation. Moreover, as foreign and French carriers did not compete on the inland waterway market, there was no distortion of competition.

The Court upheld the decision of the Commission. It held that discrimination lay not in the French legislation but in the collection of levies intended exclusively to promote export traffic, in circumstances in which foreign EC carriers had limited access to the market and could not derive from the supposed promotion benefits corresponding to their financial contribution.[118]

3.21.3. Regulation 1017/68 since 1987

From 1987 onwards, the Commission started to apply competition rules normally in the inland transport sector, just as in other sectors, whilst in maritime transport (with the consortia regulation) and, above all, air transport with subsequent block exemption regulations derived from Regulation 3976/87, the

---

[115] OJ 1985 L 219, p. 35.
[116] See Ritter *et al.*, above n. 29, at pp. 572–3.
[117] ECJ Judgment in Case 272/85 *ANTIB* v. *Commission*, [1987] ECR 2201.
[118] See *Butterworths Competition Law*, above n. 32, Ch. 3, pp. IX/195 *et seq.*, Nos. 370–80.

Commission continued its legislative work under the Council's attentive gaze. In inland transport, all efforts were put into the application—not into the creation—of transport competition law.

The priority area of the Commission's action was railway transport. It gave far less attention to waterway and road transport.

In waterway transport, the Commission studied restrictions such as the shift system (*tour de rôle*), whereby river carriers were obliged to queue—as if they were taxis—in order to carry goods and studied some less restrictive alternatives to enable the survival of small operators.

In road transport, disparate conditions of supply, excess capacity, and keen competition between operators have made the Commission's intervention less necessary than in other far more concentrated sectors.

The attention paid to railway transport is explained in good part by the new possibilities of access to the market created by Directive 91/440/EEC,[119] and by the greater intensity of co-operation between undertakings in the creation of subsidiaries and joint railway transport services, motivated in several instances by the opening of the Channel Tunnel.

3.21.3.1. The *Eurotunnel* Cases

In 1988, a notification of restrictive agreements was submitted by the Channel Tunnel Group Ltd. and France Manche S.A. under Article 12 of Regulation 1017/68, regarding a usage contract between British Railways (BR) and the French Société Nationale des Chemins de Fer (SNCF). The main provisions of the usage contract only entered into force with the fixed link across the English Channel being constructed and opened to rail transport. The contract was expected to last for the duration of the concession, i.e., 55 years, and dealt with the use of the fixed link between the United Kingdom and France permitting the passage of passenger and freight trains operated by the railways involved and shuttle trains carrying motor vehicles and their passengers operated by the concessionaires, the Channel Tunnel Group and France Manche.

According to the parties, the contract aimed to maximize co-operation between railways and concessionaires in running their respective services. The Commission, which had published a notice summarizing the agreement neutrally without making any assessments as to the applicability of Article 5 of the regulation or Article 85 (3) of the Treaty,[120] allowed the 90-day period to elapse without raising serious doubts. In that way, the agreement obtained exemption for three years from the date of publication, according to Article 12 (2) of Regulation 1017/68 (*Eurotunnel II*).[121]

---

[119] OJ 1991 L 237. See above, Ch. 1.   [120] OJ 1988 C 292, p. 2.

[121] The *Eurotunnel I* case concerned agreements between the Channel Tunnel construction companies, which were granted a negative clearance. See *18th Report on Competition Policy*, 1978, para. 57. See the *Eurotunnel I* Comm. Dec. in OJ 1988 L 311, p. 36.

The parties subsequently requested that the exemption be extended for the duration of the contract. In order to allow a longer duration, the Commission later published a new notice in 1990[122] this time pursuant to Article 26 (3) of the regulation. This notice was similar to the standard publications made before the granting of an individual exemption pursuant to Article 19(3) of Regulation 17 and stated that the Commission intended to grant exemption for a limited period of time while inviting comments from third parties.[123]

The discussions with the undertakings on the conditions under which the Commission could authorize a greater duration continued for another four years. In 1994, the Commission published a further notice, this time in keeping with Article 19(3) of Regulation 17 and Article 26(3) of Regulation 1017/68.[124] The Commission made it known that the duration of the standard contract had been extended to sixty-five years, that it considered a priori that the infrastructural management activity was not a proper transport activity and, therefore, used as a legal basis both the inland regulation and Regulation 17 and that it intended to grant an exemption for a period of thirty years.

The final decision in this case was adopted at the end of 1994.[125] The main condition imposed by the Commission, in line with the objectives of Directive 91/440, tries to guarantee that railway undertakings other than BR and SNCF could have access to 25 per cent of the 'paths' available in the tunnel. The Commission will be re-examining the proportion of paths reserved to the French and British railways (the remaining 75 per cent) before the year 2007. The aim of the obligations imposed by the Commission is to ensure it is informed twice yearly of the proportion in which the railways involved in the agreement and third parties have, in practice, used the paths.

In spite of being apparently favourable to the interests of the notifying undertakings, *Eurotunnel III* has been challenged by SNCF and BR. They have argued before the CFI that the conditions imposed by the Commission were not justified under the applicable competition rules.[126]

---

[122] OJ 1990 C 1976, p. 2.

[123] In the case of opposition proceedings, the summary notice of the agreement notified is done on the basis of Art. 12(2) of Reg. 1017/68, neutrally, without the Commission commenting on the applicability of Art. 85(3) of the Treaty. In other exemption procedures, the publication of the summary is done pursuant to Art. 26(3) of the regulation, and the Commission shows itself generally favourable to the exemption, in anticipation of comments from interested third parties. For the differences between the exemption procedure by non-opposition and the 'own initiative' exemption procedure, see below, Ch. 6.

[124] OJ 1994 C 210, p. 15.

[125] See the Commission's decision relating to the *Eurotunnel III* case, OJ 1994 L 354, p. 66. The 30-year period starts to run from 16 Nov. 1991, one day after the expiration of the first exemption of the Tunnel use contract, which had a duration of three years (*Eurotunnel II*).

[126] SNCF and BR also requested without success interim relief measures against the Commission's decision. See the Order of the President of the CFI of 12 May 1995 in Cases T–79/95R and T–80/95R, *SNCF and BR* v. *Commission*, [1995] ECR II–1433.

3.21.3.2. Agreements regarding the combined transport of goods

Another recent favourable Commission decision relates to agreements between railway companies regarding price structures in the combined transport of goods.[127]

After an enquiry into the combined road-rail transport sector, the Commission decided to open a formal procedure and send statements of objections to several EC railway and road-rail companies concerning certain agreements and practices that the Commission considered to be illegal under the competition rules. One of the objections concerned the conclusion by the railway companies of an agreement on the establishment of a common rate structure for the sale of haulage by the railways in international combined transport. In its statement of objections, the Commission took the view that, in light of its provisions and the context in which it was to operate, the agreement infringed Article 85 (1) of the EC Treaty and Article 2 of Council Regulation (EEC) 1017/68. Following the statement of objections, the agreement was amended. The Commission seemed satisfied by the amendments and before adopting its decision it published a notice under Article 26 (3) asking third parties for comments.[128]

This decision is especially important for three reasons. First, the references to Articles 2 and 5 of Regulation 1017/68 are always accompanied by their equivalents, Article 85 (1) and (3), thus putting the Commission case-law for the first time publicly in line with the ruling of the Court in the *French Seamen* case.[129] Second, the Commission on its own initiative and without prior notification, opened a procedure for granting an exemption,[130] which is only possible in very limited circumstances under Regulation 17.[131] Third, because for the first time, the Commission interpreted strictly and in accordance with the system of Article 85, the notion of 'excepted technical agreements' present in all the transport regulations, modelled on Regulation 1017/68.[132]

In the international combined transport of goods, the Commission has also adopted a decision regarding the *Union internationale des chemins de fer* (UIC) *fiches* 2 and 3. *Fiche* 2 relates to co-operation between railway undertakings in order to provide international combined transport and defines various forms of technical and commercial co-operation between railway undertakings for the provision of such services. *Fiche* 3 deals with the relations between railway undertakings and the buyers of railway transport services in international combined transport. These services are provided by the railways either on their own initiative or on buyer's request and are sold in two ways: either by selling train

---

[127] OJ 1992 L 73, p. 38. [128] OJ 1992 C 195, p. 5.

[129] See para. 19 of the decision.

[130] In the *Eurocorde* case (see below, Ch. 4) the Commission also opened a procedure for exemption on its own initiative, but did not adopt a final decision.

[131] In particular by virtue of Art. 4(2) of Reg. 17. On the general exemption of the notification requirement for obtaining an exemption in the transport sector, see below, Ch. 6.

[132] On the interpretation of Art. 3 of Reg. 1017/68, see above, paras 3.10 and 3.11.

capacity or by selling intra-modal transport units (ITU), for example, containers. Pursuant to these agreements, the contracting parties may exchange commercial information on the relevant market, including prices, and may jointly undertake marketing studies. The Commission published a notice under Article 12(2) of Regulation 1017/68[133] and authorized the agreements after the lapse of the 90-day period following the publication of the notice.

3.21.3.3. Joint Ventures

The Commission has recently authorized the creation of several joint ventures, both for passenger and for cargo transport (in particular for combined transport and transport of new vehicles). It has also authorized an agreement of the same style relating to express mail services.

In *European Night Services* (ENS), the Commission authorized an agreement made between the British, German, Dutch and Belgian railway companies for the creation of a specialized subsidiary (ENS) which would be charged with operating railway passenger transport services on night trains between the United Kingdom and Continental Europe, through the Channel Tunnel. The agreement, notified in 1993, concerned transport markets for businessmen and tourists on four routes (London–Amsterdam; London–Frankfurt–Dortmund; Paris–Glasgow–Swansea; Brussels–Glasgow–Plymouth). ENS did not have locomotives and would buy the traction from the railway undertakings.

The Commission published a first summary of the agreement after a short while,[134] but did not grant exemption until the parties had altered their agreement as required by the Commission. Following a second publication,[135] the Commission adopted its final decision in 1994.[136]

The Commission considered that the agreement might limit competition between the parties, as well as in relation to other operators who, as a result of the agreement, would have to confront greater market entry barriers. However, the agreement had the advantage of creating some new high-quality railway transport services. Users on business or tourist travel would benefit from the competition between this new service and air transport. The Commission therefore decided to authorize the agreement for a period of eight years. With the object of allowing the possibility of other operators providing similar services, the Commission imposed the condition that such operators would always ask the Commission and, if it were technically possible, the railway undertakings would have to sell them the same services as they had undertaken to sell to their subsidiary undertaking, on non-discriminatory conditions.

---

[133] OJ 1995 C 105, p. 4.
[134] OJ 1993 C 149, p. 10.
[135] OJ 1994 C 153, p. 15.
[136] OJ 1994 L 259, p. 20. See *Press Release IP (94) 870* of 22 Sept. 1994 and *24th Report on Competition Policy*, 1994, paras 189 and 190.

Despite being favourable in appearance to the applicant railway undertakings, the Commission's decision has been the subject of an appeal to the CFI.[137]

Procedurally identical in form to the way it authorized the joint ENS subsidiary,[138] the Commission authorized an agreement between the British and French railways, and Intercontainer, for the creation of a joint subsidiary called *Allied Continental Intermodal Services Ltd (ACI)*.[139] Intercontainer itself is a joint subsidiary of twenty-four railway undertakings—including the British and French railways—specializing in combined transport of goods[140] in Europe, to the development of which the European Commission has given a priority importance. Oddly, Intercontainer as such has not been individually authorized for the time being by the Commission.

ACI will be charged with combined transport by rail of road vehicles, containers, road tankers and semi-trailers, from terminal to terminal between the United Kingdom and certain places in Italy, Spain, Switzerland, Austria, Germany and France, using the Channel Tunnel. ACI will be providing its services both directly to transport users and to other transport undertakings. The British and French railways will be providing it with the traction necessary for its combined transport trains and specialist wagons required to cross the tunnel.

The Commission considered that the agreement restricted competition between the participating undertakings and amounted to a barrier to the entry of other operators of combined transport services. However, ACI had various technical advantages and users were allowed to benefit from them: shippers would have a new and better-quality service—with up-to-date wagons and the necessary regulatory—for transporting their goods through the tunnel. ACI would, moreover, deal with the grouping of isolated consignments—which is a very important factor for the development of combined transport.

The Commission therefore decided to authorize the agreement for a period of five years as from the date the tunnel opened. With the aim of ensuring that other operators of combined transport services would be able to have access to

---

[137] Cases T–374/94, *European Night Services* v. *Commission* and T–375/94, *European Passenger Services* v. *Commission*, pending. An association of combined road-rail transport companies, the *Union internationale rail-route (UIRR)* lodged an application to intervene, which was dismissed. See the Order of the President of the first Chamber of the CFI of 9 Aug. 1995 in Case T–374/94, *European Night Services* v. *Commission*, not yet reported.

[138] In this case, the Commission published a first summary of the agreement in accordance with Art. 12 of Reg. 1017/68 in OJ 1993 C 57, p. 5, and, after raising serious doubts over the authorization and obtaining of alteration of agreements, carried out a republication in accordance with Art. 26(3) of Reg. 1017/68 in OJ 1994 C 115, p. 5, this time announcing its intention to authorize it.

[139] Commission's decision relating to the *ACI* case, OJ 1994 L 224, p. 28. See *Press Release IP (94) 762*, of 28 July 1994.

[140] Combined transport means direct, point-to-point transport which uses various inland or surface transport modes and, principally, the one involving one segment by rail: transport by rail and road, or by rail and inland waterways. Combined transport must not be confused with multimodal transport (called 'intermodal' in the US), which also implies various segments, but in different modes of transport. Multimodal transport *par excellence* is sea-land transport. On this, see below, Ch. 4.

the market and compete with ACI and Intercontainer—in a word, with national railway companies, the only ones traditionally present on the railway market—the Commission imposed the condition on French and British railways to sell every operator the same indispensable services as they had undertaken to sell ACI, including the hire of specialist wagons for crossing the tunnel which they are unable to use, on non-discriminatory terms.

Still within the ambit of transport of goods, in 1994 the Commission authorized an agreement between thirteen railway companies for the creation of a *Community of Automobile Interests (CAI)*. As a procedural novelty compared with the ENS and ACI cases, in the CAI case, the notifiers, after publishing a first summary of their agreement,[141] and having received a letter of serious doubts from the Commission, carried out a further notification of their amended agreement, again on the basis of Article 12 of Regulation 1017/68,[142] thereby opening a new procedure and enabling the Commission to grant it an automatic, individual exemption for a period of three years.[143] [144]

The CAI constitutes a framework co-operation agreement between railway undertakings for the international transport of new vehicles. The participants' objective is to create suitable conditions for the increased use of transport of vehicles by rail between the assembly factories and distribution centres. In this context, the undertakings jointly define their strategy on the market, their marketing objectives and a common rate structure. The CAI does not intervene as such in the fixing of rates which are decided for each international connection by the undertakings participating in the journey; nor does it directly provide transport services, which is the railway undertakings' exclusive responsibility.

Still considering it restrictive of competition, the Commission recognized that the agreement would be able to improve the quality and technology for organizing the transport of new vehicles by rail—merchandise particularly suitable for this type of transport—and foster the development of railway transport, which is one of the objectives of the Community transport policy.

Aside from the agreement on the CAI, the Commission has also dealt with another agreement relating to the motor industry concluded between British railways, Belgian railways and the NV Ferry-Boats shipping companies (a subsidiary of Belgian railways) and NV Cobelfret. Its object was the creation of the joint subsidiary called *NV Auto Car Europe (ACE)*, whose aim would be to transport new cars and other products, such as parts, from the factories to the dealers, by train, road, sea, and air, and provide every type of complementary

---

[141] OJ 1993 C 117, p. 8.

[142] Summary notice published in OJ 1994 C 175, p. 3.

[143] And this without the need to resort to the automatic exemption procedure, simply letting ninety days pass after the second publication. On this procedural point, see below, Ch. 6, relating to the 'automatic' exemption procedure.

[144] See *Press Release IP (94) 826*, of 8 Sept. 1994.

service to transport.[145] The Commission expressed serious doubts about the applicability of Article 85(3) of the Treaty to this agreement in its original form but is continuing its talks with the undertakings.[146] One of the reasons why the Commission perhaps did not want to authorize this agreement automatically is that it involves, for the first time, inland (railway) and maritime (ferry) undertakings competing, *inter alia*, on routes across the Channel Tunnel.

In a different area of activity, in September 1994 the Commission authorized an agreement for the creation of a *European network of express delivery services* with guaranteed delivery time. The undertakings Ducros (French), DHL (Dutch) and Elan Rindt (Germany, DHL's subsidiary) notified at the end of 1993 the agreement relating to the network, concluded between them shortly before. The agreement essentially concerns travel by road (but also by rail and air) of products of great added-value, such as clothes, perfume, spare parts, records, hi-fi appliances, within a period which ranges between 34 and 96 hours, for packed consignments of a certain size (less than 3 tons and 15m^3). The network's activities were to be gradually performed throughout the Union, first in France, Germany, Italy, Spain, the United Kingdom and Benelux and, afterwards, in all European Union countries. However, Elan Rindt and Ducros would allow each other a reciprocal exclusivity in certain markets. The two undertakings were to combine their individual networks within a European network which they would operate under a trade name and within the context of a common strategy. Price-fixing and invoicing would continue to be the responsibility of each of them. DHL, active in the international express mail sector, but not in the express delivery of small packages, or messenger sector, undertakes not to enter the market and compete with Ducros.

The Commission considered that, despite being restrictive, the agreement had economic advantages, both by increasing the participating undertakings' activity and by contributing in practice to the creation of a Community area without frontiers. The creation of a new cross-frontier transport option was considered to be beneficial to the user. The restrictions appeared indispensable, as without the exclusivity which the parties give each other the transfer of information on the respective clientele on which the agreement would be based would be impossible. Lastly, and despite the comments to the contrary advanced by a competitor, the parties' market share did not appear to enable them to eliminate competition in respect of a substantial part of the market in any part

---

[145] Summary notice published in OJ 1994 C 130, p. 3. Due to the scale of transport and other activities which the ACE is trying to conduct, the legal basis for this publication is—for the first time—threefold: Art. 12(2) of Reg. 1017/68, Art. 12(2) of Reg. 4056/86 and Art. 5(2) of Reg. 3975/87. On the multiple legal bases in the Commission's communications, see below relating to the *DHL* case.

[146] Given that, apart from transport services, the undertakings seek to collaborate in the provision of other 'complementary' services, any decision will have to be adopted on the basis of the three transport Regulations and, also, on the basis of Reg. 17.

of European territory. In conclusion, the agreement satisfied all of the conditions for the exemption.

Given that the 'air' elements of the agreement were inseparable from the inland elements, the Commission granted an exemption for a period of three years as from the notification, letting ninety days pass from the publication of the summary of the agreement without opposing it.[147]

3.21.3.4. The *DHL* case

Another notification under Article 12 of the regulation which gave rise to an automatic non-opposition individual exemption was the one concerning the acquisition by Lufthansa, Japan Airlines and Nissho Iwai of minority interests in DHL International[148] (an express courier company). The main interest of this case is that, concerning agreements involving inland and air transport modes, the legal bases for the publication had to be Article 12 of Regulation 1017/68 and Article 5 of Regulation 3975/87. Due to the different duration of the period for which exemption is granted automatically pursuant to each regulation, the exemption is to be interpreted as granted for a period of three years for inland transport-related agreements and practices, and for a period of six years for air transport-related agreements and practices.[149]

This is not the only occasion on which the Commission has published notices with a double legal basis under the transport opposition procedure.[150] For example, in cases involving sea and land transport, both Regulations 4056/86 and 1017/68 have been applied on many occasions.[151]

---

[147] See the summary notice regarding the agreement in OJ 1994 C 165, p. 10, *Press Release IP (94) 850* and *24th Report on Competition Policy*, 1994, para. 192. For the different duration of non-opposition decisions pursuant to the transport regulations, see below, Ch. 6.

[148] OJ 1990 C 258, p. 33.

[149] For a commentary on this and other procedural differences between transport regulations, see below, Ch. 6.

[150] As has already been seen when referring to the *ACE* case, in this same paragraph, this is not the only occasion on which the Commission has published communications with a multiple legal basis, following the procedures for the granting of individual exemptions under more than one transport regulation. The communications with twofold legal basis are relatively numerous. Leaving to one side the ACE case (where the legal basis is threefold), these include the case relating to the *European express delivery service network*, already discussed, where Regs 1017/68 and 3975/87 were also used, as the agreements notified referred to inland and air transport.

[151] Such was the case in the *Gulfway Agreement* case, OJ 1990 C130, p. 3, in the *Agreement 1237* case, OJ 1990 C59 p. 2, in the *Irish Club Rules* case, OJ 1991 C166, p. 6 and in the *Eurocorde* case, OJ 1990 C162, p. 13, among others. In none of these cases was the exemption automatically granted.

3.21.3.5. The *HOV-SVZ/DB* case

The second (and currently last) in the very short list of infringement decisions on the basis of the inland transport regulation relates to discriminatory railway rates bound for German ports, which dates back to 1994.[152]

This Decision has its origin in the report presented by Havenondernemersvereniging SVZ (HOV-SVZ), an association of undertakings from the Port of Rotterdam. The association submitted that the German railways (Deutsche Bahn (DB)) had for many years used their monopoly on the German railway services market to impose on the combined transport operator, Intercontainer, lower railway rates for combined transport of marine containers that passed through German ports (Bremen and Hamburg) than for this same type of transport by way of the Belgian and Dutch ports, with the object of promoting its own services. The Commission's investigation corroborated such criticisms. In particular, it was found that the price for the transport of containers shipped from Rotterdam was up to 42 per cent more than the one charged from Hamburg and, on some specialist trains, up to 77 per cent.

These differences proved particularly unacceptable, bearing in mind that the competition between other modes of transport is far greater on western itineraries (Antwerp and Rotterdam) than on the northern ones (Bremen and Hamburg) and that, in other circumstances, the prices for the western itineraries should have been the cheapest, yet, on the contrary, proved the most expensive. This had as a consequence a deterioration in the competitive situation of the combined railway transport of cargo as opposed to road transport.

In view of DB's monopoly position on the German railway market at the time of the events and of the substantial effects on competition on European markets, the Commission considered that these restrictive practices amounted to an abuse of a dominant position. Accepting the existence of DB's monopoly, the Commission stated that an undertaking which enjoys, as against its competitors, legal protection, is nonetheless prohibited, in the same way as any other, from abusing its monopoly to promote its activities and those of one of its subsidiaries (Transfracht). The result of DB's practices was consciously to prejudice the economic viability of ports of other Member States for around three years at least. It thereby compartmentalized the Community market, in disregard of one of the fundamental objectives of the Treaty, and curbed the development of railway and combined transport—which is one of the objectives of Community transport policy. The Commission decided therefore to impose a fine of 11 million ECUs.

In this same Decision, the Commission also declared contrary to Article 85(1) of the Treaty the *Maritime Container Network (MCN)* agreement, concluded between the German, Dutch and Belgian railways, Transfracht and

---

[152] OJ 1994 L 104, p. 34. See *Press Release IP (94) 259*, of 29 Mar. 1994 and *24th Report on Competition Policy*, 1994, paras 193, 194, 199, 210 and 214.

Intercontainer. MCN's object was the joint marketing of its members' combined transport services, on the basis of a common rating structure. This agreement, which was a reaction to the types of discrimination practised by the German railways, backfired on the participants, as it only served to strengthen DB even more. In view of the fact that the undertakings put an end to the agreement upon receiving the statement of objections, the Commission did not impose fines on them for having participated in it.

The Decision has been appealed by DB to the CFI.[153]

3.21.4. Unused Procedures

Some of the procedures which are present only in Regulation 1017/68 have yet to be used by the Commission. Thus, for the time being, no action has been carried out in accordance with Articles 6 and 14 (individual exemption for crisis cartels). Article 17, which empowers the Member States and the Commission to seek a meeting of the Council before the adoption of a decision to implement competition rules by the Commission, has not been used either. Neither has Article 18, which allows the Commission to conduct studies by sectors in the transport sector.[154] Finally, the regulation has never been revised in accordance with the procedure provided for in Article 31.

3.21.5. The *UIC—Travel Agencies* and the *Encompass Europe* cases.

Apart from applying Regulation 1017/68 to pure transport services, the Commission has also applied Regulation 17 on certain markets connected with inland transport.[155] The most important case to date related to the distribution of railway tickets by travel agencies.[156] This was not the first time the Commission dealt with transport intermediaries' services using the procedural resources of Regulation 17.[157]

---

[153] Case T–229/94, *DB* v. *Commission*, awaiting resolution.

[154] For this particular provision of Reg. 1017/68 which is common to Reg. 17, but has no comparable provision either in Reg. 4056/86 nor in Reg. 3975/87, see below, Ch. 6.

[155] The same has been done with markets connected with, or related to, maritime and air transport. For an additional treatment of the procedural regime of services markets connected with maritime and air transport, see below, Chs 4 and 5.

[156] The Commission's decision in the *UIC-Travel Agencies* case, OJ 1992 L 366, p. 47. See also *Press Release IP (92) 961*, of 25 Nov. 1992.

[157] See, e.g., the Decisions relating to *IATA's Passenger and Cargo Agency Programmes*, relating to agreements between IATA's member airlines on the sale and distribution of their services by means of travel agents and air freight forwarders, OJ 1991 L 258, pp. 18 and 29. For a recent action by the Commission in the field of computer reservation systems (CRSs), an area close both to transport and transport agencies, see the case relating to the *Amadeus / Sabre Agreement*. The parties finally did not conclude the agreement, which had been dealt with using the procedural rules of Reg. 17. See in this respect the *21st Report on Competition Policy*, 1991, paras 93–5.

In the *UIC* case, the Commission studied certain agreements relating to the distribution of railway tickets. UIC is an international association of railway undertakings, within which its members co-operate technically and commercially. The areas of its co-operation included the fixing of criteria for acceptance of travel agencies authorized to sell railway tickets and the conditions on which these have to be sold. The members of the UIC agreed to control and limit in their countries the number of agencies with which they should compete in the distribution of tickets on their national territory; they fixed the agents' commissions and conditions for their payment; and they prohibited agents sharing their commission with customers, something which—in 1987—the Court deemed contrary to the competition rules.[158] The effect of these agreements was to limit the commercial autonomy of travel agencies and competition between distributors, to the end-users' detriment. The Commission considered that the UIC had seriously and continually infringed Article 85(1) of the Treaty and, despite its members' formal undertaking to adapt their agreements to conform with Community law, the Commission imposed upon it a fine of one million ECUs.

The members of UIC challenged the Commission decision which was quashed by the CFI on the basis that it had been adopted under the wrong procedural regulation, namely Regulation 17 instead of Regulation 1017/68.[159] The CFI concluded that travel agency services were to be considered ancillary to inland transport within the meaning of the last sentence of Article 1 of Regulation 1017/68 and accordingly had to be dealt with under the procedural rules of this regulation. The Commission has appealed against the judgment of the CFI to the European Court, but for the moment, it is applying both Regulation 17 and Regulation 1017/68 in cases where there may be doubts as to the applicable procedural regulation.[160]

Encompass Europe was a joint venture between Encompass, a 50/50 partnership between two American companies, AMRS and CSXS, whose principal activities are in the transport industry, and ELTS BV a wholly-owned subsidiary of PTT Telecom BV, the Dutch telecom operator. The joint venture was to be the European arm of an integrated, multi-modal, global cargo logistics information system, which would provide information relating to the transport of cargo to shippers, freight-forwarders, agents, receivers, customs brokers, carriers and trading partners of all transport modes.

Historically, the provision of cargo information and booking services depended on a complicated exchange of paper between undertakings in the cargo transport industry. In recent years, a number of computer-based systems for tracking cargo movements have developed. Some of these systems are owned by individual operators and other systems are open, but limited to either one

---

[158] Case 311/85, *Vereniging van Vlaamse Reisbureaus* v. *Sociale Dienst (VVR, or Flemish Travel Agencies)*, [1978] ECR 3801. As will be seen, the ECJ has also dealt with some other cases connected with travel agents.

[159] See above n. 4.   [160] For a detailed comment on this judgment, see above, para. 3.8.

mode of transport or to a particular geographical area. There being no single industry-wide system that provides comprehensive information on the movements of cargo, Encompass Europe aimed to fill this gap, by establishing a non-biased system open to all users and suppliers of transport-related activities on a world-wide basis. The various agreements to set up this joint venture were notified to the Commission, which published a notice under Article 19(3) of Regulation 17[161] and finally cleared the agreement by means of a comfort letter.

3.22. STATE INTERVENTIONS

The Court has recently ruled on the matter of the application of competition rules in the inland transport sector. In the *Reiff* case, a German court asked the Court on a preliminary reference under Article 177 of the Treaty whether road haulage rates fixed by rate Commissions in Germany were legal.[162] The questions put before the Court referred to the compatibility of the procedures for fixing road haulage rates in Germany with Articles 85 (1), 3(g) (formerly 3(f)) and 5 of the Treaty, with the consequence that such rates could be considered null and void under Article 85(2) of the Treaty. The Court rejected the applicability of those provisions in the case at issue following Advocate General Darmon's opinion,[163] as the members of the aforementioned commissions were not undertakings as such, nor was there state intervention on prices and transport conditions aimed at strengthening a prior restrictive agreement.

Even more recently, the Court has commented in a way very similar to its *Reiff* judgment in a ruling that the procedures of the rate commissions for price-fixing in waterway transport in Germany are not contrary to Article 85 of the Treaty.[164]

In other cases which have not been decided,[165] similar issues were raised in respect of price-fixing commissions for other types of inland transport.

---

[161] OJ 1992 C233, p. 2.
[162] Case 185/91, *Bundesanstalt für den Guterfernverkehr* v. *Gebruder Reiff*, [1993] ECR I–5801.
[163] Opinion of Adv. Gen. M. Darmon of 14 July 1993 in Case C–185/91, *Reiff*.
[164] Case C–153/93, *Germany* v. *Delta Schiffahrts und Speditionsgesellschaft*, [1994] ECR I—2517.
[165] See Cases C–48/92 *Wimmer*, C–77/92, *Rhode & Liesenfeld* ; and C–293/92 *Schaare* v. *Rappe*.

4

The Shipping Sector

Section I: Rules of Competition: Regulation 4056/86

4.1. THE ORIGINS AND CONTEXT OF REGULATION 4056/86

4.1.1. Introduction

Regulation 4056/86[1] contributes both to the process of establishing the instruments for the implementation of Articles 85 and 86 of the Treaty in the transport sector and also to the development of a first ever Community maritime transport policy. The maritime regulation, the second in the series of three which followed Regulation 141/62,[2] above all serves to implement the Treaty competition rules. However, for historical reasons, it also voices the first political decisions taken by Member States within Council in matters relating to the organization of liner markets, markets of vital importance to Community foreign trade.

Although it was already evident and recognized in 1962 that the Community needed to adopt a competition regulation for maritime transport, there was no real impetus for the measure until the *French Seamen* judgment in 1974.[3] Until then, the Commission had not insisted that the Council grant it powers to implement the competition rules effectively in the sector. Perhaps this was because of the Commission's experience of negotiating Regulation 1017/68[4] with the Member States, which made it suspicious of the conditions the Council would require (particularly, that maritime provisions would also deviate significantly from orthodox competition rules).

Work on preparation of a competition regulation in maritime transport started in 1979. It was already clear by then that the main purpose behind the measure was not to defend free competition in maritime transport but rather to formalize in EC legislation acceptance of the 'status quo' in international and EC maritime transport, thereby accepting the liner conference system—the international cartel structure which has dominated international liner trade since the final quarter of last century—in Community competition law.

---

[1] Council Reg. (EEC) 4056/86, of 22 Dec. 1986, laying down detailed rules for the application of Arts 85 and 86 of the Treaty to maritime transport, OJ 1986 L 378, p. 4.

[2] OJ 1962 124, p. 2753, Spec. Ed. 1959–62, p. 291. See above, Ch. 2.

[3] Case 167/73, [1974] ECR 359. See above, Ch. 2.

[4] For this Reg., see above, Ch. 3, Section II.

4.1.2. The history of conferences[5]

The first successful liner conference was the Calcutta Conference. The conference was made up of liner steamer owners[6] offering services between the United Kingdom and Calcutta who established a common tariff with uniform rates in 1875 and a binding system of deferred rebates for shippers in 1877.[7] The first liner conference was thereby created with the main features which have always characterized these owner cartels. The system thought out by the British shipping companies grew and quickly became international. Within a few years, with members from all industrialized nations, conferences would literally cover all maritime routes of the world.

The basic question of the acceptability of conferences was raised publicly on both sides of the Atlantic at the beginning of this century. The United States opted for the regulation and control of the activities of liner conferences. In 1916, they adopted their first Shipping Act,[8] which prohibited closed conferences (in other words, those which did not accept any shipping company applying to become a member) and deferred rebates. The 1916 Act, which still applies to domestic trade, was replaced by the Shipping Act 1984.[9] The 1984 Act applies to United States foreign trade and is more tolerant to shipping cartels than its predecessor. The United Kingdom preferred the '*laissez faire*' approach, permitting conferences to exist and operate without any public control. The British position was widely accepted in Western Europe, where conferences saw a far more peaceful existence from the time they were created. Governments tolerated them and even encouraged them and, in general, they were excluded *de facto* or *de jure* from the application of competition law.

From the 1960s, developing countries also started to criticize the conference system, which they considered a relic of a colonial past which made their rates more expensive and prevented the development of their merchant fleets. The result of their pressure was the adoption in 1974 of UNCTAD's Code of Conduct for Liner Conferences[10] which enshrined, *inter alia*, the cargo-sharing formula on the basis of a 40/40/20 split.[11]

---

[5] On this matter, see, in general, Marx, Daniel Jr., *International shipping cartels: a study of industrial self-regulation by shipping conferences.* (Princeton University Press. Princeton, New Jersey, 1953); Herman, Amos, *Shipping conferences.* (Lloyd's of London Press. London, 1983), and the summary of Sir Leon Brittan at his conference 'The EC's competition policy for liner shipping set in its commercial and political context', European Maritime Law Organization, London, 23 Oct. 1992.

[6] Steamer vessels gradually replaced sailing ships in international maritime trade as from the mid-19th century and made possible modern liner shipping.

[7] For the concept of deferred rebates, see below, para. 4.2.5.2.

[8] 46 USC 801.   [9] 46 USC app. 1701.

[10] The text of the Convention can be consulted in United Nations Conference on Trade and Development, Geneva, *United Nations Conference of Plenipotentiaries on a Code of Conduct for Liner Conferences. Held at Geneva from 12 November to 15 Dec. 1973 (first part) and from 11 March to 6 April 1974 (second part).* Volume II. Final Act (including the Convention and resolutions) and tonnage requirements. (United Nations. New York, 1975 (Document TD/CODE/13/Add.1).)

[11] The formula 40/40/20 is to be found in Art. 2(4) of the UNCTAD Code. In practice, it

4.1.3. The EC attitude to liner conferences and the UNCTAD Code[12]

The Member States of the Community participated in the Conference of Plenipotentiaries of the United Nations which led to the adoption of the Code of Conduct but failed to take a common stance on the Code. The Commission, for its part, was at first against the Code and threatened to bring the Member States which had signed it before the European Court under Article 169 of the Treaty. In fact, the provisions of the Code raised problems of compatibility with a certain number of provisions of the Treaty of Rome, including Article 7 (now Article 6)—by discriminating in favour of national shipping companies—and Articles 85 and 86—by unconditionally accepting their collusive agreements. The division in Community ranks was resolved five years later with the adoption of Council Regulation 954/79/EEC, dubbed the 'Brussels Package',[13] under which the Member States were authorized to ratify the UNCTAD Code provided they made certain reservations. It was the 'Brussels Package' which enabled the Code to enter into force in 1983, nine years after its adoption.

The 'Brussels Package' sought to reconcile the contradictory requirements of the UNCTAD Code and the EEC Treaty, mainly eliminating the former's discriminatory aspects. In competition law, the question was whether it was possible to reconcile the Liner Code (which accepted these competition-restricting shipping cartels) with Article 85 (which prohibits them). The answer to this question was given in the last recital of Regulation 954/79. On the one hand, it recognized the stabilizing role of conferences, assuring reliable services to shippers, and implicitly granted them a block exemption. On the other hand, in the recitals it announced a proposal for a regulation on the implementation of the rules of competition to maritime transport, which would enable infringements of Articles 85 and 86 of the Treaty in this sector to be punished. The first draft of what would end up as Regulation 4056/86 had to wait until 1981[14]—seven years after the *French Seamen* judgment and the adoption of the UNCTAD Code. It was marked by the approach advanced in the last recital of the 'Brussels Package' (with its prejudice in favour of conferences) and by the procedural rules of Regulation 1017/68. The negotiation of Regulation 4056/86 lasted five years. The first draft regulation for block exemption and application and implementation of the rules of competition was amended in 1985[15] (almost at the time

allocates 40% of cargoes carried by conferences to the national shipping lines of countries at each end of a route, and the remaining 20% to third country conference lines (conference 'cross-traders'). In theory, it should have been used for poorer countries to develop their merchant fleets upon preferential conditions.

[12] On this point, see also, above, Ch. 2.

[13] Council Reg. (EEC) 954/79, OJ 1979 L 121, p.1.

[14] The draft and an explanatory memorandum are to be found in Document COM (81) 423 final, of 13 Oct. 1981. The draft was also published in OJ 1981 C 282, p. 4.

[15] See Document COM (85) 90 final, of 14 Mar. 1985, entitled 'Progress towards a common transport policy—Maritime transport', in Annex II-5 of which the amendments of the original 1981

of the Court's judgment in the common transport policy case between the Parliament and Council[16]) and finally adopted on 22 December 1986, to enter into force on 1 July 1987.

As stated before, Regulation 4056/86 deviates notably from the orthodoxy of European competition law. Its more or less avowed aim was not to assure a system of undistorted competition but to maintain and tolerate the *status quo* of the liner conferences in existence in Western Europe since 1875. For this reason, the regulation contains, together with purely procedural provisions (applying and implementing the competition rules), other provisions which have as their object the authorization *sine die*[17] of liner conferences and their traditional practices. Regulation 4056/86 thus repeats the pattern of Regulation 1017/68 (the first regulation to deal with both application and exemption at the same time) although the substantive elements in Regulation 4056/86 are far more numerous and economically important.

4.2. THE PROVISIONS OF REGULATION 4056/86

4.2.1. Scope of the shipping Regulation

In accordance with Article 1(2), Regulation 4056/86 'shall apply only to international maritime transport services from or to one or more Community ports, other than tramp vessel services'.

The Regulation is, therefore, not applicable to cabotage traffic,[18] [19] nor to 'tramp' services, which are meticulously defined.[20] The definition of 'tramp' services drastically limits excluded services: the Council has set as a condition for the non-application of Regulation 4056/86 that 'the freight rates are freely negotiated case by case in accordance with the conditions of supply and demand'. Only when this condition is satisfied will the shipping services be able to escape the rules of the regulation. This means that a price cartel between tramp owners, or any agreement which limits their freedom to negotiate indi-

---

proposal are contained. The Commission proposed other last minute modifications in Documents COM (86) 676 final (OJ 1986 C 324) and COM (86) 744 final (OJ 1987 C 17).

[16] Case 13/83, *Parliament* v. *Council*, [1974] ECR 1513.

[17] This is one of the most polemic—and possibly illegal—aspects of the regulation.

[18] The inapplicability of the *procedural* rules of the shipping regulation does not mean that Arts 85 and 86 are inapplicable, but that they are only applicable by way of the less satisfactory procedures of Arts 88—for the national authorities of the Member States—and 89 of the Treaty—for the Commission. See above, Ch. 2, and below, Ch. 6.

[19] Note that Reg. 3975/87 did not apply either to air cabotage until the Council approved the third package of liberalizing measures. See Council Regs (EEC) 2408/92 and 2410/92 (OJ 1992 L 240, pp. 8 and 18). Despite the agreement on the gradual liberalization of maritime cabotage services by virtue of Council Reg. (EEC) 3577/92 (OJ 1992 L 364, p. 7, amended by OJ 1993 L 173, p. 33), Reg. 4056/86 has not been amended.

[20] Art. 1.3.a) of Reg. 4056/86.

vidual prices, will fall within the scope of application of the regulation and may be investigated and punished by the Commission.[21]

4.2.2. The exception for technical agreements

The basic lines of the exception for technical agreements in inland transport also characterize the exception of certain technical agreements, generally considered non-restrictive, in the maritime sector.[22] It will be remembered that it was argued that the exceptions in transport competition law are—and cannot be other than—purely declaratory in nature (a kind of 'block negative clearance', as they have sometimes been described). If, in practice, the agreements enumerated in Article 2 of the shipping regulation restrict competition in the way provided in Article 85, the exception will not apply. It was also pointed out that agreements between competitors are rarely purely technical and that the same goes (perhaps even more so) for Article 2–type agreements. The substantive reasons for exception simply reflect the reasons which justify non-application of Article 85(1) or, to put it another way round, the agreements quoted in Article 2 are only lawful when they are not restrictive. The inclusion of this provision in the transport regulations could therefore be misleading.

The list of activities in Article 2 of Regulation 4056/86 takes as a model that of Article 3 of Regulation 1017/68 (save for one of the activities quoted in the latter which is not quoted in the former[23]). Some of the wording has, however, suffered translational changes and changes in nuance, even some substantive changes of note. The shipping regulation, which is very similar in form to the inland regulation, refers in paragraphs (a) to (f) of Article 2(1) to agreements on standardization, to the exchange or pooling of means of transport and transport facilities, to the organization of successive or supplementary maritime transport operations, to the co-ordination of transport timetables for connecting routes, to the consolidation of individual consignments, and to the establishment or application of uniform rules on transport tariff structures.

It is worth observing, however, that Article 2(1)(b) of Regulation 4056/86 differs from Article 3(1)(b) of Regulation 1017/68 in that the former specifically mentions the possibility of exchanging not only transport vehicles (vessels, in this case), but also 'space on vessels or 'slots'.[24] Article 2(1)(f) of Regulation 4056/86

[21] As will be seen below, when referring to technical agreements, this is not the only provision of the Reg. the scope of which is narrower than might at first sight appear.

[22] For a more detailed treatment of 'technical agreements' under EC competition rules see above, Ch. 3, Section II. As for Art. 3(2) of Reg. 1017/68, Annex XIV, Section G.11 (b) of the Agreement of the European Economic Area (EEA) provides that Art. 2(2) of Reg. 4056/86 (which allows the list of technical agreements to be enlarged) is inapplicable for the purposes of such agreement. As has already been said, the reasons for this adaptation are unclear.

[23] In particular 'the use, for journeys by a single mode of transport, of the routes which are the most rational from the operational point of view' (Art. 3[1][d] of Reg. 1017/68).

[24] This provision has served as a basis to argue—contrary to the Commission's opinion—that, as joint capacity utilization activities, which are the main ones of liner consortia, are already duly

also differs from Article 3(1)(g) of Regulation 1017/68 in that the inland Regulation clearly specifies that the establishment of common rules on the structure of transport tariffs must not be used to 'determine the prices and conditions of transport', while the silence of the maritime Regulation may make it appear more comprehensive towards 'technical' price-fixing than its inland counterpart.

4.2.3. Liner conferences and the block exemption

The main substantive content of Regulation 4056/86 is the block exemption in favour of specific agreements of liner conferences. Granting this exemption was the Council's main objective in adopting the regulation.

This exemption unusually was granted by the Council on a proposal by the Commission. It differs substantially in its systematic arrangement from the group exemptions which were granted by the Commission rather than the Council. The exemption of conferences is extremely concise and lacks detailed lists of 'white' and 'black' clauses which characterized the previous Commission exemption regulations, instruments which aimed both to delimit precisely the ambit of the exemptions and to make sure that the defined agreements satisfied the four conditions of implementation of Article 85(3). The reason for this surprising conciseness may be that—contrary to Commission practice—the exemption was granted without previous experience in the individual application of Article 85(3) to conferences, which is why neither the Commission in its proposals, nor the Council in its deliberations were able—or perhaps willing—to devise a more detailed exemption.

The exemption is subject to various requirements, both formal and substantive. Some are necessary to *enjoy* the exemption and others are necessary to *maintain* it. Within the first group one should distinguish two sets of conditions: first, the conditions for being a liner conference for the purposes of the exemption, and, second, the conditions on which the specific activities of the conferences can be authorized, with the peculiarity that those conditions and these activities are basically the same.[25] Within the second group, a distinction should in turn be made between the requirements defined by the regulation itself for maintaining the exemption (attached obligations) and those which must be complied with due to imperatives of the Treaty (i.e., those of Article 85[3]). Sharing the characteristics of both these types of conditions a *sui generis* requirement, Article 4, sets out a condition upon which the enjoyment and the maintenance of the block exemption depend.

---

authorized, the adoption of a block exemption for these was unnecessary. For the consortia in general, see below, Section II.

[25] For an explanation of this paradox, see below.

4.2.3.1. Definition of 'liner conference'

Article 3 of the regulation starts by providing that '(a)greements, decisions and concerted practices of all or part of the members of one or more liner conferences . . .', in certain conditions, are exempt from the prohibition contained in Article 85(1). Consequently, the first requirement for the exemption of restrictive agreements between sea carriers is that such carriers belong to one or more liner conferences which fall within the scope of the definition contained in Article 1(3)(b) of the regulation.

Article 1(3)(b) follows the UNCTAD Code, and defines 'liner conference' as being:

a group of two or more vessel-operating carriers which provide international liner services for the carriage of cargo on a particular route or routes within specified geographical limits and which has an agreement or arrangement, whatever its nature, within the framework of which they operate under uniform or common freight rates and any other agreed conditions with respect to the provision of liner services.

Various consequences regarding the legal form of the conferences, the activity of their members and the geographical scope, basic features, and characteristic content of the conferences can be gathered from the EC and the United Nations definition.

Dealing with the legal form and degree of formality for their creation, the regulation does not lay down any requirement for liner conferences. Regardless of the fact that, in practice, conferences are generally created by means of very elaborate, written agreements, there is nothing to stop, for the purposes of Regulation 4056/86, a conference being created by means of a purely oral agreement or even by means of a 'gentlemen's agreement'.

The definition of Article 1(3)(b) of Regulation 4056/86 refers to 'a group of two or more vessel-operating carriers', which introduces a first limitation on the type of shipping company capable of benefiting from the group exemption of Article 3 of the regulation. The agreements between carriers who do not operate vessels ('Non-Vessel-Operating Carriers' or NVOCs), although subject to the regulation, are ineligible for the exemption. The participation of shipping companies of this type in conferences is not foreseen by the regulation and is not authorized in principle.

The Article 1(3)(b) definition coincides to a great extent with the scope of application specified in Article 1(2) of the regulation and, in referring to 'international liner services' excludes both restrictive agreements in non-liner shipping and in specialized neo-bulk transport—which certainly cannot be called 'conferences'—and cabotage conferences.

The Article 1(3)(b) definition refers, like the Code of Conduct, only to freight conferences (exclusively for the carriage of cargo). The definition, therefore, excludes restrictive agreements between passenger shipping companies such as ferry operators from the Article 3 exemption.[26]

In terms of the geographical scope of the conferences, the definition of conference of Article 1(3)(b) of Regulation 4056/86 requires the members of a conference to provide services 'on a particular route or routes within specified geographical limits . . .'. Neither the regulation nor the Code specify, however, the way in which conferences will have to be geographically delimited; shipping companies are free to designate the routes covered by the conferences and to determine the ports between which their activities will remain subject to the tariffs and conditions of the conference. In practice, the monopolistic character of the conferences has meant that, wherever due to geographical and infrastructural circumstances the shipowners have considered that there was an homogeneous and distinct market for their services, a liner conference has been created.

With respect to the characteristic content of liner conferences, Article 1(3)(b) of the regulation requires the member carriers qualifying for the block exemption to operate 'under uniform or common freight rates and any other agreed conditions with respect to the provision of liner services'.[27] Given that the regulation has to take into account the Code of Conduct,[28] above all when borrowing one of its definitions, it is necessary to study Chapter IV of the United Nations Convention, relating to freight rates and, in particular, Article 13, which deals with the tariffs of conferences in order to understand the meaning of 'uniform or common freight rates'. Article 13 states:

1. Conference tariffs shall not unfairly differentiate between shippers similarly situated. . . .

2. Conference tariffs should be drawn up simply and clearly, containing as few classes/categories as possible, depending on the [necessities of each trade, and specifying a freight rate for each[29]] commodity and, where appropriate, for each class/category . . .

Rates within the tariffs therefore have to be non-discriminatory and unique for each product or class within the tariff. The preparatory works of the Code of Conduct show that it was not the intention of its draftsman to give a distinct flavour to each such term but only to insist that rates would have to be the same irrespective of the identity of the offeree (uniform rates) or of who within the

---

[26] The 1981 draft regulation referred, however, to 'liner services for the carriage of cargo or passengers' within the definition of conference, as a result of which it would have authorized passenger conferences. The literal adaptation of the Community definition to the UNCTAD Code in 1985 meant a reduction in the scope of application of the exemption to cargo conferences.

[27] This requirement comes from the definition of a liner conference under the UNCTAD Code, which Reg. 4056/86 reproduces literally.

[28] See the third recital of the regulation.

[29] By mistake, the text in brackets does not appear in the English version of the Liner Code printed under the auspices of UNCTAD, cited above, n. 10. The other linguistic versions of the Code contain the omitted words.

conference offers (common rates).[30] This way of fixing transport prices acts as an identifying characteristic of EC-type conference inspired directly by the UN description. For this reason, the Commission has interpreted that agreements between shipowners establishing differential rates and agreements between conferences and outsiders with the same aim cannot be considered conferences in the sense of the definition of the regulation and therefore do not have the benefit of the Article 3 exemption.[31]

Shipping lines have contested the Commission's interpretation, arguing that each of the terms 'uniform' and 'common' has a distinct meaning and that 'common freight rates' are not the same as 'uniform freight rates'. Neither, they argue, would the construction of 'stability' given by the Commission (basically, freight rate stability) be correct; stability has a much broader sense under the regulation and can be achieved without uniform rates.[32] This matter has been referred to the CFI and to the European Court.[33]

4.2.3.2. Application of block exemption

The second part of the applicability 'test' of the block exemption in favour of liner conferences is found in Article 3 of the regulation. This provision has the particularity of referring to certain typical activities of conferences which are, as well as being authorized restrictive agreements, partly conditions for the application of the exemption. As a consequence of this peculiar formulation, and unusually for Community competition law, Article 3 requires the existence of minimal—although fairly substantial—competition restrictions between members of conferences for those restrictions to be permitted.

The Article 3 exemption appears to cover a cumulatively high number of agreements, primarily defined by reference to the participating undertakings (all or only part of the members of one or more conferences[34]) and thereafter by reference to their objectives (rate-fixing and, as the case may be, one or more of

[30] The uniformity of rates has been considered by the preparatory studies of the UNCTAD Code as an advantage of the conferences for users. The only derogations from the principle of equality of tariff treatment for all shippers on the part of the members of the conferences are included in the Code itself and reflected in Reg. 4056/86. They concern the rebates granted to users who have concluded loyalty agreements with conferences. See Arts 7 and 8 of the Code and Art. 5(2) of the Reg. For loyalty agreements, see below, para. 4.5.5.2

[31] See the Commission's decision in the case relating to the Trans-Atlantic Agreement (TAA), OJ 1994 L 376, 1.

[32] The arguments are summarized in the *TAA* decision, above.

[33] The CFI will have to deal with this question in the appeal against the *TAA* decision, Case T–395/94 *Atlantic Container Lines and others* v. *Commission*, pending. For its part, the ECJ will consider the matter within the context of a preliminary reference under Art. 177 of the Treaty, Case C–339/95, *Compagnia di Navigazione Marittima and others* v. *Compagnie Maritime Belge and others* (the *SUNAG* case), pending.

[34] In fact, agreements would be able to take place: between all members of a conference; between part of the members of a conference; between all members of various conferences and between part of the members of various conferences.

five other objectives). The exemption thus appears here as a wide umbrella of the fullest cover for shipping companies, not without interpretative difficulties.[35]

4.2.3.2.1. *Agreements authorized as exemption requirements*

Article 3 stipulates that agreements between all or part of the members of a conference are authorized when their objective is 'the fixing of rates and conditions of carriage and, as the case may be, one or more of the [ ] objectives . . .' which it enumerates. Article 3, therefore, requires and at the same time authorizes rate-fixing and also appears to require the conclusion of other restrictive agreements between the members of a conference, with the object that both rate-fixing and the other restrictive agreements enumerated be authorized. The paradoxical requirement of rate-fixing[36] is formulated not only in Article 3, which grants the exemption, but also in Article 1(3)(b)—which defines the way rates must be fixed in EC conferences—and, in a more qualified and implicit way, in Article 5(4), which defines the obligations of conferences in relation to publicity of tariffs. Consequently, it is immediately clear that Article 3 goes far beyond the normal authorization of specific activities which would not need to be carried on by the conferences for the exemption to apply. Instead—with its concomitant provisions—Article 3 sets a strict limit on the scope of the exemption it contains. This interpretation is supported by the hermeneutical principle that exceptions to general rules—in this case the Article 85(1) prohibition—have to be interpreted strictly. Not to require rate-fixing, or not to demand it in the precise way described in the conference definition, would be to take Article 3 as a 'maximum limit of restriction' without a minimum. Such an interpretation would widen the scope of application of Article 3 to such an extent that it would become a 'blanket exemption' for all type of restrictions of competition in liner shipping. The Treaty does not permit such broad exemptions from its fundamental rules without a clear delimitation and justification of the exemption for each and every type of exempt agreement.

On the other hand, in the structure of Regulation 4056/86, only the restrictions on competition capable of strongly limiting competition produce the desired beneficial effects, chiefly stability of rates.

The exemption of conferences also raises the interpretative question of whether discriminatory rating on the basis of the type of cargoes which characterizes liner conferences has been authorized by Regulation 4056/86. The regulation, in requiring members of conferences to offer uniform or common rates,

---

[35] Cf. Temple Lang, J., 'Current issues in maritime competition law'. (Notes for a lecture, London, Oct. 1992. European Maritime Law Organization), and Rakovsky, C., 'Sea transport under EEC competition law'. *Annual Proceedings of the Fordham Corporate Law Institute, 1992*, (Transnational Juris Publications/Kluwer, New York/Deventer, 1993), pp. 845–906, *inter alia.*

[36] Paradoxical in Community competition law but not given the political objectives and the 'codist' background to the Regulation.

does not specify the way these are to be calculated. The Code of Conduct and the history itself of maritime conferences show, however, that in liner shipping the obligation of non-discrimination implicit in the requirement of uniformity is applicable exclusively in respect of shippers of the same commodity. Under the UNCTAD Code, there are no acts of discrimination when the shippers pay different rates for the same maritime transport service, if the products transported are different, above all in terms of their value. The Commission itself, in its 1985 Communication, implicitly accepted the traditional practice of discrimination by reference to the products transported, on the basis of 'what the market (of the product) will bear'.[37]

The answer under EC competition law to this question is not obvious. It may be thought that logically, beyond rate-fixing, the discrimination inherent in the tariffs of conferences amounts to an additional factor which deserves explicit treatment within Regulation 4056/86. The truth is that neither the Articles, nor the recitals of the regulation refer to this conference practice which only by reference to the UNCTAD Code[38] can be considered implicitly authorized by Article 3 of the regulation. Even the Code does not justify it. Moreover, this discrimination might in certain circumstances amount to an abuse of the conferences' dominant position. If so, it could be attacked—without the need to withdraw the exemption—by the Commission directly and by prejudiced users before national courts.[39]

Within the second part of the 'test' for applying the liner conferences block exemption, the question arises whether

(1) rate-fixing, without any other further restrictive activity, is sufficient for the conference to benefit from the exemption; or
(2) whether apart from this type of restrictive agreement, it is necessary to carry out at least another of the activities enumerated in sub-paragraphs (a) to (e) in Article 3 of the Regulation, for the block exemption to be applicable.

Although it has been said that the Commission has already opted, pragmatically, for the first wider interpretation, according to which the mere fixing of rates would be sufficient for the exemption to apply,[40] the Commission has never formally and publicly dealt with this matter. Under Article 3, conferences must have as their objective 'the fixing of rates and conditions of carriage, and, as the case may be, one or more of the [ ] objectives . . .' which it enumerates. The literal interpretation of this requirement would make it possible to conclude both that fixing rates is sufficient—putting the emphasis on the circumstantial nature of the other agreements: 'as the case may be'—*and* that other restrictive

---

[37] 1985 Communication and proposals, see above, n. 15, para. 69.
[38] See Art. 12(b), in fine of the UNCTAD Code.   [39] Cf., Temple Lang, above n. 35.
[40] See Green, N., 'Competition and maritime trade: a critical view' *European Transport Law*, Vol. 23, No. 5, pp. 612–28, at p. 622.

activities are required—putting the emphasis on the additive nature of the conjunction 'and': 'the fixing of rates. . . and [i.e., plus] one or more of the [ ] objectives . . .' enumerated.

Bearing in mind that the block exemption is stated in the recitals to be justified largely because conferences 'contribute generally to providing adequate efficient scheduled maritime transport services', mere rate-fixing, although indispensable, is insufficient (of itself) to obtain such economic advantages. Moreover, the nature of a pure rate agreement appears different to that of a codist liner conference which, traditionally, includes an element of rationalization derived from market sharing. Finally, if that were enough, faced with the two interpretative options already outlined above, Commission doubts would have to be resolved by limiting to the utmost the scope of the exemption and, consequently, the second of the interpretations would prevail.

In conclusion, to be eligible for the block exemption shipping companies must not only determine rates but also carry out one or more of the further activities or restrictive agreements listed in sub-paragraphs (a) to (e) of Article 3.[41]

4.2.3.2.2. *Agreements authorized by the exemption*

Apart from freight rate-fixing agreements, Article 3 of Regulation 4056/86 enumerates five types of agreement which have been expressly authorized, provided the conditions considered above are fulfilled. These agreements may refer to the supply of services (rationalization agreements, sub-paragraphs [a] to [d]) or be complementary to agreements on prices ('pooling' agreements or 'pools', sub-paragraph [e]).

Article 3 of the Regulation authorizes a first group of agreements with the following objectives:

(1) the co-ordination of shipping timetables, sailing dates or dates of calls;
(2) the determination of the frequency of sailings or calls;
(3) the co-ordination or allocation of sailings or calls among members of the conference;
(4) the regulation of the carrying capacity offered by each member.

The object of all of these agreements between the members of a conference is to influence the supply and market in liner shipping services by means of:

(1) the determination of the number of sailings (temporal delimitation of supply) and of calls (geographical delimitation of supply); and
(2) the distribution and co-ordination of sailings and calls and—concomitantly—the operational patterns of the vessels (leading to market sharing).

---

[41] In a similar sense, cf. Rycken, W., 'European anti-trust aspects of maritime and air transport (Part I)'. *European Transport Law*, Vol. 22, 5, 1987, pp. 483–504, at p. 493.

The exemption specified in Article 3(a) to (d) raises two main issues in terms of its scope of application.

The first question refers to the lawfulness of geographical market-sharing agreements derived from, or inherent in, the exemption in favour of 'the co-ordination or allocation of sailings or calls among members of the conference' (Article 3[c]). Although the term 'ports' is not employed by the regulation, conference members may, by means of distributing sailings and calls, manage territorially to share the markets they cover. The Commission has not commented to date on whether the Article 3 exemption authorizes agreements which lead to the territorial exclusivity of some members of conferences on certain sectors or ports. In any case, geographical market sharing by reference to the borders of the EU Member States served by the conferences, or by reference to the nationality of the shipping companies (such as, for example, if each company undertakes to call exclusively at ports of the country in which their vessels are flagged) would be directly contrary to a basic principle of EC law; namely, the establishment of an internal market without internal frontiers.[42] Geographical market sharing could not be authorized by the exemption without the exemption becoming incompatible with the Treaty itself.

The second question which arises in respect of the scope of application of the exemption is whether, by means of 'the determination of the frequency of sailings or calls' (Article 3[b]) and 'the regulation of the carrying capacity offered by each member' (Article 3[d]) conferences are authorized to reduce substantially the supply of capacity with the aim of increasing the general level of rates. This question is of great importance as regards the acceptability of so-called 'stabilization agreements' under EC competition law.[43] The Commission considers that it is not possible to allow conferences to reduce considerably or alter substantially the offer of liner shipping services on markets in which they operate. The Commission's reasons are various and make reference to the non-existence of such practices in the conferences of the UNCTAD Code, to the emphasis of the regulation on aspects of matching supply to the geographical and seasonal variations in demand, to the avowed impossibility of authorizing price-fixing agreements together with capacity-reducing agreements in other sectors of the economy and to the need to interpret exemptions in a way compatible with Article 85(3) of the Treaty.[44] Shipping companies have construed Article 3(d) of the regulation much more widely, pointing out the fact that conferences were created essentially to deal with overcapacity and uneconomical rates. This matter is *sub judice* in the appeal of the *Trans-Atlantic Agreement* decision.[45]

The last paragraph of Article 3(e) of Regulation 4056/86, having identified agreements relating to the control of supply and market sharing, authorizes

---

[42] See, e.g., Arts 3(c) and 7a of the Treaty.   [43] See below, para. 4.3.3.3.
[44] See the Commission's Decision in the *TAA* case, see above, n. 31, at paras 359–70. See also Temple Lang, 'Current issues . . .', above n. 35.
[45] See above, n. 31.

certain agreements complementary to freight rate agreements, in particular, agreements on 'the allocation of cargo or revenue among members'. It refers, without naming them, to the pooling agreements of which Article 2 of the UNCTAD Code talks. The Article 3 reference to agreements between some of the members of a liner conference clearly refers to the common practice in codist conferences of establishing pools in which not all of their members necessarily participate. Pooling agreements are different from 'rationalization' agreements (in actual fact, mostly market sharing agreements) and are generally considered complementary to agreements on rates. This is, in any case, the angle of Article 3, which requires from the outset a common level of rates for validly establishing a pool or distribution agreement. Note that pools of cargoes, of revenues, or mixed pools, are deemed to be authorized by this provision. In spite of being the most extreme anti-competitive device, liable to eliminate all competition—including competition in the quality of the service—pooling agreements have been authorized by the Council, undoubtedly with the intention of tolerating the type of agreement which best fosters tariff observance within the codist conferences, whilst serving to put into practice the sharing of the cargoes according to the 40/40/20 formula.

4.2.3.2.3. Ancillary agreements

The list of agreements set out in Article 3 of Regulation No. 4056/86 poses as a self-contained list. At first sight, therefore, agreements of conferences would not be eligible for the exemption unless they fit within one of the five categories. While identifying the principal types, Article 3 is insufficient to take account of many of the commonest conference agreements, which can be very complex and elaborate. The question arises therefore, whether other provisions not specifically identified in Article 3 can be considered authorized bearing in mind the need to interpret the exemptions strictly.[46]

Ancillary agreements deriving naturally from principal agreements which have been authorized must also, in principle, be authorized. In the case of Article 3, what has to be understood by ancillary or derived restrictions will be determined in light primarily of the basic aims and justification of the exemption and, secondly, the immediate background and legislative history of the regulations. As the regulation is such a close descendant of the UNCTAD Code, it is normal to accept as exempt not only the (already quoted) agreements which are inherent in, or consequent upon, the main objectives of the conferences, but also those which are typical of traditional conferences pursuant to the description given them in the Code. In any event, whether a non-specifically authorized provision is ancillary (and, therefore, lawful) will depend on how necessary the

---

[46] See the recent judgments of the ECJ of 24 Oct. 1995 in Case C–70/93, *BMW* v. *ALD Auto Leasing*, not yet reported, at para. 28, and in Case C–266/93 *Bundeskartellamt* v. *Volkswagen AG and VAG Leasing*, not yet reported, at para. 33. See also Case T–9/92, *Peugeot* v. *Commission* [1993] ECR II–493, at para. 37.

restriction in question is and, following economic analysis, on how indispensable it is for the aims recognized by the Regulation.

Of the agreements which may be considered ancillary because the Code regulates them are agreements relating to conference membership (entry, withdrawal, suspension and expulsion) and internal regulations (administration, voting and self-policing).

Regulation 4056/86 does not provide for exemption of specific agreements on the admission of new members to conferences. In referring in its third recital to the UNCTAD Code of Conduct, the regulation appears, however, to opt clearly for toleration of the traditional system of closed liner conferences which have always characterized liner trades other than those of the United States. Consequently, Regulation 4056/86 has to be interpreted as *tolerating (without imposing)* closed liner conferences, in which a new member's entry is left to the will of the existing members. This supposes a deviation from the Commission's practice regarding trade associations.[47] The regulation adopts a pragmatic point of view, and accepts closed conferences on condition that shipping trade routes in which they operate are open to third-party competition and every shipping line so wishing is able to establish a regular service as an outsider. The availability of the option to operate a non-conference service without restrictions is therefore, in the system of the regulation, the escape valve which allows closed conferences and other internal clauses of the conferences to be tolerated, such as clauses or agreements relating to suspension and expulsion of conferences.

Conferences generally provide for a procedure to be followed in the event of their members wishing to cease belonging to them, whether by withdrawing from the trade or by becoming independent shipping companies. The commonest withdrawal clauses provide for an obligation on an outgoing member to inform the secretariat or administrative body or the other members of the conference of the intention to leave. Until a given notice period expires, the line in question will not be considered effectively untied from the conference and will have to honour its obligations to it, in particular the financial ones. The rules of comparative law regulating the conferences' agreements and practices usually provide limitations on the discretion of members of conferences to determine the notice period. Regulation 4056/86 is silent on this matter. For reasons of consistency with the UNCTAD Code[48] and because the conferences exemption requires agreements to be complementary to rate agreements,[49] the Commission has declared that notice periods of up to three months are always consistent with the regulation[50] and has accepted clauses of up to a maximum of six months.[51]

---

[47] See, generally, the Commission's Decision in the *Cauliflower* case, OJ 1978 L 21, p. 23.

[48] See Art. 4(1) of the UNCTAD Code.

[49] See above, para. 4.2.3.2.1.

[50] This period is the one generally considered reasonable in the USA, in Canada, and in Australia.

[51] In particular in the EAC/CMB case. On this, see below, para. 4.3.2.

In freight conferences with relatively little operating co-ordination between the members, the Commission takes the view that the notice period should not exceed three months. If the conferences[52] wish to submit to periods greater than those outlined, it may be advisable for them to notify their agreements and justify the need for longer periods to the Commission, in order to avoid that national courts may declare them null and void.

4.2.3.2.4. Inter-conference agreements

Article 3 of Regulation 4056/86 authorizes certain '[a]greements, decisions and concerted practices of *all* or *part* of the members of *one* or *more* liner conferences'. The agreements between *all* of the members[53] and between *part* of the members[54] of a liner conference have been considered above. The agreements between *all* of the members and between *part* of the members of *several* liner conferences must now be considered. Although apparently highly restrictive, a literal reading of the exemption makes it clear that the Council and Commission sought to authorize at least certain agreements or practices involving more than one conference.

By referring to agreements, decisions, and practices between all the members of more than one conference, Article 3 unequivocally points to agreements between conferences. It, therefore, has to be interpreted in the same way for inter-conference agreements as it is for the agreements of the members of a single conference. Nevertheless, it does not appear possible to oblige all members of an agreement between conferences to practice uniform or common rates. By definition, if all shipowners who are privy to an agreement between various conferences are subject to the same rates within their respective geographical areas, they would constitute a single conference and the reference to more than one conference would lack meaning. It appears that, for there to be various conferences, there have to be various levels of rates for the same products in each conference's geographic jurisdiction. In the case of agreements between conferences, the members of each conference have to keep their rates uniform or common within their geographic jurisdiction but may agree with the members of another or other conferences the maintenance of general or specific differences between their respective rates, something which is not possible within a single conference without stepping outside the EC definition. The laxity of the exemption in this respect is, undoubtedly, open to much criticism.

If, with regard to prices, the exemption appears to enable conferences to reach flexible agreement on their rates, the requirement of carrying on other activities

---

[52] In the case of consortia, the Commission has generally maintained the six month notice maximum but has accepted longer initial periods of 18 or even 30 months in some cases, during which period the lines may agree not to leave the consortium. See below, para. 4.4.4.3.

[53] E.g. the basic agreement on uniform or common rates.

[54] In particular, pooling agreements.

(also restrictive, but more clearly beneficial than the fixing of rates[55]), holds for agreements between conferences.

The wording of Article 3 finally raises problems of interpretation regarding possible agreements authorized between part of the members of several conferences. It should not be thought that, by the mere fact of belonging to a conference, shipping companies are authorized to fix transport prices and conditions in any traffic. Virtually all liner shipping companies belong to one conference or another, which is why, if it is so interpreted, all their agreements, wherever they are put into practice, would be exempt by virtue of Article 3. This interpretation is absurd and has to be dismissed.[56] The only logical way of interpreting this 'cumulative option' is by allocating it implicit geographical limits: only agreements between members of adjacent liner conferences would be exempt, provided the other Article 3 conditions are satisfied. In practice, such agreements do not appear to exist. In their generosity, the Commission and the Council preferred to adopt the widest formula possible, without stopping to think of the logical possibility or real existence of agreements which would meet the terms of the exemption.

4.2.4. The condition of non-discrimination

As stated above, as a *sui generis* requirement, Article 4 of Regulation 4056/86 enunciates a condition at the same time both precedent and subsequent, on which the enjoyment and maintenance of the block exemption depends. It requires members of conferences not to discriminate between countries and between the ports they serve.[57] The consequence of non-compliance with the condition is automatic nullity although the regulation stipulates that this nullity applies only to parts of the agreement which are void provided they are severable from the whole.

Article 4 makes block exemptions granted by Regulation 4056/86 subject to the condition that, within the Community, conferences do not apply discriminatory tariffs and conditions 'which differ according to the country of origin or destination or port of loading or discharge', 'in the area covered by the agreement'. It thereby appears to seek port equalization, a traditional practice of conferences the object of which is to eliminate geographical competition between conference shipping companies which operate out of adjacent ports. In this context, the requirement of non-discrimination for purposes of tariffs is contradictory. On many occasions conferences cover various neighbouring European

---

[55] See above, para. 4.2.3.2.1. in matters relating to the need to carry on restrictive activities to qualify for the exemption in Art. 3 of Reg. 4056/86.

[56] Temple Lang, above n. 35, has mentioned the impossibility of such interpretation and criticized the wording of Art. 3.

[57] Art. 4.1. of the regulation was modelled on Art. 79(1) of the EEC Treaty.

countries and ports of various Member States and the requirement of non-discrimination on the basis of the country of origin or destination is discriminatory as such, since there is discrimination when like is treated differently and when unlike is treated identically. The concept of discrimination in Article 4 of the regulation is clear. However, by requiring that different ports and countries have to be treated equally by conferences, the regulation considers non-discriminatory that which would normally be considered discriminatory.

The Article 4 condition is subject to an important reservation; if discriminatory tariffs and conditions between countries and ports covered by the same conference are justifiable for economic reasons, the block exemption is, or continues to be, applicable. The regulation does not give any guidance on the economic reasons which could provide such justification. The truth is that, with the addition of this reservation, the condition no longer operates automatically; the economic justification for discriminatory acts has to be examined before they can be condemned under Article 4.

For all of the above reasons, and despite its categoric formulation, the condition does not appear, in principle, to prevent any conference ceasing to enjoy the exemption.

Referring explicitly to the infringement by conferences of the condition of non-discrimination, Article 4(2) of Regulation 4056/86 provides that Article 85(1) and (2) applies to conference agreements in their entirety only when provisions contrary to Article 4 are non-severable from the agreement as a whole. The principle of severance, commonly applied in relation to restrictive clauses in complex agreements which have been subject to an infringement procedure, generally does not apply to block exemptions. In other Commission exemption regulations, the infringement of certain conditions makes the exemption automatically void in its entirety. It is this automatic operation which apparently the shipping regulation specifically tries to avoid.[58] In the absence of sufficient precision in the regulation, it should be asked whether the Commission and national courts and competent authorities are required to apply the principle of severance only in cases of discrimination under Article 4 and whether they are able, therefore, in other cases to declare the nullity of all of the conference agreements when any one of them is void regardless of whether it is severable or otherwise. This is especially important, given that conferences engage in restrictive practices which have not been specifically exempted by Article 3.[59] Thus, it is necessary to decide whether the presence of an additional restrictive clause or of new restrictive agreements not authorized by a block exemption renders the block exemption wholly inapplicable.

---

[58] One could describe Art. 4 as a 'black clause' without the usual consequences that clauses of this type have in European competition law. The inclusion of discriminatory clauses in a conference agreement would not automatically imply its total illegality.

[59] See above, para. 4.2.4.2.3., and below, paras 4.32. and 4.3.3.

There are two possible solutions to this question.[60]

On the one hand, it can be argued that where there is no provision governing the combination of exempted and non-exempted restrictions there is no basis for concluding that the block exemption should be deprived of effect.[61] The Court has stated that only those parts of an agreement which are prohibited by Article 85(1) must be considered void.[62] The elements of agreements which benefit from a block exemption and are therefore not prohibited by Article 85(1) may be allowed to stand, like non-restrictive elements, if they can be separated from the prohibited parts of the agreement.

On the other hand, there is an argument to be made for the view that where an additional restrictive element or agreement reinforces the restrictive effect of an agreement which, standing alone, would benefit from a block exemption, that reinforcement should entail the loss of the exemption. Block exemptions are enacted on the basis that in general the restrictions in question fulfil the criteria for exemption. In arriving at that conclusion, the Commission (or, in the case of Regulation 4056/86, the Council) considers those restrictions by themselves. It does not conclude that those restrictions in combination with others generally fulfil the Article 85(3) criteria. Moreover, the combination of the block-exempted restrictions with other restrictions may result in a very different competitive and economic situation from that envisaged by the Commission or the Council in enacting the block exemption. In relation to the question of severance, it may be considered that the character of the agreement or of the elements meeting the block exemption criteria is affected by the presence of additional restrictions. In such a case, the exempted restrictions should therefore not be treated as harmless clauses which are, if possible, to be protected from nullity, but as restrictions the effect of which must be examined within their whole context.

That reasoning would support the view that, in general, where the relevant regulation makes no specific provision for the combination of restrictions, and the parties to an agreement (which, standing alone, meets the conditions of a block exemption) enter into additional restrictive agreements which may have an influence on the restrictive effect of the first agreement, the block exemption should not apply. Instead, the entire agreement must be examined in its context by the Commission with a view to determining whether individual exemption is possible. In relation to Regulation 4056/86, the loss of the exemption should follow from the existence of additional restrictive elements not only in the

---

[60] I have borrowed these ideas from Richard Lyal and David Wood.

[61] Some block exemptions, although not all, provide that no restrictions other than those referred to in the regulation are permitted and that the presence of another restriction entails loss of the exemption. See Comm. Reg. 1983/83/EEC regarding exclusive distribution agreements (OJ 1983 L 173, p.1). Other regulations contain 'black clauses' whose presence also entails the loss of exemption.

[62] See Case 56/65 *Société Technique Minière* v. *Maschinenbau Ulm* [1966] ECR 235 and Case 319/82 *Sociétéde vente de ciments* v. *Kerpen & Kerpen* [1983] ECR 4173.

conference agreement itself but also in other agreements entered into by the parties whether among themselves or with other lines.

The Court will soon have to decide on this issue.[63] Until now, in every case that the non-exempted restrictive clauses or agreements of liner conferences have come to its attention, the Commission, pragmatically, has opted for attacking exclusively such clauses or agreements, without putting into question the validity of the exemption as a whole.[64]

4.2.5. Obligations attached to the block exemption

The obligations form part of the requirements to maintain the exemption once the shipowners have complied with the conditions for obtaining it. Infringement of the obligations does not cause immediate loss of the Article 3 block exemption but puts it at indirect risk. The Commission is not sanctioned to apply Article 85(1) without previously adopting an act denying a liner conference the benefit of the exemption, when an obligation attached to exemption is infringed.[65]

Article 5 of Regulation 4056/86 sets out five obligations. The last three (services not covered by the freight charges, availability of tariffs, notification to the Commission of the conciliators' recommendations and arbitration awards) are common in nature, and require conferences to carry out or refrain from carrying out certain types of conduct. The first two do, or may, imply engagement in restrictive practices, which are exempt from the prohibition of Article 85(1) of the Treaty by virtue of Article 6 of the regulation. The first (consultations with transport users) has the unusual feature in competition, but quite common in the maritime transport field, of requiring restrictive practices or agreements with customers. The second (loyalty arrangements), without requiring the restrictive arrangements to which it refers, obliges conferences to see that, when they conclude such arrangements, they comply with a series of requirements.

4.2.5.1. Consultations with transport users

Article 5(1) of Regulation 4056/86, which requires consultation with users, is modelled on Article 11(1) of the Code of Conduct of the United Nations. It is, however, even more general and vague in nature, save for the specific mention of loyalty agreements as the subject of consultation. In relation to the procedure for consultations, the regulation provides only that consultations are to be held whenever requested by users and conferences. The legal interpretation of this

---

[63] One of the questions submitted to the ECJ in the context of the *SUNAG* case, above n. 33, relates to the problem of severability in the face of restrictive agreements which may exceed what is authorized by Art. 3 of Reg. 4056/86.

[64] See below, paras 4.3.2. and 4.3.3.

[65] For the character of either requirement, see below, Ch. 6.

requirement involves looking at the UNCTAD Code to define more clearly both the content of the consultations[66] and the procedure to be followed.[67] Despite the literal tenor of the obligation, and despite its apparent absolute nature, it is difficult in practice to require conferences to consult formally with each and every user so requesting. It appears more logical that, without collective representation (which need not be limited exclusively to shippers' councils but may include shippers' associations of any other type) or, in the absence of a sufficient, individual economic interest, conferences should not be required to consult individual users. Common sense would dictate a *de minimis* rule for the holding of consultations.

4.2.5.2. *Loyalty arrangements*

Loyalty arrangements with users are the main method used by liner conferences to eliminate competition from independents. Their origin goes back to the birth of conferences.[68] The systems of binding or 'loyalizing' customers are threefold: deferred rebates,[69] the dual rate system,[70] and the system of immediate rebates.[71] The last two are known as contractual systems, as opposed to the deferred rebates system, in which traditionally no contract existed but only a unilateral offer on the part of the conferences to return a certain percentage of the freight rates to loyal shippers. Service contracts between liner conferences and shippers, nowadays common in trade with the United States, are not loyalty agreements[72] and have been neither provided nor authorized by the regulation.[73]

[66] See Art. 11(2) and (3) of the UNCTAD Code in conjunction with Arts 14 (general freight-rate increases), 15 (promotional freight rates), 16 (surcharges) and 17 (currency changes), *inter alia*.

[67] See Art. 11(4) and (6) of the UNCTAD Code. See also the consultation procedure provided by the Commission in its Consortia Regulation, below, para. 4.7.4.

[68] For a fuller description of conferences' loyalty agreements, see UNCTAD. *The liner conference system. (A Report by the UNCTAD Secretariat)*. (Document TD/B/C.4/62/Rev.1). (United Nations. New York, 1970), paras 114–155.

[69] Within the deferred rebates system, the rebates obtained by a shipper who has not used independent services during a given period of time (called loading period, generally of three or six months) are given to them after a further period of similar length (deferment period) in which he will have to continue being loyal to the conference, on pain of losing the accumulated rebates, not only during the loading period, but also in the deferment period. In this way, the reward for past loyalty is conditional on future loyalty.

[70] Another way of binding shippers to conferences is to offer them lower rates if they sign an exclusive sponsorship contract with member shipping companies. Within this system, the only one permitted in the USA until the adoption of the Shipping Act 1984, both the contractual and non-contractual rates appear in the tariff.

[71] A system similar to the one described in the previous note is known as the immediate rebate system, within which the tariff contains a single freight for each product or for each class / category and specifies the percentage of rebate which is given to loyal shippers on these rates.

[72] The Shipping Act 1984 does not allow loyalty agreements (which do not enjoy competition law immunity and can only be authorized if they fulfil common competition standards for approval), but does allow service contracts, which are fundamentally different from the former. See the Shipping Act 1984, s. 3 (21), 46 USC app. 1702 (21).

[73] According to the Commission, service contracts between an *individual* shipping company and their customers are not, in principle, restrictive of competition, and do not need an exemption. Their

Regulation 4056/86 formulates certain obligations for conferences in order that they continue to qualify for the exemption of Article 3 and their loyalty arrangements qualify for the exemption of Article 6. Conferences are not required to offer loyalty agreements (the regulation says 'shall be entitled'); only to negotiate and conclude them in a certain way, if they choose to offer them.

The first general requirement laid down by the regulation (as well as the Code of Conduct[74]) is that each conference determines, by means of consultations with the users' organizations, the form and terms of their loyalty agreements.[75] The second general requirement is that agreements provide safeguards making explicit the rights of the users and the members of the conference. The UNCTAD Code, and the regulation with it, raised the need to end the unilateral and non-binding nature which the conferences had given to their loyalty rebates,[76] substituting it by a bilateral and, implicitly, written contractual system. However, neither the UNCTAD Code, nor the regulation expressly enunciate this last requirement and may rather suggest the contrary.[77]

With respect to specific conditions, the regulation establishes, first, that conferences wishing to conclude loyalty agreements with users have to offer either a system of immediate rebates,[78] or the option between a system of immediate rebates and deferred rebates; and, secondly, that the conferences, having consulted users, have to establish two lists.

The *first* list will specify the cargoes and any portion of cargo which may have been agreed with the users to be excluded from the scope of application of the loyalty agreement. The regulation states that '100% loyalty arrangements may be offered but may not be unilaterally imposed'.[79]

The 100 per cent loyalty arrangement has to be understood to comprise the

possible conclusion by individual members of the conferences does not alter either the uniformity and commonness of the rates, as the nature of the price in the service contracts (*long-term contracts* by definition), is fundamentally different from that of the freight rates. Collectively, Art. 3 of Reg. 4056/86 only allows conference members to fix *freight rates*. This provision should not be construed as a blanket acceptance of horizontal price-fixing in all its forms, including the fixing of the economic conditions under which their members will enter into service contracts with shippers. Also bear in mind that, unlike rates, service contracts are not subject to any sudden fluctuation at all, and are stable *per se*. Therefore, the widening of the exemption to possible agreements of the members of conferences on service contracts is not justified within the structure of Reg. 4056/86, which relies on the 'stabilizing' role of cartels in order to justify their authorization to control fluctuating freight rates. The Commission's views have been disputed by shipping lines within the context of the *TAA* case—see below, para. 4.3.3.3.

[74] Art. 7(1) of the UNCTAD Code.
[75] Note that Art. 5(2) of the regulation talks of 'transport users´ organizations' (not of transport users) and of 'conference' (not conferences).
[76] See the 10th recital of Reg. 4056/86.
[77] In fact, the regulation stipulates that agreements 'shall be based on the contract system *or any other system which is also lawful*', but it is difficult to imagine how the general and the specific conditions of the loyalty agreements can be complied with without being subject to a contract, and not only a verbal one but a written one.
[78] Interpreting the regulation in the light of the UNCTAD Code, under the terms 'system of immediate rebates' reference is made both to actual immediate rebates and to the dual rate system.
[79] Art. 5(2)(b)(i).

general cargo carried by sea on conference routes, for which the user is allowed to elect the carrier. Obligations (1) to carry not general cargo but bulk cargo and other cargoes which can be sent by bulk or specialized carriers; (2) not to transport goods by land or air in the conference's zone of operations and (3) to carry with the conference even cargoes over which the user does not have the right to elect the carrier are excessive. They are equivalent to loyalty obligations of over 100 per cent and may be abusive. The 1985 draft regulation proposed in Article 5(2)(d) that loyalty agreements cover only cargoes for which the user is able to elect the carrier, in accordance with the contract of sale of such goods, with the aim of preventing conferences abusing users by obliging them to ship with them goods sold on free-on-board terms (FOB), free alongside ship (FAS), ex works or similar. This provision did not go into the final version of the regulation.[80]

The possibility of excluding portions of cargo from the scope of application of the loyalty agreements was included in the 1985 draft regulation because of the insistence of some shippers' councils and some governments proposing, since 1983, that a maximum loyalty limit not exceeding 70 per cent of the cargoes be fixed. The discussion on whether it was desirable to impose such limit went on until the end of 1986 when the compromise formula quoted was agreed ('but may not be unilaterally imposed'). With it, an option between the 100 per cent fidelity and fidelity at a smaller percentage, and between immediate and deferred rebates, was granted, not an option between concluding 100 per cent loyalty agreements or not concluding them at all.

In the *second* list, the circumstances in which the conference will dispense users from its loyalty obligation are to be specified and will necessarily have to include the case of consignments being dispatched from or to a port situated in the conference's area, but not advertised as a loading port; and the case where the waiting time at port exceeds a period to be determined after consulting the interested users from each port.[81]

The Articles of the regulation are silent about the consequences for users of using the services of non-conference shipping companies without dispensation. Only the tenth recital of the regulation, unaltered since 1981, and relating to substantive provisions different from the ones finally adopted in 1986, refers to users' disloyalty, and talks of

the right of a conference to impose penalties on users who seek by improper means to evade the obligation of loyalty required in exchange for the rebates, reduced freight rates or commission granted to them by the conference . . .

---

[80] See also Art. 7(3)(a) of the UNCTAD Code of Conduct and the Report of the UNCTAD Secretariat, above, n. 68, pp. 19–20, paras 132 *et seq.*

[81] The regulation requires only that these two circumstances be included, as a minimum, and appears to refer to the desirability of conferences accepting other cases of dispensation. See Art. 8 of the UNCTAD Code.

If the legality of loyalty agreements is accepted, it appears logical to allow conferences to take civil action against disloyal users. The 1985 draft regulation provided, for example, that '[t]he penalties shall not exceed two thirds of the freight charge on the particular shipment, computed at the rate provided under the agreement'.[82] The traditional sanction for disloyalty has been the loss of discounts. This provision of the draft regulation shows how, in the Commission's mind, the punishment for disloyalty would have to be light, purely economical in nature and directly connected with the 'act of disloyalty'. The regulation does not authorize taking any other type of reprisals—for example connected with the quality of the service—against disloyal users.[83]

4.2.5.3. Services not covered by the freight charges

In accordance with Article 5(3) of Regulation 4056/86:

Transport users shall be entitled to approach the undertakings of their choice in respect of inland transport operations and quayside services not covered by the freight charge or charges on which the shipping line and the transport user have agreed.[84]

This is an original obligation of the regulation (it does not stem from the UNCTAD Code) and implies that members of conferences may not make the conclusion of a maritime transport contract conditional upon the use by shippers of the inland transport and quayside services of conference lines. Therefore, members of conferences cannot offer all-inclusive packages of services without giving users the option of contracting non-maritime services separately with the undertakings of their choice.

The Commission believes that nothing in Article 5(3) suggests that members of conferences can or have to offer common inland or multimodal rates. However, shipping lines have relied on this provision to maintain the opposite view.[85]

4.2.5.4. The obligation to publish tariffs

Article 5(4) of Regulation 4056/86 is a direct consequence of Article 9 of the Liner Code, which it paraphrases while adding certain new elements. The reference to the obligation to set out 'the exact extent of the services covered by the freight charge in proportion to the sea transport and the land transport'

---

[82] Art. 5(2)(g) of the 1985 draft regulation, above n. 15.

[83] Cf., the Commission's Decision in the *CEWAL* case, OJ 1992 L 34, p. 20, para. 86.

[84] The regulation does not define what 'quayside services' means, but they must include all those services which are carried out at port, with the exception of the operations of loading and unloading the cargo, which may be considered directly connected with the maritime transport and can be legitimately invoiced as freight.

[85] In particular, within the context of the *FEFC* case. See below, para. 4.3.2.

insists on aspects of the Article 5(3) obligation and puts Article 5(4) in line with the eleventh recital of the regulation which, unaltered since 1981, justified this obligation as follows:

users must at all times be in a position to acquaint themselves with the rates and conditions of carriage applied by the members of the conference, since in the case of inland transports organized by [carriers[86]], the latter continue to be subject to Regulation 1017/68.'

Unlike other systems, such as the United States which require conferences to file their tariffs with a public regulatory agency, Regulation 4056/86 is less interventionist and more self-regulatory. It is enough for it that the member shipping companies make their tariffs available to the users at their offices or at their agents', or sell them at a reasonable cost. In both systems, the conferences are required to respect the published tariffs although the penalty for infringement varies substantially on either side of the Atlantic. Whilst in the United States it is penalized by fines, in the EC it may trigger the automatic inapplicability of the exemption.[87]

4.2.5.5. The obligation to notify recommendations and awards

The fifth and last obligation which Regulation 4056/86 imposes on conferences is to be found in Article 5(5) whereby:

Awards given at arbitration and recommendations made by conciliators that are accepted by the parties shall be notified forthwith to the Commission when they resolve disputes relating to the practices of conferences referred to in Article 4 and in points 2 and 3 above.

Oddly, this obligation does not concern awards and recommendations relating to all the requirements to which conferences are subject but only to the condition of non-discrimination and the obligations relating to loyalty agreements and services not covered by the freight charges.[88]

As explained by the eleventh recital of the regulation, in its second part, the aim of the obligation is:

---

[86] The English version of the 11th recital of Reg. 4056/86 refers to 'shippers' (a category of transport users) instead of 'carriers' (i.e., the providers of the liner shipping services). All the other linguistic versions of the regulation refer to carriers, which appears to be the right term. Philip Rutley, in his article 'International Shipping and EEC Competition Law', *European Competition Law Review*, Vol. 12, 1991, pp. 5–18 has argued the opposite.

[87] The loss of the commonness and uniformity of rates would make a conference whose members are in breach of the tariff fall outside the definition of liner conference, thus the exemption for liner conferences would not be applicable to them. See the *TAA* decision, above, n. 31, at para. 348. On the ambit and interpretation of Art. 3, see above, para. 4.2.3.1.

[88] The reason for this is unknown. The 1981 draft regulation referred only to awards and recommendations concerning the condition of non discrimination.

to enable [the Commission] to verify that conferences are not thereby exempted from the conditions provided for in the Regulation and thus do not infringe the provisions of Articles 85 and 86.

In accordance with Article 26 of Regulation 4056/86, the procedure of notification of awards and recommendations has been developed by the Commission in Article 1 of Regulation 4260/88.[89] To date, only two notifications in compliance with this obligation have been made.[90]

4.2.5.6. Consequences of breach of obligations

Breach of the Article 5 obligations may always cause withdrawal of the block exemption from defaulting liner conferences, following the procedure provided for in Article 7(1) of the regulation.[91]

If either of the first two obligations is breached, the situation is more complex. Because of the dual nature of consultations with shippers and loyalty arrangements, which are at the same time obligations connected to the Article 3 block exemption and restrictive agreements exempted pursuant to Article 6, breach of the terms of Article 5(1) and (2) of the regulation does not only put at risk the Article 3 exemption but makes the Article 6 exemption for loyalty agreements inapplicable. Such a breach may also affect agreements derived from consultations between conferences and users.[92]

Breach of the third obligation relating to services not covered by the freight charges on the part of individual members of the conferences may also trigger the indirect loss of the conference block exemption. Breach also involves engagement in types of conduct which, in appropriate circumstances, might be subject to Articles 85(1)(e) and 86(d) of the Treaty.

Finally, breach of the fourth and fifth obligations, relating to the availability of tariffs and to the notification to the Commission of arbitration awards and conciliators' recommendations, appears only liable to trigger the two-phase procedure of Article 7(1) of the regulation, with a view to the withdrawal of the exemption.

Pursuant to Article 19(2)(b) of the regulation, in all cases of breach the Commission is also authorized to impose fines on shipping companies who default in their obligations.

---

[89] Reg. (EEC) 4260/88, OJ 1988 L 376, p. 1. For this Reg., see below, Ch. 6.

[90] One in 1991 within the framework of the *CMB/EAC* case (see below, para. 4.3.2.) and the other in 1995 in relation to the *SUNAG* case (see above n. 33).

[91] See below, para. 4.2.8.1.

[92] See below, para. 4.2.7. The question of whether the irregularity of the Art. 5(1) and (2) agreements prevents the application of Art. 6 of the Reg. has not been touched upon as yet by the Commission, nor decided by the CFI and the ECJ. In its Decision relating to the *CEWAL* conference, above, n. 84, Arts 2 and 5, the Commission condemned as abusive certain loyalty agreements, and recommended to the conference to bring them into line with the Art. 5(2) requirements, without clarifying whether the Art. 6 exemption was applicable or otherwise.

4.2.6. The requirements of Article 85(3)

The second group of requirements for maintaining exemption comes under Article 85(3) of the EC Treaty, the conditions of which have to be complied with at all times by liner conferences. Two theories in respect of the Article 85(3) conditions can be advanced.

The first is that, given the extreme conciseness of Regulation 4056/86 in justifying and formulating the exemption requirements, the regulation has to be interpreted as implicitly requiring the four Article 85(3) conditions to be complied with *ab initio* before enjoying the exemption.[93]

The second is that, due to imperatives of legal certainty, once the requirements of the regulation are fulfilled the exemption applies, irrespective of effective compliance with the Article 85(3) conditions. The Commission would be obliged to withdraw the block exemption before taking action against a conference which meets the requirements of the regulation—although not those of the Treaty—before applying Article 85(1) to it even in the most flagrant cases of infringement of Article 85(3).

These two theories will be discussed in detail later on, in the context of Articles 6 and 7 of Regulation 4056/86.

4.2.7. Agreements exempted by Article 6

Article 6 of Regulation 4056/86 authorizes agreements between conferences and users on rates, conditions, and quality of liner services—but not on any other matters—provided they flow from conference obligations. Agreements between users are also authorized but only to the extent that they are necessary to conclude agreements with conferences, or indispensable for any of the activities described in Article 5(1) and (2).

The first problem raised by this provision is to define its scope. The twelfth recital of the regulation might suggest that only agreements directly derived from consultations, necessarily general in nature, are exempt but not, for example, individual loyalty agreements between a conference and the users. This interpretation is not convincing. First, Article 6 would be devoid of substance if it did not permit individual loyalty agreements derived from agreements between conferences and users' associations. Second, the terms of the Articles are sufficiently wide to cover individual agreements and, in case of doubt, they prevail over the recitals.

The second problem raised by Article 6 is that it grants a block exemption without demanding that any substantive requirement be satisfied. It might, therefore, be thought that Article 6 authorizes conferences unconditionally to conclude those types of agreement. The only consequence for breach of Article

---

[93] See Temple Lang, above, n. 35.

5(1) and (2) seems to be the possible withdrawal, jointly or separately, of the Article 6 and Article 3 exemptions in the event of irregularities in consultations or loyalty agreements. Contrary to this opinion, however, it is suggested that Article 6 cannot be interpreted as allowing conferences unconditionally to conclude Article 5(1) and (2) type restrictive agreements—distinct from, and in addition to, the agreements authorized by Article 3. Rather, it appears that the conditions for applying the exemption have to be found in Article 5(1) and (2), to which Article 6 implicitly refers. The terms of those provisions, therefore, act as conditions for applicability of Article 6. Given the distinct nature of loyalty agreements and of the additional restrictions they involve, and given also the distinct nature of the Article 6 block exemption, infringement of Article 5(1) and (2) must cause automatic loss of the exemption.

Observance of the essential formalities of Article 5(1), unlike the Article 5(2) requirements, is not a public policy requirement (*garantie d'ordre public*)[94] but guarantees protection to users who would be prejudiced if the exemption did not apply. Article 5(1) must implicitly allow users to ratify the *results* of consultations, even if these have been conducted irregularly.[95]

The form and content of loyalty agreements have, as authorized restrictive agreements (not merely as conference obligations), to comply with the terms of Article 5(2). These, in turn, act as conditions for the application of Article 6 and as public policy requirements with the aim not only to defend users but to maintain effective competition outside the conference and prevent loyalty agreements causing excessive harm to independent third parties. Infringement of these conditions would cause the immediate inapplicability of the Article 6 exemption and the agreements would be exposed to the consequences of breach of Article 85(1). Withdrawal of the Article 6 exemption would only be appropriate where loyalty agreements, while complying with the requirements of the regulation, produce effects incompatible with Article 85(3), not where the Article 5(2) requirements are infringed. The exemption would then be inapplicable. It would not need to be withdrawn in order to apply Article 85(1).

If one considered the Commission to be obliged to withdraw the Article 6 exemption in order to penalize conferences which have infringed Article 5(2) by imposing irregular loyalty agreements, conduct even more restrictive of competition and prejudicial to customers and competitors than that already authorized by the shipping regulation would, at least temporarily, be permitted.

It therefore appears logical to conclude that the regulation implicitly establishes the automatic inapplicability of the exemption—a stricter penalty than the

[94] See immediately below.

[95] In such case it should be wondered whether, once the applicability of the exemption is accepted, action might be taken against a conference which is in breach of the terms of Art. 5(1), due to infringement of its obligation. It appears logical to think that, irrespective of the applicability of the Art. 6 exemption 'by validation' of the users, the Art. 5(1) obligation would not have been complied with, and that the Commission would be authorized to take action against the conference in the way provided in Art. 7(1).

non-automatic withdrawal of the Article 6 exemption, or even the withdrawal of the Article 3 exemption—in cases in which Article 5(1)[96] and Article 5(2) are infringed.

The third problem raised by Article 6 is that in authorizing agreements between conferences and users, and particularly between users, it appears to go beyond the scope of application prescribed in Article 1(2) of the regulation (as interpreted by the Commission in the light of Regulation 141).[97] Although a clear intrusion into a Regulation 17 area, this does not however amount to the procedural systems overlap which occurs in relation to the application of Regulation 1017/68.[98] In any case, exemption for agreements between users only extends to the matters envisaged in Article 6. Article 6 does not therefore cover the activities of shippers' councils in general,[99] nor those of other associations of shippers created with the aim of consolidating cargo and obtaining quantitative rebates.

Finally, Article 6 does not prevent the application of Article 86 of the Treaty to conferences in a dominant position which conclude loyalty agreements—be they regular or irregular.[100]

4.2.8. Monitoring of exempted agreements

Article 7 of Regulation 4056/86 establishes the supervisory rules for the agreements exempted by Articles 3 and 6 and provides for the circumstances in which the Commission is empowered to withdraw on an individual basis the benefit of the block exemption from liner conferences and other exempt agreements which do not already satisfy the conditions of Article 85(3) of the Treaty.

Article 7 contains two paragraphs, the first relating to measures in the event of breach of one or more of the obligations attached by Article 5 to the Article 3 exemption and the second relating to the supervening infringement of the conditions of Article 85(3) of the Treaty.

4.2.8.1. Breach of an obligation

In accordance with Article 7(1) of the regulation, should the obligations attached to the exemption be infringed, the Commission may act against the members of the offending conferences and, during a preliminary phase, address recommendations to them. The Commission is unable to withdraw the block exemption directly for breach of an obligation.

---

[96] But remember the possibility of 'validation' by the users.

[97] See above, Ch. 3, Section I.   [98] See above, Ch. 3, Section II.

[99] For the origin and function of shippers' councils, see Herman, 'Shipping conferences', see above n. 5, Ch. 7.

[100] This was what the Commission did in its Decision in the *CEWAL* case, above, n. 83. On this, see below, para. 4.3.2.

During a second phase, if the recommendations have not been observed, and depending on the gravity of the breach concerned, the Commission may adopt the following decisions:

(1) A decision prohibiting, or else directing the members of the conference to carry out, certain acts;
(2) A decision granting them an individual exemption, with or without conditions and obligations, while withdrawing the benefit of the block exemption which they enjoyed;[101]
(3) A decision in which the block exemption is simply taken away from them.

In any case, the Commission is always empowered to impose fines upon conferences infringing the Article 5 obligations. For this it is not required to address a prior recommendation.

4.2.8.2. Supervening infringement of the basic conditions for exemption

Article 7(2) is one of the most difficult provisions to understand in the regulation. However, despite its formal differences to similar provisions of other block exemption regulations, it does not—nor cannot—differ substantively. If each and every one of the Article 85(3) conditions is not satisfied, the Commission is not only authorized, but may be required[102] to withdraw the exemption from the conferences or the other block-exempted agreements.

The exemption withdrawal procedure is reserved exclusively for exempted agreements. This clarification is not trite. It is not enough for agreements between shipping companies and between shipping companies and users to be self-proclaimed conference or loyalty agreements or agreements of another authorized type. For the Commission to be able to employ the procedure and for the shipping companies and users to be eligible for the interim protection it provides them from Commission sanctions and automatic nullity, the conditions for the application of the exemption need to be satisfied.

An important issue which should be raised with respect to Article 7(2) read in connection with Article 3 is whether formal compliance with the conditions enunciated in the regulation is sufficient as such to enjoy the exemption, even in cases where, since its inception (1 July 1987, or the date the conference was created) liner conferences do not, clearly, comply with the Article 85(3) conditions. Think, for example, of a monopolistic conference upon whose trade routes there are no independent companies nor alternative options of transport.

In its judgment in the *Tetra Pak I* case,[103] the CFI, motivated by reasons of

---

[101] Art. 7(1) in conjunction with Art. 11(4) and Art. 13(1) of Reg. 4056/86.

[102] For the Commission's obligations in matters of their exclusive jurisdiction, in general, and within the transport regulations, in particular, see below, Ch. 6.

[103] Judgment of the CFI in Case T–51/89, *Tetra Pak Rausing SA* v. *Commission*, [1990] ECR II–309, and the Conclusions of Judge Kirschner in the same case, [1990] ECR II–312.

system and legal certainty, appears to opt for the automatic solution of adhering exclusively to the text of the secondary legislation to judge on the applicability of a block exemption.[104] Certainly, the system and effectiveness of the block exemptions, and legal certainty for undertakings are important objectives. Nevertheless, in light of the unonerous nature of the exemption requirements under Article 3 (particularly given the lack of an 'exclusion threshold' expressed in terms of market share) and in light of the preamble itself (the thirteenth recital of which states that 'there can be no exemption if the conditions set out in Article 85(3) are not satisfied') it could be maintained that, in order to enjoy the Article 3 exemption and force the Commission to withdraw the exemption, the Article 85(3) conditions would have to be complied with, at least *prima facie*, at any given time. This would serve to alleviate the doubts which, due to the regulation's permissive nature, there might be about the legality of the exemption. At national level, it would require judicial bodies to adopt a more active role than the one they have played up to now in the interpretation of the block exemption regulations.[105]

It appears clear that the general objective of Article 7(2) type provisions is to permit the revocation of an exemption when changes have occurred in the initial situation of the agreements which serve to make the agreements incompatible with Article 85(3). As will have been noted, the title of this paragraph starts from this premise.

Article 7(2) does not contain an exhaustive catalogue of the circumstances in which the Commission is able to withdraw the exemptions of Articles 3 and 6,[106] as can be seen in Article 7(2)(b).[107] Any reason based on Article 85(3) is valid to open this procedure. There is no question that the emphasis is on the withdrawal of the exemption of the *conferences* for infringement of the *fourth condition*, especially when it is motivated by *acts of third countries*, but it is erroneous to think that the regulation only allows the exemption of conferences to be withdrawn in the limited Article 7(2) circumstances. Regulation 4056/86 cannot prevail over Article 85(3) of the Treaty.

The Article 7(2) procedure is, therefore, applicable to all cases in which, for any reason, liner conferences and other agreements which meet the requirements of Articles 3 and 6 of the regulation do not already comply with the Article 85(3) conditions. The text of Article 7(2)(b)(ii) briefly refers to the infringement of the first two exemption conditions.[108] Although it does not refer to the

---

[104] See paras 29 and 37 of the judgment.

[105] On these questions, see Temple Lang, J., above n. 35, and Lieberknecht, O., *Annual Proceedings of the Fordham Corporate Law Institute, 1992*. (Transnational Juris Publications—Kluwer, New York–Deventer, 1993), pp. 939–948, at p. 943.

[106] Cf., Temple Lang, above n. 35, and Rakovsky, above n. 35, p. 883.

[107] 'Special circumstances [to initiate the procedure which may lead the Commission to withdraw the exemption] are, *inter alia*, created by . . .'

[108] Among the special circumstances likely to activate the withdrawal procedure are those which result from 'acts of conference which may prevent technical or economic progress or user participation in the benefits'.

third condition (indispensability of the restrictions), the exemption may also be withdrawn for infringement of this requirement.

The Article 7(2)(b)(i) reference to 'acts . . . *resulting* in the absence or elimination of actual or potential competition . . .' cannot be interpreted as allowing the Commission to withdraw the exemption only when the elimination of competition has *effectively* occurred but must be interpreted consistently with Article 85(3)(b) which requires exempted agreements not 'to afford [the] undertakings the *possibility* of eliminating competition in respect of a substantial part of the [market]'.[109]

The regulation clarifies that the Commission's procedures relating to agreements which do not already meet the Article 85(3) conditions will be initiated by complaint or on its own initiative. The specific procedural rules are those of Section II of the regulation, similar to those of Regulation 17.[110]

However, when the elimination of competition by acts of a third country occurs, by virtue of Article 7(2)(c)(i), first part, the Commission is required to consult and, where appropriate, to negotiate with such State.[111] The contacts with third countries will, therefore, be carried out in two stages. The first (consultation) may be conducted by the Commission without the Council's assistance. The second stage (negotiation) has to be carried out on the Council's 'directives' or instructions. Procedurally, it is logical to think that, although enjoying greater freedom in these cases, if the Commission had to apply Article 7(2)(c)(i), it would follow in broad lines the procedure described in Article 9.[112] The consultations and negotiations do not interrupt the exemption withdrawal procedure, which is to be handled contemporaneously, as the Council and Commission stated in a joint declaration at the time of adopting the regulation.[113]

The measures the Commission is able to adopt are the same in all cases: make recommendations to the conferences and, where appropriate, to the users; adopt

[109] Cf., Rakovsky, above n. 35, pp. 883–884.

[110] See Art. 7(2)(a) of Reg. 4056/86. For the latter's procedural rules, see below, Ch. 6.

[111] In accordance with the Agreement on the European Economic Area (EEA), Annex 14, Section G.11 (e), when the competition rules of such Agreement are applicable in maritime transport, the provisions of Art. 7(2)(c)(i) of Reg. 4056/86 will be adapted, by adding to them three paras whereby first, if any of the Contracting Parties intends to undertake consultations with a third country, it shall inform the EEA Joint Committee; second, whenever appropriate, the Contracting Party initiating the procedure may request the other Contracting Parties to co-operate in these procedures; and third, if one or more of the other Contracting Parties object to the intended action, a satisfactory solution will be sought within that Joint Committee. If it were not possible to reach an agreement, appropriate measures may be taken to remedy subsequent distortions of competition. These three paras have also been added as para. 4 to Art. 9 of Reg. 4056/86 in its EEA version. See below, n. 138.

[112] See below, para. 4.2.10.

[113] Annex III of the Minutes of the Council Meeting of 22 Dec. 1986, Fifth Declaration. The period of consultations and negotiations, according to the Council and Commission, should not exceed three months, during which the Commission is to prepare the formal institution of the proceedings.

a decision prohibiting or, on the contrary, directing the conferences and, where appropriate, the users, to carry out certain acts; withdraw on an individual basis the benefit of the block exemption, granting at the same time an individual exemption, with or without obligations or conditions; or, simply, take away the benefit of the block exemption.

4.2.9. The abuse of a dominant position

4.2.9.1. Article 8 of the Regulation as a procedural provision

Article 8, entitled 'Effects incompatible with Article 86 of the Treaty', was added at the last stage of negotiations for the adoption of Regulation 4056/86. It did not appear in any of the two main Commission drafts. Its title was drafted on the lines of, and is very similar to, Article 7(2) ('Effects incompatible with Article 85(3)'), to which it also bears certain fundamental similarities.

Article 8 consists of three paragraphs. The first paragraph is apparently of a purely declaratory and general character but is targeted, like the other two, at liner conferences and has to be read in this context. Having described in Article 7(2) the block exemption withdrawal procedure infringement of the Article 85(3) conditions, Article 8 makes it clear that, in the case of Article 86 offences, it is not necessary to adopt a preliminary decision (implicitly, of block exemption withdrawal) and that the prohibition of abuses of a dominant position is directly applicable (because—it could have been added—abuses cannot be exempted and as a matter of course are not covered by the exemption).

The provisions of Article 8(2) and (3) are procedural in nature and are also explicitly targeted at liner conferences. Similarly to Article 7(2), they provide for the possibility of withdrawing the block exemption when conferences abuse a dominant position but, unlike that provision, paragraphs 2 and 3 of Article 8 are simple.

From all of the Article 8 provisions it is clear that the consequences of abuse of a dominant position for liner conferences may be twofold. On the one hand, conferences are likely to be penalized directly by it. On the other, the abuse may justify withdrawal of a block exemption by decision of the Commission.

4.2.9.2. Market definition and dominant positions

In long-haul or deep-sea liner traffic, the Commission[114] has defined the market by studying the substitutability between different types of transport services on the same routes and between services of similar technical features offered on

---

[114] Despite having always come to similar conclusions, the Commission has significantly refined its analysis of the market from 1992 to 1994 (i.e. from the date of its Decisions on West Africa to its *TAA* Decision, above, n. 44). Paras 27–70 of the latter are the best example of its current stance.

different maritime routes. The Commission's definition of services market therefore comprises a technical and a geographical analysis. The geographical aspects
of the definition of the services market must not be confused with the definition
of the geographical market.[115]

In the transport sector, the services which have the same technical features
but cover different geographical areas are not normally substitutable and, therefore, do not form part of the same services market.[116]

In its technical analysis, the Commission has distinguished various types of
cargo transport services which, contrary to the general predicates of Regulation
4056/86,[117] have proved difficult to substitute for liner shipping, at least in the
specific cases it has studied. Examples include air transport, non-liner or 'tramp'
transport, or specialized 'neo-bulk' transport, which resembles in its technical
features bulk transport.[118] Within the liner shipping market itself, the
Commission has differentiated between containerized transport services (by container vessels) and conventional services ('break-bulk') which, in many trades and
for many types of cargo, are incapable of substitution.[119]

In its geographical analysis of the liner services market, the Commission has
centred on the geographical substitutability between, on the one hand, technically substitutable services offered on maritime routes in which restrictions on
competition have occurred and, on the other hand, technically substitutable services offered on other alternative routes, for the purposes of defining a homogeneous services market. Thus, for example, the Commission has accepted the
substitutability between certain maritime services with origin or destination at
North European ports—which would constitute in specific cases a market[120]—

[115] In defining the liner shipping market, the Commission has used geographical criteria both
when studying the *services* market and when studying the *geographical* market. However, as will now
be seen, the geographical ideas which are used in each case are different (substitutability of routes,
in one case, areas of marketing, in another) and correspond to the two classic aspects of the definition of the market applied in Community competition law (i.e., product/services market and geographical market).

[116] In its Decision in the *TAA* case, above n. 44, para. 59, the Commission gives as an example
the containerized liner services between Rotterdam and New York and between Rotterdam and
Hong Kong, which would form part of different services markets.

[117] See the 8th recital of Reg. 4056/86.

[118] For the peculiarities of specialized transport, see the Comm. Dec. in the *TAA* case, above, n.
44, paras 47–9.

[119] The Commission considered that, in trades with Africa, the containerized and conventional
services were substitutable and formed part of the same market. However, in the North Atlantic it
considered them non-substitutable and forming part of two separate markets. See the Comm. Dec.
in the *TAA* case, above, n. 44, paras 44–6 and 51. This market definition has been challenged by
the shipping lines participating in the TAA.

[120] Note that, as has been pointed out above, the geographical market is defined in liner shipping by analysing the substitutability between the services *on maritime routes in which restrictions on competition occur* and the services offered on other alternative routes. The definition of the geographical
services market will, therefore, vary by reference to the zone in which the effects of an anti-competitive agreement or practice make themselves felt, and will be carried out *case-by-case*. The
Commission may therefore, in a specific case, take into consideration all the services out of North
European ports and, in other cases, take into consideration, for example, the services out of the ports

and has dismissed the substitutability between the latter and the services out of or bound for the Mediterranean at least for the users situated within the Northern European geographic market.[121]

The Commission has preferred in its decisions in the maritime sector to study the substitutability of supply more as a structural characteristic of the market, as potential competition, than as a criterion for defining the market.[122]

The geographical definition of the market is carried out by the Commission by studying the zone of sale or distribution of the services which form part of the same market. The geographical market is the area in which the former are marketed, which equates to the catchment areas of the ports from, or to which, the services are offered.

The next stage of analysis under Article 86 is to assess the existence of a dominant position. The criteria for the existence of a dominant position in maritime transport are the same as in other industries, and relate basically to market structure, the structure and performance of undertakings and their conduct on the market.[123]

In relation to the market structure criterion, market shares and potential competition are especially important.[124] Market shares are a very important factor at the time of examining a dominant position.[125] A large share is necessary, but not always sufficient, to examine the existence of a dominant position.[126] However, market shares of 75 per cent or more during a relatively long period of time are sufficient in themselves to conclude the existence of a dominant position.[127] Market shares of between 40 per cent and 65 per cent also constitute a clear sign of domination over the market but have to be corroborated with data about the market share of the most direct competitors, the market features (*inter*

of a single North European country, or even out of a single port. See the judgment of the ECJ in Case C–179/90, *Porto di Genova* v. *Siderurgica Gabrielli*, [1991] ECR I–5009, para. 15.

[121] See the Comm. Dec. in the *TAA* case, above n. 44, paras 63–66. Owing to the difficult conditions in Mediterranean ports, there may be some degree of substitutability between the services in these two areas for shippers situated in Southern Europe.

[122] The conclusions on the power of an undertaking implicated in anti-competitive practices will be the same whether other undertakings capable of increasing their capacity or entering the market as effective competitors are included within the definition of the market—so as to lower the first undertaking's market share—or whether the possibility of competing undertakings entering is considered as a characteristic capable of reducing the significance of the undertaking's market share. See below.

[123] See Ritter, L., Braun, D. and Rawlinson, F. *EEC competition law. A practitioner's guide.* (Kluwer. Deventer, 1991), pp. 278 *et seq.*

[124] Other factors to be borne in mind when studying the structure of the maritime transport market are the relative size of the shipping companies or groups of shipping companies compared with their closest rivals, the stability of their market share in time, the maturity of the liner transport market (e.g., the last technological revolution began in 1970), etc. See Ritter, *ibid*, pp. 281–2.

[125] Case 27/76, *United Brands* v. *Commission*, [1978] ECR 207, pp. 281–2.

[126] Case 85/76, *Hoffmann–Laroche* v. *Commission*, [1979] ECR 461, pp. 520–1. A monopolist is, by definition, dominant. Judgment of the ECJ in Case 127/73, *BRT* v. *SABAM II*, [1974] ECR 313, p. 316.

[127] *Hoffmann–Laroche* Judgment, *ibid.*

alia, the existence or otherwise of potential competition, and its intensity) and the structure, resources and conduct of the undertakings.[128]

With respect to potential competition, especially that derived from 'mobility of fleets', the Commission has, in the formal decisions it has so far taken, considered it of little importance. The Commission's administrative practice has demolished the presumption of the regulation, contradicting again in particular terms what has been stated in the regulation in general terms. The regulation, oddly, is based chiefly on the supposed mobility of vessels when considering the fourth condition of Article 85(3).[129] According to the Commission, potential competition is effective only when it amounts to a direct and certain threat, or at least credible, for undertakings which are already on the market and when the shipping companies capable of entering the market are also capable of leaving it without suffering excessive losses. Irrespective of the major investments required by the establishing of a maritime transport service, which make entry difficult in most cases, the Commission has pointed to the difficulties in withdrawing from a trade without suffering major losses, not only of money, but also of commercial reputation.[130] The Commission has not, therefore, given credence to certain economic theories which have tried to find in liner maritime transport a typical case of a 'contestable' market.[131]

Within the framework of liner conferences it is necessary, finally, to dwell on the idea of joint dominant position. In accordance with Article 86 of the Treaty, '[a]ny abuse, *by one or more undertakings*, of a dominant position . . .' is incompatible with the common market and is prohibited. The prohibition, therefore, applies both to a single undertaking's individual abuses and to the collective abuses of various undertakings, acting jointly. Despite the clarity of this requirement, precedents in the form of Commission administrative practice and the Court jurisprudence is minimal. The CFI referred in its judgment in the *Italian Flat Glass* case[132] to the terms of Article 86 and indicated that it could not be ruled out, in principle, that two or more economically independent entities were, on a specific market, united by economic ties such that they enjoyed a joint dominant position in relation to other operators on the same market. For its interpretation, the CFI relied specifically on Article 8 of Regulation 4056/86, which

---

[128] *Hoffmann–Laroche* Judgment, *ibid*, paras 41, 53–6, 59–60 and 67, in which the Court gives an account on the undertaking's different market shares in different vitamins covered by the proceedings. See also the case law quoted by Ritter, above n. 123, p. 280, n. 90.

[129] See the 8th recital of Reg. 4056/86.

[130] See the Comm. Dec. in the *TAA* case, above, n. 44, para. 182.

[131] In liner shipping, this theory has been defended, *inter alia*, by Davies, J. E. 'Competition, contestability and the liner shipping industry', *Journal of Transport Economics and Policy*, Sept. 1986, pp. 299–312. The Commission has neither accepted the theories which see the liner market an example of 'empty core' in which a system of free competition would not be feasible. For a defence of this theory, see Sjostrom, W. 'Collusion in ocean shipping: a test of monopoly and empty core models'. *Journal of Political Economy*, 1989, pp. 1160–79; and, by the same author, 'Anti-trust immunity for shipping conferences: an empty core approach'. *Antitrust Bulletin*, Summer 1993, pp. 419–423.

[132] Joint Cases T–68/89, T–77/89 and T–78/89, *Società Italiana Vetro et al v. Commission* ('*Flat Glass*'), [1992] ECR II–1403, paras 357 and 358.

shows how liner conferences, which are agreements between economically independent undertakings, can also abuse a dominant position.[133] With its precedent, the CFI has indirectly classified liner conferences as the prototype of a group of independent undertakings, whose ties enable them to abuse a joint dominant position and has smoothed the path for the Commission to apply Article 86 whenever conferences enjoy a dominant position. In practice, of the three decisions in which the Commission has condemned abuses of a collective dominant position, two of them refer to maritime transport: the one relating to the Franco-African Shipowners' Committees and the one relating to the CEWAL liner conference.[134]

4.2.10. Conflicts of international law

In its Article 9, Regulation 4056/86 basically provides for an internal and inter-institutional procedure to consult and negotiate with third countries[135] when a 'conflict of international law' of a certain importance arises but does not define what 'conflict' means, nor what 'important Community trading and shipping interests' means.

The existence of a conflict, as well as the importance of the interests at stake, will have to be judged by the Commission, under the judicial supervision of the CFI and the European Court. In this, the Commission appears to enjoy great discretion. It alone is competent to decide firstly whether the circumstances required by Article 9(1) exist. Private individuals are not formally entitled to ask the Commission to initiate consultations, unlike in the case of infringements of Articles 85 and 86, which may form the subject of a complaint by any natural or legal person who claims a legitimate interest.

In the case of conflict, the procedure for contacts with third countries is in two stages:

(1) The first is the consultation stage. Once the existence of a conflict is corroborated, the Commission consults 'at the earliest opportunity' with the authorities of the third countries, and informs the Advisory Committee created by virtue of Article 15 of the Regulation of the outcome of the consultations.

---

[133] *Flat Glass* Judgment, *ibid.*, para. 359. For an analysis of the concept of joint dominance and of the subsequent case-law on the matter see Soames, T. 'An analysis of the principles of concerted practice and collective dominance: a distinction without a difference', *European Competition Law Review*, Vol. 17, No. 1, Jan. 1996, pp. 24–39.

[134] For these, see below, paras 4.3.3.4. and 4.3.2., respectively. The first of the Commission's decisions condemning a joint dominant position was the decision relating to the *Italian Flat Glass* case, OJ 1989 L 33, p. 44, which was partially annulled by the CFI in the case quoted above. Originally, the *TAA* case had a joint dominance aspect but the Commission dropped that part of its case.

[135] Article 9 was drafted keeping the USA in mind. The greater North American tolerance towards shipping cartels as from 1984 left this provision without specific aim.

(2) The second stage, of negotiation, is not compulsory. If the first stage has produced its results and the Commission has resolved the conflict with third countries by means of consultations, the negotiation of agreement is unnecessary. If agreements have to be negotiated, whether to formalize the results of the consultations, or from scratch:

(a) The Commission shall make recommendations to the Council, which shall authorize the Commission to open negotiations (Article 9[2], first part);

(b) The Council will define the 'directives' or negotiating instructions to which the Commission would have to adhere (Article 9[2], second part). In exercising its powers, it shall act 'in accordance with the decision-making procedure laid down in Article 84(2) of the Treaty' (Article 9[3]), in other words, at the present time, by a qualified majority;

(c) The Commission shall conduct the negotiations within the framework of the 'directives' referred to, consulting with the Article 15 Advisory Committee.

This procedure has never been used.[136] [137]

4.3 THE APPLICATION OF REGULATION 4056/86

Unlike the remaining regulations of the 1986 maritime legislative package, from its entry into force on 1 July 1987, Regulation 4056/86 has been applied by the European Commission on numerous occasions.[138]

---

[136] The only time there have been consultations between the Commission and the Member States and a group of developing countries from West and Central Africa was pursuant to Council Reg. 4058/86/EEC, of 22 Dec. 1986, on co-ordinated action to safeguard free access to cargoes in ocean trades, OJ 1986 L 378, p. 21. On the situation in trades between Europe and West and Central Africa, see below, paras 4.3.2. and 4.3.3.4.

[137] In accordance with the Agreement on the European Economic Area (EEA) Annex 14, Section G.11 (h), when the rules of competition of such Agreement are applicable in maritime transport, the provisions of Art. 9 of Reg. 4056/86 are to be adapted by adding a para. 4 to them, by virtue of which, first, if any of the Contracting Parties intends to undertake consultations with a third country, it shall inform the EEA Joint Committee; second, whenever appropriate, the Contracting Party initiating the procedure may request the other Contracting Parties to co-operate in these procedures; and third, if one or more of the other Contracting Parties object to the intended action, a satisfactory solution will be sought within that Joint Committee. If it were not possible to reach an agreement, appropriate measures may be taken to remedy subsequent distortions of competition. These three paras have been also added to Art. 7(2)(c)(i) of Reg. 4056/86 in its EEA version. See above, n. 112.

[138] Regs 4057/86 and 4058/86 have been applied on only one occasion each, whilst Reg. 4055/86 has been applied half a dozen times. For these Regs, see above, Ch. 1.

4.3.1. The 'Irish Club Rules' Agreement

In September 1990, the Commission received an individual exemption application from liner shipping companies parties to an agreement relating to the transport of cargo between Continental Europe, on the one hand, and Ireland and Northern Ireland, on the other, called the 'Irish Club Rules'.[139] The agreement did not amount either to a conference or a consortium but only to a framework discussion agreement between members on rates (including multimodal sea-land ones) and conditions of transport in general. At the beginning, the Commission did not agree to authorize it but, after the parties had altered it (by eliminating, *inter alia*, matters relating to multimodal tariffs) it announced its intention to do so[140] and finally authorized it by means of a comfort letter.[141]

4.3.2. Application to agreements and practices of conference members: withdrawal from conferences, fixing of prices in inland transport and abuse of a dominant position

In the case of *Compagnie Maritime Belge (CMB)* v. *East African Conference (EAC)*, the Commission dealt with the problem of the legality of certain agreements between the members of a conference which are not included amongst the activities enumerated in Article 3 of Regulation 4056/86 but which are included in the UNCTAD Code (in particular, the notice clauses for withdrawal from a conference).[142] The Commission accepted that the requirement of a notice period for withdrawing from a conference amounts to a standard and reasonable clause in conference agreements in which shipping lines agree on schedules, calls, and, in general, the distribution of capacity and the sharing of the market between its members. These clauses, however, must not go beyond that which is strictly necessary for the maintenance without disruption of the service offered by the members of the conferences. The Commission established that the time which a member of a conference has to observe before withdrawing from it without penalties must not exceed six months, or even less in some cases, and must be able to be given at any time.[143]

The DSVK/FEFC case was the first time the legality of the extension of liner conferences' power to inland transport was formally raised. The origin of the case was the complaint lodged in April 1989 by various German industrial and business organizations and by the German Shippers' Council (Deutsche Seeverladerkomitees, DSVK) against the Far Eastern Freight Conference (FEFC). The German users accused the FEFC of having fixed not only the rates

---

[139] OJ 1991 C 166, p. 6.   [140] OJ 1993 C 263, p. 6.
[141] See *23rd Report on Competition Policy*, 1993, para. 233.
[142] On these clauses in general, see above, para. 4.2.3.2.3.
[143] See the *Press Release IP (93) 739* of 9 Sept. 1993 and *23rd Report on Competition Policy*, 1993, paras 230 and 231.

of the maritime transport services offered by their members, but also the prices of the port handling services and those of the inland transport within mixed voyages.

The Commission sent a statement of objections to the conference in December 1992.[144] In June 1994, shortly before adopting its final decision, the Commission presented a Report to the Council in which it explained its favourable attitude to multimodal transport and contrary to the fixing by the conferences of inland transport prices, a restrictive activity unjustifiable in itself, in the absence of co-operation of any other type between the shipping companies.[145]. In its final Decision,[146] the Commission denied that Regulation 4056/86 authorized the fixing of inland transport rates as a supplement to the fixing of maritime rates when the members of liner conferences offer multimodal sea-land rates[147] and refused an individual exemption for activities of this type. In the light of various mitigating circumstances, the Commission decided to impose on the FEFC's members a token fine of 10,000 ECU.[148] The conference lines appealed the Commission's Decision before the CFI.[149]

In the third case under this heading, the Commission had to deal with the abuse of a dominant position by the members of a liner conference.

The case of the *Associated Central West Africa Lines (CEWAL)*, falls within the scope of the procedures handled by the Commission since 1987, relating to shipping trades with Central and West Africa[150] and has its origin in the applications presented by the Danish Government and the Danish Shipowners' Association on the basis of Regulation 4056/86 (complaint against the practices of conferences and Shipowners' Committees present in trades between Europe and West Africa[151]) and Regulation 4058/86 (request for a co-ordinated action against certain African countries). The Council and Commission dealt with the applications in parallel, first adopting a decision to open negotiations with cer-

---

[144] See *Press Release IP (93) 7*, of 6 Jan. 1993.

[145] Document SEC (94) 933 final, of 8 June 1994.

[146] OJ 1994 L 378, p. 17. See especially paras 73–91 of the Decision.

[147] As had already been anticipated in the *19th Report on Competition Policy* in 1989, para. 27. One of the arguments of the Commission was that the scope of the exemption contained in Art. 3 could not be wider than the scope of Reg. 4056/86 itself. The regulation only covers 'international maritime transport services from or to one or more Community ports. . .' (see above, para. 4.2.1.). The Commission's interpretation of the scope of Reg. 4056/86 may have been reinforced by the interpretation made by the ECJ of the scope of Council Reg. 4055/86/EEC, applying the principle of freedom to provide services to international maritime transport (OJ 1986 L 378, p. 1). Reg. 4055/86 applies to 'maritime transport services between Member States and between Member States and third countries', much like Reg. 4056/86. The Court of Justice has made clear that the definition of maritime transport service ceases with the arrival at port, thus it does not extend to the inland transport of the goods that have been unloaded from the vessel. See the ECJ Judgment of 5 Oct. 1995 in Case C–96/94, *Centro Servizi Spediporto* v. *Spedizioni Marittima del Golfo*, not yet reported, at paras 51 and 52.

[148] See *Press Release IP (94) 1260*, of 21 Dec. 1994.

[149] Case T–86/95, *Compagnie Générale Maritime et al* v. *Commission*, yet to be decided.

[150] See the *17th Report on Competition Policy* in 1987, para. 47.

[151] Eleven Committees (between France and West Africa) and four conferences: COWAC, MEWAC, UKWAL and CEWAL.

tain African countries on the basis of Regulation 4058/86[152] and, later on, two decisions on the basis of Regulation 4056/86 against some of the shipping companies and conferences which kept these trades closed to competition. The first of the competition decisions was the one relating to the French West African Shipowners' Committees of April 1992,[153] which was followed by the one of December 1992 relating to several liner conferences.[154] This last decision was the first one directed against a liner conference and mainly affected CEWAL, which brings together various liner shipping companies operating between Northern Europe and Zaire.

The Commission found, on the one hand, that the members of the CEWAL, COWAC and UKWAL conferences had infringed Article 85 of the Treaty by means of a market-sharing agreement by virtue of which each shipowner undertook not to compete on the geographical territory of the conferences to which it did not belong and therefore to compete as an independent. This undertaking was, therefore, equivalent to a non-competition agreement between the conferences and their potential outside competitors. The Commission did not impose fines for this reason. On the other hand, the Commission found that CEWAL's members had abused their joint dominant position in order to eliminate competition from two competing shipping companies—Grimaldi (Italian) and Cobelfret (Belgian), G&C. The abuses consisted, first in the participation in implementation of an exclusivity agreement over the traffic in CEWAL's favour, whereby a Zairian quasi-governmental agency would put all of the cargoes exclusively into the conference's hands. Second, it involved the systematic utilization of 'fighting ships' against G&C. This ancient anti-competitive practice, traditionally used by liner conferences to destroy their independent competitors, is universally condemned. It consists in offering selectively low rates, different to the published tariff, when and only when the independent line is present on the route in order to deprive the independent of its customers. The rates are then returned to the level prior to the independent's arrival.[155] Third and finally, the abuses consisted in the imposition of 100 per cent fidelity agreements—including goods sold free on board (FOB)—and in the use of blacklists to enable reprisals against users using independent vessels in the form of reduced quality of service. The Commission imposed fines of more than 10 million ECU. The decision has been appealed before the CFI.[156]

[152] Council Decision of 20 Oct. 1987 (unpublished). Despite its apparent initial success (see *18th Report on Competition Policy* in 1988, para. 32) the consultations between the EC and African countries were ultimately unsuccessful.

[153] See below, para. 4.3.3.4.

[154] OJ 1993 L 34, p. 20.

[155] These two first abuses found in the *CEWAL* case have been explicitly condemned in a Resolution of the OECD Council of Feb. 1987. See the references contained in the Decision, para. 67, n. 2.

[156] An application to the CFI for the implementation of the decision to be suspended on the basis of Art. 185 of the Treaty proved unsuccessful. See the CFI's judgment in Case T–24/93R, *Compagnie Maritime Belge* v. *Commission*, [1993] ECR II–543.

4.3.3. Application to agreements and practices between conference members and 'outsiders'

The conclusion of collusive agreements with independents has been one of the methods most commonly used by liner conferences to reduce outside competition from so-called 'outsiders'. Since Regulation 4056/86 came into force, the Commission has endeavoured to draw a clear dividing line between conferences and their competitors with the object of distinguishing exempt from non-exempt agreements and ensuring that conferences comply with the Article 85(3)(b) condition.

The Commission has interpreted Article 3 of Regulation 4056/86 strictly not only as a result of the principle of interpretation with regard to exceptions to general rules but also in order to segregate genuine conference agreements from surreptitious agreements between conferences and outsiders. Despite the fact that, at first sight, it appears more pro-competitive to permit agreements of this type than to risk outsiders joining conferences as full members, in practice, they serve to increase the power of conferences in the trades in which they are concluded,[157] without formally producing the characteristic advantages which the regulation attributes to conferences.[158] Anyway, the increase in power which the admission of a new conference member brings may not only raise problems for the agreements between the conference and its new member under the regulation but may also jeopardize the applicability of the block exemption to the conference as a whole.[159]

4.3.3.1. Tolerated outsider agreements

The first variety of agreements between conferences and outsiders are known as tolerated outsider agreements (TOAs), by virtue of which conferences and outsiders moderate their competitive behaviour as between each other. In a typical relationship between a conference and an outsider, the latter tries to acquire the maximum market share at the expense of the conference by, for example, offering cheaper rates below the conference tariff level and following the conference's rate movements.[160] The relationship in TOAs between conference members and

---

[157] As a general rule, if an independent shipping company concludes an agreement of this type, it is because it is not prepared to join the conference as a full member. In the absence of a greater wish for integration on the outsider's part, the 'flexibility' of the agreement enables the conference to limit the outsider's competition as much as possible (in other words, as much as the outsider himself is prepared to limit it).

[158] Principally, the stability understood as a result of rate uniformity or commonness. See above, para. 4.2.3.2.1.

[159] Cf., Temple Lang, above n. 35.

[160] Conferences are, in practice, always price leaders in their markets. Generally, outsiders fix their rates a reasonable figure below the level decided by conferences for each product, except when they are not interested in carrying a specific product, in which case they follow the conference tariff or even fix higher rates than the conference.

outsiders is bound within more or less pre-determined co-ordinates in relation to rate differentials and market shares.

A typical TOA establishes differential rates between conferences and outsiders. In practice, the determination of rate differentials effectively 'freezes' market shares. However, there have been cases in which the respective market shares of the conference and the outsiders have been agreed together with differential rates. In 1990, the Commission received notification of an agreement of this type between the members of the liner conference WITASS and the outsider *Soviet Baltic Shipping Company (BSC)*. The agreement referred to shipping trades between Northern Europe and Venezuela and consisted in an agreement to keep rate differentials, in respect of specific products and following a timetable, at pre-determined levels. The main argument used by European shipping companies which were members of the conference in order to justify the exemption was that maritime policy of EC national governments had favoured agreements of this type with East European shipping companies, companies which were accused of unfair pricing practices. A summary of the agreement was published in a 1991 Notice[161] but the Commission did not grant the exemption requested. The main reasons were twofold: first, that BSC was the only direct competitor of WITASS in this trade; the second, that it is unacceptable to relax competition rules to resolve alleged 'dumping' problems.[162] As it turned out, the shipping companies terminated the agreement and the Commission closed the case.

A more flexible type of TOA, but with results similar to those of differential rate agreements, is a *discussion agreement*. This is a framework agreement by virtue of which shipping companies which are members of conferences and outsiders[163] are able to co-ordinate flexibly their competitive conduct on the market in relation to rates and other conditions of service. On three occasions, the Commission has dealt with agreements of this type, always in United States trades. On no occasion did it authorize the agreements.

The first and most important case relating to discussion agreements related to the *Eurocorde-I* and the *Eurocorde Discussion Agreement* which were concluded in 1985 between the North Atlantic liner conferences and their main competitors. The Commission, having initiated an investigation in 1987,[164] showed itself favourable to granting an exemption subject to a series of conditions which, at that time, the Commission thought sufficient for exemption to be granted.[165] However, on the point of adopting a formal decision, the Commission discovered an additional restriction on competition which made it reconsider its

---

[161] OJ 1991 C 179, p. 6.
[162] If these existed, the right answer would be to apply Council Reg. 4057/86/EEC, on unfair pricing practices in maritime transport (OJ 1986 L 378, p. 14). See above, Ch. 1.
[163] But see the case relating to the 'Irish Club Rules', above, para. 4.3.1.
[164] See the *17th Report on Competition Policy*, 1987, para. 47.
[165] See the Commission's Notice relating to this case, OJ 1990 C 162, p. 13.

previous stance.[166] Finally, the Commission made known to the parties in January 1992 that it considered that their agreements did not satisfy the conditions of Article 85(3) of the Treaty but that, notwithstanding, it would not, in principle, act against them until 1995 at the earliest, at which stage it would revise its position. In the meantime, it would monitor market developments. The shipping lines would retain their immunity from fines (the agreements having been notified) but they would otherwise be continuing their activities at their own risk.[167] The Commission would reconsider its position if major market changes occurred before 1995. Examples included where conference membership, or participation in the Eurocorde agreements or on the market as a whole, altered, or where the parties concluded even more restrictive agreements (which they did), including 'stabilization' agreements to limit or reduce transport capacity on the routes.[168]

The Commission had to deal on another two occasions with discussion agreements, in particular in the *Agreement 1237*[169] and the *Gulfway Agreement*[170] cases. These were also concluded between members of conferences and outsider companies present on trans-Atlantic trades between Europe and the United States. Once they were notified, the Commission raised serious doubts about the possibility of authorizing them and interrupted the exemption procedure. Agreement 1237 was rescinded when the outsider participating shipping company (Maersk, a Danish line) became a full member of the conference with whose members it had concluded this agreement. The Gulfway Agreement is still in force, like the Eurocorde Agreements, covered from fines and under its members' responsibility.[171]

4.3.3.2. 'Technical' agreements

The *Far East Trade Tariff Charges and Surcharges Agreement (FETTSCA)* was concluded in 1991 between twelve members of the FEFC conference and six independents in trades between Europe and the Far East. One of the objectives of the agreement was to extend to the independent shipping companies the standard practice between conference members to fix common surcharges to be imposed on users together with common rates. FETTSCA's members also reached agreement not to give surcharge rebates. FETTSCA has not been notified to the Commission, as its members consider that this is a technical agree-

---

[166] At the time of publishing the *20th Report on Competition Policy*, 1990, the Commission was already considering what final stance to take. See para. 79 of the Report.

[167] The Commission pointed to the risk of their being declared automatically void by a national court.

[168] See the Comm. Dec. in the *TAA* case, above n. 31, paras 124 and 125. On the 'stabilization agreements', see below, para. 4.3.3.3.

[169] Notice and summary in OJ 1990 C 59, p. 2.

[170] Notice and summary in OJ 1990 C 130, p. 3.

[171] See the reference to the Gulfway Agreement in the Comm. Dec. in the *TAA* case, above n. 31, para. 122.

ment excepted by Article 2 of Regulation 4056/86. As explained above, as far as the Commission is concerned, agreements which are commercial and not exclusively technical in content, concluded moreover between direct competitors, do not satisfy the requirements of Article 2 in order to be considered not covered by the prohibition of Article 85(1) of the Treaty.[172] Consequently, the Commission initiated an infringement procedure against the members of the agreement in 1994. A decision is expected in the near future.

4.3.3.3. Stabilization Agreements

Aided by the passiveness of the authorities competent in matters of competition in maritime transport in the three major international maritime trade centres (United States, Far East and Europe), conferences and their outsider competitors on Trans-Pacific and Trans-Atlantic routes, and on routes between Europe and the Far East, decided to conclude agreements with the aim, *inter alia*, of 'freezing' a part of their transport capacity. Shipowners adopted the name 'stabilization' agreements. The first stabilization agreement—from where collusive agreements of this type take their generic name—was the Trans-Pacific Stabilization Agreement (TSA), concluded in 1988.

Following the example of the TSA, the shipowners began to consider the conclusion of similar agreements in the Atlantic and between Europe and the Far East. They did not, in fact, enter into such agreements until the Commission decided temporarily to delay action against the Eurocorde agreements. The Trans-Atlantic Agreement (TAA) is closely connected with the Eurocorde agreements,[173] and came about in view of the alleged insufficiency of the latter—to the mind of the North Atlantic shipowners—to impose the necessary discipline in the trade and obtain satisfactory rate increases both for conference shipping companies and for outsiders. The TAA was concluded in April 1992 and was authorized following vacillations by the North American authorities. It was notified to the Commission in August that same year. The main conference and non-conference shipping companies present in the Atlantic—fifteen in total—formed part of it. Their joint market share approached 80 per cent between Western Europe and the East Coast of the United States, and 70 per cent between Western Europe and all of the United States ports. The TAA provided that its members would adopt their commercial decisions jointly in areas such as pricing policy, transport conditions and capacities. With reference to maritime rates, the TAA established a double structure of price-fixing, rigid—on the lines of a conference—for former conference members, and flexible for former outsiders, each of which would be able to establish its own freight level. On the other hand, the members of the TAA, as those of the FEFC,[174] would fix and publish jointly not only maritime transport, but also inland transport

---

[172] For the interpretation of Art. 2 of Reg. 4056/86, see above, para. 4.2.2.
[173] See above, para. 4.3.3.1.   [174] See above, para. 4.3.2.

tariffs and also subjected their members' service contracts[175] to certain restrictive rules which the Commission considered to be particularly harmful to small shippers. The most restrictive and controversial aspect of the TAA, however, was its capacity management programme. This programme provided for the 'freezing' or non-utilization of up to 25 per cent of its members' transport capacity. The freezing of capacities, as in the case of the TSA, applied only to cargo destined for the United States, and mainly prejudiced European exporters. It was they who, in large number, complained vociferously about the TAA to the Commission, alleging the serious prejudice which the sudden and exorbitant increase in rates which this agreement had made possible, had caused the competitiveness of their products.

The Commission concluded that because there were two types of members within the agreement, particularly in relation to rates, the TAA could not be considered to be a genuine conference agreement falling within the scope of the Article 3 block exemption. In any event, even genuine conferences are not permitted to freeze a significant part of their members' transport capacity so as to effect rate increases or to fix inland tariffs. The Commission also examined whether the TAA complied with the conditions of Article 85(3). It concluded that it did not especially since it was very harmful to users and eliminated the competition in a substantial part of the relevant market.

The Commission finally prohibited the TAA (without imposing fines since the agreement had been notified) by decision in October 1994.[176] Previously, in July 1994, the members of the TAA concluded and notified another agreement, the Trans-Atlantic Conference Agreement (TACA), which the Commission is continuing to examine. The TACA—with respect to inland transport tariffs—could give rise to a provisional decision of withdrawal of immunity from fines.[177] The members of the TAA appealed against the Commission Decision and, in relation to the ban on fixing joint multimodal tariffs, obtained its suspension by the CFI.[178] The Commission appealed the CFI order before the European Court, but unsuccessfully.[179]

---

[175] The service contracts offered by conferences and outsiders in the US (defined in Section 3 [21] of the Shipping Act 1984, 46 U.S.C. app. 1702 [21]) are a recent innovation which clashes with the system of 'common carriage' on which the anti-trust immunity of conferences and other shipping cartels is founded. American conferences may limit their use (e.g., permitting their members only collective contracts) and even prohibit them. On the nature of service contracts, see above, para. 4.2.5.2.

[176] See above n. 31.   [177] On this type of decision in the transport area, see below, Ch. 6.

[178] Order of the President of the CFI of 10 Mar. 1995 in Case T–395/94R, *Atlantic Container Line et al* v. *Commission*, [1970] ECR II-595. See the *Commission Press Release IP (95) 243* of 14 Mar. 1995, in which Commissioner Van Miert, making the point that the order of the CFI did not prejudice the merits of the case, announced his intention to propose that the Commission withdraw the immunity from fines from the TACA agreement. See also the *Press Release IP (95) 646*, of 21 June 1995. The statement of objections that has formally opened the procedure in this case has also been attacked by the TACA member shipping lines, unsuccessfully. See the Order of the President of the CFI of 22 Nov. 1995 in Case T–395/94 RII, *Atlantic Container Line and others* v. *Commission*, not yet reported.

[179] Order of the President of the CJEC of 19 July 1995 in Case C–149/95P, *Commission* v. *Atlantic Container Line et al*, not yet reported.

The second stabilization agreement which touches European ports covers trades between Europe and the Far East, the East Asia Trades Agreement (EATA). Its fundamental objective, and even its main members, are the same as those in the TAA, although the two agreements have formal differences. The EATA is centred on the freezing of the capacity which its members offer users with the object of increasing the level of rates. The agreement was notified to the Commission in 1992,[180] then the Commission objected to its authorization and, in 1994, initiated an infringement procedure which is currently pending, and which will probably end, like the TAA matter, with a prohibitory decision.

4.3.3.4. *French West African Shipowners' Committees*

The Decision relating to the *French West African Shipowners' Committees*[181] was the first adopted by the Commission as a result of the various complaints presented in 1987 by the Danish Government and the Danish Shipowners' Association.[182] The Commission concluded that these shipping company Committees, which used to control liner traffic between France and eleven States of West and Central Africa (Benin, Togo, Congo, Senegal, Mali, Guinea, Central African Republic, Cameroon, Gabon, Niger and Burkina Faso), constituted agreements contrary to Article 85(1). Furthermore, the Commission considered that as a result the Committees held a collective dominant position which they had abused in breach of Article 86. The purpose of the Committees was to share between their members (conference and independent lines under the same umbrella) the whole of the cargoes, with the exclusion of outsiders not belonging to the Committees (*inter alia*, the Danish shipping companies which lodged the complaint). As a consequence of the elimination of competition the rates were excessive. The Commission imposed fines totalling over 15 million ECU.

4.3.4. Application to agreements and practices in maritime passenger transport

Since 1987, the Commission has examined a number of agreements and practices between ferry companies, the only sector where passenger liner transport assumes great economic importance.[183] One day after Regulation 4056/86 entered into force, various agreements between ferry lines present in the English Channel were notified to the Commission for individual exemption.[184] The notifications were transmitted to the Member States. The national competition authorities showed little sympathy to the agreements and asked the Commission not to authorize them. The Commission expressed its serious doubts in respect

---

[180] See the Notice and summary of the agreement in OJ 1993 C 97, p. 2.
[181] OJ 1992 L 134, p. 1.   [182] See above, para. 4.3.2, relating to the *CEWAL* Decision.
[183] Remember that passenger transport fully falls within the powers of control of Reg. 4056/86, without qualifying for an Art. 3 block exemption. See above, para. 4.2.3.1., n. 26.
[184] See the Notices and summaries in OJ 1989 C 17, pp. 8 and 12. See also *17th Report on Competition Policy* in 1987, para. 47.

of the agreements but did not initiate infringement procedures. It continued to study market developments in the Channel and in the ferry sector in general in greater depth aiming to acquire more experience in short-sea trades.

Again in 1989, and without presenting any formal notification, various ferry companies operating in the Channel made contact with the Commission. Their intention was to obtain the Commission's opinion about their co-operation projects to compete with the Channel Tunnel. The Commission made contact with the British Monopolies and Mergers Commission (MMC), which dealt with this matter under English national law. The MMC objected to such co-operation and the Commission did not have to intervene.[185]

Also for the Channel trades, the Commission received in 1992 a notification from *Sealink Stena Line Ltd* and from *Société nouvelle d'armement transmanche (SNAT)*, the successor of Sealink UK Ltd and the shipping division of SNCF respectively, relating to the modification and extension of the agreements notified to the Commission in 1987. The Commission published a summary of the new agreements[186] and, again, raised serious doubts about the possibility of authorizing them without alterations. The matter was finally resolved with a comfort letter once the parties had made the changes required by the Commission.

In relation to a ferry route in Scandinavia, the Commission received in July 1990 a request for individual exemption for a joint venture between the Danish national railway company (*Danske Statsbaner, DSB*) and the Swedish ferry company *Scandinavian Ferry Lines (SFL)*. The agreement concerned the operation of ferries between the ports of Helsingborg (Sweden) and Helsingør (Denmark). The service offered by the joint venture to replace the two previously offered by SFL, on the one hand, and DSB, on the other. The Commission published a summary of the agreements,[187] and let the statutory 90-day period elapse for the automatic grant of an exemption for a period of six years as from the publication in the Official Journal of the summary of the agreements.[188] The Commission considered that the joint operation of the service born out of the agreements, despite restricting competition between the members, had economic advantages and complied in general with the conditions of Article 85(3).

4.3.4.1. Freedom of access to essential facilities[189]

In 1992, the Commission received a complaint and a request for interim measures from the Irish ferry company *B&I Line plc* against *Sealink Harbours Ltd.* and

---

[185] See the *19th Report on Competition Policy*, 1989, para. 29, third part. The undertakings in question were Sealink and P&O, of which the Report makes no mention.

[186] Notice and summary in OJ 1994 C 82, p. 7.

[187] Notice and summary in OJ 1992 C 36, p. 5.

[188] See *Press Release IP (92) 396*, of 18 May 1992, and the *22nd Report on Competition Policy*, 1992, Annex III, h).

[189] See Temple Lang, J. 'Defining legitimate competition: Companies' duties to supply competitors and access to essential facilities.' *Annual Proceedings of the Fordham Corporate Law Institute, 1994.* (Transnational Juris Publications/Kluwer, New York/Deventer, 1995), pp. 245–313.

Sealink Stena Ltd. regarding the *port of Holyhead.* According to the Irish company, Sealink had infringed Article 86 of the Treaty in fixing a new schedule for the departures of its vessels which would disrupt B&I's services. The Commission agreed to take interim measures against Sealink. The Commission understood that there was evidence that, in its capacity as Holyhead's port authority, Sealink authorized changes in the departure times of its own ferries which could have seriously prejudiced B&I. The Commission pointed out that, as a consequence of Article 86, 'a company that both owns and uses an essential facility, in this case a port, should not grant its competitors access on terms less favourable than those which it gives its own services'. It therefore ordered Sealink to change in part its departure times.[190]

Again, in April 1993, the Commission had to decide on a complaint and a request for interim measures against *Stena Sealink* about the *port of Holyhead.* The complainant undertaking was—this time—*Sea Containers Ltd.,* which maintained that the defendant had abused its dominant position as the owner and operator of that port in proposing the development of the port which would allegedly reduce its capacity and in not allowing it access to start a high-speed ferry service, thus protecting its own services against the competition. In October 1993, Stena Sealink allowed Sea Containers access to the port on conditions which the Commission judged reasonable and non-discriminatory. However, the Commission considered it necessary to adopt a formal decision to reject the request for interim measures with the aim of clarifying certain points of law to the ferry operators and interested third parties and avoiding the reproduction of similar complaints relating to the port of Holyhead every year.[191]

In May 1995, the Commission intervened in a case involving access to essential facilities in the ferry sector for the third time. In November 1994, *Irish Continental Group (ICG),* an Irish ferry operator, applied to the *Chambre de Commerce et d'Industrie de Morlaix (CCI Morlaix)* for access to the French *port of Roscoff,* for the purpose of commencing a ferry service between Ireland and Britanny in the summer of 1995. The port of Roscoff was, for the time being, the only port capable of providing adequate port facilities in France for a service of that kind. The market accounted for around 100,000 passengers in 1994. Only one French ferry company was operating between Ireland and Brittany. In December 1994, CCI Morlaix and ICG had already negotiated and agreed in principle on the question of access to Roscoff and on a number of technical issues. Following the agreement in principle, IGC announced its services to Roscoff and began to take bookings. However, in January 1995 the CCI Morlaix indicated its wish to suspend negotiations. ICG complained to the Commission and asked for the

---

[190] Comm. Dec. of 11 June 1992, unpublished in the OJ, and appearing in the Common Market Law Reports, [1992] CMLR 255. See especially paras 42 and 43. See also *Press Release IP (92) 478,* of 11 June 1992 (from which the citation is made), and the *22nd Report on Competition Policy* , 1992, para. 219.

[191] OJ 1994 L 15, p. 8. On the Decision, see also *Press Release IP (94) 5,* and the *23rd Report on Competition Policy* in 1993, para. 234.

adoption of interim measures against the CCI Morlaix. In spite of this, further negotiations took place but no agreement was reached between the parties, in particular as to the date to commence operations. The Commission decided that, *prima facie*, the CCI Morlaix had abused its dominant position as the operator of the port of Roscoff by refusing ICG at that stage access to the port facilities there, in violation of Article 86, and risked causing serious and irreparable harm to the Irish ferry operator. For that reason, the Commission ordered the CCI Morlaix to take the necessary steps to allow ICG access to the port by mid-June 1995. The Commisssion also hoped that both parties would find a suitable solution to the pending technical problems.[192]

4.3.4.2. Public undertakings and Article 90 of the EC Treaty

The Commission acted on two occasions against Spain for continuing even after its accession to the EC (and by way, *inter alia*, of the State-owned shipping company *Transmediterránea*) a regional policy (reductions in the air and maritime transport tariffs reserved to residents on the Canary and Balearic Islands) and a social policy (reduction in rates for the elderly) which discriminated on the basis of nationality by being made available only to Spanish citizens. On the first occasion, the matter was solved following the Commission's decision,[193] by an amendment of the relevant Spanish provisions, to extend the aforementioned benefits to all nationals of the Member States of the Community.[194] On the second occasion, in which the measures favouring Spanish elderly persons—20 per cent discounts to pensioners or those aged over sixty—had taken the appearance of a unilateral concession by Transmediterránea, the Commission considered that the granting of such advantages exclusively to persons of Spanish nationality was not based, as the Spanish Government alleged, on strictly commercial criteria. As the Spanish State was the 95 per cent-owner of Transmediterránea shares, the Commission concluded that, at least its refraining from putting an end to a measure falling within Article 7 of the EEC Treaty—now Article 6 of the EC Treaty—was contrary to Article 90(1) and initiated an infringement procedure against Spain pursuant to Article 90(3).[195] The case was disposed of when the conditions of the granting of rebates were modified to extend them to all EC citizens.[196]

In another case, this time in Northern Europe, the Swedish group Stena and its subsidiaries lodged a complaint against Denmark for infringing Article 90(1)

---

[192] The Comm. Dec. has not been published in the *OJ*. See the *Press Release IP(95)492*, of 16 May 1995.

[193] OJ 1987 L 194, p. 15.

[194] Ley 33/1987, *Boletín Oficial del Estado* of 24 Dec. 1987, amending previous legislation (*Boletín Oficial del Estado* 312 of 30 Dec. 1981). See the *18th Report on Competition Policy*, 1988, para. 309.

[195] See the *22nd Report on Competition Policy*, 1992, para. 523. For the initiation by complaint of this case, see the *21st Report on Competition Policy*, 1991, para. 334.

[196] *23rd Report on Competition Policy*, 1993, para. 364.

of the Treaty, and asked the Commission for the adoption of an Article 90(3) decision to put an end to this infringement. The Danish authorities had refused, on the one hand, to allow Euro-Port, a Stena subsidiary, to build a new port immediately adjacent to the port of Rødby (Denmark) and, on the other, to operate within the current facilities of that port.[197] The Commission judged that the denial of access to the *port of Rødby* prevented the complainants establishing a ferry line with the port of Puttgarden, in Germany, and had the object of protecting the monopoly of the Danish (DSB) and German (DB) railways, which offered a joint maritime transport service on the same route. The Commission, therefore, concluded that the refusal was incompatible with Article 90(1) read in conjunction with Article 86.[198]

4.3.5. Agreements and practices in related sectors

The Commission has intervened over the last ten years in various cases relating to agreements and practices in sectors neighbouring maritime transport, utilizing the common rules of Regulation 17.[199] The sector closest to maritime transport where these rules are applied is that of port and quayside services, where, for now, the Commission has not intervened directly, although it has reserved the right to do so in the future.[200] In the marine insurance sector, the Commission has intervened both in matters referring to insurance of contractual and some third-party liabilities arising from the operation of vessels, and in matters relating to ship hull and machinery insurance.[201] In the freight 'futures' contracts sector, the Commission studied an agreement between four intermediation companies (later also joined by shipowners, shipping agents, and other freight transport related companies) for the creation of an exchange for such contracts, called 'Baltic International Freight Futures Exchange' (BIFFEX). The Commission decided that the agreement was not restrictive of competition in the sense of Article 85(1).[202] In the 'offshore' platforms sector, the Commission also intervened in one case.[203] The Commission has also received various notifications and complaints relating to the activities of ship classification societies, without having decided formally on them for the time being.[204]

---

[197] See the *22nd Report on Competition Policy*, 1992, para. 522.

[198] OJ 1994 L 55, p. 52.

[199] For the applicability of Reg. 17 in all sectors not directly connected with the provision of maritime transport services, see above, Ch. 2.

[200] See the Comm. Dec. in the *DSVK/FEFC* case, above n. 146, paras 7 and 9.

[201] *P&I Clubs Decision (International Group Agreement)*, OJ 1985 L 376, p. 2, and *LUA/ILU* Decision, OJ 1993 L 4, p. 26. The members of the P&I Clubs have applied for a renewal of their individual exemption. See the relevant Comm. Notice in OJ 1995 C 181, p. 16.

[202] OJ 1987 L 222, p. 24.

[203] *Stena / Houlder Offshore* Case. See the *19th Report on Competition Policy*, 1989, para. 70.

[204] The activities of these companies do not come within the scope of application of Reg. 4056/86, nor are they eligible as purely technical agreements under its Art. 2.

Section II: Liner Consortia: Commission Regulation (EC) 870/95

4.4. THE CONTAINER REVOLUTION[205]

The container revolution, the second and last great technological revolution in liner shipping,[206] began in the mid-1970s and continues today. The widespread use of containerized liner services brought with it the economic concentration of the liner shipping sector which reduced the number of services and individual companies and, also, forced surviving shipping companies to tighten their links of co-operation. The container revolution, therefore, led to major structural changes, new forms of operation and new forms of co-operation between shipowners. The shipping companies made use of old types of agreement adapted to the new situation. Transshipment agreements, straight chartering agreements (in this case, of container 'slots') and joint service agreements evolved with the containerization and nowadays constitute the industrial basis for operation of scheduled services on many routes. The containerized version of joint services are liner consortia.[207]

4.5. CONFERENCES AND CONSORTIA

The process of change which occurred in liner shipping while containers were being massively introduced in new shipping trades were characterized by what shipowners called an 'orderly approach, broadly respecting the positions of other Conference lines and also effecting the change within established Conference structure'.[208] One of the key instruments of the conferences' internal reorganization were the liner consortia, industrial co-operation agreements which allowed the shipowners to adapt to the new scale of shipping operation and face jointly the necessary capital investments. Meanwhile, conferences were maintained as the traditional forum for cartel control over rates and market-sharing between shipping lines. Nowadays and despite the disuse of their most integrated

---

[205] See Van Ginderachter, E. and Durande, S. 'EC Reg. 870/95: the consortia block exemption.' *European Maritime Law Organization.* 5th Annual Conference, London 6–7 Oct. 1995 (to be published in *European Transport Law*). See also Clough, M., 'The Devil and the Deep Blue Sea (EC Competition Law and Liner Shipping Consortia)'; *European Competition Law Review*, Vol. 16, No.7, Oct. 1995, pp. 417–27.

[206] The first took place in the second half of the 19th century, with steamships. See above, para. 4.1.2, n. 6.

[207] For a definition of consortium, see below, para. 4.7.

[208] See St Johnston, K. 'The place of conference shipping during the 1990s'. Speech delivered during The Singaport Conference, Singapore, 3 Apr. 1989. St Johnston was President of CENSA, the association of European and Japanese shipowners, in the 1980s.

varieties, the consortia af all kinds continue being the preferred form of industrial co-operation between shipping companies, generally within conferences although, in recent years, an increase in the trend to join in consortium has also been observed between outsiders.

The Commission has also shown itself favourable to authorizing liner consortia. The pre-existence of the block exemption of conferences made its task technically harder, and forced it to pay particular attention to the clear delimitation of the scope of application of Regulation 4056/86 and the exemption of liner conferences, on the one hand, and of the Regulation and exemption of consortia, on the other.[209]

The only criterion for distinguishing a consortium which fixes prices on a route in which a conference does not exist, from a genuine conference (bearing in mind that there is nothing in theory to stop an agreement between shipping companies being either) appears to be the stabilizing effect of the conferences. The true conference would be capable of producing the typical stability of conferences in the trades it covers. A consortium which produces the same type of stability would at the same time be a conference. In the end, a specific analysis would show that only a consortium with market power comparable to that of a conference would be eligible for the exemption of Article 3 of Regulation 4056/86.[210] In practice, given the limits imposed on consortia in terms of their market shares,[211] it is to be hoped that a situation in which both capacities— consortium / conference—and both exemptions coincide in a single agreement does not arise.

4.6. LEGISLATIVE HISTORY

When adopting Regulation 4056/86, the Council invited the Commission to study the situation of consortia as regards the competition rules and to consider presenting new proposals, if necessary.[212] The Commission, for its part, undertook to present within one year a report to the Council on whether to grant a block exemption to consortia and to present appropriate proposals, if necessary. In the meantime, the Commission invited the shipping companies to notify their consortium agreements.

---

[209] See Temple Lang, above n. 35.

[210] The above can be illustrated with an example: The market share of a conference being the clearest evidence of its power, a consortium which holds a minimum market share (e.g. of 5%) on a route where a conference does not exist could not be considered a conference. On the contrary, in the absence of a conference, a major market share (e.g. over 50%) would allow a price-fixing consortium to be considered a conference at the same time, provided it complied with all the requirements of Reg. 4056/86.

[211] Note, however, that strictly speaking the Commission's thresholds are not market shares. See below.

[212] See the *16th Report on Competition Policy*, 1986, para. 37.

Following many problems, mainly due to the lack of co-operation between shipping companies, the Commission in 1990 presented its report with a legislative proposal.[213] The Commission asked the Council to delegate it the powers necessary to adopt an exemption regulation independent of Regulation 4056/86. Despite being consistent with standard practice in matters of competition,[214] the Commission's proposal had a cool reception at the Council, as the Member States preferred to discuss and adopt directly within the Council either an amendment of Regulation 4056/86 or a substantive exemption regulation for the consortia, as they had done in the case of liner conferences. After one and a half years of negotiation,[215] after presenting a modified draft enabling regulation,[216] and after the Commission had undertaken, in December 1992, to follow a series of directives which had been the subject of discussion within the Council,[217] the enabling Regulation 479/92/EEC of the Council was finally adopted on 25 February 1992.[218]

Regulation 479/92 followed the lines of Regulation 3976/87, the enabling regulation authorizing the Commission to grant several block exemptions in air transport, but did not anticipate the substantive content of the future Commission Regulation, except in the sense that it excluded rate-fixing. This was embodied in the guidelines presented by the Commission to the Council. Regulation 479/92 also provided for the procedure for adopting the substantive regulation.[219]

The Commission published a draft substantive exemption regulation in March 1994[220] and, following certain amendments, adopted the final version of the regulation one year later.[221]

---

[213] Document COM (90) 260 final, of 18 June 1990.

[214] The block exemptions on the basis of Art. 87 of the Treaty have generally been adopted by means of enabling regulations in which the Council would delegate to the Commission the drafting of the substantive exemption regulations.

[215] During which the Commission advanced some of the requirements which it had the intention of imposing on consortia. See the *20th Report on Competition Policy*, 1990, para. 78.

[216] Presented to the Council on 5 Dec. 1991.

[217] The guidelines for the drafting of the substantive exemption regulation were published in the *21st Report on Competition Policy*, 1991, Annex II. See also para. 41 of the Report, reporting on the Commission's conversations with Parliament and the Council on the conditions and obligations which would have to be imposed upon the consortia.

[218] OJ 1992 L 55, p. 3. See the review on the content in the *22nd Report on Competition Policy*, 1992, para. 289.

[219] See Arts 4 and 5 of Reg. 479/92.

[220] OJ 1994 C 63, p. 8. See also the *23rd Report on Competition Policy*, 1993, para. 140.

[221] Comm. Reg. (EC) 870/95, of 20 Apr. 1995, OJ 1995 L 89, p. 7. See *Press Release IP (95) 409*, of 28 Apr. 1995.

4.7. COMMISSION REGULATION (EC) 870/95

4.7.1. Exemption system

To define the categories of agreements to which the exemption is applicable, the regulation:

(1) limits the agreements to which it refers on the basis of its characteristics in terms of the operation;
(2) limits geographically the agreements on the basis of the trades in which they apply;
(3) defines exhaustively exempted activities;
(4) excludes certain activities, the performance of which also brings with it the loss of the exemption; and finally,
(5) imposes three groups of conditions before starting to enjoy and maintain the exemption, the infringement of which causes automatic loss of the exemption.

Once the foregoing requirements are complied with, and once they enjoy the exemption, the consortium agreements between shipping companies are also subject to:

(1) a series of obligations, the infringement of which may lead (indirectly and non-automatically, unlike the conditions) to withdrawal of the exemption individually; and
(2) compliance with the four conditions of Article 85(3) of the Treaty; the supervening infringement of the four conditions would also lead the Commission to withdrawing the exemption individually.

4.7.2. Definition of consortium

In accordance with Article 1 of Regulation 870/95:

'consortium' means an agreement between two or more vessel-operating carriers which provide international liner shipping services exclusively for the carriage of cargo, chiefly by container, relating to a particular trade and the object of which is to bring about co-operation in the joint operation of a maritime transport service, which improves the service which would be offered individually by each of its members in the absence of the consortium, in order to rationalize their operations by means of technical, operational and/or commercial arrangements, with the exception of price fixing.

A consortium is defined as a group of shipping companies, at least two of which operate vessels. A crucial argument for authorizing consortia is that the capital investments necessary to establish a containerized service are plentiful. The Commission indirectly requires such investments to be made in order to qualify for the exemption and does not allow pure consortia of sea carriers which do not operate vessels (non-vessel-operating carriers, NVOcs). The definition also refers to scheduled cargo services *chiefly by container*, allowing shipping companies to use—together with fully cellular lift-on/lift-off container vessels—other types of vessels which combine container capacity with conventional or roll-on/roll-off capacity. The *majority* of the capacity, however, has to be used for containerized cargo.

As a first condition enshrined in the definition of consortium, the group of shipping lines seeking to qualify for the exemption may only do so provided they improve the services which each of them individually used to offer on the route in question.[222]

Article 3(2) of the regulation authorizes those activities of the consortia with which the Commission had already characterized the consortia in its 1990 Report as well as some others added subsequently. If these activities are classifiable as 'white activities'—mirroring the traditional terminology of EC block exemptions—Article 4 of Regulation 870/95 also defines a 'black activity': the inclusion of 'freezing' or substantial reduction of capacity agreements, which triggers the direct inapplicability of the exemption. The regulation undoubtedly wanted to avoid the exemption of 'stabilization' agreements which have arisen in some trades,[223] but has respected the ability of consortia adapting their capacity to temporary fluctuations in demand.[224]

The price-fixing agreements are also not only excluded from the exemption but, if concluded, prevent the agreement between shipowners falling within the definition of consortium and enjoying the exemption, *in toto*—as if the inclusion of a 'black clause' were involved.[225]

---

[222] The improvement of the new service would have to be gauged by reference to its frequency, type of vessels, supply of general and specific capacity for certain types of cargo (e.g., reefer cargo), the number of ports served, the transit time of the merchandise, etc. The most ostensible improvement for purposes of fitting within the definition would arise when the members of the consortium did not previously offer their individual services separately on the route (provided their agreement falls under Art. 85(1) of the Treaty, which may not always be the case; e.g., if the consortium members opened a completely new route, they would be creating a new market, rather than restricting competition; see above, Ch. 2).

[223] See above, para. 4.3.3.3.

[224] See Art. 3(2)(b) of the regulation, the 7th recital of which, in any event, recognizes that one of the essential characteristics of a consortium is that of making adjustments of capacity between its members.

[225] As explained by the recitals, in the case of a consortium the members of which form part of a conference, the rate-fixing activity is covered by the conferences' block exemption. In the case of outsider consortia, or consortia which operate on a route where a conference does not exist, the regulation suggests that the parties request an individual exemption. See the 9th recital of Reg. 870/95.

4.7.3. Conditions of exemption

The conditions of the exemption are arranged into three groups.

The first group[226] formulates an 'optional condition'. Of the three circumstances it describes, at least one has to exist before the condition is deemed fulfilled. Thus, the consortium has to:

(1)   either be brought within a conference in which its members have the right of independent action in matters of rates ('independent rate action');[227]
(2)   or be brought within a conference allowing the consortium to offer its own service arrangements enabling it to compete with the other members of the conference in matters relating to the quality of the services;[228]
(3)   or operate in trades where there is effective competition, actual or potential, between the members of the consortium and non-members, irrespective of whether a conference operates on that route or otherwise.

Whilst the first two options are aimed exclusively at consortia which operate within a conference, the third one is applicable to any type of consortia. Effective competition, in this case, is measured by reference to the consortium's relative market power in its direct trades. If a consortium of outsiders has to contend with a conference on its routes, the condition would be satisfied even if it was the conference as such which eliminated the competition (in which case the Commission would have to act against the conference, but not against the consortium).

The second group[229] elaborates on the condition of Article 85(3)(b) of the Treaty, relating to the non-elimination of competition in respect of a substantial part of the market. The regulation recognizes in the seventeenth recital that, for the purposes of defining the market in individual cases, substitutable transport services which are valid alternatives should be taken into account, but clarifies in the sixteenth recital that, for the purposes of the block exemption, and for reasons of legal certainty, the basis taken should be the shares of the consortia on the direct trade between the series of ports they connect, calculated on the overall basis of all those ports. According to Article 6(1), the shares will be calculated by reference to the volume of goods carried.[230] The maximum shares

---

[226]   Art. 5 of Reg. 870/95.

[227]   This reference may seem, but is not an inconsistency of the Commission with its own interpretation of the expression 'uniform or common freight rates' in the definition of conference. However, see the Commission's arguments in the *TAA* Decision, above n. 31, paras 350–5.

[228]   Note that EC service arrangements are *sui generis*, in that they do not deal with prices. For the system of ordinary (US-style) service contracts under Community competition law, see above, para. 4.2.5.2, n. 73.

[229]   Art. 6 of Reg. 870/95.

[230]   The percentage is to be calculated, therefore, at a portion of the total volume of general cargo carried (freight tonnes or twenty-foot equivalent units, TEUs) in each series of ports, not as an average of the percentages available to the consortium at each port it connects (unless it is a weighted

vary, depending on whether the members of the consortia belong or otherwise to a liner conference, and will have to be less than 30 per cent in the first case and less than 35 per cent in the second case.[231] The regulation provides for an opposition procedure of the type of the Commission's block exemption regulations for consortia which exceed these percentages and do not exceed 50 per cent.[232] Consortia which exceed this last percentage will have to be notified by

average). The following chart, which has been prepared by David Wood, may help in calculating the trade share for consortia:

Test: trade share in respect of the ranges of ports calculated by reference to the volume of goods carried
Calculation: take a weighted average of the port pair percentages involved
Steps:
   (i) calculate Eastbound (EB) and Westbound (WB) total volumes carried on the basis of each port pair included in the range of ports served (eg. Boston/NY/Norfolk—Bremerhaven/Rotterdam/Le Havre = 9 port pairs)—♥
   (ii) calculate, for each port pair, the volume carried by the members of the consortium—♠
   e.g. Boston/NY/Norfolk—Bremerhaven/Rotterdam/Le Havre

Eastbound

Port Pair	Total Volume	Consortium Volume
Boston/Bremerhaven	A	X
Boston/R'dam	B	Y
Boston/Le Havre	C	Z
etc		
Total	♥(E)	♠(E)

Westbound

Port Pair	Total Volume	Consortium Volume
Boston/Bremerhaven	A	X
etc		
Total	♥(W)	♠(W)

   (iii) calculate the percentage carried EB and WB by the consortium members—
      (i) ♠(E)/♥(E) = ♦%EB
      (ii) ♠(W)/♥(W) = ♣%WB
   (iv) calculate the overall trade share (EB and WB) by adding the consortium's EB and WB volumes and dividing by total EB and WB volumes—

$$\frac{(♦\%EB \times ♥(E)) + (♣\%WB \times ♥(W))}{♥(E) + ♥(W)}$$

or

$$\frac{(\%\ \text{share of trade EB} \times \text{total volume EB}) + (\%\ \text{share of trade WB} \times \text{total volume WB})}{\text{total volume EB} + \text{WB}}$$

This may also be summarized as—

$$\frac{\text{Consortium Volume EB} + \text{Consortium Volume WB}}{\text{Total volume EB} + \text{WB}}$$

---

[231] Art. 6(1) of Reg. 870/95. Consortia which lie below these percentages will be in the 'white zone' of the exemption.
[232] Art. 7 of Reg. 870/95. These consortia would be in the 'grey zone' of the exemption.

the ordinary exemption procedure of Regulation 4056/86.[233] However, as a transitional provision, existing consortia which have a share of trade of more than 50 per cent were eligible for the special opposition procedure for a six month period as from the entry into force of the regulation.[234] Thus, in practice, virtually all of the existing consortia (provided they comply with the other conditions for exemption, in particular, those of Article 8 of Regulation 870/95) will benefit from the opposition procedure, and probably very few,—not to say none—will be left out of the exemption.

The third group[235] is made up of four conditions, three relating to the content of the agreements and one borrowed from Regulation 4056/86 relating to non-discrimination, all of which, without options or differences between types of consortia, has to be complied with for the block exemption to apply. The consortium must:

(1) allow its members to offer individual and individualized service arrangements[236] (adapted to the users' needs);[237]

(2) give member companies the right to withdraw from the consortium without financial or other penalty, in particular without obliging the leaving company to withdraw definitely or temporarily from the consortium trades. This right is subject to a maximum six months' notice which may be given after an initial period of eighteen months has elapsed as from the entry into force of the agreement; in the case of highly integrated consortia, the notice may be given after thirty months;[238]

(3) permit, when the consortium operates with a joint marketing structure, each member to market its services independently, subject to giving a maximum of six months' notice;[239]

(4) not discriminate (neither the consortium nor its members) in the sense of Article 4 of Regulation 4056/86.[240]

4.7.4 Obligations of members

The obligations which Article 10 of Regulation 870/95 imposes on the consortia are similar in part to the obligations which Article 5 of Regulation 4056/86 imposes on liner conferences.

[233] See the 21st recital of Reg. 870/95. These consortia would be in the 'dark grey zone', if not 'black'.

[234] Art. 13(4) of Reg. 870/95.

[235] Art. 8 of Reg. 870/95.

[236] See the EC definition of service arrangement in Art. 1 of Reg. 870/95, which, as stated before, does not include the fixing of rates as an element.

[237] Art. 8(1). This condition has to be read with Art. 5 of Reg. 870/95. In complying with it, consortia whose members participate in a liner conference will also, logically, comply with the condition of Art. 6 of the regulation.

[238] Art. 8(2), second part, of Reg. 870/95. According to the regulation, a highly integrated consortium must have 'a net revenue pool and/or high level of investment due to the purchase or charter by its members of vessels specifically for the purpose of setting up the consortium'.

[239] Art. 8(3) of Reg. 870/95.

[240] Art. 8(4) of Reg. 870/95, which reproduces the text of said provision of Reg. 4056/86.

Three of the five obligations imposed on conferences, with various modifications, are imposed on the consortia: that of holding consultations with transport users and their organizations;[241] that of making available the consortium's transport conditions[242] and that of notifying arbitration awards and the conciliators' recommendations to the Commission.[243]

The fourth and last obligation, that of giving within a period of at least one month information to the Commission proving the compliance with the conditions and other obligations on the part of the consortia,[244] is an original provision of Regulation 870/95 and is accompanied by provisions on the limited use of information obtained by the Commission as a result of the application of the regulation and on the obligation of professional secrecy of the Commission and the authorities of the Member States, their officials and other servants.[245]

4.7.5. Miscellaneous provisions

In accordance with Article 6 of Regulation 479/92, the consortia regulation empowers the Commission to revoke individually the block exemption of consortia which:

(1) have effects incompatible with Article 85(3) of the EC Treaty (in particular with the last of its conditions, in other words, when the competition outside the conference where the consortium operates, or outside the consortium, is insufficient);[246]

(2) repeatedly infringe the obligations attached to the exemption;[247]

(3) have effects incompatible with Article 86;[248]

Lastly, the Regulation foresees in its final provisions that:

(1) the exemption shall apply with retroactive effect to consortia existing at the date of its entry into force, from the time they have satisfied the exemption conditions;

---

[241] The obligation to consult with users (Art. 9[1] of Reg. 870/95) differs from the one imposed on conferences both in the consultation procedure—far more developed in the case of consortia—and in its subject-matter—limited to the activities of consortia, which excludes the main topics of consultation with conferences, including rates. As in the case of conferences, the obligation to consult is accompanied by a block exemption for agreements between the consortia members and transport users which may result from the consultations (Art. 10 of Reg. 870/95).

[242] Art. 9(2) of Reg. 870/95

[243] Art. 9(3) of Reg. 870/95. The consortia regulation does not contain obligations similar to the ones imposed by Reg. 4056/86 on conferences in matters relating to loyalty contracts (Art. 5[2] of Reg. 4056/86) and services not covered by the freight charges (Art. 5[3] of Reg. 4056/86).

[244] Art. 9(4) of Reg. 870/95.   [245] Art. 11 of Reg. 870/95.

[246] Art. 12(1) of Reg. 870/95.

[247] Art. 12(2) of Reg. 870/95. Note that the requirement of 'repetition' in the infringement does not exist in Art. 7(1) of Reg. 4056/86. See above, para. 4.2.8.1.

[248] Art. 12(3) of Reg. 870/95. Art. 12(4) specifies that withdrawal may take place, in particular, where the effects incompatible with Art. 85 and Art. 86 result from an arbitration award.

(2)   Article 85(1) of the Treaty will not be applicable to the period prior to the
       entry into force of the regulation when consortia which do not comply with
       the conditions of the regulation at the time of its entry into force are
       amended within the first six months of application of the regulation, and
       the amendments are notified to the Commission within that same period.[249]

Following Council Regulation 479/92, Regulation 870/95 has a limited duration of five years, in other words to 20 April 2000.[250] Like the first two versions
of Regulation 3976/87, Regulation 479/92 provided in its Article 2(1) for the
limited duration of the regulation granting substantive exemption. The
Commission, following the example of air transport, did not want to risk in 1990
asking the maritime authorities of the Member States for a delegation of powers
unlimited in time, on the lines of those of Regulations 19/65/EEC and
2821/71—something which in air transport it did not obtain until 1992[251]—and
wisely limited the duration of the delegation to five years. Before the end of that
period it will have to negotiate with the Council an amendment of the present
regulation or a new enabling regulation. Despite its limited duration, the substantive regulation will be reviewable by the Commission during its five years of
validity.[252]

---

[249] Art. 13, second and third parts of Reg. 870/95.
[250] Art. 13, first part of Reg. 870/95.
[251] See Reg. (EEC) 2411/92, OJ 1992 L 240, p. 19.
[252] Art. 2(2) of Reg. 479/92.

5

The Air Transport Sector

5.1. BACKGROUND

5.1.1. The regulation of international air transport and liberalization in the EC

International air transport has traditionally been regulated on the basis of the Convention on International Civil Aviation of 7 December 1944 ('the Chicago Convention'),[1] to which all EU Member States and most other countries in the world adhere. That Convention is predicated on the principle that every State has complete sovereignty over the airspace above its territory (Article 1). As a result no scheduled air services are allowed over or into the territory of a State unless that State has authorized those services (Article 6).

The International Air Transport Agreement[2] defines certain 'freedoms', i.e., activities which may be the subject of such authorization. The International Air Services Transit Agreement grants two of these freedoms which are essentially of a technical nature: the first freedom implies the right of overflight without landing, and the second freedom enables aircraft of Contracting States to make technical stops (e.g., for the purpose of refuelling) in the territory of other States. Of more commercial relevancy are the third, fourth and fifth freedoms, also referred to as 'traffic rights': the third freedom is the right to carry passengers and freight from the airline's home State to another State and the fourth freedom is the right to carry passengers and freight to the home State. The fifth freedom is the right to carry passengers and freight from one State to another, neither of which is the airline's home State, but normally as an extension of an air service which begins or ends in the home State. Subsequently other freedoms have been developed, such as the sixth freedom which is the linkage of a fourth with a third freedom service, thereby enabling airlines to carry passengers and freight from one State via their home State to a third state.

Third, fourth and (more rarely) fifth freedom traffic rights for international air services are negotiated on a bilateral basis between two States. The world is now spanned by a network of thousands of such bilateral Air Service Agreements.

---

[1] United Nations Treaty Series, 1948, 296.
[2] Both the International Air Transport Agreement and the International Air Services Transit Agreement were adopted at the same time as the Chicago Convention. Whereas the latter has been widely ratified, the former was not.

Typically those agreements enable each State to designate one airline which is substantially owned and controlled by its nationals, to operate third and fourth freedom air services to the other State. The airports served are usually exhaustively enumerated in the agreement; the addition of other airports would require renegotiation of the agreement. Bilateral Air Service Agreements often oblige the designated airlines to share their capacity in equal parts, to consult or even to agree on schedules and tariffs and to share revenues in proportion with the capacity mounted by each carrier.[3] In the typical case the airlines operating an air service between two States would agree for a particular season on the capacity each would offer on their schedules and on the fares to be charged and they would compensate the airline carrying fewer passengers or less freight by a revenue transfer. While there may be some justification for such a regime in cases where the two airlines involved operate under very different conditions, from a competition perspective it is characterized by regulatory barriers to entry to the market and by market-sharing and price-fixing.

In recent years some bilateral Air Service Agreements have provided for a less restrictive regime. More liberal agreements allow designation of several airlines on services between the two States or on individual routes, they enable the airlines to follow more competitive pricing strategies and they no longer discourage attempts to increase market share at the expense of the other airlines.

Inspired by the deregulation of air transport in the United States, the Commission has moved in the Community to apply the principles underlying the internal market and to develop a more liberal regime for the air transport sector pursuant to Article 84(2) of the EC Treaty. Regional airlines served as a precursor.[4]

Initial proposals[5] for a more ambitious programme, subsequently updated,[6] encountered considerable resistance from the major airlines and this was reflected by the position of most Member States in the Council. Nevertheless, a first 'civil aviation package'[7] for intra-Community scheduled air passenger transport entered into force on 1 January 1988. Its adoption by the Council was to a large extent prompted by action by the Commission under the competition

---

[3] Capacity and tariffs are usually subject to approval by the aeronautical authorities of both States concerned.

[4] Dir. 83/416 authorizing certain inter-regional air services between Member States, OJ 1983, L 237, as amended by Dir. 86/216, OJ 1986, L 152 and Dir. 89/463, OJ 1989, L 226; revoked by Art. 16 of Reg. 2343/90, OJ 1990, L 217.

[5] Contribution of the EC to the Development of Air Transport Services, Document COM(79) 311 final, *EC Bulletin* suppl. 5/79.

[6] Progress Toward the Development of a Community Air Transport Policy, Document COM(84) 72 final ('Second Memorandum'), and proposed legislation published in OJ 1984, C 182.

[7] Council Dir. 87/601 on fares for scheduled air services between Member States; Council Dec. 87/602 on the sharing of passenger capacity between air carriers on scheduled air services between Member States and on access for air carriers to scheduled air service routes between Member States, OJ 1987, L 374.

rules pursuant to Article 89 of the EC Treaty,[8] following on confirmation by the European Court, in the *Nouvelles Frontières* case,[9] that the competition rules applied to the air transport sector. The political consensus was helped by a promise by the Commission to grant, at least initially, generous block exemptions for agreements between airlines.

The rules embodied in the first package supplanted more restrictive rules in bilateral Air Service Agreements between Member States and marked the first step towards a more liberal regime. The first package enabled Member States to designate several of their airlines to operate certain air services, created some new traffic rights, relaxed the requirement to share capacity on a 50/50 basis and loosened regulatory supervision of tariffs. Liberalization of the sector in the Community was conceived of as a gradual process allowing industry sufficient time to prepare itself for the changed environment.

Some further progress was made by a second liberalization package[10]—still essentially in the form of more liberal bilateral regimes—and by rules on freight air services.[11] The establishment of a genuine internal market for air transport, comprising freedom of establishment and freedom to provide services, had to wait until a third liberalization package[12] which became effective on 1 January 1993. These rules entitle the nationals of a Member State which satisfy the conditions laid down in the package to establish an airline either in their own Member State or in another Member State. They remove capacity restrictions and create traffic rights on substantially all routes within the Community, subject *inter alia* to exceptions for some regional services and services governed by a public service obligation. Tariffs are essentially released from Member State supervision, subject only to ex-post control of very low or excessive tariffs. This liberalized regime opens up market access and sets airlines free to compete on intra-Community routes.

Community liberalization is not complete deregulation, in the sense that a residual amount of regulation continues to apply. Restrictions on the commercial freedom of airlines, however, have now been lifted to a very large extent and are not significantly more onerous than in many other industries. Considerable industry losses over the period 1990–93 led some observers to question whether liberalization had been an auspicious development. An in-depth review of the industry confirmed that liberalization is a key element of the effort to improve the competitiveness of European airlines: the single market

[8] Argyris, N., The EEC Rules of Competition and the Air Transport Sector, *Common Market Law Review*, 1989, 5, 8–11.

[9] Joined cases 209 to 213/84, *Ministère public* v. *Asjes and others*, [1986] ECR 1425.

[10] Council Regs 2342/90 on fares for scheduled air services and 2343/90 on access for air couriers to scheduled intra-Community air service routes and on the sharing of passenger capacity between air carriers on scheduled air services between Member States, OJ 1990, L 217.

[11] Council Reg. 294/91 on the operation of air cargo services between Member States, OJ 1991, L 36.

[12] Council Regs 2407/92 on licensing of air carriers, 2408/92 on access for air carriers to intra-Community air routes, and 2409/92 on fares and rates for air services, OJ 1992, L 240.

provides the necessary platform to face rivals on a global scale and competition is an indispensable stimulus for cost reduction.[13]

Even though air services within a single Member State had been excluded from the first and second liberalization packages, they are now included—subject to limitations on market access during a transitional period ending on 1 April 1997—in the third package.

The Community's liberalization policy has up to now excluded extra-Community air transport. During the early liberalization discussions, it was generally recognized that the specific features of routes to third countries required a different approach from the intra-Community area. Transport in that area is governed by bilateral Air Service Agreements with third countries which are not a party to the Community's policy-making process and which often do not share the objectives of liberalization. Nevertheless it is clear that such bilateral agreements between a Member State and a third country may conflict with Community law, in particular when they deny airlines from other Member States the opportunity to be designated to operate air services between the contracting States and when they encourage or require the conclusion of restrictive agreements between the airlines operating air services between the contracting States (e.g., agreements requiring the setting up of revenue pools or other forms of market-sharing, or requiring airlines to agree on tariffs).[14]

Under Article 234 of the EC Treaty, Member States are required to attempt to remove such inconsistencies with Community law from bilateral agreements with third countries. The Commission furthermore in 1992 made a proposal[15] asserting Community competence over air transport relations with third countries which would enable the negotiation of traffic rights for the Community as a whole. It expected that such an approach would facilitate the removal of provisions which are not compatible with Community law, reflect the external dimension of the internal market and enhance the Community's negotiating position. The proposal encountered substantial difficulties in Council. Following the more recent ruling by the Court of Justice[16] on the competence of the Community to agree the GATT, GATS and TRIPS agreements, in which the Court concluded that the Community and its Member States shared the competence to conclude international agreements on trade in services, Member States are probably even less enthusiastic to grant negotiating authority to the Community. The Commission's efforts now seek essentially to persuade Member States of the advantages of Community negotiations in terms of increased bargaining power *vis-à-vis* the major trading partners.

The Commission's efforts to develop an external air transport policy met with

---

[13] *Expanding Horizons*, A Report by the Comité des Sages for Air Transport to the European Commission, Jan. 1994, and the Commission's response in Document COM(94)218 final.

[14] Case 66/86, *Ahmed Saeed*, [1989] ECR 803 (recitals 47–49).

[15] Document COM(92)434 final, *Air Transport Relations with Third Countries*.

[16] Opinion 1/94, [1994] ECR I—5267.

some success in relation to its immediate neighbours. Norway and Sweden took over the *acquis communautaire* in respect of the second package and air cargo liberalization,[17] and subsequently in respect of the third package.[18] That agreement was superseded by the European Economic Area, which extended Community legislation to Norway, Sweden, Finland, Iceland, Austria and Liechtenstein[19] although on 1 January 1995 Sweden, Finland and Austria became full members of the EU, which left the scope of the European Economic Area rather limited.

5.1.2. Competition rules and air transport

In 1962, Council Regulation 141[20] removed the transport sector from the scope of Regulation 17[21] pending the formulation of a common transport policy. As a result, the Commission did not have in the air transport sector the extensive powers to investigate suspected infringements, to take binding measures to stop infringements, to impose penalties and to grant exemptions to valuable forms of co-operation which it enjoys in other sectors. Until the development of a common air transport policy, the Commission had to rely on its residual powers under Article 89 of the EC Treaty which did not permit effective enforcement of the competition rules. The adoption of the first package of air transport liberalization measures, in 1987, cleared the way for effective application of the competition rules. Enforcement of these rules by the Commission, following similar procedures to those under Regulation 17, was acknowledged to be an essential component of the liberalization packages: the creation of opportunities to compete under these rules would be useless if airlines could conclude restrictive agreements or abuse dominant positions in order to frustrate the effect of the liberalization measures. Therefore the first package included two regulations adopted pursuant to Article 87 of the EC Treaty.

Regulation 3975/87 laying down the procedure for the application of the rules on competition to undertakings in the air transport sector[22] grants the

---

[17] Agreement between the EEC, the Kingdom of Norway and the Kingdom of Sweden on Civil Aviation, OJ 1992, L 200. The Agreement entered into force on 6 July 1992, OJ 1993, L 105.

[18] The third liberalization package was incorporated into the Agreement by an amendment published in OJ 1993, L 212.

[19] Agreement on the EEA between the EC, their Member States, the Republic of Austria, the Republic of Finland, the Republic of Iceland, the Principality of Liechtenstein, the Kingdom of Norway, the Kingdom of Sweden and the Swiss Confederation, OJ 1994, L 1; the third package legislation was subsequently incorporated into the Agreement by two decisions of the EEA joint committee published in OJ 1994, L 85 and 160.

Switzerland subsequently decided not to join the EEA. An agreement similar to the earlier arrangement with Norway and Sweden is in the process of being negotiated—cf. Documents SEC (93) 1437, (94 (91) and (95) 344.

[20] OJ 124 of 18 Nov. 1962, p. 2753 (Spec. Ed. 1959–62, p. 291).

[21] OJ 13 of 21 Feb. 1962, p. 204 (Spec. Ed. 1959–62, p. 67).

[22] OJ 1987, L 374, as amended by Reg. 1284/91, OJ 1991, L 122 and by Reg. 2410/92, OJ 1992, L 240. *Corrigenda* in OJ 1988, L 30 and OJ 1989, L 43.

Commission powers similar in effect, if not in procedure, to those under Regulation 17 to carry out investigations, terminate infringements, and grant individual exemptions. Regulation 3976/87 on the application of Article 85 (3) of the Treaty to certain categories of agreements and concerted practices in the air transport sector[23] enables the Commission to issue block exemptions in respect of certain categories of agreements defined in the regulation.

The eventual adoption of block exemptions covering significant forms of co-operation between airlines, also in matters of commercial relevance, was perceived to be an essential component of the liberalization process. Even though the enabling regulation empowers but does not oblige the Commission to adopt block exemptions (Article 2 of Regulation 3976/87 refers to 'may' rather than 'shall'), the Commission in effect committed itself to do so in the first package. The Council also defined the contents of these block exemptions in considerable detail in the enabling regulation under the first and second packages (Article 2(2)), thereby reducing the Commission's discretion to define the most appropriate conditions itself. It is to be noted that, in contrast to the situation under the first and second liberalization packages, the enabling regulation under the third package no longer lists the conditions to be included in the block exemptions but simply defines the categories of agreements for which block exemptions may be issued. Regulation 3975/87 has been complemented by a procedural regulation, dealing mainly with the organisation of applications to the Commission and of hearings in competition procedures.[24] Regulations 3975/87 and 3976/87 are jointly referred to hereafter as the 'competition regulations'.

5.2. SCOPE OF THE REGULATIONS

5.2.1. Geographical scope

In line with the scope of the liberalization measures, the competition regulations were limited under the first and second packages to international air transport between Member States. Berlin was initially excluded from the scope of the regulations on account of a communication from the Government of the Federal Republic of Germany which was attached to the first and second liberalization packages and which drew the attention to the fact that the allied powers had reserved competence over civil aviation in the city. That reservation became moot as a result of the German unification and was not restated in the third liberalization package.

---

[23] OJ 1987, L 374, extended under the second package by Reg. 2344/90, OJ 1990, L 217, and under the third package by Reg. 2411/92, OJ 1992, L 240. *Corrigendum* in OJ 1993, L 79.

[24] Comm. Reg. 4261/88 on the complaints, applications and hearings provided for in Reg. (EEC) 3975/87 laying down the procedure for the application of the rules on competition to undertakings in the air transport sector, OJ 1988, L 376.

The inclusion of domestic air services under the third package warranted an extension of the scope of the competition regulations to air transport within a single Member State, so that they now apply to all air transport between Community airports.

Presumably 'airport' has the same meaning as under the market access regulation, i.e., an area which is open for commercial air transport operations. Transport which is not between airports (e.g., to private helicopter pads or balloon flights) may not be caught by the competition regulations.

Even though the Commission has the power to enforce the competition rules in respect of domestic services, restrictions on competition relating to those services will not always be caught by these rules, in particular because they will not necessarily have a significant effect on trade between Member States[25] and could consequently escape the application of Articles 85 and 86. The required effect on trade between Member States could nevertheless arise, for example, where practices confined to a single Member State aim to eliminate a competitor, whose disappearance would alter the structure of competition within the Community.[26] An effect on trade between Member States could also result from practices which divert traffic to a domestic air service and away from an international air service, or vice versa. These situations are likely to become more common as airlines start offering cabotage services in other Member States as part of their network. An effect on trade between Member States could further be found where the domestic air service affected by the restrictive practice is closely linked to air services to other Member States, e.g., because the flight in question continues to another Member State or because many passengers on the domestic air service transfer to international services.

Fifth freedom air services within the Community are caught by the competition regulations, even if they are operated by carriers registered in third countries. For the competition regulations to apply, it is not necessary that all carriers involved are actually in the business of providing air transport between Community airports; it is sufficient that the restrictive practice is implemented in the Community. As a result, actions to exclude a third country carrier from Community markets could be caught by the competition rules.

In the same way that the liberalization measures are limited to intra-Community transport, the competition regulations do not at present apply to air transport between the Community and a third country.[27] The Court of Justice has nevertheless confirmed that Articles 85 and 86 do apply in that situation, although the Commission cannot avail itself of its normal investigation and enforcement powers: action can only be taken by Member States' authorities

---

[25] It is to be noted that international flights between Member States always affect trade between Member States: Case 66/86, *Ahmed Saeed*, [1989] ECR 803 (recital 28).

[26] Cf., Cases 6 and 7/73, *Commercial Solvents*, 6 and 7/73, [1974] ECR 223, at 252–3.

[27] With the exception of Norway, Sweden and the other EFTA states which took over the competition regulations as part of the *acquis communautaire*—see above.

pursuant to Article 88 of the Treaty[28] or by the Commission pursuant to Article 89 of the Treaty.[29] Provided a prior decision has been taken under Articles 88 or 89 establishing the existence of an infringement of Article 85(1), national courts can hold an agreement to be void under Article 85(2). National courts, however, are empowered to apply Article 86 without prior decision under Articles 88 or 89.[30]

Following the Court's opinion in the 1989 *Ahmed Saeed* case, the Commission has proposed that air transport to third countries be included within the scope of Regulation 3975/87 and that the Commission be enabled to adopt block exemptions in that area.[31] That proposal would allow the Commission to give effective guidance on the application of Articles 85 and 86 in respect of air transport to third countries and to increase legal certainty for agreements with redeeming features by protecting them from the application of Article 85(1). In this manner, the risk of national courts holding certain common but acceptable restrictive agreements to be void, such as the worldwide IATA airport slot allocation exercises, or prohibiting as abusive tariffs applied by a dominant airline and discussed with other airlines[32] under circumstances where tariff consultations could be covered by a block exemption, would be reduced. The proposal would also enable the Commission to legitimize the actions of Member States' aeronautical authorities approving tariffs which result from consultations which now technically violate Article 85(1).[33] The Commission's proposal provides for consultations and negotiations with third countries in the event that a breach of Community competition law is the result of legislation or administrative action by a third country or of the provisions of the applicable bilateral Air Service Agreement. The progress of the Commission's proposal in the Council appears to depend on the result of discussions on external policy in relation to air services.

---

[28] It is to be noted that most Member States have not designated authorities with the competence to apply Art. 88 in the air transport sector.

[29] Under that provision the Commission can record an infringement (which may assist in the case of litigation before national courts) but cannot order its termination or impose penalties. For the considerations underlying the use of Art. 89 in respect of various third countries, see B. Van Houtte, Competition Aspects, in: H. A. Wassenbergh (ed.), *External Aviation Relations of the European Community*, (Deventer-Boston, 1992).

[30] Case 66/86, *Ahmed Saeed*, [1989] ECR 803 (recitals 19–33).

[31] Document COM(89)417 final, OJ 1989, C 248, as amended by COM(91)183 final, OJ 1991, C 153. That proposal initially also provided for applicability of Regs 3975/87 and 3976/87 to cabotage air services. That aspect of the proposal has become moot as a result of its inclusion in the third liberalization package.

[32] *Ahmed Saeed* (above n. 30), (recital 44).

[33] In its *Ahmed Saeed* judgment (above n. 30, recital 49), the Court held that the approval by the aeronautical authorities of tariff agreements contrary to Art. 85(1) is not compatible with Community law and in particular with Art. 5 of the EEC Treaty. The Court also pointed out that aeronautical authorities must refrain from taking any measure which might be construed as encouraging airlines to conclude tariff agreements contrary to the Treaty.

5.2.2. Substantive scope

Regulations 3975/87 and 3976/87 apply to all forms of air transport, including the carriage of passengers and freight by both scheduled and charter services. Air transport which is incidental to another activity (for example, aerial publicity or photography)[34] is probably subsumed under that other activity and is therefore caught by Regulation 17. The competition regulations do not apply to multi-modal air/land transport operations as a whole; overland sectors are subject to Regulation 1017/68 and the air sector is subject to the competition regulations applicable to the air transport sector.[35]

The Commission has traditionally adhered to a very narrow construction of the exclusion of transport from the scope of Regulation 17, which was brought about by Regulation 141/62.[36] Agreements and practices which do not directly relate to the provision of transport services continue to be covered by Regulation 17. Since Regulation 3975/87 essentially seeks to close the gap created by Regulation 141,[37] it does not apply to agreements and practices which are ancillary to air transport. Consequently, the Commission examined practices relating to ground handling services[38] and computer reservation systems[39] on the basis of Regulation 17 rather than Regulation 3975/87. Regulation 3976/87 is of a more hybrid nature and enables the Commission to adopt block exemptions in respect of agreements which relate directly to air transport as well as some agreements covering ancillary activities.[40] Agreements and practices which relate to the marketing rather than to the provision of transport services also fall outside the scope of Regulation 141/62 and hence continue to be caught by Regulation 17. The Commission took the view that restrictions in the market for agency services are caught by Regulation 17 rather than by Regulation 3975/87, even though the agent acts on behalf of an air carrier.[41] As a result, the Commission was able to examine restrictions relating to agency services in respect of air services to third countries. Likewise, marketing practices such as frequent flier programmes and override commissions should arguably be examined under Regulation 17 rather than under Regulation 3975/87. Finally, agreements and practices which relate to the demand for transport services rather than to their provision are caught by Regulation 17. That conclusion would apply, for example, to abuses of a dominant position on the demand side.

---

[34] The situation is unclear for air mail. Even though air transport is incidental to the delivery of letters, air mail is listed in (f) of the Annex to Reg. 3975/87.

[35] Decision DHL, OJ 1990, C 258.   [36] See above, notes 20–1.

[37] As reflected in the second 'whereas' clause of Reg. 3975/87.

[38] Decision *Olympic Airways*, OJ 1975, L 46.

[39] Decision *London European-Sabena*, OJ 1988, L 317, with extensive justification of the applicability of Reg. 3975/87.

[40] In Document COM(86)328 final, the Commission had maintained a clear separation between air transport properly speaking and ancillary activities, the latter to be included in Council Reg. 2821/71. The Council did not maintain that distinction.

[41] Decisions *IATA Passenger and Cargo Agency Conferences*, OJ 1991, L 258.

A recent ruling by the Court of First Instance on the applicability of Regulation 1017/68 on inland transport[42] puts into question whether the narrow construction of Regulation 141 adhered to by the Commission is justified. Since the judgment in question relies heavily on the wording of the inland transport regulation, which is materially different from the air transport regulation, the question is still open.[43]

5.3. THE COMPETITION RULES IN THE LIBERALIZATION PROCESS

Articles 85 and 86 and the merger regulation apply to the air transport sector with the same effect as they do to other industries. Therefore the concepts of restriction of competition, abuse of a dominant position and effect on trade between Member States are employed in the same manner as in other sectors. In view of the recent introduction of competition law enforcement, of the highly regulated nature of the industry[44] and of the interplay with the gradual liberalization of the industry, however, it was appropriate to clarify the operation of competition rules in the air transport sector and to adopt, somewhat unusually in the area of competition law, industry-specific legislation. It can be expected that, as the effects of liberalization become more concrete, the need for this industry-specific legislation will be reduced.

Effective application of the competition rules in the air transport is not merely an objective in itself. Competition policy is particularly important in order to support the liberalization process[45] when the latter is understood as the relaxation of controls over industry so that airlines are set free to compete. Effective application of the competition rules is required to prevent companies from obstructing the progress of liberalization. Market participants must not be allowed to conclude agreements on prices rather than avail themselves of the opportunity to pursue independent pricing strategies; they must not deny new entrants the market access opportunities created by the liberalization process, for example, by agreeing to exclude newcomers from essential infrastructures such as airports or computer reservation systems, or by targeting newcomers by means of abusive business practices such as predatory fares.

The maintenance of a competitive market structure was acknowledged to require particularly effective intervention by the Commission. Therefore

---

[42] Judgment of 6 June 1995 in case T–14/93, *Union internationale des chemins de fer* v. *Commission*, not yet published.

[43] See discussion above, Ch. 3.

[44] The high degree of regulation affects the possibility for airlines to react rapidly and autonomously to crisis events. This prompted the Commission to address a Communication to Member States on measures, also under the EEC competition rules, which had to be taken to support the air transport industry at the time of the Gulf war. Document C(91)422 final, *21st Report on Competition Policy*, 1991, para. 40.

[45] *20th Report on Competition Policy*, 1990, para. 69 and *21st Report*, 1991, para. 40.

Regulation 3975/87 has been amended to enable the Commission to take interim measures when it has clear *prima facie* evidence that certain practices are contrary to Article 85 or 86 and have the object or effect of directly jeopardizing the existence of an air service,[46] and where recourse to normal procedures may not be sufficient to protect the airline or air service concerned.[47] Interim measures can consist of an order not to implement the practices at issue and may include such other instructions as are necessary to prevent certain practices until a substantive decision on the alleged infringement is taken.

The interim decision may initially apply for a period not exceeding six months. That initial decision can be taken on the basis of an informal consultation of the Advisory Committee on Agreements and Dominant Positions in Air Transport: Article 8(5) of Regulation 3975/87 is disapplied, which implies that the Advisory Committee need not meet physically, or if it meets that it need not be convened with fourteen days' notice[48] and that the Commission does not need to report to it in writing (eliminating the need for attendant translations). As a result, the time required for adoption of an interim decision is considerably reduced. The Commission may renew the initial decision, with or without modification, for periods not exceeding three months; in such case the Commission reverts to the normal Advisory Committee procedure. Interim decisions cannot give rise to a fine but they may impose periodic penalty payments to compel compliance.[49] Also in order to streamline interim measures procedures, the Commission has been considering an amendment to the hearing regulation 4261/88[50] to accelerate the conduct of hearings in urgent cases but the regulation has not yet been modified.

5.4. AGREEMENTS WHICH DO NOT NORMALLY RESTRICT COMPETITION

5.4.1. Regulation 3975/87 Annex list

Certain agreements are deemed not to have an appreciable impact on the competitive behaviour of the parties in the market because they relate to technical co-operation which is remote from the market.[51] Such agreements escape the application of Article 85(1). Article 3 of Regulation 3975/87 reflects this posi-

[46] In Document COM(90)167 final, the Commission contemplated in particular predatory fares, excessive capacity or frequency, frequent flier programmes and override commissions as practices which could give rise to interim measures when they have the required object or effect on competition.

[47] New Art. 4a of Reg. 3975/87, as inserted by Council Reg. (EEC) 1284/91, OJ 1991, L 122.

[48] The Commission nevertheless undertook to convene the Advisory Committee with at least 48 hours notice and to make a detailed oral presentation of draft decisions to the Committee.

[49] Art. 13(1)(e) of Reg. 3975/87 as amended by Reg. 1284/91, above n. 47.

[50] Comm. Reg. 4261/88, OJ 1988, L 376.

[51] Cf., Comm. Notice about co-operation between enterprises, OJ 1968, C 75, *corrigendum* OJ 1968, C 84.

tion and confirms that Article 85(1) does not apply to agreements to the extent that their sole object and effect is to achieve technical improvements or co-operation. The Annex to the Regulation lists—non-exhaustively—the following common agreements :

(a) The introduction or uniform application of mandatory or recommended technical standards for aircraft, aircraft parts, equipment and aircraft supplies, where such standards are set by an organisation normally accorded international recognition, or by an aircraft or equipment manufacturer;
(b) the introduction or uniform application of technical standards for fixed installations for aircraft, where such standards are set by an organisation normally accorded international recognition;
(c) the exchange, leasing, pooling, or maintenance of aircraft, aircraft parts, equipment or fixed installations for the purpose of operating air services and the joint purchase of aircraft parts, provided that such arrangements are made on a non-discriminatory basis;
(d) the introduction, operation and maintenance of technical communication networks, provided that such arrangements are made on a non-discriminatory basis;
(e) the exchange, pooling or training of personnel for technical or operational purposes;
(f) the organisation and execution of substitute transport operations for passengers, mail and baggage, in the event of breakdown/delay of aircraft, either under charter or by provision of substitute aircraft under contractual arrangements;
(g) the organisation and execution of successive or supplementary air transport operations, and the fixing and application of inclusive rates and conditions for such operations;
(h) the consolidation of individual consignments;
(i) the establishment or application of uniform rules concerning the structure and the conditions governing the application of transport tariffs, provided that such rules do not directly or indirectly fix transport fares and conditions;
(j) arrangements as to the sale, endorsement and acceptance of tickets between air carriers (interlining) as well as the refund, pro-rating and accounting schemes established for such purposes;
(k) the clearing and settling of accounts between air carriers by means of a clearing house, including such services as may be necessary or incidental thereto; the clearing and settling of accounts between air carriers and their appointed agents by means of a centralised and automated settlement plan or system, including such services as may be necessary or incidental thereto.

Caution is required as certain of these agreements are liable, in some circumstances, to affect the parties' competitive behaviour in the market. The joint fixing of inclusive rates for successive air transport operations (item (g), which closely corresponds to a similar exception in Article 3 of Regulation 4056/86 applicable to maritime transport) would indeed fall outside the scope of Article 85(1) where the participants are individually unable to offer carriage over the entire journey; their co-operation could then more properly be understood to imply a subcontracting relationship, whereby one party issues the ticket or airway bill and holds itself out as the main contracting party. If that is not the case and they are actual or potential competitors, the co-operation would become commercially relevant and could no longer be considered to have as its sole effect the achievement of technical improvements.

Likewise, the establishment of uniform conditions governing the application of transport tariffs (item(i)) could also exceed the sole achievement of technical improvements, not only where they directly or indirectly fix fares and conditions, but also where they would, for example, have the effect of making tariffs unavailable to certain users or of discriminating between users.

Item (j) refers to the operation of the interline system which in itself is not considered to be restrictive of competition. Some concern might be warranted if the interline system encouraged excessive reliance on co-operation with competitors and prevented any change in the respective market position of participants.[52] However, interline arrangements in the airline industry are not normally linked with obligations to rely on a competitor's capacity or to refrain from introducing additional capacity. In so far as the interline system enables airlines to offer their customers access to each others' networks and frequencies, it may be regarded as a pro-competitive instrument. However, the tariff coordination process which is not a necessary component of the interline system but traditionally operates in conjunction with that system, does restrict competition and has been allowed only under the conditions set out in a specific block exemption.[52a]

5.4.2. Code-sharing agreements

Code-sharing occurs where airlines agree to use a joint airline designator code (for example, SR/SK) for flights operated by one of them. The code-sharing enables both participants to hold out the flights as their own. That common commercial practice may have implications under legislation on unfair commercial practices, on market access or on computer reservation systems[53] but it does not necessarily in itself raise concerns under the EC competition rules. The situation could be different if, by ancillary agreement, the airlines restrict their commercial freedom with respect to schedules, fares, or capacity or agree to share revenue and/or costs for the code-shared service. In that situation, the appraisal under the competition rules would focus on these aspects of the co-operation, according to the rules set out below.

5.4.3. Blocked space agreements

Blocked space agreements essentially amount to the sale by one airline of a part of its capacity on a given air service to another airline. That other airline then

---

[52] Cf., Comm. Dec. *Rolled zinc products and zinc alloys*, OJ 1982, L 362.

[52a] See below para. 5.5.5.

[53] Council Reg. 2299/89 on a code of conduct for computerized reservation systems, OJ 1989, L 220, as amended by Reg. 3089/93, OJ 1993, L 278, requires code-sharing flights to be clearly identified and to be treated as connecting flights.

has a number of seats available for resale in its own name on the first airline's flights, and can identify that capacity as its own by giving it a proper flight number with its own airline designator code. The airline which books the blocked space would normally carry the risk of the inventory, i.e., it has to pay the first airline even if it does not sell the seats.

Blocked space agreements in themselves do not necessarily have an appreciable effect on competition.[54] However, where the blocked space agreement does have an effect on the competitive behaviour of the parties, Article 85(1) would be relevant. That conclusion would apply in particular where the airline buying the blocked space is, in fact or in law, prevented from concluding similar agreements with other airlines or from operating the air service at issue itself. Such may be the case, for example, in the presence of an exclusivity provision, possibly also in the case of an agreement for an unusually long duration or in the case of a reciprocal blocked space agreement, where the parties would be at risk of upsetting their relationship if they start independent operations. An effect on the parties' competitive behaviour is also more likely where they are not exposed to other airlines operating the service in question. Certain ancillary agreements could also bring the transaction under Article 85(1), for example, where the two airlines co-ordinate prices or where they are restricted as to the territories in which they can sell their share of capacity. Finally, where the airline which books the blocked space does not really carry the risk of inventory, for example, because of a provision for buy-back by the carrying airline of unsold seats, it is closer to a joint operation and restricts competition for the reasons set out in the following paragraph.

5.5. AGREEMENTS WHICH RESTRICT COMPETITION

5.5.1. Joint operations

As a variation on blocked space agreements, airlines may agree to share the risks and rewards of air services by means of joint operations. Those arrangements consist in the operation, by one airline, of an air service whereby another airline shares in both the costs and risks of that service. The second airline does not normally operate the service in competition with the first airline[55] but reimburses part of the operating costs and correspondingly receives part of the

---

[54] Blocked space agreements are akin to supply or original equipment manufacturer (O.E.M.) contracts which are common to most industries; where these agreements do not contain restrictions preventing the purchaser from acquiring the goods from anyone else or from producing them himself, and where they do not contain restrictions on the resale or use of the goods, they do not normally violate Art. 85(1).

[55] Although it is normally not precluded from doing so, the second airline usually does not operate independent services in competition with the joint operation. Tariffs are normally set in agreement by the partner airlines.

revenue of that service. Joint operations are often identified by a joint airline designator code. The non-operating airline can market the service under its own code.

A series of such agreements was notified to the Commission[56] which took the view that they do not amount to a form of concentration[57] because they are limited in scope to co-operation in respect of one or a few individual air services rather than constituting an independent economic entity and because they are limited in time to relatively short periods and do not necessarily imply the permanent withdrawal of the non-operating airline from the air service at issue.[58]

Even where the participating airlines are not precluded by agreement from competing with each other, the sharing of costs and revenues creates a powerful disincentive—normally stronger than in the case of code-sharing or blocked space agreements—to operate and market the service concerned independently of each other. In that sense, joint operations are considerably more restrictive than looser forms of co-operation such as code sharing or blocked space agreements. The Commission nevertheless takes a favourable view under Article 85(3) of some of these agreements, in particular when the air service is operated by a small airline which is based at one end of the route but has no effective marketing presence at the other end. The second airline is established at the other end of the route and helps to market the service in the catchment area of that airport. The air service concerned typically is a new one, whose operation carries considerable risk, and is of such low density that the second airline is reluctant to plan individual operations. In those circumstances, the Commission authorized a few agreements[59] for a limited time—normally three years—after which the air service is expected to have developed sufficiently to sustain two competing airlines. In other circumstances the Commission would require the participating airlines to envisage individual operations or to organize less restrictive arrangements, such as blocked space agreements.

On the basis of that experience the Commission has adopted a block exemp-

---

[56] Air France–Air Inter, OJ 1989, C 190 (*exploitation croisée*); Air France–NFD (Nürnberg/Paris, München–Lyon, München–Marseille); Air France–Iberia (Paris/Bilbao and Santiago de Compostela); Air France–Alitialia (Paris/Milano, Paris/Turin); Air France–Brymon (Paris/London City Airport); Air France–Sabena (Brussels/Paris, Bordeaux, Toulouse, Lyon, Marseille); Aer Lingus–Sabena (Dublin/Brussels); London City Airways–Sabena (London City Airport/Brussels), all published in OJ 1989, C 204; British Midland–Sabena (Birmingham/Brussels), OJ 1990, C 29; Aer Lingus–Lufthansa (Dublin/Manchester and Birmingham/Frankfurt), OJ 1990, C 108; Maersk–Lufthansa (Copenhagen/Köln), OJ 1991, C 124; Maersk–Sabena (Brussels/Billund), OJ 1991, C 235.

[57] Although joint operations are often improperly called 'joint ventures', they are in reality a form of specialization agreement akin to manufacturing arrangements which benefit from a block exemption under conditions set out in Comm. Reg. 417/87, OJ 1987, L 53, as amended by Comm. Reg. 151/93, OJ 1993, L 21.

[58] Cf., Comm. Notice regarding concentrative and co-operative operations under the merger control regulation, OJ 1994, C 385.

[59] Air France–NFD, Air France–Brymon, London City Airways–Sabena, Lufthansa–Maersk, Sabena–Maersk, above n. 56.

tion for joint operations.[60] In accordance with the terms of the Council's enabling regulation[61] the block exemption is limited to routes which were not previously operated by the parties or by other airlines and to low-density routes (capacity below 30,000 seats per year in each direction, or below 60,000 on longer distances). The block exemption only covers the situation where the sharing of costs and revenues is necessary to provide the operating airline with financial and marketing support. That dual justification is reflected in two requirements: the operating airline must not yet be offering a significant capacity at one of the airports involved (90,000 seats per year, which implies that it does not have an adequate presence on the market in the catchment area of that airport) and the operating airline must be relatively small (Community turnover not in excess of 400m ECU, which implies that it is less likely to take the risk of developing a new service independently).

The block exemption limits the restrictive effects of the joint operation to a minimum: the agreement must not prevent the parties from operating additional services on their own account nor from independently determining the fares, capacity, and schedules of those additional services. Either party must be able to terminate the joint operation at reasonably short notice and in any event the duration of the joint operation must not exceed three years—after which it is hoped that the route is sufficiently developed to sustain independent and competitive services. Obviously the Commission maintains the possibility of exempting on an individual basis joint operations which do not fit the conditions set out in the block exemption. Likewise, where a plausible argument is made for extension of the joint operation beyond the duration foreseen in the block exemption, approval on an individual basis will be possible.

Where in particular circumstances the joint operation would not be exposed to effective competition by other airlines operating to the same or nearby airports or by other modes of transport, the Commission in accordance with Article 7 of Regulation 3976/87 retains the possibility to withdraw the benefit of the block exemption.

5.5.2. Revenue pool agreements

Of more historical interest, at least in so far as intra-Community transport is concerned, is co-operation in respect of an air service by means of a revenue pool. Those arrangements are more common in situations where airline capacities are constrained by regulatory ceilings. In the typical case they amounted to a transfer by one airline of part of its revenue in respect of an air service to another airline as compensation for not competing in respect of that air service or for allowing the first airline to exceed its share of capacity. Even in the absence of capacity constraints a revenue pool could be an anti-competitive

---

[60] Art. 3 of Comm. Reg. 1617/93, OJ 1993, L 155.
[61] Council Reg. 2411/92, OJ 1992, L 240; *corrigendum* published in OJ 1993, L 79.

device designed to deprive the more competitive carrier of the additional profits it has earned by attracting a greater number of passengers to its flights. In
such a case the incentive to compete with the other airline would be considerably reduced.

The first liberalization package, during the period of which there were still
significant capacity constraints within the Community, included a block exemption[62] for revenue pools subject to strict conditions requiring the transfer of revenue to be made in compensation for the loss incurred by the receiving parties
in scheduling flights at less busy times of the day or during less busy periods.
Stringent rules on the direction and the amount of the transfer of revenue made
revenue pools unattractive for intra-Community transport, and the block exemption was not renewed during the second package.

5.5.3. Co-ordination of schedules

The objective of ensuring a satisfactory supply of services at less busy times of
the day, during less busy periods or on less busy routes can be attained without
financial compensation by (bilateral) co-ordination of schedules. This exercise
enables airlines to complement each others' schedules in order to offer users a
choice of frequencies throughout the day or the week at convenient times or in
order to facilitate interline connections.

In recognition of this consumer benefit a block exemption[63] applies to the
joint planning and co-ordination of schedules. The conditions imposed by the
block exemption essentially seek to preserve the airlines' freedom of individual
action. Schedule co-ordination with a view to ensuring service at less busy times
must not be binding; however, parties can agree to a binding arrangement on
schedules to facilitate interline connections, so that passengers can be guaranteed easy and rapid transfers. The co-ordination must not prevent participants
from introducing additional capacity or frequencies; however, in the framework
of schedule co-ordination to facilitate interline connections an agreement on
minimum capacity is authorized so that the interline partner can rely on a certain volume of feeder traffic. Participants are not allowed to share capacity under
this provision of the block exemption.[64] The schedule co-ordination must not
prevent participants from changing their planned capacity or influence the
schedules adopted by carriers not participating in the co-ordination. The parties
must be able to withdraw from the co-ordination by giving three months' notice.

---

[62] Art. 3 of Comm. Reg. 2671/88, OJ 1988, L 239.
[63] Art. 2 of Comm. Reg. 1617/93, OJ 1993, L 155.
[64] This condition implies that the air services for which the schedules are co-ordinated must not
be operated jointly or under blocked space or code-sharing arrangements.

5.5.4. Airport scheduling and slot allocation

Airlines also co-ordinate their schedules in the larger context of (industry-wide) airport scheduling and slot allocation. This exercise is based on twice-yearly meetings organized by the International Air Transport Association, during which airlines worldwide[65] co-ordinate their schedules in such a manner as to have airport slots (i.e., a reserved time during which their aircraft can use an airport's infrastructure, such as runways and gates) available at appropriate times for departure and arrival of their services. As a function of the airlines' tentative schedules, airport slots are allocated. As a result the demand for airport capacity is co-ordinated so as to avoid conflicting use of infrastructure.

Co-ordination is in practice rather flexible and relies on mutual good faith, so that in most cases reasonable demand for airport slots can be satisfied. The system works best, however, when all airlines have an equal stake: at the time when all participating airlines had a strong influence over the allocation of slots at their home base, the slot allocation exercise was unlikely to leave any significant participants strongly dissatisfied. Now that there are more 'new entrant' airlines which cannot rely on a strong position at their home base in order to reciprocate possible unfavourable treatment at other airports, it becomes more difficult to ensure a satisfactory outcome of the allocation process. More fundamentally, the system is under considerable pressure because airport capacity is difficult to expand. Increasingly the lack of airport slots, in particular at the busiest airports but also elsewhere at the most attractive times of the day, operates as a barrier to entry. At several of the major airports in the Community it is practically impossible for new entrants to offer air services at peak times, and at some of the most congested airports new entrants even find it difficult to offer anything other than a less than optimal schedule.

Since airport scheduling and slot allocation rely on agreement between airlines[66] and reduce access to essential infrastructures, to the possible disadvantage of competitors, they restrict competition. IATA guidelines which govern the scheduling process include certain rules on priorities for the allocation of slots which favour some airlines or categories of airlines over others. Most controversial of these rules is the absolute priority given to 'historical precedence' (also denoted as 'grandfather right'): an airline using a particular slot during a season

---

[65] The necessity to organize airport scheduling as a single exercise on a worldwide basis, which cannot be split up into separate regional scheduling exercises, effectively illustrates the practical difficulties raised by the limitation of the Commission's enforcement powers to intra-Community air transport. As a result, the Commission is not able to grant a block exemption to slot allocation and airport scheduling in so far as that activity relates to air transport between the Community and third countries.

[66] Historically IATA airport scheduling was driven by airline demand rather than by airport supply. As a result the rules under which airport capacity is allocated to airlines have been defined by the airlines themselves rather than by the suppliers of that capacity. In some countries public authorities supervised this process but it was in almost all Member States administered by the air transport industry.

is entitled to continue using it during future corresponding seasons; it may change the type of service, type of aircraft, even the destination and still enjoy the right to use the slot to the exclusion of other interested airlines. While historical precedence maintains the stability of the established airlines' networks and schedules, it undeniably makes it more difficult for new entrants to start competing services.

Nevertheless, the existing airport scheduling and slot allocation system is acknowledged worldwide as an efficient means to accomplish an extremely complex task. Even though alternatives exist (auctioning the right to use slots during a certain period, allowing airlines to own and trade slots, administrative allocation)[67] these have not been extensively tested in an international environment and may not be demonstrably superior to the existing system. The merits of an allocation system based on grandfather rights have been recognized in Council Regulation 95/93 on common rules for the allocation of slots at Community airports.[68] However, that regulation also attempts to create additional opportunities for new entrants by increased transparency and tighter organization of allocation procedures. Special safeguards are introduced to ensure neutrality and non-discrimination in that process. New entrants should also benefit from priority to obtain slots which become available, *inter alia* through a rule obliging incumbent air carriers to give up slots which they do not use sufficiently. The Commission will report on the effectiveness of these rules as instruments to maintain adequate opportunities for access to congested airports.

The common rules in the recent Council Regulation were preceded and are still mirrored by largely parallel requirements set out in a block exemption. While the block exemption has lost much of its significance as a result of the adoption of common rules in the Council regulation, it still serves a dual role. First of all, the block exemption applies to non-co-ordinated airports on which the Council rules do not impose substantive obligations. However, these airports are also uncongested, so that slot allocation is unlikely to give rise to problems. Second, the Council rules leave some scope for industry-wide (IATA) and local (guidelines reflecting local conditions) rules defined by the airlines which complement the rules set out in the Council Regulation. Those complementary rules must respect the conditions laid down in the block exemption.

In addition, it should be borne in mind that the Council Regulation (as secondary legislation) is without prejudice to the competition rules in the EC Treaty, as witnessed by the recitals to the regulation. Consequently, the application of the Council rules cannot lead to a result which would be inconsistent with the competition rules. Since the rule of historical precedence in the Council Regulation merely echoes the (identical and pre-existing) industry rule in the IATA guidelines, it would appear that the Council Regulation cannot confirm

[67] For a comprehensive study of alternative slot allocation systems carried out for the Commission, see Scicon, S. D. *Study on Airport Slot Allocation*, (London, 1991).

[68] OJ 1993, L 14.

grandfather rights in a situation where these would not benefit from an exemption under Article 85(3). It is questionable, therefore, whether the Council Regulation is effective in protecting historical rights at an airport where effective competition is severely jeopardized.

The block exemption[69] imposes a number of conditions with a view to increasing the transparency of the IATA-sponsored airport scheduling and slot allocation mechanism, removing elements of discrimination and facilitating access for new entrants to congested airports. These conditions are closely aligned to the conditions set forth in the Council Regulation. The consultations must be open to all interested airlines. The Commission and the Member States concerned must be invited to attend the consultations.[70] The airlines attending the consultations must have access to precise information on the existing situation, on outstanding requests for slots, on slots available and on the allocation criteria. The allocation criteria must not discriminate on the basis of nationality, identity, or mode of operation of the carrier. The allocation may defer to historical precedence; however, new entrants must be entitled to 50 per cent of new or unused slots.

The existence of a Council regulation based on the transport provisions of the EC Treaty does not prevent the withdrawal of the block exemption, pursuant to Article 7 of Regulation 3976/87, in cases where the airport scheduling and slot allocation process has effects which are incompatible with Article 85(3), in particular where an airport is so congested that historical precedence leads to the elimination of competition. The block exemption[71] provides that withdrawal may take place where the conditions attached to the block exemption have not been sufficient to enable new entrants to obtain such slots as may be required at a congested airport in order to establish schedules which enable these carriers to compete effectively with incumbent carriers on any route to and from that airport and competition on those routes is thereby substantially impaired.[72] In such cases the withdrawal of the block exemption relates only to the congested airport in question.

To date, few complaints under this provision have been filed, although no doubt the mere existence of the possibility of withdrawal induces airlines to avoid situations of severe conflict. The improvement of slot allocation procedures as a result of the common rules laid down by the Council are likely to strengthen opportunities for new entrants; and the Council Regulation itself is

---

[69] Art. 5 of Comm. Reg. 1617/93, OJ 1993, L 155.

[70] Comm. notice published in OJ 1993, C 177.

[71] Art. 6(iii) of Comm. Reg. 1617/93, OJ 1993, L 155.

[72] The precise nature of residual competition which obviates recourse to the withdrawal procedure is not defined in the regulation. No doubt the Commission would take into account the number of competitors; the definition of 'new entrant' in the Council rules suggests that the Commission would expect the new entrant to face at least two competitors operating direct services. Other relevant factors would include the intensity of competition and the existence of competition by indirect air services or by other modes of transport.

currently undergoing review. If those changes do not prove to be sufficient to safeguard competition at congested airports, the question arises whether the block exemption can be maintained in the long term.

5.5.5. Tariff co-ordination agreements and interlining

Airlines co-ordinate tariffs at regular meetings involving either all operators in certain regions (multilateral meetings organized by IATA at the level of, for example, Europe) or active on a route or set of routes (so-called bilateral meetings, for example, covering all airlines operating between Germany and the U.K.).

The detrimental effects of tariff co-ordination on price competition are unmistakable. In particular for fully flexible tariffs and on routes where the competition from indirect air transport or from other modes of transport is less intense, the existence of tariff co-ordination is liable to lead to prices being set at a compromise level which is higher than it needs to be for low-cost airlines. Price leadership can be discouraged. In situations where the industry wants to raise the general price level, tariff co-ordination provides a forum to launch and steer a trend towards price increases. Tariff co-ordination also leads to a more homogeneous tariff structure, in which all airlines offer comparable products. Consultations on tariffs also help airlines to maintain artificial relationships between tariffs on routes to nearby points and between tariffs on direct and indirect services. Finally, tariff co-ordination facilitates the maintenance of cross-subsidies between business and leisure fares and between feeder and long-haul services which might not withstand the pressure of more intense price competition.

Nevertheless, tariff co-ordination is an established industry practice which in many cases used to be warranted by the regulatory authorities' insistence that airlines only submit tariffs for approval which had been the subject of consultation or even agreement. Within the Community, the first liberalization package did not require tariff co-ordination but it obliged airlines to file tariffs and provided that such filings could be made either individually or jointly following consultations.[73] Tariff consultations were authorized under the competition rules for the purpose of preparing joint fare filings and subject essentially to requirements of a procedural nature.[74] However, it was already made clear at the time that tariff co-ordination within the Community was justified essentially because of its putative beneficial effects on interlining.[75]

[73] Art. 4(1) of Council Dir. 87/601 on fares for scheduled air services between Member States, OJ 1987, L 374.

[74] Art. 4 of Comm. Reg. 2671/88, OJ 1988, L 239.

[75] Fifth whereas clause, see n. 68, p. 12. 'Interlining' denotes a form of co-operation between airlines whereby one airline can issue a ticket comprising sectors on which another airline has to effect carriage. The result is that users can purchase a single ticket comprising carriage by different airlines. Often the fare for the overall journey is lower than the sum of fares for the different sectors. Usually interlining is combined with the possibility to change reservations from one airline to another. For a comprehensive description of the interlining system, see Comm. Dec. *British Midland v. Aer Lingus*, OJ 1992, L 96/34–35.

Tariff co-ordination appears to facilitate interlining in two ways. First, tariff consultations enable airlines to fix their tariffs at the same level. That simplifies administrative procedures for the interchangeability of tickets. Second, participants in tariff consultations gain insight into the tariff structure of other airlines. This insight enables them to be confident that other airlines' tariffs are sufficiently high for their own share of constructed joint fares to be profitable. As a result airlines do not need to negotiate agreements with each potential interline partner about each joint fare to be offered. Their confidence in the worldwide tariff structure enables airlines to subscribe to a multilateral interline agreement, i.e. they give other airlines the general authority to issue tickets on their behalf and to include their services in joint fares, without having to negotiate their share of joint fares in advance. While both reasons certainly facilitate interlining, they are not indispensable for some form of interlining to continue.

While the restriction of price competition which is the result of tariff co-ordination is caught by Article 85(1), the Commission has been receptive to the benefits arising from interlining. Passengers can buy a single ticket providing for transportation by different carriers, for example, leaving on the issuing airline and returning on another airline serving the same route, or leaving on the issuing airline and continuing to destinations not served by that airline; airlines can complement their networks and frequencies, which is of particular value to smaller airlines or airlines based in peripheral locations. The relaxation of price controls within the Community and the corresponding increase in the scope for price competition reduced the negative effects of tariff co-ordination. On the other hand, the possibility for smaller and peripheral airlines to have access to other airlines' networks and frequencies improves their competitive position. As a result, tariff consultations continued to be allowed after the first package, but the justification shifted from the need to prepare joint tariff filings to the need to promote interlining relationships.

In order to enhance the justification of tariff co-ordination under Article 85(3), the possibility to interline was made mandatory for the approval of consultations on public passenger and cargo tariffs for scheduled air services under the competition rules in the second liberalization package.[76] It should be noted that the Commission is presently considering whether to remove the benefit of the block exemption for cargo rates and to maintain the exemption only for passenger tariffs.[77]

Currently[78] tariff consultations are allowed on the condition that all attendants—even if they do not actively participate in the discussions—accept to interline with all other carriers operating routes which are the subject of the co-ordination. The duty to interline means that participants must allow other airlines to issue a single ticket including carriage over their own routes; the

---

[76] Art. 3(1)(b) of Comm. Reg. 84/91, OJ 1991, L 10.
[77] Notice published in OJ 1995, C 322.
[78] Art. 4 of Comm. Reg. 1617/93, OJ 1993, L 155.

applicable tariffs are those of the carrying, not of the issuing airline. The duty to interline applies at each of the tariff categories which was the subject of consultation, even if the participants did not reach a consensus on the applicable level of the tariff. It does not require that the beneficiary of interlining applies identical tariffs to the airline which has to grant interlining authority. The duty to interline extends to changes of reservations onto other airlines' flights; in the event that the tariffs are different, a refund or extra payment can be made in accordance with applicable IATA resolutions.

The duty to interline can be overridden by considerations of a technical or commercial nature, for example, insolvency of the carrying airline, but any restriction of interlining authority must have been notified to the airline involved and must remain proportional to the technical or commercial difficulty which justifies it. Where such a difficulty arises, the airline involved may be able to offer a bank guarantee for a reasonable amount or to agree to a unilateral interlining agreement so as to limit the financial exposure of the other airline.

Tariff consultations must not go beyond the aim of facilitating interlining. Therefore, revenue enhancement is not a proper objective of tariff consultations; price initiatives must be taken by individual airlines, subject to subsequent consultations, rather than be concerted in advance of marketing.[79]

The block exemption furthermore requires that airlines maintain their freedom of independent action, for example, co-ordination must not prevent airlines from applying different tariffs. Coordination also must not extend to certain elements of tariffs, such as agents' remuneration. In addition, the block exemption imposes a number of procedural conditions which are mainly intended to enable the Commission to monitor the co-ordination process. In particular, the Commission must be invited to tariff consultations and is to receive a full report on those consultations.[80]

Notwithstanding the benefits which accrue from interlining and the conditions laid down by the block exemption, the fact remains that tariff co-ordination entails a significant restriction on price competition. The question may arise in some circumstances whether the conditions of Article 85(3) are fulfilled, in particular whether there are sufficient consumer benefits outweighing the reduction in price competition and whether all restrictions are indispensable for the stated benefits. Pursuant to Article 7 of Regulation 3976/87, the Commission may withdraw the benefit of the block exemption from tariff co-ordination where it has effects which are incompatible with Article 85(3). Accordingly, the block exemption may be withdrawn where tariff consultations lead to the absence of price competition on any route or group of routes.

At the time of adoption of the first package, however, the Commission indicated that it recognized that after tariff consultations, airlines may file at least some identical fares. It expressed the view that the fact that these filings are iden-

---

[79] *23rd Report on Competition Policy*, 1993, para. 238.
[80] Commission notice published in OJ 1993, C 177.

tical does not on its own constitute sufficient evidence of a concerted practice contrary to Article 85. Presumably withdrawal of the block exemption will therefore require evidence of some form of positive action beyond tariff consultations with a view to discouraging price competition. The increasing prominence of price competition in the air transport sector raises the question whether this generous regime in favour of tariff co-ordination can be maintained in the long term. As Community airlines are building global networks, the justification of tariff co-ordination as a component of the interlining system is likely to diminish.

5.5.6. Tariff construction rules

The Commission has also examined the industry-wide tariff construction rules. These relate, for example, to the conversion of tariffs between different currencies, the relationship of fare levels on related routes to each other, and restrictions on the sale of tickets outside the country where travel originates. The Commission took the view that these rules have an effect on price levels and therefore do not qualify as technical agreements which are outside the scope of Article 85(1).[81] It objected in particular to restrictions on the purchase of tickets outside the country where travel originates, which amounts to a form of market segmentation and prevents the consumer form obtaining the best terms for transport arrangements. The Commission saw no justification for these restrictions on price competition and insisted on airlines' freedom to set and market any tariff in accordance with their own commercial policy; as a result these restrictions were removed from travel within the Community, Norway and Sweden.[82] The Commission is currently examining other restrictions with a similar effect (the requirement imposed by airlines that passengers respect the 'sequential use of coupons').

5.5.7. Ground handling services at airports

The first two liberalization packages contained block exemptions in favour of agreements for the supply of ground handling services at airports.[83] Even though these agreements are not generally restrictive of competition, Council had included them in the enabling Regulation. The block exemptions essentially required that these agreements do not bind users to a single supplier. They did so by means of a ban on exclusivity clauses and excessive notice periods for terminating agreements.

It was doubtful whether these block exemptions served a useful purpose because the conditions they imposed were designed to remove any restrictive features of the agreements, thereby actually obviating the need for an exemption.

---

[81] See above, para. 5.4.1. [82] *23rd Report on Competition Policy*, 1993, para. 237.
[83] Comm. Regs 2673/88, OJ 1988, L 239, and 82/91, OJ 1991, L 10.

In addition, the block exemptions were not a suitable instrument to address the source of lack of choice for users, i.e., the monopoly arrangements instituted by law or administrative action at many airports. Therefore, the block exemptions were not renewed in the third liberalization package.

In order to deal with the issue of ground handling monopolies, the Commission initially considered a directive under Article 90 which would have required Member States to allow multiple providers of ground handling services at major airports.[84] Subsequently the Commission changed course and proposed a draft directive, based on Article 84(2) of the EC Treaty, which establishes the right to self-handling.[85] It should be noted that the Commission justified reliance on Article 84(2) on the grounds that airport handling is an integral part of air transport, where in the competition area it has traditionally taken the opposite view.

5.5.8. Computer reservation systems

Discussions on the first liberalization package coincided with the start-up of two joint ventures between European airlines to develop and operate sophisticated computer reservation systems which would replace the obsolete systems operated by individual airlines. Computer reservation systems (CRS) enable travel agents to have access to up-to-date information about participating airlines' schedules and fares and to make instantaneous bookings.

Taking into account the benefits of the new generation of CRS for airlines, passengers, and travel agents alike and the considerable investment required and the technological difficulties to be overcome to develop these systems, the Council included CRS in the enabling regulation.[86] Experience in the United States has shown, however, that CRS can be used to distort competition by restricting airlines' access to the system or some of its functions or by discrimination in the display of airlines services.[87] The effects of such action on airlines' sales could be quite significant. Regulatory authorities, both in North America and in Europe, intervened to curb abuses by the operators of some CRS. Drawing on the work carried out by the European Civil Aviation Conference,[88] the block exemption included a number of obligations designed to regulate the

---

[84] Doc. SEC(93)1896 final; see also Dussard-Lefret, C. and Federlin, C., 'Ground Handling Services and EC Competition Rules', *Air and Space Law* Vol. 19, No. 2, 1994, 50.

[85] Doc. COM (94) 590 final of 13 Dec. 1994.

[86] Although arguably the joint ventures setting up CRS are concentrative and could be subsumed under the merger control regulation. Reg. 4064/89 was however not yet adopted at the relevant time.

[87] For a full account of early experiences with CRS, see Ehlers, P. N., *Computerized Reservation Systems in the Air Transport Industry*, (Deventer, 1988).

[88] Eventually culminating in the ECAC code of conduct for Computer Reservation Systems, Paris, 1989 which in turn inspired Council Reg. 2299/89 on a code of conduct for computerized reservation systems, OJ 1989, L 220 (some provisions of the code were clarified by means of an Explanatory Notice published in OJ 1990, C 184) which was subsequently amended by Council Reg. 3089/93, OJ 1993, L 278.

conduct of CRS rather than the contents of the joint venture agreements themselves.

The Commission granted an exemption[89] in favour of the key restrictions of the joint venture agreements (duty of partners not to compete and regulation of the distribution of CRS by giving partners exclusive territories). The regulation essentially sets out two series of conditions. A first series is intended to avoid distortions of competition between airlines. The regulation mainly requires that all air carriers must be able to participate in the marketing function of the CRS, that the services of participants are displayed without bias, that fees are reasonable, cost-related, and non-discriminatory and that airlines must be able to terminate their participation at reasonable notice. Another set of conditions ensures that competition between CRS is maintained. Airlines must not be prevented from participating in other systems. Travel agents must not be prevented from subscribing to other systems, they must be able to terminate their agreement with reasonable notice, and they must not be exposed to incentives to use a particular CRS ahead of others.

Notwithstanding these conditions, the CRS market remains highly concentrated. Most of the major Community airlines are partners in one of the two European joint venture agreements. Travel agents in their territories tend to prefer the system in which the local airline has an interest and other CRS find it difficult to penetrate that market. In particular, where a well-established local airline refuses to participate in other CRS, the latter may find that they cannot offer an attractive product to local travel agents.

With a view to facilitating market access, the Commission intervened in order to obtain undertakings from the major airlines with an interest in a CRS to participate on non-discriminatory terms in competing CRS.[90] That intervention eventually gave rise to a legislative obligation on airlines owning a CRS not to discriminate against a competing CRS by refusing that CRS to distribute its services under substantially the same conditions as its own CRS.[91]

A duty to participate in competing CRS could also arise under Article 86. Where a dominant airline refuses to participate in a CRS which competes with another CRS in which it holds an interest without having objective commercial or technical reasons to do so, it may be abusing its dominant position by impeding the development of competition.

5.5.9. Strategic alliances

Recent years have seen the development of loosely knitted strategic alliances between airlines. Those arrangements fall short of outright mergers and, in

---

[89] Comm. Reg. 2672/88, OJ 1988, L 239, renewed and amended by Reg. 83/91, OJ 1991, L 10 and by Reg. 3652/93 in OJ 1993, L 333.

[90] *21st Report on Competition Policy*, 1991, paras 93–5 (for further details see J. Temple Lang, *Air Transport in the EEC—Community Antitrust Law Aspects*, (1991 Fordham Corporate Law Institute), 287, 317–22) and *23rd Report*, 1993, para. 239. [91] Art. 4 of Comm. Reg. 3652/93, OJ 1993, L 333.

particular, preserve the participants' identity and autonomy. They constitute a framework within which the participating airlines are committed to developing extensive co-operation in technical, commercial, and operational areas. Typically, the alliance will endeavour to attain economies of scale by joint equipment purchasing and maintenance, insurance, personnel training etc. Route networks and schedules may be co-ordinated, thereby mimicking a single large airline's. Often the alliance is supported by small shareholdings by each of the parties in the others.

The assessment of these complex forms of co-operation differentiates between the framework agreement and its implementation. Where the framework agreement creates a structure likely to be used for commercial co-operation by enabling the parties to influence each other's strategy and conduct in the market, it is caught by Article 85(1).[92] If parties can make a plausible argument that co-ordination will generate significant benefits, the framework agreement is likely to be acceptable unless they possess considerable market power.[93] The Commission then also assesses the actual areas of co-operation in implementation of the framework agreement on their merits. Co-operation wholly in the technical field normally is not caught by Article 85(1).[94] Where the co-operation is commercially relevant, it will have to satisfy the tests of Article 85(3). Difficulties would arise where the co-operation eliminates competition on a route or where the partners control access to essential facilities. If that were the case, ways would have to be found of stimulating competition and of safeguarding the position of third parties.[95]

---

[92] Cases 142 and 156/84, *B.A.T. and Reynolds* v. *Commission* (*Philip Morris* case), [1987] ECR 4487 (recital 38).

[93] The Commission examined an alliance between Air France and Lufthansa, large airlines dominating adjacent markets. It insisted on the elimination of a co-ordination committee composed of middle management with operational responsibilities, but accepted the establishment of contacts at Board level where general trends are discussed. *20th Report on Competition Policy*, 1989, para. 106.

[94] See above, para. 5.4.1.

[95] In its review of the joint shareholding by Lufthansa, JAL, and Nissho Iwai in DHL, the Commission insisted on certain undertakings with a view to safeguarding access by DHL's competitors to Lufthansa's and JAL's capacity on non-discriminatory terms. OJ 1990, L 258, and *21st Report on Competition Policy*, 1991, paras 88–9.

More recently the Commission examined the possible joint venture airline Premair, OJ 1995, C 262, and the alliance between Lufthansa and SAS, OJ 1996, L 54, p. 28. In the latter case the Commission has insisted *inter alia* on the freeze of frequencies on routes dominated by the two parties, on the availability of slots at airports where the partners have very strong positions, on mandatory interlining and participation in frequent flier programmes, and on the termination of agreements providing for commercial co-operation with other airlines.

5.6. AIR TRANSPORT MERGERS

5.6.1. General

The merger control regulation[96] applies to air transport even in areas which are not covered by Regulation 3975/87, such as transport to third countries.[97] As a result, mergers between two non-Community airlines which operate air services to the Community could have to be notified to the Commission.

When examining under Article 1(2) of the merger control regulation whether a merger has the Community dimension required for review under the regulation, the Commission has to allocate airline turnover to the Community and to particular Member States. In its first decision under the regulation in the air transport sector[98] the Commission listed three possible methods of making that allocation: revenue can be allocated to the final destination point outside an airline's home base, it can be split on a 50/50 basis between the country of origin and that of final destination, and it can be allocated to the country in which the tickets generating the revenue have been sold. Results would only differ in marginal cases. In the subsequent cases the Commission has not had to take a decision on the preferred method. It would appear that as a rule an allocation method based on the origin of turnover corresponds most closely to the approach followed in other industries. However, in some situations that method may not accurately reflect the cross-border nature of air transport and it cannot be excluded that other allocation methods may be used in appropriate cases in order to meet the objective of the regulation, i.e., monitoring mergers involving substantial activities in the Community which are not confined to a single Member State.

The liberalization of Community air transport and increasing competition from third country airlines have increased pressure on Community airlines to reduce their costs, rationalize their networks, expand their customer base and increase their scale to a level comparable with that of major airlines worldwide and in particular in the United States. The traditional structure of European industry, comprising a rather large number of carriers which are confined to relatively small-scale operations—concentrating essentially on transport to and from their home country rather than ensuring a presence on routes throughout the Community—is no longer adequate. Adaptation to this new environment is leading to a restructuring of the Community airline industry which, in so far as it is likely to improve the performance of the industry, can be welcomed.

---

[96] Reg. 4064/89 on the *Control of Concentrations between Undertakings*, OJ 1990, L 257.

[97] See above, para. 5.2.1.

[98] Dec. *Delta-Pan Am*, n. 99 below, discussed by Lange, D. and Weitbrecht, A., European Merger Control in the Air Transport Industry, in *Zeitschrift für Luft- und Weltraumrecht*, 1992, 41. This issue was not considered in detail in the Commission's Notice on the allocation of turnover under the merger regulation, OJ 1994, C 385.

Even though the restructuring process is likely to reduce the number of independent airlines, it will not necessarily imply a reduction of competition overall. On the contrary, liberalization is expected to lead to a more intense confrontation of the remaining airlines. The traditional pattern of duopoly routes served by less efficient carriers protected against competitors is giving way to open routes on which the carriers are exposed to actual or potential competition from several efficient operators. With that perspective, the Commission has cleared a number of airline mergers, usually subject to conditions safeguarding at least potential competition on the main markets affected.[99] While the analysis in each of these cases hinged on the specific facts of the merger and on the economic and regulatory background of the operation, some common themes emerge.

The function of competition review in airline merger cases appears to be twofold. First, it must ensure that the restructuring process does not go so far as to jeopardize the competitive structure of the Community airline industry and lead to unacceptably high levels of concentration. Second, care must be taken to avoid dominance over important individual markets—routes, airports, or catchment areas of airports—by a single powerful airline.

Assessment of a merger between airlines therefore requires analysis of different sets of relevant markets.[100] First, overall concentration of the Community industry as a whole is measured by reference to the Community market[101] with a predominantly geographic dimension, denoting the reservoir of potential competition by suppliers of air transport within the Community. In view of the relatively low degree of concentration of the Community industry as a whole at present, this element of the analysis has not given rise to serious concern to date. Second, the impact of a merger on air transport users is measured by reference to the various product markets affected, denoting the air services for which demand is expressed. The starting point for product market definition is the route on which the air service is operated. Depending on the facts of each case,

---

[99] British Airways–British Caledonian, IP(88)131, *18th Report on Competition Policy*, point 81; Air France–Air Inter–UTA, IP(90)870, *20th Report on Competition Policy*, point 116; KLM–Transavia, IP(91)658, *21st Report on Competition Policy*, points 90–92. (These three operations were reviewed under Arts 85 and 86 prior to the entry into force of the merger control regulation and have not given rise to a full decision). See also the Commission's concern about the possible merger between Lufthansa and Interflug, *20th Report on Competition Policy*, point 114. A full review under the merger regulation was carried out in Delta–PanAm, decision of 13 Sept. 1991; Air France–Sabena, decision of 5 Oct. 1992; British Airways–TAT, decision of 27 Nov. 1992, upheld by the Tribunal of First Instance in case T–2/93, judgment of 19 May 1994, [1994] ECR II-323, and in Swissair—Sabena, decision of 20 July 1995, OJ 1995, C 165. The Commission also carried out a review under Art. 22 of the merger Regulation of the effects on the Belgian market of the merger between British Airways and DanAir—see judgment of 24 March 1994 of the CFI in case T–3/93, [1994] ECR II-121. (The full text of decisions under the merger Regulation is available to interested parties upon written request to the Commission of the European Communities, DG IV, Merger Task Force, 200 rue de la Loi, B-1049 Brussels).

[100] Cf., n. 110 and accompanying text.

[101] Which may be extended to third countries, where there are no barriers to entry by airlines of these countries to the Community market—*vide* European Economic Area and, in the longer term, other third countries with access to the Community market.

services by means of indirect flights, by charter services, from nearby points of origin or to nearby points of destination, or by other modes of transport may have to be taken into account if they are genuine alternatives for the direct air service.[102] Account must be taken of the fact that demand for air transport services is not homogeneous: business travellers are less likely to use slower or less convenient means of transport than leisure travellers. On routes where business travel constitutes an appreciable segment of demand, markets will tend to be defined narrowly. Finally, the position of the merged airlines is also assessed by reference to the airports they serve, reflecting their use of airport infrastructure (for example, slots). This assessment largely coincides with the measurement of the market power of the merged airlines *vis-à-vis* travel agents,[103] as denoted by their share of all sales of air transport out of the catchment areas of the airports affected.

5.6.2. Past, present, and future

In the initial stages of the liberalization process, the Commission approved merger operations which gave rise to high shares of individual route or airport markets, while concentration of Community industry remained low. Some of these operations were characterized by special circumstances, such as the poor financial condition of the acquired airline[104] or the confinement of the participants to narrow segments of the market which prevented them from building a comprehensive network.[105] In those cases, the Commission essentially insisted on compensation for the increase in market power by the creation of genuine opportunities for competition to develop in respect of those individual markets where a risk of dominance existed.

This compensation often took the form of commitments by the Member States concerned to accelerate the liberalization process, for example, by allowing competition on routes not yet covered by market access regulations. These undertakings were accompanied by commitments by the merged airline to abstain from certain action or to take positive action with a view to facilitating the development of competition, for example, by surrendering licences, limiting the usage of airport facilities or refraining from taking an interest in remaining competitors. In one operation which was subsequently abandoned by the partners, the Commission raised doubts about the need to allow an interest in an airline by two rather than by one competitor.[106] The difficulty of these cases

---

[102] Case 66/86, *Ahmed Saeed*, [1989] ECR 803 (recitals 39–42).

[103] The Court ruling in Case 322/81, *Michelin* v. *Commission*, [1983] ECR 3461 (recital 42) confirms that, in the case of a multiproduct firm whose products are not interchangeable at the level of consumers, it may nevertheless be appropriate to assess the firms's aggregate position at the level of dealers.

[104] British Caledonian and Sabena mergers, see above n. 99.

[105] Air Inter/UTA and Transavia mergers, see above n. 99.

[106] British Airways/KLM/Sabena, *20th Report on Competition Policy*, 1990, para. 108.

resulted to a large extent from the fact that the airlines involved were based in the same[107] or in adjacent geographic markets, thereby considerably reinforcing or extending the market power of the merging airlines; operations involving airlines based in distant markets[108] would no doubt only give rise to conditions in respect of the routes linking these markets.

The future is likely to see more operations involving airlines based in different home markets. Also, market access opportunities can be expected to make most Community route and airport markets more competitive.[109] Therefore, many airline mergers are unlikely to give rise to a negative assessment under the competition rules. On the other hand, increasing congestion may create dominance of some airport markets which would be difficult to remedy. Lack of slots may inhibit the effective use of route market access opportunities. In any event, the completion of the internal market has exhausted the possibility of stimulation of potential competition by anticipating further liberalization as a condition for allowing airline mergers.

Future mergers which raise serious issues of dominance may well require more far-reaching commitments by the merging airlines to safeguard competition. Reliance on the 'contestability' of air transport markets can no longer be deemed to be an adequate substitute for genuine competition in a mature environment. Finally, as the restructuring process continues, the concentration of Community industry as a whole is bound to increase. High concentration levels, such as those which now give rise to concern in the United States, must be avoided, and therefore it is doubtful whether the largest Community airlines would be allowed to merge with each other even if there is no dominance of any individual product market.

5.7. ABUSES OF DOMINANT POSITIONS

Control of abuses of dominant positions is of high importance in the air transport sector. On the one hand, many of the major Community airlines inherited dominant positions from the earlier regulatory regimes: most Member States conducted their air transport policy with a view to putting their 'flag carriers' in the strongest possible position on their home market. On the other hand, these dominant airlines often have the power, by means of control of essential facilities and by their overwhelming weight in their local market, to hinder the development of competition.

[107] This may be due to some extent to the fact that it is easier to consolidate the networks, operations, and labour forces of airlines sharing the same base. It is also due to Member States' reluctance to allow airlines from other Member States to take an interest in their airlines, invoking the circumstance that third countries might object under the provisions of bilateral Air Service Agreements to passage of ownership of non-nationals of the first Member State. Effective realization of the freedom of establishment will be one of the main objectives of the Community's assumption of competence to negotiate bilateral agreements with third countries—see above, para. 5.1.1.

[108] TAT merger, see n. 99.

[109] This is already the case for most transatlantic markets: cf., Delta–PanAm decision, n. 99.

As noted above in relation to airline mergers, relevant market definition is a fairly complex exercise in the air transport industry.[110] The relevant market is defined as a function of the alleged abuse: it consists of those products or services which constrain the possibility of committing the abuse concerned. Depending on the precise nature of the conduct at issue and on the target of the abuse, relevant markets can consist of one route or a set of routes; for this exercise one has to take into account, where appropriate, services by means of indirect flights, by charter services, from nearby points of origin or to nearby points of destination, or by other modes of transport, if there is evidence that these alternatives provide genuine competition for the direct air service. The relevant market may also focus on sales of air transport in a certain area, or on an airport or airport system. Occasionally the Commission may look at several of these relevant markets in the same decision.[111]

Where the abuse relates to a specific activity the existence of competition for other activities or in other areas is not inconsistent with dominance in respect of the activity concerned. It is therefore possible for an airline to be dominant in respect of a specific route, even though it is quite small in comparison with other airlines and exposed to competition in respect of other services. The Commission has tended towards relatively narrow market definitions; usually the definition of the relevant market is a relatively controversial exercise and there is a great need for economic evidence (for example, data on traffic development following changes to the relative prices applied in nearby relevant markets) to support market definitions.

In its decisions to date, the Commission has had little difficulty in finding that dominance existed. The Commission accepted the existence of dominance on the market for computer reservation systems—excluding other reservation methods—in Belgium with a market share below 50 per cent,[112] no doubt reflecting the necessity of guaranteeing non-discriminatory access to an essential marketing tool. In another case dominance was found on the market for the provision of air transport between London (Heathrow) and Dublin—excluding other modes of transport and other London airports and notwithstanding the presence of two other airlines on the route—and on the market for the sale of tickets for that service in both Ireland and in the United Kingdom.[113] In that case the airlines' share of each of the markets defined was in excess of 50 per cent and there existed both regulatory (restrictive policy on market access) and practical (lack of slots at congested airport) barriers to entry.

In view of the frequent occurrence of tight oligopolies and parallel behaviour in route markets, the concept of joint dominance is arguably particularly

[110] On the technique of relevant market definition in the air transport sector, see B. Van Houtte, Relevant markets in air transport, *Common Market Law Review*, 1990, 521.

[111] Comm. Dec. *British Midland* v. *Aer Lingus*, OJ 1992, L 96.

[112] Comm. Dec. *London European* v. *Sabena*, OJ 1988, L 317.

[113] Comm. Dec. *British Midland* v. *Aer Lingus*, OJ 1992, L 96.

relevant in the air transport sector. However, that is not reflected in the Commission's practice to date, no doubt because of the legal uncertainty still surrounding the concept of joint dominance.

Examples of abuse in the Commission's practice to date include tying access to a computer reservation system with the provision of ground handling services, denying access to a computer reservation system with a view to discouraging the competitor from operating a particular air service, exerting pressure on a competitor to increase its tariffs[114] or to align tariffs with those of the dominant airline, charging excessive tariffs which bear no reasonable relation with the airline's long-term fully allocated costs, charging predatory fares with a view to eliminating a competitor from a market,[115] and denying interline facilities to a competitor, thereby forcing it to operate under an unusual handicap which is not imposed on other competitors.[116] In the latter case, it should be noted that the Commission did not impose a permanent duty to interline because that could have the perverse effect of encouraging smaller airlines to continue relying on the dominant airlines' frequencies and networks, rather than building up extensive networks and high frequencies by themselves. The duty to interline was limited to two years during which the small airline could gain commercial standing and attract interest from travel agents and passengers for its air service without being under a competitive disadvantage. There is a need to clarify more precisely the circumstances under which tariffs would be held to be predatory.[117] When frequent flier programmes, override commissions, and excessive capacity or frequency,[118] are practiced by a dominant airline without persuasive business justification and if they have a significant adverse effect on the development or maintenance of competition, they are liable to constitute an abuse in the sense of Article 86.

[114] See n. 112 (imposing a fine of 100,000 ECU).

[115] Case 66/86, *Ahmed Saeed*, [1989] ECR 803 (recitals 43–4). It should be noted that tariffs are also subject to disapproval by aeronautical authorities under Reg. 2409/92 on fares and rates for air services, OJ 1992, L 240 (for transport within the Community) and under the relevant provisions of bilateral Air Service Agreements (for transport to third countries).

[116] See above n. 111 (imposing a fine of 750,000 ECU); *20th Report on Competition Policy*, points 73–6.

[117] See Soames, T. and Ryan, A. 'Predatory Pricing in Air Transport', *ECLR*, 1994, 151.

[118] See above n. 46.

6

EC Competition Procedure in the Transport Sector[1]

6.1. APPLICABLE LEGISLATION

One of two broad types of competition procedure may apply in the transport sector, depending on the type of transport activity involved.

6.1.1. Transitional rules

Certain transport operations have not yet been made subject to detailed rules for the application of Articles 85 and 86 of the Treaty. This is the case for tramp and cabotage shipping and air transport between the EU and third countries.[2] In these sectors, the transitional rules for the application of EC antitrust law apply.[3]

(1) Under Article 88 of the Treaty,[4] before legislation pursuant to Article 87 is adopted, Member States can apply Articles 85 and 86 (including the granting of individual exemptions) in accordance with national law, i.e., rules of procedure vary depending on the Member State in which EC substantive rules are to be applied.

(2) Under Article 89:

1. Without prejudice to Article 88, . . . (o)n application by a Member State or on its own initiative, and in co-operation with the competent authorities in the Member States, who shall give it their assistance, the Commission shall investigate cases of suspected infringement of these principles. If it finds that there has been an infringement, it shall propose appropriate measures to bring it to an end.

2. If the infringement is not brought to an end, the Commission shall record such infringement of the principles in a reasoned decision. The Commission may publish its decision and authorise Member States to take the measures, the conditions and details of which it shall determine, needed to remedy the situation.

---

[1] I am grateful to John Temple Lang, Richard Lyal and David Wood for their comments on earlier drafts of this part. I am also indebted to Berndt Langeheine and Alain Alexis, from whom I borrowed some ideas.

[2] See above, Chs 4 and 5.

[3] For a general comment on Arts 88 and 89 of the Treaty, see Schröter, H., in Groeben, H. von der, Thiesing, J., and Ehlermann, C., *Kommentar zum EWG Vertrag*, (4th Ed. Vol. 2: Arts 85–109, Nomos. Baden-Baden, 1991), pp. 2514–27.

[4] Art. 88 is also the legal basis for the application of Arts 85(1) and 86 of the Treaty by Member States' competition authorities in economic areas subject to Reg. 17, before the Commission initiates a procedure, according to Art. 9(3) of Reg. 17.

Under this provision requests by natural or legal persons do not give rise to procedural rights. Formally, only Member States can request the Commission to investigate alleged infringements. However, nothing prevents the Commission from initiating a procedure on its own, on the basis of the information provided by private complainants. The Commission lacks its standard powers of investigation[5] and must rely on Member States to enquire into alleged infringements. For their part, Member States must assist the Commission in performing its task, as required by Article 5 of the Treaty. Undertakings involved in the infringements have the right to be heard.[6]

The Commission must follow a two-step procedure to declare the existence of an infringement. First, the Commission must propose (to the undertakings or to Member States) appropriate measures to put an end to the infringements it discovers. Secondly, if such measures are not effective, the Commission must publish a reasoned decision alleging the infringement in which it may authorize the Member State to take the specific measures it prescribes. Decisions must be implemented by Member States. Note that EU national administrations are 'authorized'—not obliged, apparently—to take the measures proposed by the Commission in its decision. However, in appropriate circumstances, Article 5 of the Treaty might well oblige them to take such measures.[7] The Commission cannot impose fines in these cases.

This unsatisfactory procedure under Article 89 has been followed by the Commission on several occasions, but without ever having reached the stage where a formal decision has been adopted.[8]

6.1.2. The applicability of specific procedural regulations for non-excluded forms of transport, by reference to the mode of transport (inland, maritime, or air)

Transport operations other than those mentioned in the previous section are subject to specific procedural rules. Different rules apply to different modes of

[5] For the Commission's powers of investigation in competition cases, see, in general, Kerse, C. S., *EC Antitrust Procedure*, (3rd Edn, Sweet & Maxwell, London, 1994), Ch. 3, and Ortiz Blanco, L., *EC Competition Procedure*, (Clarendon Press. Oxford, 1996). Chs 4, 5 and 6 and the bibliography quoted there.

[6] The general principle of respect for the rights of the defence obliges the EC institutions, before they adopt measures which may affect individuals, to allow them to make known their point of view, even when there is no explicit provision so requiring. See ECJ judgment in Joined Cases C–48/90 and C–66/90, The Netherlands and *PTT* v. *Commission*, [1992], ECR I–565, at para. 37, citing Case C–301/87, *France* v. *Commission*, [1990] ECR I–351.

[7] For an interpretation of Art. 5 of the EC Treaty which supports this view, see Temple Lang, J., 'Community Constitutional Law: Article 5 EEC Treaty'. *Common Market Law Review*, Vol. 27, No. 4, 1990, pp. 645–81.

[8] In particular in the air transport sector, during negotiations and before adoption of Reg. 3975/87 (see Ch. 5). See *Bulletin of the EC* No. 7/8–1986, para. 2.1.60; *Bulletin of the EC* no. 7/8–1978, para. 2.1.90; *16th Report on Competition Policy*, 1976, para. 36; and *17th Report on Competition Policy*, 1977, para. 46. See Ritter, L., Braun, W. D. and Rawlinson, F., *EEC Competition Law: A Practitioner's Guide*, (Kluwer. Deventer. 1991), pp. 599 *et seq.*

transport. Regulation 1017/68 applies to inland transport and to services ancillary to inland transport operations.[9] Regulation 4056/86 applies to international (non-cabotage) maritime transport, except tramp shipping.[10] Regulation 3975/87 applies to air transport between EU airports.[11] In procedural terms, the three transport regulations are almost identical, and they are in most respects similar to Regulation 17.

Restrictions on the demand side of transport, i.e., imposed by transport users, who are acquirers (not providers) of transport services, and transport by means of pipelines and fixed installations are subject to Regulation 17.[12]

The following pages seek to provide a comparative account of the procedures contained in the transport regulations insofar as they differ from the standard Regulation 17 procedures.[13]

6.2. COMPETENT AUTHORITIES

As in other sectors, the application of Articles 85 and 86 of the Treaty in transport does not fall under the exclusive competence of the Commission. The three transport regulations provide for individual exemptions under Article 85(3) to be granted only by the Commission,[14] but the application of Articles 85(1) and 86 remains within the competence of national authorities until the Commission has initiated a procedure, thereby reserving competence to itself in a particular case.[15] On the other hand, the existence of the numerous block exemptions in the transport sector should not obscure the fact that Articles 85(1) and 86 are directly applicable in national courts,[16] subject to the doctrine of provisional validity.[17] The same principles apply in sectors covered by Regulation 17 and in the transport field.

The application of competition rules by the Commission and by Member State authorities and national courts in transport has some features of its own.

As a general rule, Member States have at least two administrative departments dealing with competition matters for transport: the national competition authority and the transport authority. Their relative weight varies from country to country. In general, however, competition authorities can be said to tend to be less sensitive to industrial policy (or protectionist) arguments than their transport colleagues and this ambivalence may be found in national decision-making and policy-making.

An additional problem may be the application at national level both of

---

[9] See above, Ch. 3, Section II.

[10] See above, Ch. 4.

[11] See above, Ch. 5.

[12] As stated above, Ch. 3, Section I.

[13] On procedural rules in Reg. 17, in general, see among others, Kerse, above n. 5, and Ortiz Blanco, above n. 5.

[14] Art. 15 of Reg. 1017/68; Art. 14 of Reg. 4056/86; and Art. 7 of Reg. 3975/87.

[15] See below, para. 6.2.2.4.

[16] See above, Ch. 2.

[17] See below, para. 6.5.2.

legislation exempting transport from national competition law and of Articles 85 and 86.[18] Whenever restrictive activities exempted by the former fall foul of the latter a conflict may arise. Although, according to the doctrine of supremacy, EC law should prevail in such a case of conflict, in practice, national authorities may be called upon to apply simultaneously a national exemption and a Community prohibition and national judges tend to be more aware of national law than they are of EC law.

The opposite could also arise. Restrictive agreements authorized under EC law might be prohibited under national competition law. Although the European Court has maintained that the enforcement of national competition law must not compromise the uniform application of EC law,[19] it has not ruled on this specific problem.[19a] The Commission considers that EC block exemptions should, in principle, be respected by national authorities while applying their domestic competition law, so that possibly stricter national rules should not be enforced against agreements exempted under EC law.[19b] For the rest, nothing prevents the Commission itself from acting against an exempted agreement, withdrawing any given block exemption on the national authorities' initiative.

National courts are obliged to apply EC competition rules in all sectors of the economy, including transport. For the moment, although the Commission has excluded the transport sector from the Notice on co-operation between the Commission and national courts for the application of competition rules,[20] the same principles apply. However, judges and national courts do not yet enjoy in the transport sector the extensive body of case-law which exists in other sectors. They may not be in a position, therefore, to decide on the provisional validity of agreements, on the applicability of a particular block exemption[21] or on the applicability of the conditions for exemption under the Treaty, capabilities which are a pre-condition for the effective solution of transport cartel cases. The application Article 86 might, on the other hand, be easier.

With the object of remedying this situation, the Commission plans to publish a specific notice on co-operation with national courts in competition matters in transport.[22]

---

[18] This possibility is available, for example, in Germany where national transport is not subject to the Act against Restraints of Competition (*Gesetz gegen Wettbewerbsbeschränkungen (GWB)*).

[19] ECJ judgment in Case 14/68, *Walt Wilhelm* v. *Bundeskartellamt*, [1969], ECR 1.

[19a] This question was raised, but remained unanswered, in the judgments of the ECJ in Case C-70/93, *BMW AG* v. *ALD Leasing* and in Case C-266/93, *BundesKartellamt* v. *Volkswagen*, not yet reported. The German Federal Court of Justice asked the European Court to rule on whether a restrictive agreement allowed under EC competition law by means of a block exemption could nevertheless be considered unlawful under German competition law.

[19b] Advocate General Tesauro, in his Opinions of 24 November 1994 in the cases cited in the previous note, held the same view.

[20] OJ 1993 C 39, p. 6 last para.

[21] National courts cannot apply Art. 85(3), but they can judge whether a given agreements falls within the scope of a block exemption. See in particular ECJ judgment in case 63/75, *Fonderies Roubaix* v. *Fonderies Roux*, [1976] ECR 111 at 118.

[22] Comm. Notice on co-operation between the Commission and national courts, last para.

In the meantime, the general Notice, which is based on the procedural system of Regulation 17, can play a significant role in the transport sector. For example, the co-operation procedure for submitting questions to the Commission while national court proceedings are stayed could, and indeed should, be fruitfully applied in the transport sector in order to clarify matters on which information and legal guidelines might not be readily available for national courts.

Finally, the ambivalence and inconsistencies which occur at a national level are reproduced at Community level, this time within the Commission between the Competition and Transport Directorates General (DG IV and DG VII). Although DG IV takes the leading role in competition matters, DG VII must not be underestimated. In particular, it is capable of persuading the Commission to take account of considerations uncommon in the competition field. The intervention of DG VII also restricts the ability for DG IV to employ mechanisms to shorten its decision-making procedures.

6.3. THE INFLUENCE OF REGULATION 17

The transport regulations mirror more or less closely many of the procedural provisions of Regulation 17. They also contain a significant number of specific features. Most of these features derive from Regulation 1017/68, which paved the way for Regulation 4056/86 and Regulation 3975/87. The similarities between the general regime put in place by the Regulation 17 implementing rules (Regulations 3385/94 and 99)[23] and the transport implementing rules (Regulations 1629 and 1630/88 and Regulation 4261/88)[24] are even greater.

The mark of Regulation 17 is to be seen not only in the provisions of the different transport regulations, but also in the precedents and case-law of the European Court and the CFI on specific procedural matters in relation to the implementation of Regulations 17, 27 and 99, and in the administrative practice of the Commission over the last thirty years or so which, in principle, apply to transport procedures. Examples could include: the need for a formal decision to withdraw immunity from fines; the possibility of adopting interim measures; the right of access to files; the *AKZO* and *AM&S* procedures; the *Transocean* requirements, etc. In general, all precedents, all case-law and all administrative practice concerning Regulation 17 and its implementing rules are applicable.

[23] Comm. Reg. (EC) 3385/94, OJ 1994 L 377, p. 28, which has substituted Reg. 27 of the Commission, relating to the form, content and other procedures of applications and notifications made in accordance with Reg. 17 of the Council, and Reg. 99/63/EEC, OJ 1963 127, p. 2268, Spec. Ed. 1963–4, p. 47, relating to the hearings provided for in Reg. 17.

[24] Comm. Reg. (EEC) 1629/69 and 1630/69, OJ 1969 L 209, pp. 1 and 11, Spec. Ed. 1969 II, pp. 371 and 381 (with Forms I, II and III); Comm. Reg. (EEC) 4260/88, OJ 1988 L 376, p. 1 (with Form MAR); and Comm. Reg. (EEC) 4261/88, OJ 1988 L 376, p. 10 (with Form AER). Reg. 1629/68, 4260/88 and 4261/88 were amended with a view to developing the competition rules of the Agreement on the EEA by Comm. Reg. (EEC) 3666/93, OJ 1993 L 336, p. 1.

6.3.1. Powers of investigation, enquiries into economic sectors and professional secrecy

The Commission's powers of investigation under the transport regulations are identical to those in other areas governed by Regulation 17. In particular, requests for information and inspections are subject to the same rules.[25]

In spite of two of the regulations only being recently adopted, the Commission's powers in sea and air transport are not restricted in time as regards the information that can be requested or the documents to which the Commission may have access. The Court has confirmed that if such a limitation is not explicitly set out in implementing legislation, the Commission's powers of investigation must be understood as extending to activities prior to the entry into force of the implementing legislation.[26]

Like Regulation 17,[27] the transport regulations impose on Member States the obligation to adopt, within a reasonable time, all appropriate measures to enable the Commission's agents to carry out investigations at an undertaking's premises even if the undertaking opposes.[28]

The rules on confidentiality, i.e., those relating to the use of information obtained by the Commission during its procedures,[29] and the obligation of professional secrecy on the part of the Commission and Member States, their officials and servants,[30] are also reflected in the transport regulations.[31] According to the latest case-law,[32] the Commission's obligations extend also to the information obtained following a notification by undertakings with a view to obtaining an individual exemption.

However, not all the transport regulations mirror Regulation 17 with regard to fact-finding. Whilst that regulation and Regulation 1017/68 contain a provision on 'enquiries into economic sectors',[33] the sea and air transport regulations do not.[34] Had the Commission had the opportunity to avail itself of such a

---

[25] See Arts 19, 20 and 21 of Reg. 1017/68; Arts 16, 17 and 18 of Reg. 4056/86; and Arts 9, 10 and 11 of Reg. 3975/87, which are the equivalents of Arts 11, 13 and 14 of Reg. 17.

[26] See ECJ judgment in Joined Cases 97–99/87, *Dow Chemical Iberica* v. *Commission*, [1989] ECR 3165, at para. 61. In this case, the issue at stake was an inspection on the basis of Reg. 17 one year after such regulation entered into force in Spain. The fact that conduct can be *investigated* does not mean that such conduct can be *punished*, at least in the sea and air transport sectors. See below para. 6.3.4.

[27] See Art. 14(6) of Reg. 17.

[28] See Art. 21(6) of Reg. 1017/68, Art. 18(6) of Reg. 4056/86 and Art. 11(6) of Reg. 3975/87.

[29] Art. 20(1) of Reg. 17.   [30] Art. 20(2) of Reg. 17.

[31] Art. 27(1) and (2) of Reg. 1017/68; Art. 24(1) and (2) of Reg. 4056/86; and Art. 17(1) of Reg. 3975/87. It is worth noting that, no doubt by mistake, Art. 24(1) of the maritime transport regulation refers only to Arts 17 and 18 (inspections), missing out Art. 16 (requests for information).

[32] Case C–67/91, *Dirección General de Defensa de la Competencia* v. *Asociación de Bancos Españoles*, [1992] ECR I–4785.

[33] See Art. 12 of Reg. 17 and Art. 18 of Reg. 1017/68.

[34] See Regs 4056/86 and 3975/87. The first draft of Reg. 4056/86 (see Comm. Doc. COM (81) 423 final and OJ 1981 C 282, p. 4) included a mysterious 'Article 16' which had already been deleted in 1981 and no doubt contained the equivalent of Art. 18 of Reg. 1017/68. This provision

power in maritime transport, the Commission's report and draft proposal on shipping consortia might have seen the light much earlier.[35]

6.3.2. Infringement procedures

Infringement procedures in transport follow the same rules which apply in sectors subject to Regulation 17. The Commission must make its objections known (this is the moment when the Commission—if it has not already done so—withdraws Member States' competence to apply Articles 85 and 86),[36] give access to its files, and allow the undertakings suspected of a breach of the competition rules the opportunity to be heard. The case-law of the European Courts and the administrative practice of the Commission in respect of the rights of the defence apply.

Commission Regulation (EEC)/1630/69, in respect of inland transport, Section II of Commission Regulation (EEC)/4260/88, regarding maritime transport, and Section II of Commission Regulation (EEC)/4261/88, for air transport, lay down the rules for hearings in transport infringement cases. Transport rules concerning hearings are identical to those of Commission Regulation (EEC)/99/63.[37]

Finally, the Commission Decision on the implementation of hearings in connection with procedures for the application of Articles 85 and 86 of the EC Treaty, Articles 65 and 66 of the EEC Treaty and Regulation 4064/89 (the merger regulation),[38] is also applicable in the transport sector.[39]

6.3.3. Liaison with Member States

Liaison with national authorities under the three transport regulations[40] takes place in the same way as it does under Regulation 17.[41] There are, nevertheless, some minor differences.

was placed before the provision on requests for information, as in Reg. 1017/68 itself, the acknowledged model for the maritime procedural rules. The reasons for the deletion are nowhere explained or justified.

[35] The Commission complained about the lack of co-operation of shipowners while the enquiry was being made, in particular about the insufficient number of consortia agreements it could examine until 1989. See Kreis, H. W. R. 'European Community Competition Policy and International Shipping', *Fordham International Law Journal*, Vol. 13, No. 4, 1989–90, pp. 411–45, at 425.

[36] Under Art. 15 of Reg. 1017/68; Art. 14 of Reg. 4056/86 and Art. 7 of Reg. 3975/87.

[37] See the Regulations above n. 23 and 24.

[38] OJ L 395 1989, corrected in OJ L 257 1990, p. 14.

[39] Initially this decision was found in Comm. Dec. of 23 Nov. 1990, XX Rep. Com. 1990, at p.312. More recently, the Commission has published its Decision 94/810/ECSC,EC of 12 December 1994 on the terms of reference of hearing officers in competition procedures before the Commission, OJ 1994 L 330 p. 67. Art. 1 incorporates the transport regulations within the scope of its 'implementing provisions' to which the decision applies. See Art. 1(2)(c), (d), (e) in respect of inland, sea and air transport, in connection with Regs. 1630/69, 4260/88 and 4261/88.

[40] See Art. 16 of Reg. 1017/68; Art. 15 of Reg. 4056/86 and Art. 8 of Reg. 3975/87.

[41] Art. 10 of Reg. 17.

The transport regulations foresee that national authorities for both competition and transport will participate in Commission procedures. Thus, Member States have generally designated two competent authorities in the field of transport, with which the Commission liaises.[42] Officials from the competition and the transport fields also participate in the Advisory Committee meetings.[43] There is one Advisory Committee for each mode of transport.[44] In cases where more than one transport regulation applies, the Commission should summon more than one Committee at the same time, and officials from the competition authorities, plus officials from the transport authorities, competent for each mode of transport involved, may participate in the consultation.

For historical reasons, the Commission has a reinforced obligation of liaison with the Council in inland transport competition procedures. In these cases, the Commission is obliged to wait until the expiry of twenty days after the inland transport Advisory Committee has delivered its opinion, before it can adopt a final decision. If required by any Member State during that period, the Council must be convened to examine with the Commission any questions of principle concerning inland transport policy which may be involved. The Commission may not adopt its decision until after that meeting, and must take into account any policy guidelines which emerge from it.[45]

6.3.4. Fines and periodic penalty payments

The regime for fines and periodic penalty payments under the transport regulations[46] is almost identical to the general regime under Regulation 17.[47] The provisions on review by the Court (and now, for competition cases, by the CFI), on the unlimited jurisdiction of the Court within the meaning of Article 172 of the Treaty to review Commission decisions imposing economic sanctions in the transport sector,[48] and on the unit of account to be used[49] are exactly the same.

However, one of the transport regulations shows differences that merit some comment. Contrary to what is provided by Article 15(5) of Regulation 17,

---

[42] Written communications may be addressed to one of them for delivery to both, or via the Member States' permanent representations, for distribution to the competent national departments.

[43] See Art. 16(4) of Reg. 1017/68; Art. 15(4) of Reg. 4056/86; and Art. 8(4) of Reg. 3975/87.

[44] Aside from the 'Reg. No.17 Committee', which might also be called upon to comment on mixed cases (in which other services are involved, aside from pure transport services).

[45] Art. 17 of Reg. 1017/68. For a detailed critique of this provision, see above, Ch. 3, Section II.

[46] See Arts 22 and 23 of Reg. 1017/68; Arts 19 and 20 of Reg. 4056/86; and Arts 12 and 13 of Reg. 3975/87.

[47] Arts 15 and 16 of Reg. 17.

[48] Art. 17 of Reg. 17; Art. 24 of Reg. 1017/68; Art. 21 of Reg. 4056/86 and Art. 14 of Reg. 3975/87.

[49] Art. 18 of Reg. 17; Art. 25 of Reg. 1017/68; Art. 22 of Reg. 4056/86 and Art. 15 of Reg. 3975/87.

Article 19, second sub-paragraph, of Regulation 4056/86 and Article 12(5), first sub-paragraph, of Regulation 3975/87, Article 22 of Regulation 1017/68 does not provide for immunity from fines from the date of notification until a final decision on the applicability of Article 85(3) of the Treaty is adopted.[50] The reasons for this absence are not clear and, in the generally benign procedural context of Regulation 1017/68, the lack of immunity[51] seems to be extremely harsh *vis-à-vis* inland transport undertakings. Moreover, there seems to be no reason for distinguishing between inland transport undertakings, on the one hand, and sea and air transport undertakings, on the other.

In spite of the absence of a procedural provision granting immunity in respect of notified conduct under Regulation 1017/68, it can be argued that the case-law of the European Court justifies the view that, in general, a valid notification to the Commission deserves, and should receive, immunity in all situations.[52] In practice, the Commission has not denied immunity to an inland agreement notified on the basis of Article 12 of Regulation 1017/68.[53]

As regards 'fining policy' in the transport sector, the Commission has been reluctant to regard the novelty of the application of competition rules in transport as a mitigating factor. It has followed the general policy adopted in other sectors.[54] The adoption of implementing legislation can be a long process and carriers are generally aware of their obligations under EC competition rules.[55] Mindful of these facts, the Commission has endeavoured to impose fines at deterrent levels when faced with well-established forms of infringements in order to enhance compliance in sectors which previously have lacked effective enforcement.[56]

Another issue which might arise in respect of fines is whether, under the transport regulations—and mainly under the most recent instruments, i.e.,

---

[50] As a consequence, Art. 22 of Reg. 1017/68 does not provide for any possibility of withdrawal of such immunity either. See below para. 6.3.7.

[51] The second draft of the inland transport regulation (Document COM (68) 142 final, of 13 March 1968) already omitted this provision (and the one on withdrawal of immunity) in its Art. 18, later Art. 22 in the finally adopted text. The first draft of Reg. 4056/86 (above, n. 34) omitted these provisions as well in its Art. 20, which reproduced the text of Art. 22 of the inland transport regulation. The text was finally amended after 1985 to include them.

[52] See the ECJ judgment in Joined Cases 100–103/80, *Musique Diffusion Francaise et al* v. *Commission* (*Pioneer*) [1983] ECR 1825, at paras 92–3.

[53] The Commission has implicitly accepted the idea of an immunity which has subsumed within it the possibility of its withdrawl in the *Trans-Atlantic Conference Agreement (TACA)* case. See *Press Release IP(95) 243* of 14 March 1995. See also below para. 6.3.7.

[54] For the Commission's fining policy and the mitigating factors see Kerse, above n. 5, Ch. VII and Ortiz Blanco, above n. 5, Ch. VIII.

[55] This argument was made by Adv. Gen. Lenz in his Opinion in Case 66/86, *Ahmed Saeed* v. *ZUW* [1989] ECR 803, pointing out that the first Commission proposals for implementing legislation were made in 1981, and that in particular in air transport the Commission had initiated proceedings under Art. 89 of the Treaty on several occasions.

[56] See, e.g., the Commission Decisions in the *Shipowners' Committees* case (OJ 1992 L 134, p. 1 and in the CEWAL case (OJ 1993 L 34, p. 40).

Regulation 4056/86 and Regulation 3975/87—this type of economic sanction can be imposed for conduct which took place prior to their entry into force.[57] This question has not been considered by the European Court or the CFI. It was apparently left open by Regulation 17. Article 15(5)(b) of that regulation established that no fines would be imposed for acts taking place before notification of agreements in existence at the date of entry into force of the regulation, provided timely notification was made. It could be interpreted that conduct prior to the entry into force of Regulation 17 was subject to fines in the absence of a valid and timely notification.

None of the transport regulations contains provisions similar to Article 15(5)(b). Nor do they contain time limits for the validation of agreements, except for Regulation 1017/68 (though, even then, in a somewhat peculiar manner).

Article 30 of Regulation 1017/68 provides for its entry into force on 1 July 1968, eighteen days before the regulation was in fact adopted and twenty-two days before it was published. The regulation was given retroactive effect in order to comply with the last extension of the deadline for the adoption of a competition regulation in inland transport, pursuant to Article 2 of Regulation 141.[58] The prohibition of abuses of a dominant position was delayed until the day following the publication of the regulation and the prohibition of cartels until 1 January 1969 (though only for agreements which were in existence on the day of the publication of the regulation).[59] In practice, existing agreements had almost one year and a half to adapt to the prohibitions under the regulation although the provisions on validation lacked the clarity and flexibility of those contained in Regulation 17.[60]

Article 27 of Regulation 4056/86 provided that it should enter into force on 1 July 1987—after a six-month 'legal vacation'—without establishing a transitional regime for existing agreements. Article 20 of Regulation 3975/87 provided it should enter into force on 1 January 1988 and did not provide even for a legal vacation (it was published on 31 December 1987).

The want of a provision like Article 15(5)(b) of Regulation 17 in the transport regulations does not seem to stand in the way of the imposition of fines for conduct prior to their entry into force. On the other hand, there is no specific provision validating the imposition of such fines either. The Court's judgment in the *Dow Chemical Ibérica* case[61] may support the argument that the Commission is entitled to impose fines on any infringement of Articles 85 and/or 86 dated prior to the entry into force of the applicable regulation.[62] Moreover, Articles 85 and 86 have been applicable since 1958 under the Articles 88 and 89 procedures.[63]

---

[57] For the entry into force of the transport regulations see below.
[58] On this regulation, see above, Ch. 3, Section I.
[59] For a critique of these provisions, see above, Ch. 3, Section II.
[60] See Arts 5 and 7 of Reg. 17.   [61] See, above n. 26.
[62] Including inland transport, even before the *French Seamen* judgment. See above Ch. 2.
[63] See above, para. 6.1.1.

In spite of the arguments in favour of the possible general retroactive application of competition rules, at least since 1958, a distinction must be made between the sanctionary and the declaratory application of such rules.

In respect of sanctions, and regardless of the self-proclaimed non-criminal nature of fines under EC law,[64] the CFI and the European Court might recognize the principle of non-retroactivity of EC sanctions, on the ground that they originate not from the Treaty, but from later secondary legislation. In such a case, the Commission would only be able to impose fines from the date of the entry into force of the transport regulation involved, even if the infringements began before.

In respect of the declaratory application of the transport regulations, there is nothing to prevent the Commission from stating in a decision that particular conduct constituted a breach of Articles 85(1) or 86 notwithstanding the fact that the actual procedural regulation pursuant to which the decision was adopted had not yet entered into force at the time the conduct occurred. Articles 85 and 86 have been applicable since 1958. Furthermore, the Commission could have declared the same conduct contrary to the competition rules at any time, using Article 89 of the Treaty. The change in the procedural regime after the adoption of the transport regulations should not prevent the Commission finding that an infringement predating such regulations has occurred.

For the moment, in the few cases in which the Commission has obtained information on 'old' infringements, it has been extremely cautious. Not only has it avoided the imposition of fines but it has also adopted the approach of declaring the existence of an infringement before the entry into force of the transport implementing regulations.[65]

6.3.5. Publication of decisions. Implementing rules

The rules on publication of decisions[66] and the enabling provisions for the adoption of implementing legislation in respect of notifications and hearings[67] are identical to those in Regulation 17.[68] Following Regulation 1017/68, two Commission regulations were adopted, one for notifications[69] and one for hearings.[70] Following the adoption of Regulation 4056/86 and Regulation 3975/87, only one regulation was adopted in each case,[71] covering both notifications and

---

[64] On the nature of the Commission's fines, see Ortiz Blanco, above n. 5 Ch. VIII.

[65] See, e.g., the Commission's Decision in the *French-West African Shipowners' Committees'* case and in the *CEWAL* case, see above, n. 56.

[66] Art. 28 of Reg. 1017/68, Art. 25 of Reg. 4056/86 and Art. 18 of Reg. 3975/87.

[67] Art. 29 of Reg. 1017/68, Art. 26 of Reg. 4056/86 and Art. 19 of Reg. 3975/87.

[68] Arts 21 and 22 of Reg. 17.

[69] Comm. Reg. (EEC) 1629/69, see above, n. 24.

[70] Comm. Reg. (EEC) 1630/69, see above, n. 24.

[71] Comm. Reg. (EEC) 4260/88 (see above, n. 24) for sea transport, and Comm. Reg. 4261/88 (see above, n. 24) for air transport.

hearings in two separate sections. The content of all these Commission regulations is, save on a few details,[72] identical to Regulations 27[73] and 29.

6.3.6. Limitation periods

In the early seventies the Court pointed out the existence of a lacuna in Regulation 17.[74] With the aim of filling this lacuna, the Commission proposed and the Council adopted Regulation 2988/74 dealing with limitation periods in proceedings and the enforcement of sanctions under the EC rules on transport and competition.[75] Although this regulation was adopted long before the sea and air transport regulations, and refers exclusively to Regulation 17 and to Regulation 1017/68, its last recital specifies that '[i]t must also apply to the relevant provisions of future regulations in the fields of European Economic Community Law relating to transport and competition'.

Accordingly, the general rules on limitation periods apply in the whole transport sector, in respect of Regulations 4056/86 and 3975/87 as well as in respect of Regulations 17 and 1017/68.

6.3.7. Special procedures

Under the transport regulations, as under Regulation 17, it is possible to adopt provisional decisions withdrawing immunity from fines of notified restrictive agreements[76] and to order interim measures.[77] In all these cases the general rules apply. Nevertheless, some comments should be made.

The question arose in respect of provisional decisions whether, because of the absence of immunity from fines under Regulation 1017/68, immunity should in

---

[72] These exceptions include, among others, the provision which allows the Commission to examine a notification using a different regulation from that under which the undertakings have submitted their notification. On this point, see para. 6.6.3.1.

[73] Reg. 27 has now been repealed and replaced by Comm. Reg. (EC) 3385/94 of 21 Dec. 1994 on the form, content and other details of applications and notifications provided for in Council Reg. 17, OJ 1994 L377, p. 28, Art. 5. The new regulation entered into force 1 Mar. 1995. It substantially changes the appearance (and some of the content of) form A/B notifications and applications for negative clearance which fall under standard competition rules. At the moment the Commission has not yet decided to bring the transport regulations into line with Reg. 3385/94.

[74] In particular, in its judgments in Case 41/69, *ACF* v. *Commission, (Quinine)*, [1970] ECR 661 and in Case 48/69, *ICI* v. *Commission (Dyestuffs)*, [1972] ECR 619.

[75] Council Reg. (EEC) 2988/74, OJ 1974 L 319, p. 1.

[76] Art. 15(6) of Reg. 17 corresponds to Art. 19(4), third sub-para. of Reg. 4056/86 and to Art. 12(5), second sub-para. of Reg. 3975/87. For provisional decisions in general, see Kerse, above n. 5, Ch. VI.II and Ortiz Blanco, above n. 5, Ch. XI.

[77] On the basis of Art. 3 of Reg. 17, according to the ECJ. See order in Case 792/79R, *Camera Care* v. *Commission*, [1980] ECR 119 (see below). The corresponding articles in the transport regulations are Arts 10 and 11 of Reg. 1017/68, Arts 10 and 11 of Reg. 4056/86 and Arts 3 and 4 of Reg. 3975/87.

any event be granted by the Commission as a general principle of EC competition law. This question was answered affirmatively.[78]

A second question might then arise: if the obligation to respect a non-written immunity under Regulation 1017/68 is established, what kind of procedure should be followed by the Commission to withdraw immunity, remembering that no similar legal basis to Article 15(6) exists under the inland transport regulation?

It could be argued that, while the Commission must always grant immunity upon notification, it lacks powers to withdraw immunity since there is no written legal basis, nor parallel general principle, for such powers. However, this is probably a rather formalistic approach.

Perhaps a more logical approach, and the one that has been adopted by the Commission in practice,[79] is to say that immunity can be withdrawn, even in inland transport, following the general procedure for the adoption of these decisions.[80] Rights of defence would thereby be protected and the inland transport undertakings involved would be able to challenge the Commission's decision before the CFI. This solution could only be supported if immunity was not considered a general principle of EC competition law or if the possibility of withdrawing immunity was considered implicit in the principle of immunity itself.

As far as interim measures are concerned, the general rules fully apply in transport.[81] The Commission has used this procedure on several occasions although only once has adopted a final decision under the rules of Regulation 4056/86.[82]

In spite of the general applicability of the rules on interim measures in the transport sector, Regulation 3975/87 was recently modified to include a special procedure for interim measures in relation to certain anti-competitive practices.[83] The aim of this legislation is to safeguard the achievement of the liberalization in EC air transport.[84] It allows the Commission 'to take prompt action

---

[78] See above, para. 6.3.4.

[79] The President of the CFI seems to have implicitly accepted the Commission's solution by not raising this problem in his Order of 22 Nov. 1995 in Case T–395/94 R II, *Atlantic Container Line et al.* v. *Commission*, not yet reported, relating to the *TACA* agreement, see above n. 53. See in particular, para. 14 of the Order.

[80] The general procedure derives from the ECJ judgment in Joined Cases 8–11/66, *Cimenteries* v. *Commission*, [1967] ECR 75, and it was developed by the CFI in its judgment in Case T–19/91, *Vichy* v. *Commission*, [1992] ECR II–415.

[81] See Kerse, above n. 5, Ch. VI.I and Ortiz Blanco, above n. 5, Ch. XI.

[82] Decision of the Commission of 11 June 1992 in the *B&I Sealink-Holyhead* case, not published in the OJ, [1992] CMLR 255, adopted under Art. 10 of Reg. 4056/86. Given that the case basically involved harbour services, it might be wondered whether it would have been more suitable to use as an exclusive legal basis Art. 3 of Reg. 17, without mentioning Art. 10 of the maritime Regulation. The Commission subsequently followed this route in its Decision of 21 Dec. 1993 dismissing provisional measures in the *Sea Containers/Stena Sealink* case, OJ 1994 L 15, p. 8, and in its Decision concerning the Port of Roscoff, *Press Release IP (95) 492*, of 16 May 1995. See above para. 4.3.4.1.

[83] Council Reg. (EEC) 1284/91, OJ 1991 L 122, p.2, amending Reg. 3975/87.

[84] 1st recital and 2nd recital, 1st para., of Reg. 1284/91.

in cases where air carriers engage in practices which are contrary to the competition rules and which may threaten the viability of services operated by a competitor or even the existence of an airline company and thus cause irreversible damage to the competitive structure'.[85]

Under the new Article 4a of Regulation 3975/87:

Interim measures against anti-competitive practices

1. Without prejudice to the application of Article 4(1), where the Commission has clear prima facie evidence that certain practices are contrary to Articles 85 or 86 of the Treaty and have the object or effect of directly jeopardising the existence of an air service, and where recourse to normal procedures may not be sufficient to protect the air service or the airline company concerned, it may, by decision, take interim measures to ensure that these practices are not implemented or cease to be implemented and give such instructions as are necessary to prevent the occurrence of these practices until a decision under Article 4(1) is taken.

2. A decision taken pursuant to paragraph 1 shall apply for a period not exceeding six months. Article 8(5) shall not apply.

    The Commission may renew the initial decision, with or without modification, for a period not exceeding three months. In such case, Article 8(5) shall apply.

The requirements of this provision have been modelled around the conditions for interim measures established by the Court.[86] However, the provision's scope of application is somewhat different.

The first condition for interim measures to apply, as under the Court's jurisprudence, is that there is a *prima facie* infringement of competition rules. The second condition prescribed by the European Court and the CFI—that the likelihood of serious and irreparable harm makes the adoption of interim measures urgent—has been developed in detail in Article 4a of Regulation 3975/87. Furthermore, Article 4a relates only to the situation where the existence of a competing air service is, or is capable of being, endangered; only one of the possible situations in which, under the other transport regulations and Regulation 17, interim measures can be applied. Practices in the air transport which have a different object or effect must be dealt with under the general rules established by the EC Courts. For example, interim measures adopted by the Commission against an air transport undertaking for abusive exploitation of its customers must be adopted under Articles 3 and 4 of Regulation 3975/87[87] and not under Article 4a of Regulation 3975/87.

---

[85] 2nd recital, 2nd para., of Reg. 1284/91.

[86] See the ECJ order in the *Camera Care* Case (above n. 77) recently interpreted by the CFI in Case T–44/90, *La Cinq* v. *Commission* [1992] ECR II–1.

[87] As already stated, articles 3 and 4 of Reg. 3975/87 constituted the general legal basis for the adoption by the Commission of interim measures in air transport and have a content similar to that of Art. 3 of Reg. 17, which serves as a legal basis for the adoption of interim measures in other sectors.

6.4. THE PARTICULARITIES OF THE TRANSPORT PROCEDURES

While sharing these similarities with the general procedures under Regulation 17 and its implementing regulations, the transport regulations also present significant differences, some of which have been pointed out by the CFI in its *UIC* judgment.[88]

The main difference lies in the absence of individual negative clearance[89] in two of the three transport regulations[90] and in the way Article 85(3) proceedings are handled. Regulation 1017/68 already contained special features,[91] which, since it was the model for Regulation 4056/86[92] and Regulation 3975/87,[93] became the rule in transport.

Other differences concern the use of recommendations[94] and the degree of formality required for resolving cases,[95] but these are in practice unimportant differences.

The justification for a special procedural regime in transport and for its privileged treatment under Article 85(3), is in what the different regulations call the 'distinctive features' or the 'distinctive characteristics' of the various modes of transport.[96] No indication whatsoever is given in the regulations about the concrete features that justify a different treatment for transport under competition law, except in the air transport regulation, where reference is made to a wide network of bilateral agreements.[97]

6.5. NEGATIVE CLEARANCE AND ARTICLE 85(3)

All the transport regulations contain 'block negative clearance' provisions, as the 'exceptions' for 'technical agreements' have been described.[98] The inland and sea transport regulations, however, do not contain provisions on individual negative clearance like those contained in Article 2 of Regulation 17.[99]

The initial omission of negative clearance from the inland transport regulation could either be seen as intentional or as inadvertent.[100]

---

[88] See the judgment of the CFI in Case T–14/93, *Union internationale des chemins de fer(UIC)* v. *Commission*, 6 June 1995, (not yet reported).

[89] As opposed to 'en bloc' clearance. As has been seen, each transport Reg. contains an 'exception' for certain purely technical agreements—which is more or less equivalent to a 'block negative clearance'.

[90] See para. 6.5. [91] See above, Ch. 3, Section II.

[92] See 17th recital of Reg. 4056/86. [93] See 5th recital of Reg. 3975/87.

[94] See below, para. 6.8. [95] See below, para. 6.9.

[96] See 4th recital of Reg. 1017/68; 6th, 15th, 17th and 18th recital of Reg. 4056/86; and 3rd recital of Reg. 3975/87. [97] See 3rd recital of Reg. 3975/87.

[98] See above, Ch. 3, Section II in respect of Art. 3 of Reg. 1017/68.

[99] Although specific provisions of both regulations—undoubtedly by mistake—refer to 'negative clearance pursuant to Art. 85(3) of the Treaty'. See the English version of Art. 23(3) of Reg. 4056/86. In Reg. 1017/68 reference is made to Arts 5 and 6 of that Reg. instead of Art. 85(3) of the Treaty. As stated before, Art. 5 is the inland transport mirror of that provision of the Treaty. See above, Ch. 3, Section II. As to Art. 6 of Reg. 1017/68, see also Ch. 3 Section II.

[100] See above, Ch. 3, Section II.

The aim of the Commission and the Council might have been to encourage carriers' own assessment of competition rules, so that only clear-cut restrictive agreements were notified. If this was the case, the Commission and the Council probably thought that this absence gave a more favourable treatment to trans-port undertakings than Regulation 17.

In fact, the situation is just the reverse. It is most impractical for inland and sea transport undertakings to be denied the right to apply formally to the Commission in order to ascertain whether their agreements are restrictive;[101] whether a particular practice is abusive[102] or whether a given block exemption is applicable.[103]

Moreover, it is contrary to the policy considerations behind both transport regulations[104] not to give inland and sea transport undertakings the right to ask for the assistance of the Commission in clarifying by means of a formal decision whether their agreements are fully in conformity with the rules of competition, or whether the latter simply do not apply.

In conclusion, the 'pure mistake theory' for Regulation 1017/68—due to the haste with which it was prepared[105]—and the mechanical repetition of the pro-visions of the latter in Regulation 4056/86 is the most consistent explanation for the absence of negative clearance in the inland and shipping regulations.

The practical implications of the lack of a legal basis for the adoption of for-mal decisions granting negative clearance are, nevertheless, of little importance. In particular, it should be noted that:

(1)   on request, the Commission can, in effect, issue a negative clearance by means of a comfort letter using its powers granted by Regulations 1017/68 and 4056/86; and that,

(2)   in any event, the practical difference between a formal decision granting negative clearance and a comfort letter to the same effect is less acute than in the case of an individual exemption.[106]

---

[101] This would be particularly useful in the case of alleged technical agreements, which might be put before the Commission for consideration. See the 16th recital of Reg. 1017/68 and the last recital of Reg. 4056/86. The 13th recital of the inland regulation also talks about 'the needs of undertakings for certainty in the law'.

[102] E.g., certain practices by dominant transport undertakings *vis-à-vis* their customers and com-petitors.

[103] Like infringement decisions themselves, decisions granting negative clearance help to clarify the legal status of specific agreements whose coverage by the inland and maritime transport block exemptions may be unclear.

[104] See 16th recital of Reg. 1017/68 and last recital of Reg. 4056/86. The 13th recital of the inland regulation also talks about 'the needs of undertakings for certainty in the law'.

[105] Its second draft was discussed only for a few months, see above Ch. 2.

[106] Although this issue has not been addressed definitively by the ECJ, negative clearance deci-sions do not impede the application of Art. 85(1) by national courts; nor do they prevent national competition law from being applied to the same agreement. See in particular Kerse, above n. 5, pp. 212–13 and the views quoted there.

Unlike Regulations 1017/68 and 4056/86, Regulation 3975/87 contains a provision on negative clearance (Article 3[2]). Form AER, annexed to Regulation 4261/88 can be used for this purpose.[107]

Two points should be made on this issue.

First, form AER contains the usual options between 'A' (application for negative clearance) and 'B' (notification with a view to obtaining an individual exemption) in the old Regulation 27 form A/B.[108] The use of both options (A, or alternatively B), which used to be the case with most submissions under form A/B, could create problems. In such cases, the Commission should examine whether the agreement under consideration meets the test of Article 85(1), and only if *prima facie* it so appears, it would be obliged to publish a summary of the agreement under Article 5(2) of the regulation.[109] Later clearance would be complicated. In fact, under the three transport regulations, if the Commission changed its mind after the publication, and considered that Article 85(1) did not apply, or the parties modified it to make it harmless, quite paradoxically, the Commission should raise opposition, because Article 85(3) cannot be applied to an agreement not falling within the prohibition of Article 85(1). In this situation it would be necessary to send a 'serious doubt letter' based precisely on these grounds. For reasons of legal certainty, the Commission should also take action to clear the agreement, either formally or informally.[110]

As stated, under Regulation 1017/68 and Regulation 4056/86 clearance cannot be formal. This is possible only in air transport. Under Article 3(2) of Regulation 3975/87 , as under Article 2 of Regulation 17, the Commission 'may', but is not obliged, to adopt a formal decision whenever it is requested to do so, contrary to other provisions in the transport regulations, including the air transport regulation.[111]

Secondly, if the Commission opts for a formal decision, one might think that, contrary to Regulation 17, Regulation 3975/87 would not oblige it to publish a summary of the agreement to be cleared, because Article 16(3) of the regulation refers exclusively to the need to publish a notice before adopting individual exemption decisions but not before adopting negative clearance decisions.[112]

This might simply illustrate a preference of the Commission for informal

---

[107] See Complementary Note to Reg. 4260/88 and Reg. 4261/88. The note is common to both forms, MAR and AER.

[108] For this form, in its old and new version, see Kerse, above n. 5, Ch. II and Ortiz Blanco, above n. 5, Ch. III. The old form A/B has been replaced with a new version, to be found in Reg. 3385/94, on the form, content and other details of applications and notifications provided for in Council Reg. 17, cited above, n. 73. The new form is essentially a detailed series of questions which must be answered by notifying parties. The explicit choice between A and B is no longer made.

[109] For the nature of the statements in opposition procedures' notices, see para. 6.6.3.1.

[110] For the informal conclusion of Commission procedures, see Kerse, above n. 5, Ch. VI. and Ortiz Blanco, above n. 5, Ch. X.

[111] See below, para. 6.9.

[112] Art. 19(3) of Reg. 17 obliges the Commission to publish a notice before adopting a decision under Art. 85(3) of the Treaty and under Art. 2 of the Regulation.

solutions in these types of cases. Form AER is actually in keeping with both the old and the new form A/B in this respect.[113] In any event, it is more than probable that if the Commission, for any reason, wanted to adopt a negative clearance decision, it would follow the standard practice under Regulation 17. In fact, the very aim of such a decision clarifying a legal or economic point of contention, could be better achieved with prior notice to interested parties as provided for in Article 16(3) of the air transport regulation, which copies Article 19(3) of Regulation 17.

With regard to exemptions, as already stated,[114] the transport sector is characterized by the widespread application of block exemptions which cover most of the traditional restrictions of competition existing in the various modes of transport, especially in sea and air transport.

The most remarkable feature in respect of individual exemptions, apart from the possibility of granting them under two procedures,[115] is the non-mandatory nature of notifications.[116] This has repercussions in respect of the provisional validity of agreements in the transport sector[117] and in respect of retroactive validation.[118]

6.5.1. Exemption from notification

Although Regulation 17 and 1017/68 share a preoccupation with ensuring effective supervision and simplifying administration as far as possible[119] (and this aim must be considered to underlie Regulation 4056/86 and 3975/87, which closely follow the inland regulation's procedural provisions),[120] they contain some different nuances.

Regulation 17 considers that it is 'necessary to make it obligatory, as a general principle, for undertakings which seek application of Article 85(3) to notify to the Commission their agreements, decisions and concerted practices'.[121]

Meanwhile Regulation 1017/68 states that 'it is for the undertakings themselves, in the first instance, to judge whether the predominant effects of their agreements, decisions or concerted practices are the restriction of competition or the economic benefits acceptance as justification for such restriction and to decide accordingly, on their own responsibility, as to the illegality or legality of such agreements, decisions or concerted practices'.[122]

---

[113] See pt VII of the Complementary Note to form AER. The Complementary Note to old form A/B contained the same statements, but—as stated—a prior publication is required by Reg. 17 in other sectors of the economy. The introduction of the new form A/B in Reg. 3385/94 also indicates that many applications and notifications will be dealt with informally by means of a comfort letter.

[114] See above, Chs 4 and 5. [115] See above, para. 6.5.3.
[116] See next para. [117] See above, para. 6.5.2.
[118] See above, para. 6.7.2.
[119] See the 2nd recital of Reg. 17 and the 13th recital of Reg. 1017/68.
[120] See the 17th recital of Reg. 4056/86 and the 5th recital of Reg. 3975/87.
[121] 3rd recital of Reg. 17. [122] 14th recital of Reg. 1017/68.

Regulation 4056/86 and Regulation 3975/87 follow the inland regulation, and point out that 'it is primarily the responsibility of undertakings to see to it that their agreements, decisions and concerted practices conform to the rules on competition, and consequently their notification to the Commission need not be made compulsory'.[123]

Under Regulation 17, only certain agreements with 'special features which make them less prejudicial for the development of the common market'[124] are exempt from notification, but—of course—not exempt from Article 85.[125] The list of agreements for which notification is not compulsory is given in Article 4(2) of that regulation.[126]

Under the transport regulations, no matter how restrictive the agreements, decisions or practices might be, they need not be notified to the Commission and they can be concluded or operated without being declared.[127] Undertakings run the risk then that their agreements may be declared retroactively void.[128] It is their own responsibility to assess this risk.

From the preambles to the transport regulations and from the preamble to Regulation 17 in respect of Article 4(2) agreements, it can be seen that exemption from notification does not mean exemption from the competition rules. Nor does it mean that notification must not or should not be made. Non-notification exposes undertakings to the unenforceability of the agreements and to administrative fines from the Commission. Accordingly—and especially in transport, where it cannot be said that agreements are always or usually harmless, unlike those falling under Article 4(2) of Regulation 17—it is important that transport undertakings notify their restrictive agreements, if they want to enjoy legal certainty. In this respect the non-mandatory nature of notifications does not help transport undertakings substantially in respect of Articles 85 and 86 and may, on the contrary, give the false impression that rules for transport differ from the general rules. This is not the case.

In conclusion, the exemption from notification cannot be considered a substantial advantage for transport undertakings and may lead to misunderstandings.

In some respects, however, the exemption from notification may be of some advantage to transport undertakings. In particular:

(1)   it allows the Commission to make its individual exemption decisions retroactive to the date of the agreement;[129]

---

[123] 18th recital of Reg. 4056/86; the 9th recital of Reg. 3975/87 is almost identical.

[124] 4th recital of Reg. 17.

[125] According to the 5th recital of Reg. 17, 'there is a need to make more flexible arrangements for the time being in respect of certain categories of agreement, decisions and concerted practices, *without pre-judging their validity under Art. 85*'. (Emphasis added)

[126] For Art. 4(2) of Reg. 17, see Kerse, above n. 5, pp.52 *et. seq.* and Ortiz Blanco, above n. 5, Ch. III.

[127] 15th recital of Reg. 1017/68.   [128] *Ibid.*

[129] See below, para. 6.7.2.

(2) it obliges the Commission to examine whether the conditions of Article 85(3) are met, even when it becomes aware of the agreements as a result of a complaint or of its own initiative;[130] [131]

(3) it increases the possibility of provisional validity applying, since there are no time limits for notification. This is a major difference with the general rules and deserves some comment.

6.5.2. Provisional validity[132]

For the purposes of assessing the validity of agreements in a national court, agreements concluded prior to the date on which the relevant EC competition regulation entered into force must be considered 'old' while later agreements must be considered 'new'. Given that Regulation 4056/86 and Regulation 3975/87 entered into force relatively recently, on 1 July 1987 and 1 January 1988 respectively,[133] provisional validity may be a major issue in maritime and air transport.

According to the Court's *Haecht II* judgment, 'old agreements' which have been duly notified must be considered provisionally valid by national courts until the Commission decides on the applicability of Article 85(3), while 'new agreements' cannot enjoy provisional validity[134]—Regulation 17 assumes that, so long as the Commission has not taken a decision, agreements, even if notified, can only be implemented at the parties' own risk.

The conclusions of the *Haecht II* judgment in respect of new agreements under Regulation 17 are equally applicable to the transport regulations. As stated, Regulation 1017/68 stresses that it is the responsibility of undertakings to assess the legality of their agreements, decisions, and concerted practices.[135] Such agreements are equally exposed to the risk of being declared void with retroactive effect.[136] The other two transport regulations follow Regulation 1017/68 in this respect.[137]

The question of 'old' transport agreements is more complicated. The later *De Bloos/Bouyer* judgment of the Court,[138] while re-affirming the *Haecht II* judgment,

---

[130] In all its transport decisions, the Commission has actually examined the four conditions. See e.g., *Shipowners' Committees* and *CEWAL*, above, n. 56.

[131] In these two points, the transport regulations are similar to Art. 4(2) of Reg. 17. See Kerse, above n. 5, pp. 43–4.

[132] For provisional validity in general, see Kerse, above n. 5, pp. 360 and see Ortiz Blanco, above n. 5, Ch. I.

[133] Reg. 1017/68 entered into force, generally, on 1 July 1968 (Art. 30(1); special provisions were contained in Art. 30(2) and (3)), so provisional validity in the inland sector is of lesser importance.

[134] ECJ judgment in Case 28/67 *Haecht II*, [1973] ECR 77. The doctrine of provisional validity was first outlined by the ECJ in its judgment in Case 13/61, *De Geus* v. *Bosch*, [1962] ECR 45 and confirmed in several other judgments before 1973.

[135] 14th recital of Reg. No.1017/68.   [136] 15th recital of Reg. 1017/68.

[137] See the 15th recital of Reg. 4056/86 and the 5th recital of Reg. 3975/87.

[138] ECJ judgement in Case 59/77, *De Bloos* v. *Bouyer II*, [1977] ECR 2359.

made it clear that provisional validity applies 'to an old agreement duly notified or exempted from notification'.[139]

It is wrong to interpret this statement in the *De Bloos* ruling, which could be misleading if taken outside its context, as establishing an unconditional presumption of validity of old agreements the notification of which is not compulsory.

The better interpretation of the judgment is that it establishes the rule that:

(1) old agreements in general be notified before the deadline set out in Article 5(1) of Regulation 17; or

(2) old agreements of the kind covered by Article 4(2) of Regulation 17 (which need not be notified within the time limits of Article 5[1], but can nevertheless be notified according to Article 5[2] of the Regulation) are notified to the Commission.[140]

National courts should consider such agreements to be provisionally valid until the Commission has decided on the applicability of Article 85(3) to them.

This interpretation is fully consistent both with the *De Bloos* judgment[141] and with the earlier jurisprudence,[142] which emphasizes the need for notification in order for the provisional validity of old agreements of any kind to be accepted. The *Haecht II* judgment is absolutely clear when it specifies that agreements exempted from notification can be declared void retroactively by a court, and not only by the Commission.[143] If provisional validity of agreements exempted from notification were unconditional and unlimited, a national court could not apply Article 85(2) to old Article 4(2) agreements, at least not until a Commission decision finding an infringement of Article 85(1) had been adopted.

Moreover, in respect of the air transport sector, this conclusion has been specifically supported by the Court in its *Ahmed Saeed* Judgment.[144] There, the Court concluded that certain old agreements between airlines, covered by Regulation 3975/87, were automatically void:

where no application for exemption of the agreement from the prohibition set out in Article 85(1) has been submitted to the Commission under Article 5 of Regulation 3975/87; or where such an application has been made but received a negative response on the part of the Commission within 90 days of the publication of the application in the

[139] Para. 15 of the *De Bloos/Bouyer* judgement, *ibid.*

[140] Implicitly, at any time before the question of its validity is challenged before a national court. It is submitted that a court should deny provisional validity to old Art. 4(2) agreements notified after (and as a consequence of) challenge in the national court in their regard.

[141] See *De Bloos/Bouyer*, at para. 14, in which it is clearly stated that provisional validity extends *from notification until the date of a Commission decision*; see equally the reply to the first question in the final ruling.

[142] See, in particular, the *Haecht II* judgment, above n. 131, especially paras 9 and 13.

[143] See *Haecht II, ibid.*, at paras 24–7.

[144] ECJ judgment in the *Ahmed Saeed* case, above n. 55.

Official Journal; or again where the 90-day time-limit expired without any response on the part of the Commission but the period of validity of the exemption of six years laid down in the aforesaid Article 5 has expired or the Commission withdrew the exemption during that period[145]

Exactly the same conclusion must be drawn in respect of inland and maritime transport, in which the applicable provisions in respect of notification are contained in Article 12 both of Regulation 1017/68 and of Regulation 4056/86.

The fact that Regulation 3975/87—and indeed Regulation 4056/86—do not contain transitional provisions on pre-existing agreements along the lines of Article 5 of Regulation 17 does not preclude the unconditional applicability of Article 85(1) and (2). As stated by Advocate General Lenz in the *Ahmed Saeed* case,[146] competition rules are not new for air carriers. The Court decided in 1974 in the *French Seamen* case[147] that transport was subject to the general rules of the Treaty (including competition rules) and the first proposal for a regulation for applying Articles 85 and 86 of the Treaty to air transport dates back to 1981.[148] The same argument applies to shipping. The last recital of the 'Brussels Package'[149] recognized in 1979 already that competition rules applied and should be implemented in maritime transport. The first Commission proposal was tabled in 1981.[150] The shipping industry was undeniably fully aware of the imminence of the application of competition rules to the sector. For the rest, Regulation 4056/86 entered into force six months after being published.[151]

Accordingly, the immediate application of Articles 85(1) and (2) cannot be denied on the grounds that carriers were unaware of the applicability of competition rules to their operations.

In summary, in spite of the lack of transitional rules in the transport sector and in spite of the special rules in the sector, so that all agreements[152] are for procedural purposes 'Article 4(2)–type' agreements—i.e., their notification is not a pre-condition for exemption—the only benefit transport undertakings derive from the doctrine of provisional validity is the fact that, they can, *at any time,*[153] obtain provisional validity by notifying their old agreements.

Without a valid notification, provisional validity cannot apply across the board to old restrictive agreements in the transport sector until the Commission

---

[145] *Ahmed Saeed* judgment, *ibid.* at para. (1) (ii) of the final ruling, p. 855.
[146] Opinion of Adv. Gen. Lenz of 28 April 1988, *ibid.* at para. 16, p. 821.
[147] ECJ judgment in Case 167/73, *Commission* v. *France*, [1974] ECR 359.
[148] Commission proposal of 10 Nov. 1981, OJ 1981 C 291, p. 4.
[149] Council Reg. (EEC) 954/79, OJ 1979 L 121, p. 1.
[150] See above, n. 34.   [151] See Art. 27 of Reg. 4056/86.
[152] As explained, according to the 4th and 5th recitals of Reg. 17, the more flexible arrangements for Art. 4(2) agreements were based on their 'less prejudicial character'. This is not the case for all types of restrictive agreements in transport, and further supports the views expressed here in respect of the limited value of provisional validity in transport.
[153] But, once again, before the question of its validity is put before a national court. See above, n. 140.

decides individually on the applicability of Article 85(3)[154] to each agreement or practice. To adopt a different interpretation would be tantamount to derogating from Article 85(2) of the Treaty. Given that many of the agreements in the sector are 'old', this derogation would extend to a high number of agreements in the shipping and air transport sector.

It is more than likely that when the Court developed the doctrine of provisional validity it thought that provisionally valid agreements would be short-lived and that the regime it proposed would be transitional, framed within Regulation 17 procedures and affecting relatively few and unimportant agreements. The relevance of provisional validity grew, however, with the maturity of the EC and the accession of new Member States; accession agreements[155]—i.e., agreements prior to the accession of new Member States having, in effect, to be treated also as 'old' agreements for provisional validity purposes.

The proposed interpretation of provisional validity, based on the non-mandatory nature of notification as laid down in the transport regulations, already goes a long way. A more generous interpretation would be almost to derogate from Article 85(2) for shipping and air transport and could hardly be endorsed by the Court—if only because it took almost thirty years for the competition rules to be implemented in transport.[156]

6.5.3. Individual exemption procedures

As we have seen already, the main contrast between the procedures under the transport regulations and the general rules of Regulation 17 is the way in which Article 85(3) proceedings are handled.

Under the transport regulations, there are two types of procedure for adopting decisions applying Article 85(3).[157]

The first type of procedure is called an 'opposition procedure', like the procedures included in certain Commission block exemption regulations.[158] The substance of the procedure in the transport regulations is, however, different.[159]

The second type of procedure is similar—if not identical—to the standard Regulation 17 procedure. It can only be used when a procedure of the first kind

---

[154] See recently the judgment of the CFI in Case T–29/92 *Vereniging van Samenwerkende Prijsregelende Organisatie in de Bouwnijverheid (SPO) and others* v. *Commission*, at para. 342, citing the judgment of the ECJ in Joined Cases 240, 241, 242, 261, 262, 268 and 269/82 *SSI* v. *Commission* [1985] ECR 3831 at paras 73–8.

[155] For the regime applicable to 'accession agreements', see Kerse, above n. 5, pp. 360 *et seq.* and Ortiz Blanco, above n. 5, Ch. I.

[156] Yet some specific forms of transport—like tramp shipping and air transport between the EC and third countries—still lack implementing rules. See above Ch. 2.

[157] This does not take into account the exemption and procedures under Arts 6 and 14 of Reg. 1017/68, to which reference was made above. See Ch. 3, Section II.

[158] For Commission opposition procedures see Kerse, above n. 5, Ch. 2.IV and Ortiz Blanco, above n. 5, Ch. X, Section II.

[159] See below, para. 6.6.9.

has not culminated in a favourable decision—because of opposition from the Commission or from a Member State—or when the Commission—generally after having considered the case within the framework of an infringement procedure—finally decides to grant an exemption, without the agreement having been notified, on its own initiative. This procedure will be referred to in the following sections as the 'own-initiative exemption procedure'.

6.6. THE OPPOSITION PROCEDURE

6.6.1. Notification of agreements

According to the sea and air transport regulations, undertakings and associations of undertakings which seek application of Article 85(3) of the Treaty in respect of agreements, decisions and concerted practices which fall within the scope of Article 85(1) and to which they are parties may seem to be obliged to notify the Commission.[160] On the other hand, the inland transport regulation, which served as a model for sea and air transport, states that, in order to obtain an exemption under Article 85(3) undertakings may notify the Commission.[161] The maritime and air transport regulations (Regulations 4056/86 and 3975/87) may impose an obligation to notify, and more closely resemble Regulation 17, which says 'shall submit'.[162] Given that neither under the inland transport regulation nor under the sea and air transport regulations notification is required for an exemption to be granted,[163] these textual differences have no real practical effect.

6.6.2. Waiving the opposition procedure

The Commission implementing regulations in transport[164] provide that applications (which in reality, under Regulation 17 terminology, are notifications) pursuant to the provisions on opposition procedure are to be submitted using specific forms. These are similar to Regulation 3385/94's (formerly Regulation 27's) form A/B,[165] and are called form II,[166] form MAR and form AER.[167] They are annexed to the relevant regulations.

---

[160] Art. 12(1) of Reg. 4056/86 and Art. 5(1) of Reg. 3975/87. The texts are identical in substance, although there are minor textual differences. The first reads 'will be lodging a claim' and the second 'will be submitting applications'.

[161] Art. 12 of Reg. 1017/68 says in particular 'will be able to send an application to the Commission'.

[162] See Arts 4(1) and 5 of Reg. 17.   [163] See below.

[164] See Art. 3(1) of Reg. 1629/69, Art. 4(1) of Reg. 4260/88 and Art. 3(1) of Reg. 4621/88.

[165] The similarity of the MAR and AER forms with the old form A/B of Reg. 27, is even greater as it served as model.

[166] Reg. 1629/69 contains three different forms : Form I, for complaints—like the old form C of Reg. 27 (now found in Reg. 3666/93); Form II, for 'applications' (in reality notifications), with a view to an Art. 5/Art. 85(3) of the Treaty decision; and Form III, for 'notifications pursuant to Art. 14(1)', or notifications of crisis cartels.

[167] Unlike the other two standard notification forms, form AER contains the option for negative

The question arises whether it would be possible for transport undertakings to request the individual application of Article 85(3) by the Commission outside the framework of the opposition procedures. In other words, could transport undertakings be allowed to waive the opposition procedure and notify their agreements under conditions similar to those applied by Regulation 17? This could have two main advantages for the undertakings. First, there would be no publication of a summary of their agreements if they accepted a Commission comfort letter in response to their notification. This might be interesting for transport undertakings which, for commercial reasons, desire confidentiality. Second, it would permit a much more flexible framework for negotiating any modifications the Commission might require before it grants an exemption. As will be seen,[168] once notified under the opposition procedure, agreements must be published in summary form by the Commission without modification. Only where an exemption is not automatically granted, and that within an 'own initiative exemption procedure', can the Commission, with the same powers and limitations as under Regulation 17, ask for the changes necessary for it to adopt a favourable decision.

However, the transport regulations do not seem to contemplate the possibility of renouncing the opposition procedure. Of the two possible exemption procedures,[169] only the opposition procedure is directly available to the parties involved.[170]

There is no doubt that the intention of the Commission and the Council in adopting the transport regulations was to allow transport undertakings to enjoy a more flexible procedural regime. However, the practical result of creating a special regime for notifications and individual exemptions has not only not served this purpose but has probably run counter to it.

In an attempt to simplify Article 85(3) procedures, the Commission might consider allowing the parties to choose between the transport opposition procedure and the common Regulation 17 procedures. Although to some extent subsidiary, the latter procedures are also present in the transport regulations .

This could bring advantages for transport undertakings. The present system's rigidities are capable of harming undertakings' interests by obliging them to undergo undesired publicity. The ability for undertakings to choose would doubtless reduce the Commission's administrative load and accelerate the preparation of decisions. Once the opposition procedure is stopped, the Commission is in any event obliged to open up a new phase of examination and follow a Regulation 17-type procedure if it wants to adopt a formal exemption decision. In addition, the Commission would be able more assiduously to resort to informal resolution of cases by means of comfort letters.

clearance : it is an air form A/B. Using the same terms of comparison, Forms II and MAR would be inland and maritime B forms, exclusively.

[168] See below, para. 6.6.6. [169] See above, para. 6.5.3.
[170] For a further discussion of possible options for the Commission, see below, Ch. VII.

If specific agreements risked not being granted an automatic exemption, the parties could elect to follow the standard competition exemption procedure and the Commission would be able—on the basis of the provisions dealing with common communications prior to an individual exemption in the transport sector[171]—to publish a summary and adopt a formal decision. The legal basis for this could be the various articles in the regulations which allow the Commission to exempt agreements on its own initiative.[172]

However, unless the transport regulations are modified, it seems unlikely that the Commission will adopt such a procedure. The rights of third parties may be compromised if transport undertakings could avoid the obligation under the opposition procedure to make their agreements public.

6.6.3. Action on notification

Once the Commission has received a notification of an agreement in the transport sector, it must examine:

(1) whether the notification is admissible;
(2) whether it is in possession of all the available evidence; and
(3) whether action has been taken (or indeed should be taken) to enjoin the agreement, i.e. whether infringement procedures have been or should be initiated under the applicable provisions in the different regulations.

Only then will the Commission proceed to the publication of a notice in the *Official Journal* 'as soon as possible'.[173] [174] Before doing so, however, the Commission may inform the notifying undertakings of its intentions to examine the notification under a different regulation from the one used for the notification.

6.6.3.1. Admissibility

Inadmissibility of a notification may arise from failure to comply with the basic procedural requirements of a notification under the opposition procedure[175] (following the requirements set out in the old Regulation 27[176]) paramount among

---

[171] Art. 26(3) of Reg. 1017/68, Art. 23(3) of Reg. 4056/86 and Art. 16(3) of Reg. 3975/87.
[172] Art. 11 of Reg. 1017/68, Art. 10 of Reg. 4056/86 and Art. 3 of Reg. 3975/87.
[173] See Art. 12 of Reg. 1017/68, Art. 12.1 of Reg. 4056/86 and Art. 5.1 of Reg. 3975/87.
[174] For the time-frame in the opposition procedures, see below, para. 6.6.5.
[175] The procedural rules of Reg. 1629/69 for inland transport, Reg. 4260/88, Section I, for sea transport and Reg. 4261/88, Section I, for air transport.
[176] Art. 4 of Reg. 3385/94 makes clear that whenever a notification or an application is incomplete, it cannot be considered to be valid. Nonetheless the Commission is under a duty to inform the undertakings of the incomplete nature of their application, failing which the incomplete application will be deemed to be effective from the date of its receipt by the Commission. Former Reg. 27 and its transport counterparts do not have any similar provision, but the Commission will probably apply the same principles. However in this case, the Commission would not be bound by any

which is the mandatory utilisation of specific notification forms for each mode of transport.[177]

Under the inland and sea transport regulations a notification may also be considered inadmissible when the agreements, decisions or practices to which it refers are clearly not restrictive of competition in the sense of Article 85(1) of the Treaty, or already enjoy exemption pursuant to Regulation 1017/68 or Regulation 4056/86, which grant exemption to certain categories of agreements.[178] Admissibility under the opposition procedures of those regulations presupposes the real possibility that the notified agreement falls within Article 85(1). If that were not the case, the Commission would be able to send a negative clearance comfort letter,[179] but it would not have the power to adopt a formal negative clearance decision.[180]

It should nevertheless be observed that the admissibility of a notification does not imply the existence of a violation of Article 85(1). The Commission could make a conclusive statement of this kind only in a final decision—an act that could be challenged before the Court (a notice not being subject to appeal)— particularly given:

(1) that the position of the Commission, if it were definitive, must be respected by a national court before which a question on the validity of the notified agreement is put; and

(2) that nothing prevents the Commission, after having published a notice pursuant to the opposition procedures, from concluding that the agreement which has been notified is not contrary to Article 85(1) of the Treaty and thus need not be exempted.[181]

Accordingly, admissibility simply implies no more than a possible applicability of Article 85(1) of the Treaty.[182]

This interpretation of admissibility is also justified on grounds of good administration. The opposition procedures, with the publication of a notice in eleven languages and short periods within which to react, are cumbersome for negative clearance. Furthermore, it is illogical that, in a context in which the notification

time limits and, lacking a legal basis, it would probably not be able to deem the application or notification inadmissible automatically.

[177] Form II in inland transport, form MAR in sea transport and form AER in air transport. See above, n. 162 and n. 163.

[178] See above, Ch. 3 Section II and Ch. 4.

[179] On this type of letter, see Kerse, above n. 5, Ch. VI, Ch. VIII and Ortiz Blanco, above n. 5, Ch. X.

[180] See above, para. 6.5.1.

[181] Opposition should be raised in this case as well, in order to avoid tacit automatic exemption of a non-restrictive agreement, which has no sense.

[182] For the most recent formula used in the Commission's opposition notices, see below para. 6.6.5. Also, see e.g., the Notice on the CIA agreement in the railway sector, OJ C 117, 28.4.1993, p. 8.

of restrictive agreements is not compulsory and where formal negative clearance is not possible, transport undertakings are encouraged to notify all their agreements, even the ones which are clearly not restrictive of competition.

The above considerations do not apply in air transport, where, as under the general regime of Regulations 17 and 3385/94, undertakings may ask for negative clearance under Article 3(2) of Regulation 3975/87 or, alternatively, for individual exemption pursuant to Article 85(3). In such a case, a notification might be considered inadmissible for the purposes of the opposition procedure, but still be treated as a formal application for negative clearance in response to which a formal negative clearance decision and not only a comfort letter may be adopted. Contrary to many other provisions in the transport regulations—including Regulation 3975/87—the term used in Article 3(2) is 'may', not 'shall'. As in Regulation 17, the procedure for 'air negative clearance' is fully flexible (i.e., informal conclusions are clearly possible) and very different from the opposition procedure under Article 5 of the air transport regulation.

The availability of negative clearance may encourage applications under Regulation 3975/87. This seems to run counter to the system in the two previous transport regulations. The reasons for the different regime existing in air transport are not clear[183] but may relate to the practical advantages deriving for air transport companies from the use of this procedural tool. The convenience of air transport undertakings in a field where extensive use has been made of block exemptions and where clearance could be specifically useful was no doubt considered during the final drafting process of this regulation.

In any event, the argument that, on the basis of a preference for self-examination, formal negative clearance was not necessary in the transport regulations—which may be no more than an *ex post facto* rationalization of a simple error as already commented[184]—has been subsumed by the administrative convenience enjoyed by air transport undertakings. The ironic result has been that a theoretically more interventionist provision in the air transport regulation has granted air carriers a more user-friendly regime than the extremely non-interventionist inland and sea transport regulations.

Further on admissibility, the fact that a notification has been made under the wrong procedural regulation does not make it inadmissible.

According to Article 4(8) of Regulation 4260/88 and Article 3(8) of Regulation 4261/88:

Where an application submitted pursuant to Article 12 of Regulation (EEC) No. 4056/86 [or Article 5 of Regulation (EEC) No. 3975/87] falls outside the scope of that Regulation, the Commission shall, without delay, inform the applicant that it intends to examine the application under the provisions of such other Regulation as is applicable to the case;

---

[183] On this type of letter, see Kerse, above n. 5, Ch. VI, VII, and Ortiz Blanco, above n. 5, Ch. X.

[184] See above, para. 6.5.

however, the date of submission of the application shall be the date resulting from paragraph 7. The Commission shall inform the applicant of its reasons and fix a period for him to submit any comments in writing before it conducts its appraisal pursuant to the provisions of that other Regulation.

In accordance to Article 15(1) of Regulation 4260/88 and Article 14(1) of Regulation 4261/88, the minimum period for submitting comments may not be less than two weeks, and may be extended.

This provision is an innovation not previously included in Regulation 27[185] which has not been picked up in the new Regulation 3385/94 (in respect of notifications subject to the general rules of Regulation 17) or Regulation 1629/69 (for notifications under Regulation 1017/68 in the inland transport sector). The Commission has used this provision explicitly on various occasions.[186]

The question arises whether, in the event that the legal basis relied on by the notifying undertaking was the general (Regulation 3385/94) or the inland transport (Regulation 1629/69) procedural regulations, the Commission would still be entitled to treat the notification under any of the other three possible regulations. The Commission has used this provision by analogy at least once with respect to an application in inland transport[187] but it has never applied it yet in sectors subject to Regulation 17. The analogous application of that requirement to notifications subject to Regulation 1017/68 has been facilitated by the fact that all three regulations basically contain the same opposition procedure. But even if the notification was made under Regulation 17, the Commission would react in a similar manner, as actions under the wrong procedural regulation might be challenged, as it was in the *UIC* case, as being an infringement of an essential procedural requirement.[188]

The Commission's letter and comments of the undertakings tend precisely to avoid this problem, permitting a preliminary discussion of the issues and possibly a consensus on the applicable procedural regime. In any event, the Commission has the last word in deciding which regulation applies, subject to the control of the CFI and the European Court.

Although, in principle, there should be no difficulty in resolving this issue, there can be cases in which the procedural possibilities and the legal rights of the parties vary from one regulation to the other. For example, retroactive

[185] Obviously, because at the time Reg. 17 was the only procedural regulation.

[186] See, e.g., in the shipping sector the notices concerning the *Gulfway Agreement* (OJ 1990 L 130, p. 3) and the Agreement 1237 (OJ 1990 C 59, p. 2). None of these agreements was exempted, however. See above, Ch. 4.

[187] See the Commission's Communication in the *Auto Car Europe* case, OJ 1994 C 130, p. 3, Part V. Despite the fact that the notification was made only in accordance with Reg. 1017/68, the Commission carried out the publication based on Regs 4056/86, 3975/87 and 17. The notice does not specify, however, whether the parties were given an opportunity to make comments on the legal basis for the publication, although this was done in all probability.

[188] See the CFI judgment in the *UIC* case, above n. 88.

decisions are always possible in the transport sector but not in other sectors[189] and the Commission is obliged to make a full investigation on a complaint within the framework of the transport regulations, but not within the context of Regulation 17.[190] [191]

The decision of the Commission regarding the applicable regulation is not a decision within the meaning of Article 173 paragraph 4 of the Treaty. Like a statement of objections[192] or access to the file,[193] it is just a preliminary step or a provisional measure which paves the way for a challengeable decision. Since it is not the culmination of a special procedure, distinct from that of the final substantive decision (i.e., not being definitive or final) and does not have the necessary adverse legal effects (because in a challenge of the main decision any procedural questions can be raised and taken up by the Court),[194] it must be concluded that it is not possible for notifying undertakings to challenge the Commission's decisions before the CFI. Once a final decision is adopted, the validity of that decision (which could be attacked for having been adopted on the basis of the wrong procedural regulation) and any procedural irregularities can be submitted to the attention of the Court, which can annul the decision on those grounds.[195]

6.6.3.2. Possession of all the available evidence

Under the opposition procedure, the Commission's obligation to publish a summary of the agreements notified by transport companies is subject to the condition that the Commission is in possession of 'all the available evidence'. Notifying undertakings are obliged to submit detailed information about their activities. The information required is specified in the three transport forms referred to above, and in a supplementary note.[196] If the information provided by the undertakings is not complete, or if it is insufficient in a given case, the Commission may ask for such information from the parties to the agreement. During that period no publication will take place.

As in other areas of competition law[197] the transport provisions allow the Commission to delay the commencement of the opposition period while information is being collected.

---

[189] See below, para. 6.7.2.   [190] See below, para. 6.9.2.

[191] For the differences between the transport regulations (in particular Reg. 1017) and Reg. 17, see the CFI judgment in the *UIC* case, above n. 88, at paras 58–64.

[192] ECJ order in Cases 60/81R and 190/81R *IBM* v. *Commission* [1981] ECR 1857.

[193] CFI judgment in Case T–7/89 *Hercules* v. *Commission* (1991) ECR II–1711.

[194] *Ibid.*

[195] The Court will probably look into the question whether the use of the wrong procedural regulation has had any bearing on the outcome of the case before the Commission, and decide accordingly.

[196] See above, para. 6.6.2.

[197] In particular, in the State aids area.

6.6.3.3. Actions against the notified agreements

The Commission is obliged to publish a summary of the notified agreements only when no action has been taken against them. Clearly the Commission is not obliged to publicize when, before notification, it has initiated formal infringement procedures against those agreements. It can be questioned, however, whether this applies to cases in which, after having studied the notification, the Commission considers it necessary to send a statement of objections to the parties and open a formal procedure.

The first point to make is that the Commission cannot be denied the right to open formal proceedings at any time, including after notification. An interpretation preventing the Commission from acting against notified agreements until publication of a notice would deny the Commission its fundamental power to apply Article 85 of the Treaty. Further, it could encourage last minute notifications after fact-finding has finished and before the Commission has formally opened proceedings against transport undertakings.[198] Accordingly, the Commisions' right to open procedures after a notification should not be denied.

The question is instead whether, having decided to open a formal procedure, the Commission is still obliged to publish a notice. As will be seen,[199] the opposition procedure is binding on the Commission and creates advantages for the undertakings concerned that cannot normally be withdrawn without solid legal grounds. In this case the text of the various provisions dealing with the transport opposition procedures appears to be unambiguous and releases the Commission from the obligation to publish a notice where—but only where—a formal procedure has been opened before publication of a notice.

The fact that the Commission can always open a procedure should not be interpreted as a *carte blanche* allowing it to frustrate the advantages and the guarantees afforded to transport undertakings by the implementing regulations. In fact, opening a formal procedure is not a decision that can be taken easily. It always necessitates solid factual and legal support, which usually comes in the form of a statement of objections,[200] a much more complex and developed document than the 'serious doubts letter' which would permit the Commission to stop the opposition procedure.[201]

6.6.4. Initiation of procedures

Under the general regime, the rules concerning the powers of the Commission and of Member States for the application of Articles 85 and 86 of the Treaty are contained in Article 9 of Regulation 17. Pursuant to this provision:

---

[198] Undertakings are normally aware of the Commission's proceedings long before such a formal step is taken.

[199] See below, para. 6.6.7.

[200] Cf., Ortiz Blanco, above n. 5, Ch. VII.

[201] See below, para. 6.6.7.

(1)   the Commission has exclusive competence to apply Article 85(3);
(2)   the national administrative authorities designated by the Member States have competence to apply Articles 85(1) and 86 in accordance with Article 88 of the Treaty;
(3)   Member State administrative authorities lose their competence whenever the Commission opens a procedure under Article 2 (negative clearance), Article 6 (individual exemption) or Article 3 (infringement) of Regulation 17. Although the Commission can open a procedure earlier, customarily the Commission has opened procedures at the time of sending a statement of objections (in infringement procedures) or at the time of publishing a notice under Article 19(3) of Regulation 17 (in negative clearance and individual exemption procedures);[202]
(4)   national judicial bodies may at any time directly apply Articles 85(1) and 86 even after the Commission has instituted proceedings.[203]

The provisions setting out the powers of Member States in the transport sector are Article 15 of Regulation 1017/68, Article 14 of Regulation 4056/86 and Article 7 of Regulation 3975/87. Those provisions differ in some respects from Article 9 of Regulation 17:

(1)   According to the inland and sea transport regulations, the Commission has sole power not only to apply Article 85(3) of the Treaty but also to impose obligations pursuant to Article 4(2) of Regulation 1017/68 and Article 7 of Regulation 4056/86. These provisions deal with the monitoring of block exempted agreements pursuant to the two regulations.[204]
(2)   The transport regulations do not cite the legal basis for the enforcement of Articles 85(1) and 86 of the Treaty by Member States, namely Article 88. This reference was omitted in Regulation 1017/68 because Member States did not then accept the applicability of Articles 85, 86 and 88 to transport.[205] The omission was passed on to the other two transport regulations, for which Regulation 1017/68 was the model.
(3)   There is no difference between the Regulation 17 regime and the transport regimes in respect of the opening of an infringement procedure and in 'own initiative exemption' cases.[206] The situation regarding opposition procedures is different.

---

[202] The Commission has recently begun announcing in its notices that the procedure has been opened pursuant to Art. 9(3) of Reg. 17.

[203] Case 127/73, *BRT* v. *SABAM II*, [1974] ECR 313.

[204] Art. 4.2 of Reg. 1017/68 does not talk of obligations within the common meaning of Reg. 17 and of the other transport regulations. Pursuant to it, in certain cases, undertakings 'may be required to make such effects cease'.

[205] However, they had no difficulty in taking Art. 87 as a legal basis for Reg. 1017/68. See above, Ch. 3, Section II.

[206] For 'own initiative' exemptions, the procedure of which mirrors closely the exemption procedure under Reg. 17, see below, para. 6.7.

In opposition procedures the transport regulations reserve exclusive competence for the Commission to apply Articles 85(1) and 86 after it has sent a 'serious doubts letter'. This is the latest possible moment at which competence can be withdrawn from Member States since the Commission can initiate proceedings before then.

The question is whether, as in the case of Article 19(3) of Regulation 17, under current practice, the Commission should open a procedure at the time of publishing a notice pursuant to the transport opposition procedures.

There seems to be no obligation to do so on the part of the Commission. Taking into account the fact that, in principle, the publication of a notice is not a conclusive statement about the applicability of Article 85(1), it would not be appropriate for the Commission to open such a procedure systematically before a notice is published opening the opposition period. The Commission might, in any event, consider opening a parallel formal procedure, at any time, respecting the competence of Member States until it has definitely made up its mind on the applicability of Article 85(1), be it in a serious doubts letter or before. In the latter case, an internal decision to that effect should be adopted. It does not seem that such a decision is necessary when sending a serious doubts letter. The very act of sending such a letter implies—according to the transport regulations—the withdrawal of the competence to apply Articles 85(1) and 86 from Member States.

6.6.5. Notices

Whenever the Commission finds that a notification is admissible; that it is in possession of all the available evidence and no action has been taken against the agreement, the Commission is obliged in all circumstances[207] to publish a notice with a summary of the agreement in the *Official Journal*.[208] This publication shall be made as soon as possible after the Commission has satisfied itself that those three conditions have been fulfilled.

The notice must outline the main elements of the agreement put forward in the notification. It may include elements obtained by the Commission while gathering 'all the available evidence'.[209]. The notice must not disclose the business secrets of the undertakings.[210] In order to fulfil this obligation, once it has prepared a draft notice, the Commission submits it for comments to the

---

[207] Even if a Member State has formally requested within forty-five days after receiving the notification under the provisions on co-operation with Member States that the Commission oppose an agreement. See below, para. 6.6.7.

[208] Note that, as observed above, the Commission can open a formal procedure upon notification of an agreement, in which case it is not obliged to publish a notice about it. See above, para. 6.6.3.3.

[209] See above, para. 6.6.3.2.

[210] Art. 12(2), last sentence of Reg. 1017/68; Art. 12(2), last sentence of Reg. 4056/86; and Art. 5(2), last sentence of Reg. 3975/87.

undertakings. In this case, the Commission is not bound by the two weeks' minimum period for comments provided for by the procedural regulations.[211] Comments should refer to confidentiality issues, not to substantive issues nor to the manner in which the agreements have been summarised.[212]

The notice is then translated into the eleven official working languages of the Community and published in the *Official Journal.*

In practice, the triple examination prior to the publication of a notice, plus the administrative work associated to it, may mean that notices are published several months after the notification is made.

These notices tend to be short (legal arguments are not fully developed).[213] They contain a final paragraph, intended to make them neutral, in contrast to standard Article 19(3) notices under Regulation 17 and 'own initiative exemption' notices under the transport regulations. In these two types of notices the Commission announces its intention to exempt the agreements made public in the notice.[214] In the transport opposition notices the Commission states that it has before it an agreement which *prima facie* could fall within the prohibition of Article 85(1)[215] and has not, at this stage, formed any view on the applicability of Article 85(3) of the Treaty. Finally, the Commission invites interested third parties and Member States to submit their comments on the summarised agreement within thirty days.[216]

6.6.6. Grant of exemption

The Commission may decide, after having received comments from interested third parties and Member States, that the agreement falls within the terms of Article 85(1) of the Treaty and fulfils the conditions for an individual exemption. In such a case, the Commission will not raise serious doubts as to the applicability of Article 85(3) and an individual exemption will be granted.

Any individual exemption under the opposition procedures implies two Commission decisions: first, the decision not to raise serious doubts; secondly, the individual exemption itself.

The decision not to raise serious doubts is a real Commission decision,

---

[211] Art. 11(1) of Reg. 1629/69; Art. 15(1) of Reg. 4260/88 and Art. 14(1) of Reg. 4261/88 do not apply to this type of letter, which are of a much less important nature than those referred to by those provisions.

[212] In this respect, note that the Commission is sovereign, in deciding on the contents of its notices, subject to judicial control of its acts. Moreover, it seems difficult that a notice could affect any legal rights of the parties. The Commission is, nevertheless, obliged to act objectively whilst summarizing the agreements. A biased summary which would encourage opposition from third parties would not fulfil this condition. The final decision in any such case does not seem to be challengeable for this reason, anyway.

[213] This might prove an inconvenience if an automatic exemption were finally granted by positive administrative silence.

[214] See below, para. 6.7.2.   [215] On the meaning of this assertion see above, para. 6.6.3.1.

[216] About the intervention of Member States, see below, para. 6.6.7.

although its character is purely internal. The adoption of this decision is the moment at which the Commission opens a formal procedure and informs Member States that they can no longer apply Articles 85(1) and 86 to the notified agreement. The Commission also informs the undertakings of its decision not to raise serious doubts before the ninety days' period expires. The actual decision exempting the agreements notified under the opposition procedure is automatically adopted on the day that the period expires, not on the day the Commission decides internally not to raise serious doubts. The only challengeable decision is, accordingly, the tacit automatic individual exemption. In order to fulfil its obligations under Article 190 of the Treaty the Commission informs the notifying undertakings of its reasons to authorize their agreements in the letter in which they are notified of the Commission's decision not to raise serious doubts. The structure of this letter resembles that of a formal decision, i.e. it contains adequate factual and legal grounds. The Commission publishes a press release each time an individual exemption of this kind takes place.[217] [218]

Conditions and obligations cannot be formally attached to an individual exemption granted in the absence of opposition, although the Commission may state that its positive view is based on specific assumptions regarding the conduct of the undertakings. If the Commission wants to impose conditions and obligations by decision, it is obliged to raise serious doubts and follow the standard Regulation 17-type procedures for 'own-initiative exemptions' under the transport regulations.[219] One of the problems of the opposition procedures is precisely that they do not give the Commission any flexibility to make its decisions formally subject to specific requirements. In certain cases, the Commission has nevertheless made clear that it reserves the right to monitor the exempted agreements and ask for information about them during the period of the exemption.[220]

The question also arises whether—as is normal practice under Regulation 17—the Commission may ask for modifications of agreements notified under the opposition procedures, in order to make them compatible with Article 85(3) of the Treaty. This generally allows the Commission to negotiate with undertakings terms on which an agreement might be exempted.

No reference to this possibility is made in the provisions dealing with the transport opposition procedures. A rigid interpretation that obliged the Commission to summarize and publish literally without modification what is first notified by the undertakings would be, first, against the interest of undertakings and, secondly, against the purported aims of the opposition procedures, i.e., administrative simplification. The Commission would be obliged to raise serious

---

[217] But not each time a serious doubts letter is sent. This may cause problems for third parties. See below, para. 6.6.7.

[218] See, e.g., *Press Release IP (92) 396* of 18 May 1992, in which reference is made to an individual exemption granted under the opposition procedure in favour of a joint venture agreement in the ferry routes between Denmark and Sweden (DSB/SFL, Helsingor-Helsingborg).

[219] See below, para. 6.7.　　　　　　　　　　[220] See the *Press Release* referred to in n. 218.

doubts even in cases in which, with slight modifications of the notified agreements, they could qualify for exemption and successfully pass through the opposition procedure (if third parties and Member States' comments did not persuade the Commission to the contrary).

The Commission has taken a flexible approach and when modifications to agreements have been accepted by the parties and notified, it has not objected to the automatic approval of the revised agreements.[221]

However, the Commission is not entitled to oblige undertakings to make modifications to their agreements under the opposition procedure.[222] If the parties are not ready to follow the Commission's advice, the Commission is obliged either to publish a notice and then raise serious doubts, or to open a formal procedure against the agreement, avoiding the publication of a notice. In both cases, the Commission will insist in having modifications made if the parties want to avoid an infringement decision. The outcome may be an 'own initiative' individual exemption the content of which would not basically differ from what could have been an opposition procedure individual exemption, had the parties agreed to modify their agreements at the outset.

In the absence of opposition, individual exemption is granted in favour of the notified agreements, insofar as they conform with the description given in the application. The exemption covers the time already elapsed and extends for a maximum of three years—in inland transport—or six years—in sea and air transport—from the date of publication in the *Official Journal* of the notice concerning the agreements.

The difference between the inland and the sea and air transport regulations may cause inconvenience in cases which involve several modes of transport, and other services subject to Regulation 17 where the opposition procedure does not exist. In one case,[223] and this is not the only example involving a multiple legal basis,[224] the Commission had to apply at the same time Regulation 1017/68, Regulation 3975/87 and Regulation 17. The Commission did not raise serious doubts and the notified agreements were exempted for three years in respect of inland activities and for six years for air transport activities. Other services were dealt with in a comfort letter by the Commission. Cases like this can be worked out in the same manner, but the Commission and the Council should consider the establishment of uniform procedural rules for all modes of transport, preferably by simply applying Regulation 17 to agreements in the transport sector.[225]

---

[221] Again, see the *Press Release* on the DSB/SFL case.

[222] As a matter of fact, it does not have such a right within the Reg. 17 exemption procedure, either.

[223] Comm. Notice on the *DHL* case, OJ 1990 L 258, p. 33.

[224] E.g., in the Case *NV Auto Car Europe (ACE)* the Commission published a Notice (OJ 1994 C 130, p. 3) with a triple legal basis: Art. 12(2) of Reg. 1017/68, Art. 12(2) of Reg. 4056/86 and Art. 5(2) of Reg. 3975/87. See above, Ch. 3, Section II.

[225] See conclusions in Ch. 7, below.

6.6.7. Opposition: 'Serious doubts' letters

The Commission may, before the end of the ninety-day period, notify the parties to the agreement that there are serious doubts as to the applicability of Article 85(3) of the Treaty.

Pursuant to Article 12(4), first sub-paragraph, of Regulation 4056/86 and Article 5(4), first sub-paragraph, of Regulation 3975/87, the Commission 'shall do so if requested by a Member State within 45 days of the forwarding to the Member State of the notification', in accordance with Article 15(2) of Regulation 4056/86 and Article 8(2) of Regulation 3975/87 respectively (co-operation with Member States). Member States must justify their request 'on the basis of considerations relating to the competition rules of the Treaty'. In the context of transport cases this is especially important. As already explained,[226] the competent national authorities comprise both the national competition and transport authorities. National transport authoritie equally are obliged to argue on competition law grounds. They are also obliged to ask the Commission to oppose the exemption on competition law grounds and not on considerations of transport policy.

This rule is not to be found in Regulation 1017/68, Article 12(4), first paragraph, which states:

If, within the 90-day limit, the Commission notifies applicants as referred to in the first sub-paragraph of paragraph 3 [serious doubts letter], it shall examine whether the provisions of Article 2 [Article 85(1)] and of Article 5 [Article 85(3)] are satisfied [Parentheses added].[227]

With respect to the possibility for Member States to require the Commission to oppose exemption, the sea and the air transport regulations[228] borrow elements of the Commission's opposition procedures in certain block exemption regulations adopted under Regulation 1017/68, the first one being Commission Regulation (EEC) No. 2349/84, of 23 July 1984[229] now superseded.[230] Article

---

[226] See above, para. 6.2.

[227] The second part of Art. 12(4) of Reg. 1017/68 is identical to the second part of Art. 12(4) of Reg. 4056/86 and Art. 5(4) of Reg. 3975/87. These provisions oblige the Commission to consider an 'own initiative' individual exemption when it has raised serious doubts concerning an agreement. For 'own initiative' individual exemptions, see below, para. 6.7.

[228] The first draft text for a maritime opposition procedure, apart from mentioning directly Art. 85(1) and (3), contained exactly the terms of Reg. 1017/68. The first maritime opposition procedure was later modified and it set the pattern for the air transport regulation, the first version of which, above, n. 148, did not contain such a provision either. See Art. 11(4), 1st sub-para. of the 1st draft of Reg. 4056/86, above, n. 34, of 1981. The 2nd draft, of 1985 (COM [85] 90 final, OJ 1985 C 212, p. 9) did not contain any modification of the purely procedural rules in the future regulation, but its final text included the novelty referred to above.

[229] OJ 1984 L 219 p. 15; *Corrigendum* in OJ 1984 L 280, p. 32.

[230] Reg. 2349/84 has been replaced by Comm. Reg. (EEC) 240/96, OJ 1996 L 131, p.2, which deals with technology transfer agreements. The opposition procedure in this new regulation is

4(5) and (6) of this regulation, and similar provisions in other Commission regulations providing for opposition procedures[231] state:

5. The Commission may oppose the exemption. It shall oppose exemption if it receives
   a request to do so from a Member State within three months of the transmission to
   the Member State of the notification referred to in paragraph 1 or of the communication referred to in paragraph 4. This request must be justified on the basis of considerations relating to the competition rules of the Treaty.
6. The Commission may withdraw the opposition to the exemption at any time.
   However, where the opposition was raised at the request of Member State and this
   request is maintained, it may be withdrawn only after consultation of the Advisory
   Committee on Restrictive Practices and Dominant Positions.[232]

Under the sea and air transport opposition procedures, the period for a Member
State to induce opposition is shorter than in Commission block exemptions
(forty-five days as opposed to three months) but the period starts to runs from
the date of receipt by Member States of the notification by the parties, pursuant
to the procedural co-operation mechanisms between the Commission and
Member States. Accordingly, the starting-point of the forty-five-day period is different from the starting-point for the ninety-day period for the Commission to
oppose automatic exemption. In practice, several weeks may elapse between the
end of the first and the beginning of the second period.[233] Member States can
also make comments on the notice within thirty days of its publication.

   If required by Member States within the forty-five-day period, the Commission must raise serious doubts. That obligation does not arise when Member
States make critical comments on a given agreement within the thirty-day period
following its publication in the *Official Journal*.

   One might question whether it serves any purpose to publish a notice concerning the agreement, once opposition has been required by national authorities. It might be thought unnecessary, time-consuming, and potentially
misleading, since where a Member State has requested the Commission to raise
serious doubts the Commission is obliged to proceed correspondingly and no
automatic exemption will be granted. This approach would also have procedural advantages for the Commission: a notice being unnecessary, the
Commission could avoid the administrative work which it entails.

   The Commission, however, has adopted a much stricter approach, and even
in such circumstances it publishes a notice. There are several reasons for this:

---

somewhat different from former opposition procedures. In particular, the deadline for the
Commission to oppose automatic exemption has been shortened to four months, instead of six.

   [231] On the Commission's opposition procedures in some block exemption regulations, see Kerse,
above n. 5, Ch. II.IV and Ortiz Blanco, above n. 5, Ch. XI.

   [232] For a comment on the differences between the Commission's opposition procedures and the
Council transport opposition procedures, see below, para. 6.6.9.

   [233] See above, para. 6.6.5.

(1) the opposition procedure of Article 12 is mandatory. This is clear from the wording of this provision ('shall publish'). There must be solid legal grounds for any deviation from this obligation, which must be satisfied in every case unless the Commission first opens a formal procedure against the notified agreement;

(2) the opposition procedure creates advantages for the undertakings concerned and cannot be disregarded for reasons of administrative convenience for the Commission. The main advantages are strict time-limits and automatic exemption in case of failure of the Commission to react within these time-limits (though these advantages do not apply if a Member State has opposed);

(3) in particular, publication of a summary of the application triggers the commencement of the ninety day period for the Commission. Without such a time-limit the Commission would be free to raise serious doubts at any time;

(4) the previous point is of considerable importance in two cases:

(a) the Member State subsequently withdraws its request; here—without publication—the ninety-day period would not even have started (to the disadvantage of the undertaking);

(b) in spite of its obligation to react, the Commission—for whatever reason—does not raise serious doubts (here again the undertakings would not enjoy the advantages flowing from the ninety-day time-limit);

(5) the same conclusions must be drawn not only in respect of requests from Member States, but—all the more so—in respect of complaints from third parties. The receipt of a complaint would, in any event, not be sufficient for the Commission not to publish a notice summarizing a notified agreement, since the Commission is only released from its obligation to publish where it has opened proceedings under Article 10;[234]

(6) a consistent application of the looser approach would mean that publication would also be superfluous when the Commission already knows from the outset that it will raise serious doubts. This was certainly not the intention of the drafters of the provisions dealing with transport opposition procedures, and is not in line with the substance of those provisions;

(7) for the Commission, publication allows third party comments and helps to assess the Member States' objections.

Finally, note that a request from a Member State to raise serious doubts under Regulation 1017/68, on inland transport, is not binding on the Commission, although the Commission may react in the same way as in the sea and air transport sectors.

[234] See above, para. 6.6.3.3.

Serious doubts letters are not challengeable decisions of the Commission. Like statements of objections themselves, they do not prejudice or alter the legal position of the parties in a definite way, nor are they final acts in an independent procedure. They are—even more so than statements of objections—preliminary steps or preparatory acts towards a final Commission decision. In the case of serious doubts letters, moreover, the Commission is automatically obliged to consider whether an individual exemption can be granted after the opposition procedure has been interrupted.[235]

Serious doubts letters are fairly short (normally no more than five pages) and contain a summary of the facts and an embryonic reasoning on the basis of Article 85(1) and (3). They are not as elaborated as a statement of objections. In practice, if after examining the possibility of an individual exemption outside the opposition procedure the Commission decides not to grant exemption, it will be obliged to address a statement of objections to the parties. In this case, a serious doubts letter would be a preliminary step before a statement of objections.

The Commission may, of course, combine a serious doubts letter with a statement of objections, when it has sufficiently considered the reasons against an individual exemption. The joint serious doubts letter / statement of objections could be issued not only pursuant to the rules applicable in substantive infringement procedures, but also in preliminary decision procedures (withdrawal of immunity from fines) and in interim measures procedures.[236] In such cases, the Commission will clearly indicate the double legal nature of the document sent to the undertakings.

A serious doubts letter has several consequences. First, the notified agreements lose their provisional validity—if they ever enjoyed it.[237] This is clear from the *Ahmed Saeed* judgment.[238] The Court stated that whenever after the formal notification of an agreement in the air transport sector (and by extension, in all transport sectors, where similar rules apply) the Commission raises serious doubts within the ninety-day time-limit, national courts must consider such agreements automatically void.

Secondly, the Commission is obliged to consider further whether an exemption can be granted. This requirement is included in the three regulations,[239] though the drafting is much clearer in the inland transport regulation.[240] In spite of the different wording, there is no reason to believe that the intentions of the Council were different in the sea and air transport regulations.

The Commission will carry out its examination largely in the standard way of Regulation 17. Given the fact that the notified agreements, as they stand, seem

---

[235] See below, para. 6.7. on 'own initiative' exemption procedures.

[236] On these two special procedures in the transport sector, see above, para. 6.3.7.

[237] On the conditions for provisional validity in the transport sector, see above, para. 6.5.2.

[238] On this judgment, see para. 6.5.2.

[239] See Art. 12(4), 2nd sub-para. of Reg. 1017/68; Art. 12(4), 2nd sub-para. of Reg. 4056/86; and Art. 5(4), 2nd sub-para. of Reg. 3975/87.

[240] See Art. 12(4) 1st sub-para. of Reg. 1017/68.

not to merit exemption, the Commission might suggest changes, or impose conditions and obligations to render them compatible with Article 85(3).[241] If that is not possible, the Commission must follow the standard infringement procedures under the transport regulations. Both 'own initiative exemption' procedures and infringement procedures are virtually identical to exemption and infringement procedures under Regulation 17.[242]

Lastly, the Commission must inform Member States of the delivery of a serious doubts letter, pursuant to the co-operation provisions in the transport regulations.[243]

The Commission is not obliged to make public its opposition to the automatic exemption of an agreement. This might mislead third parties who, having read the notice concerning the agreement, and having no evidence of the opposition of the Commission, can genuinely think that silence from the Commission means acceptance of the agreements three months after they have been summarized in a notice in the *Official Journal*. In order to avoid this problem, the Commission might in the future consider the publication of a press release or a short notice in the *Official Journal* when a serious doubts letter has been sent and refer to the follow-up of notices under the transport opposition procedures in the *Annual Report on Competition Policy*.[243a]

6.6.8. Withdrawal of a non-opposition exemption

According to the sea and air transport regulations:

If the Commission finds, after expiry of the 90-day time limit, but before expiry of the six-year period, that the conditions for applying Article 85(3) are not satisfied, it shall issue a decision declaring that the prohibition in Article 85(1) is applicable. Such decision may be retroactive where the parties concerned have given inaccurate information or where they abuse the exemption from the provisions of Article 85(1).[244]

The inland transport regulation is identical, except for the length of the exemption (three years) and the reference to its Articles 2 and 5 (instead of Articles 85[1] and [3] of the Treaty).[245]

The last part of this provision has been borrowed from Article 8(3) of Regulation 17. The transport regulations refer only to the possibilities under (c) (incorrect information) and (d) (abuse of the exemption).[246] Reference is not made

---

[241] For the 'own initiative' individual exemption procedure, see below, para. 6.7.
[242] Minor differences might exist in respect of informal settlements. See below, para. 6.9.2.
[243] See above, para. 6.3.3.   [243a] See conclusions in Ch. 7, below.
[244] See Art. 12(3), 2nd sub-para. of Reg. 4056/86; and Art. 5(3), 2nd sub-para. of Reg. 3975/87.
[245] See Art. 12(3), 2nd sub-para. of Reg. 1017/68.
[246] The problems raised by the interpretation of the actual meaning of 'abuse of the exemption' are common to Reg. 17 and the transport regulations. For the withdrawal of individual exemptions and an interpretation of Art. 8(3) (d) of Reg. 17, in general, see Ortiz Blanco, above n. 5, Ch. XI.

to (b) (breach of an obligation), because the opposition procedures do not provide for obligations,[247] nor to (a) (change in the basic facts underlying the decision).

Regardless of the lack of a more specific provision, the Commission can always withdraw the exemption whenever the basic facts underlying a decision change in such a way that the conditions of Article 85(3) are not fulfilled, whether or not the undertakings have taken an active role in those changes. The legal basis for this action is the Treaty itself which only allows exemptions when the four conditions apply. The failure of secondary legislation to deal with all possible cases of non-fulfillment of those conditions cannot be interpreted as a *numerus clausus* limiting the reasons for which an exemption can be withdrawn.[248]

The adoption of a decision must be preceded by infringement proceedings in which the undertakings are given the opportunity to be heard on the matters to which the Commission has taken objection.[249]

Contrary to the Commission's opposition procedures in other fields,[250] once it has raised serious doubts against a notified agreement in transport the Commission cannot, by withdrawing its opposition, effectively accept the applicability of Article 85(3). In this case, the opposition of a Member State or its own opposition obliges the Commission to go through a standard individual exemption procedure at the end of which a formal decision can be adopted.[251] [252]

The transport opposition procedures do not contain provisions on the renewal or modification of non-opposition exemption decisions.

In respect of renewals, apart from the possibility of granting them as 'own initiative' individual exemptions, the general rules apply. The parties may apply for renewal. They need not use the standard transport notification forms.[253]

---

[247] See above, para. 6.6.6.

[248] In the sea transport field, in respect of the withdrawal of Arts 3 and 6 block exemptions, see, the commentary on Art. 7 in Ch. 4.

[249] Art. 26(1) in conjunction with Art. 12(3), 2nd sub-para. of Reg. 1017/68; Art. 23(1) in conjunction with Art. 12(3), 2nd sub-para., of Reg. 4056/86; and Art. 16(1) in conjunction with Art. 5(3), 2nd sub-para. of Reg. 3975/87.

[250] Under Art. 4(6) to (8) of Comm. Reg. (EEC) 2349/84 and Comm. Reg. (EC) 240/96 (above, n. 229 and n. 230) and similar provisions in the Commission block exemptions that contain an opposition procedure:

6. The Commission may withdraw the opposition to the exemption at any time. However, where the opposition was raised at the request of a Member State and this request is maintained, it may be withdrawn only after the consultation of the Advisory Committee on Restrictive Practices and Dominant Positions.

7. If the opposition is withdrawn because the undertakings concerned have shown that the conditions of Art. 85(3) are fulfilled, the exemption shall apply from the date of notification.

8. If the opposition is withdrawn because the undertakings concerned have amended the agreement so that the conditions of Art. 85(3) are fulfilled [satisified in Regualtion 240/96], the exemption shall apply from the date on which the amendments take effect.

9. If the Commission opposes exemption and the opposition is not withdrawn, the effects of the notification shall be governed by the provisions of Reg. 17.

[251] Note that the regulations say 'shall'. See below, para. 6.9.1.

[252] On this procedure, see below, para. 6.7.

[253] The judgment of the ECJ in Case 75/84, *Metro* v. *Commission II*, [1986] ECR 3021 established that within the Reg. 17 procedure, it was not necessary to use form A/B. There is no reason to believe that this doctrine does not apply in the transport sector.

A summary of the request must be published and the renewal will be granted for an additional period (three or six years) if the Commission does not raise serious doubts.

In respect of modifications, non-opposition individual exemptions, like 'own-initiative' individual exemptions, can only be modified by the Commission by a new decision after hearing the parties to the agreement and interested third parties.

The Commission would send the parties a document similar to a statement of objections, informing them of the modifications it would require before granting the extension. The undertakings participating in the agreements would be able to reply as in infringement proceedings[254] although the need to hold an oral examination may not be apparent. In such a case, the Commission might lack the powers to modify a previous exemption just by issuing a new 'own-initiative' decision before which it would, in any event, be obliged to hear the parties.[255]

With respect to third parties, the modification of an exemption would be subject to the obligations of prior publicity requirements which must be fulfilled before an exemption will be granted. The Commission would have to publish a notice containing a summary of the agreement and allow thirty days for the interested third parties to make observations before adopting its decision.[256]

6.6.9. Comparison with other block exemption regulations

The opposition procedures contained in the Council regulations laying down detailed rules for the application of Articles 85 and 86 in the transport sector are substantially different from the opposition procedures contained in the Commission block exemption regulations in certain areas covered by Regulation 17.

The basic difference relates to the nature of the decisions adopted in each case. In the transport sector, the opposition procedure appears to be the only way for an undertaking to notify an agreement to the Commission in order to obtain an individual exemption. In the Commission's opposition procedures, the parties do not formally ask for an individual exemption. Rather, paradoxically they ask the Commission to apply a block exemption to their agreements, on an individual basis. Transport opposition procedures lead to individual exemptions, while Commission's opposition procedures extend the benefits of a given block exemption to notified agreements, on a case-by-case basis. In other words, transport non-opposition decisions are real individual exemption decisions applying Article 85(3) of the Treaty, while non-opposition decisions pursuant to the

---

[254] See Arts 26(1) and 13(1) and (3) of Reg. 1017/68; Arts 23(1) and 13(1) and (3) of Reg. 4056/86; and Arts 16(1) and 6(1) and (3) of Reg. 3975/87.

[255] Though the provisions dealing with such decisions do not limit their possible scope. See Art. 11(4) of Reg. 1017/68, Art. 11(4) of Reg. 4056/86 and Art. 4(3) of Reg. 3975/87.

[256] See Art. 26(3) of Reg. 1017/68, Art. 23(3) of Reg. 4056/86 and Art. 16(3) of Reg. 3975/87.

Commission's block exemption regulations are decisions to apply a given block exemption individually, pursuant to the powers[257] of the Commission under such regulations.[258] [259]

Transport opposition procedures also differ from block exemption opposition procedures in that they are open to comments from interested third parties. Within thirty days, such persons (and Member States, as well) may address comments to the Commission. This is not the case for Commission opposition procedures, in which only Member States are involved.

Another difference relates to the time frame of the two types of procedures. The point of departure of the opposition period is different in both procedures: the date of publication of a notice in the *Official Journal*, in the case of transport; the date of receipt or the date shown on the postmark of the notification, in the case of Commission block exemptions. Note that information *must* be complete in both cases. In the block exemption opposition procedures, the opposition period of six months[260] will otherwise not begin to run. In the transport opposition procedures, the notice opening the ninety-day opposition period is not published until all the available necessary evidence has been obtained by the Commission.[261]

Member States have forty-five days to voice their opposition after they receive a transport notification and three months in the case of a Commission block exemption notification.

The length of the exemption period differs as well: three or six years in the case of transport; the period of validity of the relevant Commission block exemption regulation, in the other cases.

The consequences of opposition also vary. Opposition in transport entails automatic examination of the conditions of Article 85(3); then, if necessary, an infringement procedure. Opposition under the Commission block exemptions opens a period of discussion with the undertakings that may lead to the with-

---

[257] It has been questioned whether the Commission has been granted such powers or indeed can have them. For the Commission's opposition procedures in general, see Kerse, above n. 5, Ch. 2.IV and Ortiz Blanco, above n. 5, Vol. 2, Ch. V.II.

[258] See Art. 4(1) of Comm. Reg. (EC) 240/96 and similar provisions in other Comm. Regs containing an opposition procedure.

[259] The nature of the decisions under the opposition procedures of the Commission is the subject of debate but it seems clear that they are not standard individual exemptions. It could be argued that they are decisions to extend the scope of a given block exemption to agreements not previously covered. However, this is not quite so, because the block exemption would not be applicable to identical agreements, after the non-opposition decision, unless they were notified and authorized following the opposition procedure. For a general discussion of the Commission's opposition procedures, see Kerse and Ortiz Blanco, above n. 5.

[260] See Art. 4(3)(b) of the old Comm. Reg. (EEC) 2349/84, and corresponding provisions in other Commission block exemptions. Note that the new Comm. Reg. (EC) 240/96 provides for a 4-month period for opposition, and that its Art. 4(3) refers the question of the completeness of a notification to Art. 4 of Comm. Reg. (EC) 3385/94.

[261] For the need to gather all the 'available' evidence before publishing a notice under the transport opposition procedures, see above, para. 6.6.3.2.

drawal of the opposition at any time.[262] In that case, the effects of notification are governed by Regulation 17,[263] i.e., the parties enjoy immunity from fines from the moment of notification, at least for conduct within the terms of their agreement. Withdrawal of opposition does not exist in transport. Once a serious doubts letter has been sent, a new procedure begins. There is no way to revoke such a move.[264]

The issues just referred to are of some importance within the context of the new block exemption for maritime consortia,[265] because the Commission has included an opposition procedure along the lines of the opposition procedures in Regulation (EEC) 2349/84 and other Commission block exemption regulations.[266]

Within the consortia opposition procedure the applicable notification form will be form MAR, which might be modified to enable the parties to specify clearly whether they claim that their application may benefit from the consortia opposition procedure,[267] or whether their application must be considered a standard notification under Article 12 of Regulation 4056/86.

Under the consortia opposition procedure, the applicant shipping companies will also enjoy immunity from fines. Opposition can be withdrawn at any time. As a result, without departing from the opposition procedure, a favourable decision could be achieved through the imposition of conditions and obligations, arising out of discussions between the Commission and the parties, or through modification of the agreements. If neither conditions and obligations, nor modifications, could make the Commission change its mind, an infringement procedure should be opened.

Since this is a procedure of a different nature, publication of a notice and automatic examination of the conditions in Article 85(3) do not seem necessary, as would be the case under the standard procedure in Article 12 of Regulation 4056/86. The letter informing the parties to the notified consortium that the Commission opposes automatic extension of the block exemption is not equivalent to a serious doubts letter, for the purposes of Article 12 of Regulation 4056/86. In conclusion, it is important that the parties make a clear choice when submitting an application.

---

[262] See Art. 4(6) of Comm. Reg. (EC) 240/96 and corresponding provisions in other block exemption regulations. Withdrawal makes the block exemption applicable from the date of notification or, if amendments have been introduced into the agreements, from the date on which the amendments take effect. See Arts 4(7) and (8) of Comm. Reg. (EC) 240/96 and corresponding provisions in other block exemption regulations.

[263] See Art. 4(9) of Comm. Reg. (EC) 240/96 and corresponding provisions in other block exemption regulations.

[264] This is yet another inconvenience of the transport opposition procedures.

[265] Comm. Reg. (EC) 870/95, OJ 1995 L 89, p.7.　　　[266] See Art. 8 of Reg. 870/95.

[267] Form A/B was modified in order to adapt it to the Commission's opposition procedure. See Comm. Reg. (EEC) 2526/85 OJ 1985 L 240, p. 11, modifying Reg. 27. Form MAR has not yet been modified with a view to adapt the consortia Regulation opposition procedures, although many notifications have been received by the Commission regarding consortia.

6.6.10. Acceleration of procedures

One of the most common criticisms of the Commission's administrative practice is that its procedures are extremely long. The Commission has reacted to this criticism and has undertaken to speed up its decision-making process, first, in cases involving non-concentrative structural joint ventures, then also in all other cases.[268]

The basic commitment of the Commission towards notifying undertakings is to inform them within a short period—two months in the case of joint ventures—of its intentions *vis-à-vis* the notified agreement. If the information given by the undertakings is complete, the Commission will react:

(1)   by sending a comfort letter, in straightforward authorization cases (negative clearance or individual exemption);

(2)   by sending a 'warning letter', when its intention is to prohibit the agreement; or

(3)   by announcing its intention to adopt a formal decision authorizing the agreement.

In cases under (1) and (3) the Commission will inform the parties of the estimated date for a final decision.

The new administrative instructions have been designed to fit within the framework of Regulation 17, which differs substantially from the transport regulations in respect of notifications. Accordingly, they have to be adapted, as necessary, within the framework of the transport regulations.

In light of the first letter envisaged in the new instructions, and taking into account the fact that in most cases a notice in the *Official Journal* will follow notification, the Commission will inform the parties of its initial assessment of the notified agreement when sending to the parties a draft notice for comments on the confidentiality of the information it contains.[269] The Commission's initial views will be qualified by a clear indication that they are subject to future comments from interested third parties regarding the notice.

Within the ninety-day opposition period, the Commission may fail to react to the agreement,[270] in which case an exemption will be granted. Otherwise it will send a serious doubts letter.[271] In the latter case, the Commission will indicate the date of a prospective final decision on the agreement.

---

[268] See *Press Release IP (92) 1009* of 8 Dec. 1992, summarizing Sir Leon Brittan's speech 'The Future of EC Competition Policy', and *Press Release IP (92) 1111* of 23 Dec. 1992, in which mention is made of an internal communication entitled 'Encouraging co-operation between undertakings: a new policy towards co-operative joint ventures'. These changes have been incorporated into the new 'Form A/B' found in Reg. 3385/94.

[269] Save when the Commission takes action against the notified agreement directly, opening a formal procedure. See above, para. 6.6.3.3.

[270] See above, para. 6.6.6.   [271] See above, para. 6.6.7.

6.7. 'OWN INITIATIVE' INDIVIDUAL EXEMPTION

Under the transport regulations, the Commission:

(1) must issue a decision applying Article 85(3) of the Treaty to a given agreement, decision or concerted practice, even if *it has not received a request from the parties to do so*, when it finds, after having opened an infringement procedure (following a complaint or on the Commission's own initiative), or purely on its own initiative, after investigation, that the conditions of both Article 85(1) and Article 85(3) are fulfilled by the agreement, decision or concerted practice (whether previously attacked by the Commission or not);[272]

(2) must issue a decision applying Article 85(3) of the Treaty to a given agreement, decision, or concerted practice duly notified under the opposition procedure when, after *it has opposed the automatic exemption by sending a serious doubts letter* to the parties, it finds that the conditions of both Article 85(1) and Article 85(3) are finally fulfilled by the notified agreement, decision or concerted practice.[273]

Before these provisions can be used for granting an exemption, it is necessary that the undertakings modify or amend their agreements, or otherwise convince the Commission (which may in any event impose conditions and obligations) of their merit. As a rule, if the agreements which have been the subject of an infringement procedure or of a serious doubts letter are not put in line with Article 85(3), exemption will not be granted.

6.7.1. Obligations of the Commission under Article 85(3)

The first question in respect of these two methods of granting exemptions outside the opposition procedure (both previously referred to as 'own initiative exemption' procedures) is whether from the terms in which they are drafted it can be concluded:

(1) that the Commission is obliged in all infringement procedures to justify the denial of an individual exemption; and

(2) that the Commission is always obliged to decide formally on the applicability of Article 85(3) to every agreement that comes before it for consideration.

---

[272] Art. 11(4) of Reg. 1017/68; Art. 11(4) of Reg. 4056/86 and Art. 4(3) of Reg. 3975/87.

[273] Art. 12(4), 1st and 2nd para. of Reg. 1017/68; Art. 12(4), 2nd sub-para. of Reg. 4056/86, and Art. 5(4), 2nd sub-para. of Reg. 3975/87.

In respect of (1), the answer is yes. Contrary to Regulation 17, the transport regulations oblige the Commission to assess the applicability of Article 85(3) in all the cases in which an infringement decision under Article 85(1) is envisaged.[274] Even under Regulation 17, the Commission is increasingly in favour of justifying the inapplicability of Article 85(3), even in pure infringement cases in which no request from the parties to apply such provision has been made.

As to (2), the Commission may be obliged to decide formally on agreements which merit exemption from Article 85(1) pursuant to Article 85(3) of the Treaty. This obligation stems from its exclusive competence to apply this provision[275] and from the wording of the transport regulations, which is much clearer and more compelling than that of Regulation 17. Nonetheless, the Commission will not adopt a formal decision in every case. It will often try to solve cases informally. The Commission may consider that in a given case, because of lack of Community interest, or for other reasons, a comfort letter is sufficient. However, the Commission does not seem to be able to refuse to adopt a formal decision if required by the undertakings to do so. In this respect, the rights of the undertakings are the same under Regulation 17 and under the transport regulations.

6.7.2. Procedural rules

As already stated, the applicable procedural rules in these cases are to a large extent taken from the provisions on the grant of exemption in Regulation 17.

As under that regulation,[276] before an individual exemption is granted a notice must be published, clearly stating that the Commission is in favour of an individual exemption, subject to comments from interested parties.[277] By contrast, notices in opposition procedures are neutral in respect of Article 85(3) and are not definitive in respect of Article 85(1).[278]

Contrary to Regulation 17, in which no indication is given about the possible period of validity of individual exemption decisions,[279] the transport regulations state that 'normally such period shall not be less than six years'.[280] This provision does not prevent the Commission from adopting decisions for a shorter period. It may simply oblige it to justify the adoption of a shorter period, on the basis of an assessment of the special circumstances in the case under consideration.

---

[274] See, e.g., the decisions of the Commission in the *Shipowners' Committees* and *CEWAL* Cases, above, n. 56.

[275] See below, para. 6.9.1.   [276] Art. 19(3) of Reg. 17.

[277] Art. 26(3) of Reg. 1017/68; Art. 23(3) of Reg. 4056/86; and Art. 16(3) of Reg. 3975. Mistakenly, the English version of the inland and sea transport regulations refer to 'negative clearance pursuant to Article 85(3) of the Treaty'. See above, para. 6.4.1., n. 99.

[278] See above, paras 6.6.3.1. and 6.6.5.

[279] Under Art. 8(1) of Reg. 17, such decisions must simply 'be issued for a specified period'.

[280] Art. 13(1) of Reg. 1017/68; Art. 13(1) of Reg. 4056/86; and Art. 6(1) of Reg. 3975/87.

The major difference between the transport regulations and Regulation 17 in respect of the period of validity of exemptions relates to the general possibility, under the transport regulations, of issuing retroactive exemptions. Such a possibility is restricted, under Regulation 17, to the special, less harmful agreements listed in Article 4(2) of the regulation, and to other agreements notified within certain periods.[281]

Under the transport regulations, 'own initiative exemption' decisions can take effect prior to the date of notification (in 'own initiative' procedures upon interruption of an opposition procedure)[282] or prior to the date of the decision (in pure 'own initiative' cases),[283] or when the Commission, after having investigated an infringement, finally decides to grant an individual exemption.[284] The reasons for this privileged treatment relate to the non-mandatory nature of notifications in this area,[285] which is itself justified on the 'distinctive features' of transport.[286]

In 'own initiative' exemption procedures, conditions and obligations can be imposed,[287] unlike the opposition procedures.[288] Standard rules apply. The Commission must give the parties the opportunity to make their views known in respect of any conditions and obligations the Commission envisages to impose, following the *Transocean* judgment.[289]

The question also arises whether and how the parties to an agreement can oppose an 'own initiative' exemption. This is particularly important when the Commission has not previously attacked an unnotified agreement[290] or envisages the imposition of conditions and obligations.

It is clear that the parties can attack an individual exemption pursuant to Article 173 of the Treaty, be it in its entirety or in part,[291] whenever their legal position is affected by the Commission's decision.[292]

---

[281] See Art. 6(1) and (2) of Reg. 17.

[282] Art. 11(4), last sentence, of Reg. 1017/68; Art. 11(4), last sentence, of Reg. 4056/86; and Art. 4(3), last sentence of Reg. 3975/87.

[283] The Commission can grant 'pure' 'own initiative' individual exemptions without attacking an unnotified agreement (see above, para. 6.7.). In practice, this is very unlikely. The transport regulations do, nevertheless, provide for this.

[284] Art. 12(4), 2nd sub-para., last sentence, of Reg. 1017/68; Art. 12(4), 2nd sub-para., last sentence of Reg. 4056/86; and Art. 5(4), 2nd sub-para., last sentence of Reg. 3975/87.

[285] See above, para. 6.5.1.

[286] For a critical comment on these features see above, para. 6.4. The 15th recital of Reg. 1017/68—which contains the only reference to retroactivity to be found in the preambles to the transport regulations—gives no concrete justification for allowing retroactivity. It simply states that agreements can be declared lawful retroactively in the event of a subsequent examination.

[287] Art. 13(1) of Reg. 1017/68, Art. 13(1) of Reg. 4056/86 and Art. 6(1) of Reg. 3975/87.

[288] See, above, para. 6.6.6.

[289] Case 16/74, *Transocean Marine Paint* v. *Commission*, [1974], ECR 1063.

[290] See, above, para. 6.7, point (1).

[291] See, e.g., the judgment of the ECJ in the *Transocean Marine Paint* case, just referred to, in which Transocean challenged the obligations imposed by the Commission, not the exemption itself.

[292] See the recent ECJ judgment in Case T–138/89, *Dutch Banks Associations* v. *Commission*, [1992], ECR II–2181, in which the recitals of an exemption granted by the Commission were not considered to be challengeable separately because they did not actually affect or prejudice the legal position of the parties and because the operative part of the decision (*dispositif*) was not challenged.

It is also clear that the transport regulations provide that before adopting 'own initiative' individual exemption decisions—but not before automatic non-opposition exemption decisions are adopted—the undertakings have the right to be heard 'on the matters on which the Commission has taken objection'.[293] This wording was adapted from Regulation 17[294] and refers mainly to the Commission's obligations under infringement procedures. In spite of this, it cannot be denied that undertakings, much more than interested third parties for whom notices are published, have the right to be heard even when the Commission intends to adopt decisions which are in principle favourable, as the *Transocean* judgment acknowledged. This qualification is particularly important in transport, where decisions can be adopted without prior notification to guide the Commission. That is to say, the Commission might take measures which harm transport companies' interests without a clear indication of what the undertakings concerned would consider appropriate.

For these reasons, the Commission must give the parties to an agreement which it intends to exempt the opportunity to make their views known in respect of the terms of the envisaged exemption. The Commission may ask for comments from the parties in a specific letter for these purposes. It may also ask for comments when submitting a draft notice to the parties in order to avoid disclosure of confidential business secrets.[295]

Finally, in relation to 'own initiative exemption' procedures, there is no difference between the transport regulations and Regulation 17 in respect of renewal, withdrawal and modification of this type of exemptions.[296]

6.8. THE USE OF RECOMMENDATIONS

Under Article 3(3) of Regulation 17 '[w]ithout prejudice to the other provisions of this Regulation, the Commission may, before taking a decision under paragraph 1 (infringement decisions), address to the undertakings concerned recommendations for the termination of the infringement' (Parenthesis added).[297]

The three transport regulations reproduce without variation the wording of this provision[298], which allows the Commission to adjust its reaction *vis-à-vis*

---

[293] Art. 26(1) of Reg. 17; Art. 23(1) of Reg. 4056/86; and Art. 16(1) of Reg. 3975/87, all include 'own initiative' individual exemption decisions within those giving the parties the right to be heard.
[294] Art. 19(1) of Reg. 17.
[295] Avoiding disclosure of business secrets is also required in the 'own initiative' exemption procedure. See Art. 26(3), last sentence of Reg. 1017/68; Art. 23(3), last sentence of Reg. 4056/86 and Art. 16(3), last sentence of Reg. 3975/87.
[296] The following provisions reproduce exactly the text of Arts 8(2) and (3) of Reg. 17: Arts 13(2) and (3) of Reg. 1017/68; Arts 13(2) and (3) of Reg. 4056/86; and Arts 6(2) and (3) of Reg. 3975.
[297] For the interpretation of the powers of the Commission pursuant to this provision, see the judgment of the CFI, in Case T–83/91, *Tetra Pak* v. *Commission* [1994] ECR II–755, para. 222.
[298] See Art. 11(1), 2nd sub-para. of Reg. 1017/68; Art. 11(1), 2nd sub-para. of Reg. 4056/86; and Art. 4(1), 2nd sub-para. of Reg. 3975/87.

restrictive agreements and practices and has scarcely ever been used in the general sector.[299]

Regulations 1017/68 and 3975/87 contain no other reference to recommendations in their operative parts.[300] Since they are identical in this respect to Regulation 17, it does not seem that different conclusions in respect of recommendations may be drawn under the inland and air transport regulations.

Regulation 4056/86 contains several other references to recommendations in Articles 7 (monitoring of exempted agreements) and 8 (effects incompatible with Article 86 of the Treaty). Both provisions are directly related to the block exemption for liner conferences contained in Article 3 of the Regulation. Regulation 3976/87, the enabling regulation for the grant of block exemptions in air transport-related sectors,[301] also contains a reference to recommendations in Article 7(1), setting down rules for the monitoring of the block exemptions granted under its authority.

From the above it appears that there is a twofold regime for recommendations under the transport regulations. On the one hand, under standard infringement procedures pursuant to the three basic transport regulations, rules on recommendations do not differ from Regulation 17, and the Commission can be expected to apply them in much the same way, i.e., no special use of recommendations in the transport sector should be expected, at least in normal infringement cases. On the other hand, under the rules for the monitoring of exempted agreements, the Commission is sometimes obliged to use recommendations and on other occasions it is expressly entitled to consider using them.

The Commission is obliged to issue a recommendation before withdrawing the block exemption for shipping conferences in a specific case of breach of the obligations attached to the exemption and is not entitled to withdraw it directly.[302] In air transport related sectors this rule applies not only to breaches of an obligation, but, surprisingly, even to breaches of a condition attached to the exemption.[303]

The Commission can also consider addressing recommendations under Article 7(2) of Regulation 4056/86 (effects incompatible with Article 85[3]). This provision is quite different from Article 7 of Regulation 19/65 and Article 7 of Regulation 2821/71, which contain the rules applicable to the individual

---

[299] For recommendations under Reg. 17, see Kerse, above n. 5, Ch. VI. and Ortiz Blanco, above n. 5, Ch. VII.

[300] Only the 21st recital of Reg. 1017/68 refers to recommendations in largely the same terms as Art. 11(1), 2nd sub-para. of this regulation.

[301] See, above, Ch. 5.   [302] See Art. 7(1) of Reg. 4056/86.

[303] See Art. 7(1) of Reg. 3976/87. In this situation, it is doubtful whether any of the 'conditions' imposed by the Commission on air transport undertakings pursuant to its block exemption regulations in this sector can be considered genuine conditions (the breach of which has the principal effect of rendering a given block exemption directly inapplicable, no prior decision to that effect being necessary), unless the validity of this provision is challenged in that respect.

withdrawal of block exemptions in other sectors, and is also different from Articles 7(2) and (3) of Regulation 3976/87.[304]

The maritime transport approach to the monitoring of exempted agreements for breaches of the conditions in Article 85(3) is contained in the last phrase of Article 7(2)(a) of Regulation 4056/86: the severity of the measures to be adopted by the Commission 'must be in proportion to the gravity of the situation'.

This provision simply expresses the general principle of proportionality in the application of EC law[305] and does not impose any additional obligation on the Commission when applying competition law in shipping. The Commission is entitled and obliged to assess and decide which is the most appropriate and proportionate reaction in all cases, not only in shipping. It cannot be argued that, because of the regulation's insistence on proportionality, the Commission should be more moderate in shipping than in other sectors. Proportionality cannot mean different things under Regulation 4056/86 and under Regulation 17. Accordingly, the use of the options afforded to the Commission by Article 7(2)(c)(ii) and Article 8(3) of Regulation 4056/86 (address a recommendation; withdraw the block exemption and issue an individual exemption; or plainly withdraw the exemption) and the interpretation of said provisions, is not—in fact, cannot be—different from the options and the interpretation of the Commission's powers under Article 3 of Regulation 17.[306]

In conclusion, the use of recommendations in the transport sector is subject, for the most part, to the same rules and principles applicable in other sectors. Special rules exist only for breaches of obligations and/or conditions attached to certain block exemptions in the sea and air transport sectors, where recommendations are not an alternative, but a necessary first step before withdrawal. In all other cases the general principle of proportionality applies, as in any other industry subject to the rules on competition.

6.9. THE APPARENT OBLIGATION TO DECIDE FORMALLY ON NOTIFICATION

The wording of the transport regulations differs from Regulation 17 in respect of the way the Commission must act after a notification or a complaint is submitted, or when an enquiry has been launched by the Commission on its own initiative.

---

[304] Art. 7(2) of Reg. 3976/87 replicates Art. 7 of Reg. 19/65 and Art. 7 of Reg. 2821/71. Art. 7(3) of Reg. 3976/87, however, explicitly allows the Commission to address recommendations before adopting decisions, in much the same way as Art. 3 of Reg. 17.

[305] On general principles of law in Commission's proceedings, see Kerse, above n. 5, Ch. VIII and Ortiz Blanco, above n. 5, Ch. I.

[306] On Arts 7 and 8 of Reg. 4056/86, see above, Ch. 4.

6.9.1. Exemption

According to the transport regulations' opposition and 'own initiative exemption' procedures, the Commission *shall* examine whether the conditions for an individual exemption apply and, where they do, it *shall* issue a decision applying Article 85(3).[307]

These provisions give undertakings the right to obtain a formal decision, but they do not impose an automatic obligation on the part of the Commission to decide formally on every Article 85(3) case that comes to its attention. The transport regulations are also subject to the requirements of good administration and the response of the Commission must be in line with the undertakings' demands. The regulations should not be interpreted as impeding informal solutions (mainly comfort letters) in the transport sector. The text of the transport regulations makes more explicit the principle that undertakings have the right to obtain a formal exemption decision, something over which the Commission has exclusive competence and can therefore be obliged to decide on formally.[308] This applies to individual exemptions under Regulation 17 (where the Commission has no explicit obligation to issue a formal decision) as well as to exemptions under the transport regulations (which are much more explicit than Regulation 17).

6.9.2. Complaints and 'own initiative' procedures

Under the transport regulations, whether acting on receipt of a complaint or on its own initiative, the Commission *must initiate procedures* to terminate any infringement of the provisions of Articles 85(1) or 86 of the Treaty or to enforce the rules on monitoring and withdrawal of block exemptions.[309] 'Where the Commission finds that there has been an infringement of Articles 85(1) or 86 of

---

[307] For the opposition exemption procedure, see Art. 12(4) of Reg. 1017/68; Art. 12(4) of Reg. 4056/86 and Art. 5(4) of Reg. 3975/87. As stated before, the clearest text establishing the Commission's obligation to consider an 'own initiative' exemption is in Reg. 1017/68, but it does not seem that the other two regulations can be interpreted differently in respect of such obligation. For the 'own initiative' exemption procedure, see Art. 11(4) of Reg. 1017/68; Art. 11(4) of Reg. 4056/86 and Art. 4(4) of Reg. 3975/87.

[308] See the CFI judgment in Case T–24/90, *Automec* v. *Commission II*, [1992], ECR II–2223, at para. 75. Although the CFI referred to the Commission's obligation to act formally on complaints asking for the withdrawal of an exemption under Art. 85(3) (a block exemption in this particular case), unlike complaints in respect of infringements of Arts 85(1) and 86, the same doctrine may apply in respect of the granting of an individual exemption under Art. 85(3), which is the reverse, and constitutes one of the Commission's exclusive competences under the competition regulations.

[309] Art. 10 of Reg. 1017/68 (which refers to Arts 2 [85(1) EC] and 8 [86 EC] of the Regulation); plus Art. 4(2), concerning the monitoring of the block exemption contained in Art. 4(1); Art. 10 of Reg. 4056/86 (which also refers to Art. 7 of the Regulation, dealing with measures for the monitoring of block exemptions); and Art. 3(1) of Reg. 3975/87, in conjunction with Art. 7 of Reg. 3976/87.

the Treaty, it *may by decision* require the undertakings or associations of undertakings concerned to bring such infringement to an end'.[310] This also applies to the monitoring of exempted agreements.[311] The transport provisions closely follow Article 3(1) of Regulation 17.[312]

The Commission's implementing regulations in transport also contain provisions identical to Article 6 of Regulation 99, which provides that where the Commission, having received a complaint, considers that on the basis of the information in its possession, there are *insufficient grounds* to pursue it, it *shall inform* the complainants of its reasons and fix a time-limit for them to submit any further comments in writing.[313] The transport counterparts of Article 6 of Regulation 99 must be interpreted in the light of the European Court and CFI case-law regarding this provision. In particular, in the light of the *Automec I*[314] and *Automec II*[315] cases, and more recently the *Guérin Automobiles* case.[316]

Finally, the three Council transport regulations provide that if the Commission, acting on a complaint, concludes that on the evidence before it there are *no grounds for intervention* in respect of any agreement, decision, or concerted practice, it *shall issue a decision* rejecting the complaint as unfounded. The inland and sea transport regulations refer to complaints on the basis of Articles 85(1) and 86 *and* to complaints requesting the enforcement of the rules on monitoring of exempted agreements, i.e., requesting the withdrawal of the block exemptions in the inland and sea transport sectors.[317] The air transport regulation refers only to Articles 85(1) and 86[318] and within the rules on monitoring of block-exemptions in air transport there is no rule regarding rejection of complaints against block-exempted agreements.[319]

On the basis of the above transport provisions and the case-law of the European Court and CFI, several points can be made.

First, both Regulation 17 and the transport regulations allow, but do not oblige, the Commission to adopt infringement decisions, whether the procedure has been launched upon complaint or on the initiative of the Commission. The Commission may decide not to issue a final infringement decision on a complaint. It may also decide to stop an 'own initiative' enquiry or procedure, and, in general, it can also choose its priorities in the transport sector in a way sim-

---

[310] Art. 11(1), 1st sub-para. of Reg. 1017/68; Art. 11(1), 1st sub-para. of Reg. 4056/86; and Art. 4(1), 1st sub-para. of Reg. 3975/87.

[311] Art. 11(2) of Reg. 1017/68 and Art. 11(2) of Reg. 4056/86. In air transport, see Art. 7(2) of Reg. 3976/87.

[312] This provision states: '[w]here the Commission, upon application or upon its own initiative, finds that there is infringement of Art. 85 or Art. 86 of the Treaty, it may by decision require the undertakings or assocations of undertakings concerned to bring such an infringement to an end'.

[313] Art. 6 of Reg. 1630/69; Art. 10 of Reg. 4260/88; and Art. 9 of Reg. 4261/88

[314] CFI judgment in Case T–64/89, *Automec I*, [1990] ECR II–367.

[315] See above n. 308.

[316] Judgment of the CFI of 27 June 1995 in Case T–186/94, *Guérin Automobiles* v. *Commission*, not yet reported.

[317] Art. 11(3) of Reg. 1017/68 and Art. 11(3) of Reg. 4056/86.

[318] See Art. 4(2) of Reg. 3975/87.   [319] See Art. 7 of Reg. 3976/87.

ilar to other sectors.[320] However, the Commission is not entitled to refuse adopting a decision withdrawing a block exemption on an individual basis, if required by a complaint. The reason is that the withdrawal of exemptions is an exclusive competence of the Commission,[321] and neither national competition authorities nor judicial bodies can provide appropriate remedies at national level.

Secondly, the wording of the transport regulations—which obliges the Commission to 'initiate procedures' upon complaint or on its own initiative once an infringement has been detected—can be interpreted as obliging the Commission to undertake a full investigation every time it becomes aware of an infringement. Under this interpretation, the *Automec II* prerogatives of the Commission, i.e., the power to reject a complaint upon first examination, without a full enquiry, would not be applicable in transport. This is the position expressed by the Commission and by Judge Edward acting as Advocate General in the Automec II case,[322] though the Court of First Instance has not yet upheld it.

Although this interpretation is not supported by the preambles to the transport regulations, which are silent on the matter, this particular provision, if interpreted literally, would simply oblige the Commission to open a formal procedure, thus reserving for itself the competence to apply EC rules. However, there does not seem to be any policy reason to justify the automatic exclusion of the competence of national authorities, once a complaint has been made to the Commission.

In conclusion, it seems that the words 'on receipt of a complaint . . . the Commission shall initiate procedures' should be interpreted as requiring the first part of any infringement procedure (i.e., a full enquiry) to be made by the Commission before rejecting any complaint in the transport sector.

Thirdly, from a procedural point of view, the general rules concerning rejection of complaints pursuant to Articles 85(1) and 86 apply. This means that the Commission may use the three-step procedure for rejection of complaints described in the *Automec I* judgment.[323] Like under Regulation 17, as made clear in the *Guérin* judgement,[324] the Commission cannot refuse to adopt a

---

[320] See CFI judgment in the *Automec II* case, cited above n. 308, para. 77.

[321] See *Automec II,* at para. 75.

[322] See the opinion of 10 Mar. 1992 of Judge Edward acting as Adv. Gen. in the *Automec II* case, cited above n. 308, at p. 2226, points 9–12. In this case the Commission argued that the difference between Reg. 17 and the transport regulations was due, first, to the intrinsically international character of transport activities, so that a high degree of Community interest might be presumed in each case; and, secondly, to the wide possibilities of block exemption from Art. 85 under the transport regulations, so that the residual scope of application of Art. 85 deserves a stronger degree of protection. Judge Edward did not appear to find the Commission's arguments particularly convincing, but he shared its conclusions in respect of the Commission's obligation to act following a complaint.

[323] See the CFI judgment in the *Automec I* case, above n. 314. For a detailed description of this procedure, see also, Kerse, above n. 5, Ch. II. III and Ortiz Blanco, above n. 5, Ch. VIII.

[324] See above n. 316. Before the *Guérin* judgment, it was not completely clear whether a complainant had the right to obtain a formal rejection decision from the Commission beyond the right to receive an Art. 6 letter.

formal decision after the second step if the complainants make such a request.[325] Accordingly the Commission can also be obliged to issue a formal decision rejecting a transport complaint.

Fourthly, the above considerations also clearly apply to rejections of complaints requesting the withdrawal of inland and sea transport block exemptions. However, in respect of air transport it might be thought that Regulation 3976/87 does not oblige the Commission to reject formally complaints of this type, nor to inform the complainants of its reasons and fix a time-limit for them to submit any further comments in writing.[326]

In spite of this lacuna, and taking into account the *Automec II* and *Guérin Automobiles* case law,[327] there is no doubt that since the matter lies within its exclusive competence, the Commission can be obliged to decide formally on the withdrawal of a block exemption also in the air transport sector. As to the procedure, and in spite of the absence of a rule similar to Article 6 of Regulation 99/63 obliging the Commission to inform the complainants of its reasons to reject a complaint of this kind, there is no reason why the Commission should deviate from the standard *Automec I* procedure.

6.9.3. Settlements and informal conclusions

From the above it can be concluded that, in transport, the Commission generally enjoys the same powers but bears more administrative burdens than when operating under Regulation 17. The Commission must react to notifications and complaints in a more formal way in the first part of the procedure (the terms in which opposition procedure is set out and the possible obligation to make a full investigation indicate that), but may resolve matters informally without always adopting exemption or infringement decisions. The Commission has on several occasions shown that notifications and complaints that have been the subject of full investigations have been finally solved informally, by means of administrative letters.[328]

In spite of this, as in other sectors, transport undertakings have the right to obtain a formal exemption decision, because the Commission has exclusive competence in relation to individual exemptions. On the other hand, and for the same reasons, persons claiming a legitimate interest have the right to obtain a formal decision withdrawing an exemption, be it individual or *en bloc*, if the complaint is well founded. Just as under Regulation 17, other complainants cannot oblige the Commission to adopt an infringement decision, but they can compel it to adopt a formal decision rejecting their complaint.

---

[325] Before *Guérin* the lack of this specific obligation under Reg. 17 and Reg. 99 could have been considered a difference between the general provisions and the transport provisions.

[326] See Art. 9 of Reg. 4261/88, which refers only to complaints under Art. 3(1) of Reg. 3975/87 (not under Art. 7 of Reg. 3976/87).

[327] See, above n. 308 and n. 316.

[328] See, e.g., upon notification, the outcome of the *Irish Club Rules* Case (OJ 1993 C 263, p. 6: notice pursuant to Art. 23(3) of Reg. 4056/86). This case was finally settled with a comfort letter. Upon complaint, see the *East African Conference* Case (*Press Release IP (93) 739*, of 9 Sep. 93).

7

Conclusion

7.1. A CRITICAL VIEW OF REGULATION 1017/68

Regulation 1017/68 is, in many respects, a bad precedent. For example, one of the more just criticisms of the Regulation is that it establishes a privileged regime for inland transport undertakings. What in the case of agriculture and Regulation 26 was expressly provided for by the Treaty, was adopted without justification also in the transport sector. Allowing a sector of the economy differentiated regulations from the common rules applicable to other sectors in this way may serve only to encourage sectors of the economy to lobby the institutions of the Union for special competition laws that would better represent their specific concerns, market features, and competitive traditions.[1]

A further criticism of Regulation 1017/68 is that, in spite of the statement in the fifth recital which sets out the need for undertakings to be able to ascertain what rules apply in particular cases, the Council has not succeeded in adopting a clear and coherent text. The recital is apparently, then, limited to a declaration of goodwill.[2]

The scope of application of Regulation 1017/68 is also open to criticism. The scope of that regulation impinges on the territory of Regulation 17, something which was not envisaged in Regulation 141. Certain activities have been included in its scope of application with the aim specifically of excluding some related agreements from the restrictive agreements prohibition, and, in particular, services ancillary to inland transport. The unification of the procedural systems of inland transport and those ancillary services has helped a little to apply more coherently the transport regulations. Conversely, however, the unification has caused greater confusion in the EC's system of competition law for transport by causing the partial overlap of the specific procedural rules of inland transport and of the general rules of Regulation 17. This is a criticism which, to a lesser extent, also concerns the other competition regulations in transport. It is regrettable that the scope of application of all the regulations has not been defined in line with Regulation 141 and Regulation 17.

Regulation 1017/68 gives the false impression that, in the inland transport sector, the established prohibition principle under EC competition law has been so greatly weakened by numerous exemptions and exceptions that, as far as the

---

[1] See Wägenbaur, R., 'Les règles de concurrence applicables aux transports', *Cahiers de Droit Européen*, No. 6, 1970, pp. 645–62, at pp. 661–2.

[2] Cf., *ibid.*, p. 661.

practical application of the regulation is concerned, it would be more appropriate to speak of a control of abuse than a prohibition.[3]

As far as the exception for technical agreements is concerned (one of the inland transport provisions inherited by the maritime and air regulations), its practical utility is open to question. The exception lacks the normal legal certainty accorded by a genuine block exemption since, despite the impression it may give, it fails to exclude from the application of Article 85(1) the activities which are listed as 'technical agreements'. The Regulation, therefore, causes misunderstandings and creates false expectations. In the future, thought should be given to repealing Article 3 of Regulation 1017/68, Article 2 of Regulation 4056/86 and Article 2 and the Annex of Regulation 3975/87, and to clarifying the position in relation to Article 85 of the Treaty of the activities currently enumerated in the regulations, and any other activities which may fall within their scope, through Commission communications.

Furthermore, the provisions of Regulation 1017/68 bestowing a block exemption on groupings of small and medium-size undertakings may not be sufficiently reasoned for the purposes of Article 190 of the Treaty, either with respect to compliance with the conditions of Article 85(1) or those of 85(3) of the Treaty. Article 6 which, at first sight, allows exemption of crisis cartels without complying with all the requirements of Article 85(3) of the Treaty, is not free from criticism either. Moreover, the procedure it sets out is unique in EC competition law, requiring the intervention of two EU institutions to apply the competition rules individually to undertakings. The time limits set out in Article 6 are extremely vague. Moreover, it is not clear whether the procedure is really still usable. It is more than twenty-five years since its adoption and its duration is as vague as Article 6(1) itself. It might be suggested, therefore, that Articles 6 and 14 of Regulation 1017/68 be omitted from any amendment of the competition regulations.

To summarize, on the assumption that the provisions of Regulation 1017/68 cannot prevail over the general rules of the Treaty, the transport-specific competition rules can, and are, criticised for having introduced innovations which cannot be considered justifiable simply on the grounds of the special characteristics of the transport sector and, in some cases, can even be said to be contrary to the provisions of the Treaty and, therefore, illegal.[4]

---

[3] Thus, e.g., Blonk, W. A. G., 'Regulation (EEC) 1017/68 of the Council of the 19th of July 1968 applying rules of competition to transport by rail, road and inland waterway', *Common Market Law Review*, Vol. 6, No. 4, Oct. 1969, pp. 451–65, p. 457, is rather carried along by this impression.

[4] In this connection, cf., Wägenbaur, above n. 1, p. 662.

7.2. TRENDS TOWARDS AN ACTIVE TRANSPORT COMPETITION POLICY[5]

In the early days of the European Communities, the Commission's weakness and apparent lack of interest in transport matters and the lack of Community spirit shown by national transport authorities encouraged the development of the multi-faceted Community system of competition in the transport sector. Lack of interest in transport matters—undoubtedly motivated by what seemed at the time to be more pressing matters for a newly-created competition authority—resulted in Regulation 141. Failure to persuade the Council to accept common substantive and procedural competition rules resulted in the adoption of Regulation 1017/68 in its present form.

The consequences of the 1962 and 1968 events virtually paralysed the Commission up until the *French Seamen* judgment of 1974. After it, the little energy invested by the Commission in transport competition was concentrated on recovering its lost powers of investigation and sanction and establishing its arsenal of procedural weapons in maritime and air transport. For this reason, Regulation 1017/68 has been applied on relatively few occasions, the majority of them very recently.

The implementing regulation has been of little use since 1968. In the absence of the necessary political interest in the Council—which only arose with the judgment of the Court in the case between the Parliament and Council in 1985 and, above all, with the prospect of the establishment of a single market—and faced with other priorities, the Commission ignored the transport sector. The first cases show its lack of experience and scant interest in the sector. With only two exceptions—the *Tankschiffahrtskonvention* case and the *EATE* case—all decisions adopted by the Commission since Regulation 1017/68 entered into force in 1968 have been adopted since 1988. The *EATE* Decision is the bridge between two eras, one characterized by the virtual absence of implementation of competition rules in inland transport, and the other by their application on the same conditions as in other sectors, and heralded the new Commission approach towards transport.

The incursion of competition policy into the transport sector was a sign of the Commission's renewed activism in the 1980s, and of its move into areas which previously had received its insufficient attention. This development was made possible by the re-organization of the Directorate General for Competition of the European Commission, DG IV, and by the allocation of sufficient resources to transport.[6] In particular, a special division within DG IV was created in 1987

---

[5] See Ch. 2.

[6] In two successive stages, in 1984/85 and in 1986, with the aim of increasing the level of technical sectorial expertise of reporting officials or *rapporteurs* and their Heads of Division, the powers of the operating Directorates of DG IV were re-allocated. Cf. Wilks, S., 'The metamorphosis of European Competition Policy', *Russel Working Papers, No. 9.* (University of Exeter. Exeter, 1992), pp. 12–14.

which was allocated the resources and staff necessary for it to effect a coherent implementation of the competition rules in all modes of transport.

7.3. REGULATION 4056/86 AND THE POLITICIZATION OF THE COMPETITION RULES IN MARITIME TRANSPORT

As of 1974 (with the judgment of the ECJ in the *French Seamen* case and the adoption of the Code of Conduct for Liner Conferences under the auspices of UNC-TAD) and, above all, 1979 (with the adoption of Regulation 954/79, or 'Brussels Package'), and until the adoption of Regulation 4056/86, the Commission's competition policy in the maritime sector was centred upon the recovery at all costs of the powers lost in 1962 after the adoption by the Council of Regulation 141. In aiming to recover from the Council powers similar to those lost, the Commission made a number of fundamental concessions to the maritime authorities of the Member States. The most fundamental of these concessions was the authorization under EC competition law of codist liner conferences by means of a block exemption pursuant to Article 87 and Article 85(3) of the Treaty.

The lack of critical analysis of the activities of traditional liner conferences perhaps owes as much to the Commission's perception that the results of the negotiations with the Council were inevitable as to the wishes of the Commission to obtain powers of control and sanction as soon as possible. The Commission did not have the opportunity to start from scratch and to reconsider what would be the best system of implementation of the competition rules in maritime transport. That system had already been thought out in the 1979 'Brussels Package'. The Commission's work was not—as in other sectors of trade and industry—to study the market and agreements between shipping undertakings but to give legal form to something which substantively, at least, seemed resolved, i.e., the political compromise to respect the liner conference system's *status quo*. On that basis, both the substance and the form of the regulation are defective.

Article 3 of Regulation 4056/86 raises the specific question of the applicability of Article 85(3) of the Treaty to conferences—above all in view of their market power—and the general question of the compatibility of a dominant position with the requirement that competition not be eliminated.

The relationship between Articles 86 and 85(3) has been the subject of attention from the European Court and the CFI on various occasions.[7] The most recent and interesting of these is the *Tetra Pak I* Case.[8]

---

[7] See the judgments of the ECJ in Case 32/95, *Italy* v. *Council and Commission* [1966] ECR 389, relating to Reg. 19/65/EEC; in Case 85/76, *Hoffmann-Laroche* v. *Commission* [1979] ECR 461; and in Case 66/86, *Ahmed Saeed et al* v. *ZBW*, [1989] ECR 803, *inter alia*. According to them:

(1) Arts 85 and 86 have their own objectives and each is indistinctly applicable to various types of agreements when the specific conditions of either are satisfied; *cont/*

The *Tetra Pak I* judgment, despite making it clear that Articles 85(3) and 86 can be applied at the same time in the context of a block exemption, does not deal directly with one of the most fundamental questions raised by Article 3 in conjunction with Article 8 of Regulation 4056/86, namely the compatibility with Article 85(3)(b) of the Treaty of the exemption of an agreement which allows the creation of a collective dominant position.

Article 8 centres on the behaviour of conferences and glosses over the question of whether a conference agreement which creates a collective dominant position does not infringe, by definition, the fourth condition of Article 85(3) and, accordingly, regardless of the dominant conference's conduct, either it has never enjoyed an exemption or that exemption has to be withdrawn.[9] The block exemption does not even raise the question of whether a collective dominant position obtained by means of a collusive agreement is compatible with the condition that competition not be eliminated in a substantial part of the common market. This is a question which, undoubtedly, will have to be considered by the European Court and CFI in the near future.[10] In light of the *Tetra Pak* judgment, the answer could be that such collective dominance is incompatible with Article 85(3)(b).[11]

Articles 6 and 5(2) are further provisions of Regulation 4056/86 which raise problems of compatibility with the Treaty. For example, the question should be raised whether, in practice, loyalty agreements are not only incompatible with Article 85(3), but even with Article 86. Agreements and practices binding customers to undertakings in a dominant position have always been considered infringements of Article 86 of the Treaty.[12] The regulation of conference loyalty agreements and their block exemption is perplexing from the competition policy point of view. Once again, the authorization has its origin in the wish of the Commission and Council to respect the traditional practices of conferences without altering the *status quo* created by the UNCTAD Code, not in competition law considerations. The application of the competition rules in line with the Court's jurisprudence could hardly justify the exemption of agreements and practices

(2) When the conditions of both are satisfied, the Commission can proceed to apply one or the other.

(3) The fact that the conduct of an undertaking in a dominant position is subject to Art. 85(3) does not prevent the application of Art. 86.

[8] Judgment of the CFI in Case T–51/89, *Tetra Pak* v. *Commission I*, [1990] ECR II–309, and the Opinion of Judge Kirschner (acting as Adv. Gen.) of 21 Feb. 1990 in the same Case, [1990] ECR II–312.

[9] On this see, in particular, Ch. 4, above.

[10] The first Case in which this question could be resolved by the CFI is T–24/93, *Compagnie Maritime Belge* v. *Commission*, still pending, which relates to the Commission's Decision in the *CEWAL* case, OJ 1993 L 34, p. 20. In its decision, the Commission, despite finding that the conference held a dominant position, did not withdraw the block exemption.

[11] Cf., judgment of the CFI in the *Tetra Pak I* case, paras 26–8.

[12] See, *inter alia*, the judgments of the ECJ in the *Hoffmann-Laroche* Case, above n. 7, and in Case 322/81, *Michelin* v. *Commission*, [1983] ECR 3461.

with an Article 86 stigma, unless conferences are not considered generally to enjoy a dominant position allowing them to commit abuses. Such a point of view appears, however, to run contrary to what has been observed in the large majority of the markets where they operate. What appears clear is that the loyalty agreements are only safe from Article 86—like conferences themselves and their block exemption—if the conferences do not enjoy a dominant position.

Be that as it may, upon adopting the regulation, the Commission began acquiring experience from 1987 to 1990 in maritime transport. At the same time, it tried to reconcile the system of EC competition law with the paradoxes inherited from the 'Brussels Package'. In a sector where numerous restrictive agreements shelter under the protective mantle of Article 3 of Regulation 4056/86, where liner conferences control the markets and where collusion acquires many other conference-like forms, its task was not easy. Until the early 1990s, coinciding with its change of attitude in respect of the Eurocorde agreements, the Commission appeared to believe that the same attitude of tolerance could be adopted to collusion within and without conferences, provided the activities of the maritime cartels could be very directly controlled.

The Commission's interpretational maturity developed between 1990 and 1994. Almost all of the decisions implementing Articles 85 and 86 date back to this period. The Commission applied Article 3 of Regulation 4056/86 in the way in which the text, historical background, and system of the block exemptions required it to, that is, strictly. It thereby not only respected the exemption as far as was possible but did the conferences a service by giving an appearance of legality to an exemption the legality of which could be greatly questioned.

On the one hand, the Commission headed off the most flagrant abuses detected in codist conference trade (the *Shipowners' Committees* and *CEWAL* Decisions) although failing, over generously, to withdraw the protection of the block exemption. On the other hand, it adopted some of the decisions of greatest legal and economic significance to date (*TAA* and *DSVK/FEFC* Decisions).

The Consortia Regulation was also prepared at this time. Further, the Commission presented its June 1994 Communication to the Council[13] and requested a group of 'wise men' to study the inland price-fixing activities of liner conferences from the economic and legal point of view. The 'wise men's' interim report was issued at the beginning of 1996. These two reports are of great importance in outlining the future development of competition policy not only in relation to multimodal transport but also in relation to maritime transport in general.[14] The Commission has clearly given its backing to co-operation within

---

[13] Document SEC (94) 933 final, 8 June 1994, which represented the fulfilment of an undertaking given by the Commission at the Transport Council meeting of 29 Nov. 1993.

[14] Regarding multimodal transport and inland price-fixing by shipping conferences, following its June Report, the Commission accepted the proposal of the Council to create a 'Committee of Wise Men' to assist the Commission. The Committee was called 'Multimodal Group' and delivered its first *Interim Report* in Feb. 1995. In principle, the Group did not consider inland rate-fixing by shipping conferences as indispensable for the provision of multimodal transport services. The June *Report*

consortia and against 'naked' restrictions on competition which, on the pretext of maintaining a theoretically desirable stability, in fact restrict competition to an intolerable extent, without bringing any benefits. In the Commission's opinion, its policy is not only entirely in accordance with the EC Treaty but also is economically sound and beneficial to the Union, users and shipping companies included.

A new phase can be seen developing from 1995. It is characterized as follows:

(1)   by defining the limits of the scope of application of the liner conference block exemption through the judicial control of Commission decisions. This could result in the EC Courts declaring the exemption illegal;
(2)   by the expansion and extension of the Commission's interpretative approach to still untouched liner shipping practices which involve serious competitive restrictions. The Commission will have to act to obtain the necessary freedom for individual negotiation of service contracts wherever the shipping companies—members of conferences or outsiders—offer them and to apply Articles 85 and 86, by means of Regulation 17, to the non-maritime services of shipping companies (in particular port and quayside services) which have not until present been dealt with.

In the ferry sector, the adoption of the first substantive infringement decisions and strengthened Commission resolve, above all in intra-Community trade, should also be expected.

7.4. COMPETITION RULES AND THE FUTURE OF THE COMMON AIR TRANSPORT POLICY

Looking back on developments since the first package, the Commission has lived up to its mandate of putting into place, by and large on a consensual basis, a competition policy in a sector which did not have a tradition of compliance with those rules. The volume of competition legislation and the number of interventions by the Commission show that considerable attention has been devoted to this task. Overall this has been a relatively smooth process which benefited considerably from close liaison with Member States and from usually constructive relations with the airline community.

Still, the limitation of the competition regulations to intra-European flights remains a serious constraint. While it is admittedly difficult to replace the traditional system based on bilateral agreements between Member States and foreign

of the Commission and the *Multimodal Group Interim Report* have been published by the Office of Publications of the European Communities in March 1996. See European Commission, *Interim Report of the Multimodal Group*, Office for Official Publications of the European Communities, Luxembourg, 1996.

nations by a Community external aviation policy, the applicability of competition rules in this context can no longer be dismissed. While some routes to third countries are characterized by intense competition, that is not the case for most routes where market-sharing and price-fixing are still common practice. Air transport outside the Community is too important for the Community to continue to turn a blind eye to it and the need for and benefits of competition law enforcement cannot continue to be denied.

As a second conclusion, it must be pointed out that the introduction of a competition policy in the air transport sector was planned very much as a gradual process which at this stage stops well short of rigorous implementation of the competition rules. The regulatory framework will no doubt develop in the future and approximate the system established by Regulation 17 for other industries, if it is not to be absorbed by it. In some areas—notably the application of Article 85 to restrictive agreements and the grant of exclusive and special rights by Member States—enforcement activity will have to intensify. Of course the speed of progress on this road depends to a large extent on the ability of the industry to withstand the strains of adapting itself to a more demanding environment. Yet the industry should be aware that it still benefits from a relatively favourable regime and that the travelling public—in particular passengers on intra-European flights—perceives the level of competition to be fairly low. The European air transport industry has certainly not exhausted its potential for increasing efficiency and intense exposure to competition makes a decisive contribution to rationalization programmes.

The final conclusion relates to the link between developments in the industry and the focus of competition law enforcement. In the early stages of liberalization the industry was marked by the strong position of the former 'flag carriers' in their home markets. Control of dominant positions under Article 86 was therefore a clear necessity. The need for extensive co-operation in order to create a worldwide air transport system was reflected in the relatively generous treatment of agreements between airlines. The Commission recognized the need for a far-reaching restructuring of the Community's airline industry in order to adapt itself to the new liberalized environment; that position is demonstrated by its voluminous merger control practice. But as the effects of liberalization become apparent in the marketplace, the focus of competition law enforcement will doubtlessly shift. As dominant positions are eroded, one can expect there to be fewer cases of clearcut dominance. The restructuring movement is likely to continue for some time, but at some point it will reach a limit resulting from the need to maintain effective competitive market structures. Most importantly, the new players emerging from restructuring will expect to compete on their own strengths throughout the Community.

As a result the need for protecting extensive industry co-operation will be much reduced and the block exemption regime can become more orthodox. Airlines competing with each other throughout the Community are likely to be more sensitive to the grant of State aids to competitors; after the necessary restructuring operations have been completed and most carriers have ceased to be readily identifiable with a single Member State, the availability of State aids will probably also be diminished. Consequently, while it is unlikely that the transition towards a more mature competition policy in the air transport sector will be completed in the near future, all elements appear to be in place for that trend to continue in the right direction to the benefit of the air transport industry as much as of its customers.

7.5. IMPLEMENTING COMPETITION RULES: PROBLEMS AND SOLUTIONS

A brief study of the procedural provisions of Regulation 1017/68, 4056/86 and 3975/87 has shown that, contrary to the goal of the 1968 inland transport regulation (i.e., administrative simplification),[15] transport regulations appear to have further complicated Commission proceedings. This is especially true in respect of the opposition procedures, during which two publications in the *Official Journal* may be necessary before an exemption decision can be adopted. Far from providing expediency to the decision-making process, opposition procedures tend to place an additional burden on the Commission and, due to their rigidity, do not in practice achieve better results than standard Regulation 17 procedures.

The only advantage which may be gained from the procedures is enhanced transparency for the benefit of third parties of the agreements notified to the Commission. In fact, the systematic publication of a summary of the agreements notified which may affect third parties notably improves the situation of interested parties, though this is not consistent with the goal of administrative simplification.

The transparency which characterizes the first stage of the opposition procedure is lost in successive phases. Once the publication of the summary is completed, the regulations do not provide for public disclosure of the Commission's preliminary assessment nor, where the Commission does not have doubts about the agreement, the reasons why the agreement has been authorized. Third parties are unable, therefore, to exercise their rights before the CFI. Indeed, the complete factual background and legal reasoning of the decision can only be found either in the Commission's internal documents preparatory of the meeting at which the passing of the ninety-day time limit is discussed or in the letter sent to the notifying parties advising them that the Commission has decided not to object to their agreement. However, none of these documents is public or accessible for third parties.[16]

---

[15] 13th recital of Reg. 1017/68.

[16] Although, at first sight, the position of the national authorities does not appear more enviable than that of third parties, as the transport regulations do not provide for the convening of the Advisory Committees before the 90-day period has elapsed, the mechanisms for co-operation between national competition authorities and the Commission may, in practice, fill this gap.

The Commission's responsibilities in relation to infringement procedures in the transport sector are also stricter than under the Regulation 17 general procedures but the granting of greater guarantees to private individuals also adds to the Commission's administrative burden.

In order to simplify opposition procedures, it may be that the Commission should allow transport undertakings the possibility of opting out. If they so wish, and with the aim of permitting a more flexible dialogue with the Commission over the conditions that may be necessary for an exemption to be granted, the undertakings might resort to procedures similar to that of Regulation 17 which exist in all transport regulations. However, this probably could not be achieved without a review of the regulations and would be less beneficial for third parties than the present system.

The only current realistic possibility of saving time in transport opposition procedures appears to be for the Commission to initiate without delay a formal procedure whenever it does not appear possible, at first sight, to grant an exemption, in order to avoid pointless publications.

With respect to transparency following the publication of the summary of a notified agreement, two measures would appear appropriate. The first would be systematically to publish a press release or a brief notice in the *Official Journal* informing the third parties whenever a letter of serious doubts has been sent or a non-opposition exemption has been granted. The second would be for the Commission to contemplate either publishing the letter in which it has informed the notifying undertakings that it is not going to object to automatic exemption (these letters in practice contain sufficient reasoning) or announcing in the press release itself that interested third parties can obtain a copy of such letter from the Commission. In either of the cases, business secrets would have to be deleted from the letter.

Procedural problems apart, the greatest drawback of the competition regulations in the sector is the co-existence of five different procedural systems for transport and related services. Defining which regulation applies can be difficult since the borders of the modes of transport, the transport services and other value-added non-transport services offered together with the transport service by transport undertakings, are, at times, imprecise.

Regulation 141 separates carriers' restrictive agreements (which are subject to specific procedural rules) from restrictive agreements between transport users (which are subject to the general rules of Regulation 17). Demand-side cartels and dominant positions in the demand for transport services have to be dealt with under Regulation 17 despite the fact that the effects of these restrictions on competition make themselves felt throughout the transport market. This interpretation in itself, largely based on the wording of Regulation 141 and on the need to interpret the exceptions to the general rules strictly, causes a duplication of procedural systems in each modal transport market.

The Commission's view is that Regulation 17 is also applicable to activities related to transport but not directly connected with the provision of these types of services, such as seaport and airport handling activities.

Certain forms of transport are still today subject to the transitional rules of Articles 88 and 89 of the EC Treaty. For example, maritime cabotage transport and non-intra-Community international air transport.

Finally, the three procedural systems derived from the transport regulations have to be added to the equation. It is difficult to imagine a more unfortunate legal system.

The reason for this fivefold set of rules is basically the Member States' opposition to accepting the complete and immediate applicability of the competition rules to transport. The tri-modal procedural regime is due less to the particularities of each mode of transport, than to the unsatisfactory trend of the common transport policy and to the existence of other priorities in competition policy. Competition considerations were partially abandoned and, in any event, were neutralized during (1) the watering down of the procedural regulations as part of the packages of measures adopted by the Member States for the development of a common transport policy and (2) the granting of very generous block exemptions to the carriers' traditional restrictive practices. In contrast with other economic sectors subject to the Treaty rules, the adoption of competition rules for transport has been irrational and unfortunately has been treated as an ancillary instrument of the common transport policy (a policy not, until very recently, especially favourable to free competition), rather than as an instrument for the enforcement of the competition rules in the transport sector.

In conclusion, the transport procedures in EC competition law constitute an extremely complicated set of rules, highly influenced by the national transport policy of the Member States. The regulations adopted following Regulation 141 may not only appear unusual and pointlessly complicated but also contrary to the system of EC competition law. They are not justifiable by the specificity of the transport markets. They seek to create a particular *ad personam* system of law applicable exclusively to carriers in their own modes of transport.

One might wonder whether it might not have been legally wiser from the outset to treat inland transport and, of course, the other modes of transport, as subject to general procedural regulations (Regulation 17 and its implementing regulations), adopting by means of separate instruments block exemptions whenever it appeared justifiable in the light of Article 85(3) of the Treaty.

In the years ahead, it will be necessary to integrate fully the different procedural rules. The Commission will have to consider the desirability of amending the regulations in force, if not to eliminate the special procedural provisions for transport, at least to merge them in a single procedural regulation for transport along the lines of Regulation 17, whilst remedying any errors they contain. The first appears the ideal solution and would leave Regulation 17 (or a renewed version of it), as the only procedural text for the implementation of Articles 85 and 86 in all sectors of the economy subject to the EC

Treaty.[17] In parallel, the numerous block exemptions in transport would have to be segregated from the rules of procedure and collected in pure exemption regulations, specific for each mode of transport. The hypothetical regulation would thereby be left clean of substantive provisions more characteristic of block exemption regulations than of a procedural regulation.

7.6. TRANSPORT COMPETITION POLICY IN PERSPECTIVE

Transport has not reached the front line of competition policy without fuss or opposition. The transition towards greater activism on the part of the Commission has been characterized at times by the firm opposition of industry and national transport authorities. Only with the support of users and competition and consumer authorities have changes been made possible in the *modus operandi* of European carriers. The role of recent European Commissioners' charged with the competition portfolio has been crucial not only to convey to their Commission colleagues the importance to the EU of a more competitive transport industry but to convince the European capitals that competition policy in transport has undoubted advantages for the general economy of EU nations.

Against the background of Member State regulation and protectionism, the EC institutions have made efforts to promote gradually ever more pro-competitive policies. The competition regulations themselves in transport have responded to this strategy and have developed in a more dynamic fashion.

The regulations treat competition restrictions extremely generously, especially in maritime and air transport. Council Regulation 4056/86 exempts liner shipping conferences from the cartels prohibition in EC law. Naked price-fixing is, therefore, accepted by the EC institutions. Equally, the current competition rules enable airlines to consult on tariffs. However, it should be hoped that this unusual aspect of the present regulations will soon be progressively eliminated; further, that such progress should depend not only on the attitude of the Member States but also on that of the Commission—both in air and maritime transport. The current acceptance by the EU institutions of cartels in transport has to be considered as a stepping-stone towards a more competitive system in the future; not as a final endorsement of the carriers' anti-competitive agreements and practices, but as an indispensable pragmatic stage of tolerance if we are to arrive at an entirely open and competitive EU transport market.

Only from such a perspective of dynamism can the EU institutions defend themselves against the criticism that the transport regulations are indulgent and unambitious. If the present situation were to remain, competition policy in the transport sector could be considered a failure. As the transport competition

---

[17] It will be remembered that, as a matter of fact, in 1962, Reg. 17 was applicable to transport during a short period of time.

regime stands 'the institution of a system ensuring that competition in the Common Market is not distorted', one of the Community's fundamental tasks prescribed by Article 3(g) of the EC Treaty, would not be achieved in this crucial sector of the economy.

Competition rules apply under the same principles in all sectors of the economy contemplated by the Treaty, including transport. This is settled law since the Court's judgment in the *French Seamen* case in 1974. Despite the sometimes surprising features of Regulation 1017/68 and its clones, the application of the competition rules in this sector has to be considered, for all purposes, as a branch of competition law and not as a branch of the common transport policy.

This basic principle will be put to the test by carriers and users before the CFI and the European Court. The EU Courts will have to judge on the legality of the Commission's decisions and perhaps even on the legality of some of the provisions of the different regulations which have been studied here. The role of the Courts has been, and will continue to be, fundamental to the rate and development of this policy, whether affirming the applicability of the general rules of the Treaty or denying the applicability of the rules on freedom to provide services in the transport sector, declaring road haulage tariff commissions in Germany compatible with Community law or holding that the EC shares external competence with the Member States in matters relating trade in services.

Some of the Courts' decisions have parted ostensibly from the Commission's points of view, points of view which have been examined here in most detail. That is the reason why, more than in Brussels, the future course of competition policy in transport is to be found in the hands of the Luxembourg Judges.

Bibliography

Transport and competition, in general

Bauchet, Pierre et Rathery, Alain. 'La politique communautaire des transports.' *Problèmes Politiques et Sociaux*, Paris, N° 712, 8 octobre 1993, pp. 1–67.

Bayliss, B.T. 'Transport in the European Communities.' *Journal of Transport Economics and Policy*, Vol. 13, N° 1, January, 1979, pp. 28–43.

Brandt, Eberhard. 'Die europäische Verkehrspolitik auf dem Weg zum Binnenmarkt' *Schweizer Journal*, Vol. 54, April, 1988, pp. 33–36.

Braun-Moser, Ursula. *Europäische Verkehrspolitik—Chancen und Ziele*. Libertas Verlag. Sindelfingen, 1989.

Communautes Europeennes. Commission. *'Développement de la politique commune des transports.' Bulletin des Communautés Européennes*. Supplement, N° 8/71. Office de Publications Officielles des Communautés Européennes. Luxembourg, 1971.

—— 'Politique commune des transports: objectifs et programmes.' *Bulletin des Communautés Européennes*. Supplement, N° 16/73. Office de Publications Officielles des CE. Luxembourg, 1974.

Comunidades Europeas. Comisión. 'El desarrollo futuro de la política común de transportes.' *Boletín de las Comunidades Europeas*, Suplemento 3, 1993. Oficina de publicaciones oficiales de las Comunidades Europeas. Luxemburgo, 1993.

Dawson, Reginald y Renaux, Geneviève (Eds.). *EEC transport policy*. Club de Bruxelles. Brussels, 1989.

De Ferron, Olivier. *Le problème des transports et le Marché Commun*. Librairie Draz. Genève, 1965.

Degli Abbati, Carlo. *I transporti nel quadro dell'integrazione economica europea*. Publicaciones del Istituto di Geografia Economica e Trasporti dell'Università di Genova. ECIG. Génova, 1984.

—— *Transport and European integration*. Commission of the European Communities. Office for Official Publications ot the European Communities. Luxembourg, 1987.

Dousset, Jacques. *Politiques nationales des transports et politique européenne*. Schweizerische Zeitschrift für Volkswirtschaft und Statistik, Vol. 113, N° 3, September, 1977, pp. 315–324.

De Rus, Ginés. 'El sistema de transportes español en el marco de la CE.' *Papeles de Economía Española*, N° 51, 1992, pp.102–115.

Dolfen, M. *Der Verkehr im europäischen Wettbewerbsrecht*. Verlag Recht und Wirtschaft. Heidelberg, 1991.

Erdmenger, Jürgen. *Politique commune des transports des neuf:—evolution à l'intérieur—overture à l'extérieur*. Raccolta Delle Lezioni. Universita degli studi. Trieste, 1977. pp. 31–60.

Agence Europe. Europe Documents. *The European Commission's new pragmatic approach to the Common transport policy*. Agence Europe, N° 1243, 23 February 1983.

Ewers, Hans-Jürgen. *Institutional requirements for a Common market in transport services*. In The completion of the Internal market. Ed. by Horst Siebert. Institut für Weltwirtschaft an der Universität Kiel. J.C.B. Mohr (Paul Siebeck). Tübingen, 1989, pp. 150–164.

Gómez Alonso, Lorenzo. 'Los transportes en la Comunidad Económica Europea.' In: *Tratado de Derecho comunitario europeo.* Editorial Civitas, Madrid, 1986, Vol. III, pp. 459–498.

Greaves, Rosa. *Transport Law of the European Community.* Athlone Press. London, 1991.

Izquierdo de Bartolomé, Rafael. 'La política común de transportes y la incidencia de la integración de España en el transporte nacional.' *Revista de Instituciones Europeas,* Vol. 13, N° 2, 1986, pp. 375–412.

Izquierdo de Bartolomé, Rafael; Lopez Pita, Andrés; Colomer Ferrándiz, José V., *et al.* 'Política de transportes.' *Información General Española,* N° 659, 1988, pp. 5–134.

Laguna de Paz, José Carlos. 'El mercado interior de transportes. Su incidencia en el Derecho interno.' *Noticias de la Unión Europea,* vol.11, N° 121, february 1995, pp. 61–72.

Lenz, Carl Otto. 'Die Verkehrspolitik der Europäischen Gemeinschaften im Lichte der Rechtsprechung des Gerichtshofes.' *Europarecht,* Vol. 23, N° 2, April–June 1988, pp. 158–178.

McDonald, Robert. *Towards a common transport policy* European Trends (The Economist Intelligence Unit), N° 3, 1993, pp. 78–88.

Martínez Álvaro, Oscar. 'Treinta años de política de transporte en la Comunidad Europea. (IV)' *Lecturas de Transporte,* Turismo y Comunicaciones. Ministerio de Transportes, Turismo y Comunicaciones. Madrid, 1989.

Müller, Jürgen. 'Comment on H.-J. Ewers 'Institutional requirements for a Common market in transport services.' In *The completion of the Internal market.* Ed. by Horst Seibert. Institut für Weltwirtschaft an der Universität Kiel. J.C.B. Mohr (Paul Siebeck). Tübingen, 1989, pp. 165–173.

Salafranca Sanchez-Neyra, José Ignacio; González-Blanch Roca, Francisco and Summers Rivero, Francisco. *La política de transportes en la Comunidad Económica Europea.* Trivium. Madrid, 1986.

Stabenow, Wolfgang. 'Verkehrspolitik und Wettweberbsregeln in der Europäischen Wirtschaftsgemeinschaft.' *Sociaal Economische Wetgeving,* N° 7–8, July–August 1963, pp. 379–396.

Studiecentrum voor de Expansie van Antwerpen. *La politique commune des transports de la CEE. Bilan 1985–1987.* SVEVA. Antwerp, 1987.

Weinstock, Ulrich. 'Réflexions sur la politique commune des transports: du légalisme au pragmatisme.' *Revue du Marché Commun,* N° 242, December 1980, pp. 571–588.

Weyer, Heinrich. 'Gelten die Wettbewerbsbestimmungen des EWG-Vertrages auch für den Verkehr?.' *Wirtschaft und Wettbewerb,* Vol. 21, N° 1, 1971, pp. 11 et seq.

Whitelegg, John. 'The Common transport policy: a case of lost direction.' *Transportation Science,* Vol. 13, N° 4, November, 1979, pp. 343–357.

William, Ernest W. 'U.S. and Common Market transport: a comparative study' *Columbia Journal of World Business,* Vol. 11, N° 1, Spring, 1976, pp. 5–14.

Inland transport

Aberle, Gerd; Basedow, Jürgen; Dagtoglou, Prodromos, et al. *Europäische Verkehrspolitik. Nach dem Untätigkeitsurteil des Europäischen Gerichtshofes gegen den Rat vom 22 Mai 1985–Rechtssache 13/83 (Parlament./.Rat).* Max-Planck-Institut für Ausländisches und Internationales Privatrecht. Tübingen, 1987.

Alexis, Alain. 'Transports ferroviaires et concurrence. Les principaux apports de la Directive N° 91/440.' *European Transport Law*, Vol. 28, N° 4, 1993, pp. 499–516.

Alfs, M.H. 'Ausgewählte Probleme einer wettbewerbsgerechten EG–Binnenschiffahrtspolitik.' *Internationales Verkehrswesen*, N° 4, July–August 1974, pp. 135–140.

Arpio Santacruz, Marta. 'El Parlamento frente al Consejo: la sentencia del Tribunal de Justicia en materia de transportes.' *Revista de Instituciones Europeas*, 1985, pp. 789–804.

Baumgartner, J.P. 'Should we deregulate the European railways?' *International Journal of Transport Economics*, Vol. 10, N° 2, April–August 1983, pp. 385–402.

Bernardet, Maurice. *L'Europe des transports routiers: institutions, textes, perspectives.* Editions CELSE. Paris, 1990.

Blonk, W.A.G. 'Regulation (CEE) No 1017/68 of the Council of July 19, 1968 applying rules of competition to transport by rail, road and inland water way.' *Common Market Law Review*, Vol. 6, N° 4, October 1969, pp. 451–465.

Bodson, Victor. 'Perspectives de développement de la politique commune des transports.' *European Transport Law*, Vol. 5, N° 4, 1970. pp. 488–533.

Brandt, Eberhard. 'Untätigkeit in der Europäischen Verkehrspolitik. Ammerkungen zum Untätigkeitsurteil des Europäischen Gerichthofes vom 22. Mai 1985.' *Transportrecht*, Vol. N° 3, March, 1986, pp. 89–94.

Cascales Moreno, Fernando J. *Transporte internacional de viajeros por carretera en el ámbito comunitario; el Reglamento n°. 684/92 del Consejo, de 16 de marzo, por el que se establecen normas comunes en esta clase de transporte, efectuado con autocares y autobuses.* Noticias CEE/CISS, Valencia, Año 9, n° 102, julio de 1993, pp.75–79.

Close, George L. 'Inland transport services: recent developments in Community policy.' *Common Market Law Review*, Vol. 22, N° 4, December, 1985, pp. 587–614.

Crowley, James. 'Inland transport in the European Community following 1992.' *Antitrust Bulletin*, Vol. 37, N° 2, 1992, pp. 453–480.

Dousset, Jacques. 'Un arrêt capital de la Cour de Justice des Communautés Européennes au sujet de la politique commune des transports (22 mai 1985—Recours en carence du Parlement Européen contre le Conseil des ministres des transports).' *Transports*, N° 306, July–August, 1985, pp. 384–388.

Erdmenger, Jürgen. 'Die EG-Verkehrspolitik vor Gericht. Das EuGH-Urteil Rs. 13/83 vom 22.5.1985 und seine Folgen.' *Europarecht*, N° 4, October–December, 1985, pp. 375–392.

Europe Documents. 'European Commission proposals for establishment of common road transport market.' *Agence Europe*, N° 1386, 18 January 1986.

—— 'Le plan du Conseil pour réaliser le marché commun unifié des transports de marchandises par route.' *Agence Europe* N° 1416, 28 August 1986.

—— 'Programme pour une relance de la politique commune des transports.' *Agence Europe*, N° 1128, 10 December 1980.

Gamm, Otto-Friedrich Von, and Gamm, Eva Von. 'Die EWG-Wettbewerbsregeln für der Eisenbahn, Strassen—und Binnenschiffahrtsverkehr.' *Wettbewerb in Recht und Praxis*, Vol. 15, N° 1, January, 1969, pp. 19–22.

Gazette du Palais. 'Communautés européennes. Fondements de la Communauté. Libre circulation des marchandises. Transports.' Transport international (a.s. aff. PE/CCE). *Gazette du Palais*, N° 305–306, 1–2 November, 1986, pp. 13–15.

Idot, L. 'L'ouverture des transports ferroviaires à la concurrence.' *Cahiers de Droit Européen*, Vol. 31, N° 3–4, 1995, pp.263–321.

Lewis, Xavier. 'Vers le marché unique des transports.' *Revue du Marché Unique Européen*, N° 4, 1991, pp. 49–88.

Maury, B. 'La règlementation communautaire des transports.' *Revue Trimestrielle de Droit Européen*, Vol. 20, N° 2, 1984, pp. 249–288.

Maury, B. 'Cour de Justice, 22 mai 1985. Aff. N° 13/83, Parlement européen contre Conseil des CE (a.s. recours en carence).' *Cahiers de Droit Européen*, Vol. 22, N° 1, 1986, pp. 44–91.

Navigation, Ports et Industries. 'La dérèglamentation ou, mieux, la libéralisation des transports terrestres en Europe doit être progressive et maîtrisée.' *Navigation, Ports et Industries*, Vol. 58, N° 2, 25 January 1986, pp. 21–23.

Organisation for Economic Cooperation and Development. *Competition policy and the deregulation of road transport*. Organization for Economic Cooperation and Development. Paris, 1990.

Pinay, Pierre. 'Règles de concurrence et transports dans le cadre de la C.E.E.' *Annuaire Français de Droit International*, Vol. 8, 1962, pp. 781–805.

Pons de Vall, Marta. 'Eliminación de controles fronterizos en el transporte.' *Horizonte Enpresarial/ Fomento del trabajo nacional*, Barcelona, n° 2009, noviembre de 1990, pp. 56–57.

Revue Trimestrielle de Droit Europeen. Jurisprudence: Cour de Justice des Communautés européennes. Arrêt du 22 mai 1985. Parlement européen contre Conseil des Communautés européennes (aff. 13/83). *Revue Trimestrielle de Droit Européen*, Vol. 21, N° 4, October– December 1985, pp. 757–766.

Riphagen, W. 'The transport legislation of the European Communities, its relationship to international treaties and its effect on Member states.' *Common Market Law Review*, Vol. 6, 1965, pp. 291–325.

Saupe, Gerd. *Technische Vereinbarungen und Unternehmensgemeinschaften im Verkehrskartellrecht der EWG (Eisenbahn-, Strassen- und Binnenschiffsverkerhr)*. Kölner Schriften zum Europarecht, Band 16. Carl Heymanns. Köln, 1972

Steele, John R. 'Transport policy and the European Court.' *Transport*, Vol. 7, N° 2, April, 1986, pp. 77–79.

United Kingdom. House of Lords. *EEC transport policy, R/2371/77: Commission programme of priority business in the transport sector*. House of Lords. HMSO. London, 1978.

Violland, M. 'Déréglementer ou libéraliser les transports routiers de marchandises?' *Transports*, N° 313, March, 1986, pp. 131–136.

Wägenbaur, Rolf. 'Die EWG-Kartellregelung für den Verkehr vor der Verabschiedung.' *Aussenwirtschaftsdienst des Betriebsberaters*, 1968, pp. 256–258.

—— 'Wettbewerbsregeln für den Verkehr in der EWG.' *Aussenwirtschaftsdienst des Betriebsberaters*, 1968, pp. 415–424.

—— *Les règles de concurrence applicables aux transports*. Cahiers de Droit Européen, N° 6, 1970, pp. 645–662.

Maritime transport

Ademuni-Odeke. 'The Brussels Package: the United Kingdom and the EEC respond to the Code.' *Maritime Policy and Management*, Vol. 11, N° 4, 1984, pp. 233–250.

Arbault, Marie-Laurence. 'Le cabotage maritime dans la réglementation communautaire: un plagia de la libéralisation des services de transport terrestre?' *Transports*, Vol. 39, N° 368, November–December 1994, pp. 385–388.

Aspinwall, Mark. *Moveable Feast. Pressure Group conflict and the European Community shipping policy*. Avebury. Aldershot, 1995.

Bayer, Nathan J. 'Antitrust comes to maritime transport in the European Economic Community.' *Federal Bar News and Journal*, Vol. 34, 1987, pp. 299–306.

Bird, James. 'Further debate on the Treaty of Rome, Article 84, paragraph 2 as it may affect maritime transport.' *European Transport Law*, Vol. 2, N° 1, 1967, pp. 24–47.

Bonassies, Pierre. 'Le cadre institutionnel: le projet de règlement sur les conditions d'application des règles de concurrence du Traité de Rome aux transports maritimes. Aspects juridiques.' In 'Les transports maritimes à l'heure communautaire. 2e Colloque. Marseille 1,2,3 Juin 1982. Compte rendu des travaux'. *Cahiers de Documentation de la Chambre de Commerce et d'Industrie de Marseille*. Marseille, 1982, pp. 135–140.

Bredimas, A.E. 'The Common Shipping Policy of the EEC.' *Common Market Law Review*, Vol. 18, N° 1, February, 1981, pp. 9–32.

—— and Tzoannos, J. 'In search for a common shipping policy for the E.C.' *Journal of Common Market Studies*, Vol. 20, N° 2, December, 1981, pp. 95–114.

Bredima-Savopoulou, Anne and Tzoannos, John. *The common shipping policy of the EC*. North-Holland. Amsterdam, 1990.

Bright, Christopher and Easter, Caroline. 'Competition law and the Shipping sector.' *European Business Law Review*, Vol 3, N° 1, November 1992, pp. 291–293.

Brittan, Sir Leon. *Liner shipping developments and prospects for the Community*. Address by Sir Leon Brittan QC, Vice-President of the Commission of the European Communities. Institut Français de la Mer. Paris, 8 March 1991. 15 pp.

—— *The EC competition policy for liner shipping set in its commercial and political context*. Address before the European Maritime Law Organization Second Conference, held in London, 23–24 October 1992, at the Institute of Advanced Legal Studies. European Maritime Law Organization. London, 1992. 13 pp.

Carbone, Sergio M. 'Il ruolo delle norme sulla concorrenza nella disciplina dei traffici marittimi internazionali (con particolare riferimento allo Shipping Act americano e alle proposte comunitarie)'. *Il Diritto Marittimo*, 1985, pp. 703 et seq.

—— 'Traffici marittimi e Comunità Europea' Relazione introduttiva.' *Il Diritto Marittimo*, 1989, pp. 3–8.

—— 'La nuova disciplina comunitaria dei traffici marittimi.' *Rivista di Diritto Internazionale Privato e Processuale*, Vol. 25, N° 2, 1989, pp. 293–324.

Caspari, Manfred. 'EEC competition policy and maritime transport.' In 'Speeches. ESC Jubilee Symposium. The Hague 22 September 1988'. European Shippers' Councils/EVO (Dutch Shippers' Council). Zoetermer, 1988. 11 pp.

Castillo de la Torre, Fernando. *La aplicación de las normas comunitarias de competencia al transporte marítimo*. Noticias CEE/ CISS, Valencia, Vol. 9, N° 102, July 1993, pp. 81–94.

Clough, Mark and Randolph, Fergus. 'Shipping and EC competition law.' Current Legal Development Series. Butterworths. London, 1991.

Clough, Mark. 'The Devil and the Deep Blue Sea (EC Competition Law and Liner Shipping Consortia).' *European Competition Law Review*, Vol. 16, N° 7, October 1995, pp. 417–427.

Dargallo Nieto, Marita. 'Transporte marítimo y Derecho comunitario: normas de competencia y prácticas de tarifas desleales.' *Anuario de Derecho Marítimo*, Vol. 7, 1989. pp. 381–406.

Deakin, Brian M. and Seward, T. *Shipping conferences: a study of their origins, development and economic practices.* Cambridge University Press. London, 1973.

de la Cuétara Martínez, Juan Miguel. *La política de transportes marítimos en España y en la C.E.E. Comentario al Real Decreto 990/86 de 23 de Mayo.* Noticias CEE/CISS, Vol. 3, N° 26, 1987, pp. 89–93.

Devescovi, Fabrizio. *Le conferences marittime come strumento di collaborazione tra imprese.* A. Giuffré (Quaderni di Giurisprudenza Commerciale, N° 79). Milano, 1986.

Dominedo, F.M. et al. *'Conferences' marittime e mercato comune.* Cedam-Casa Editrice Dott. Antonio Milani. Padova, 1964.

Erdmenger, Jürgen. 'Seeschiffahrts politische Massanahmen der E.G.—gemeinsames Interesse—rechtliche Möglichkeiten. Shipping Policy in the European Community: common interest—legal possibilities.' *Schriften des deutschen Vereins für internationales Seerecht.* N° 30, 1978.

Erdmenger, Jürgen. 'EEC Rules—Shipping policy of the Community.' In 'Conference Report. International Symposium on liner shipping IV.' *Institute of Shipping Economics and Logistics.* Book series, N° 14. Bremen, 1988, pp. 91–105.

Erdmenger, Jürgen and Stasinopoulos, Dinos. 'The shipping policy of the European Community.' *Journal of Transport Economics and Policy*, 1988, pp. 355 et seq.

Erdmenger, Jürgen. 'Development and prospects of the maritime transport law of the European Communities.' *European Transport Law*, Vol. 23, N° 5, 1988, pp. 543–555.

——— *Liner shipping in the 1990s. Government and liner shipping. Does the EEC really promote free competition in liner trades?.* Speech before the 6th ICC Shipping Conference. Hamburg, 25 June, 1990. 13 pp.

Faull, Jonathan. 'Recent Developments in European competition policy in the maritime field.' *European Transport Law*, Vol. 30, N° 1, 1995, pp. 3–11.

Fontaine, Emmanuel. *The Commission in action: practical examples of maritime competition law application.* Address before the European Maritime Law Organization inaugural conference on 'EEC maritime competition law', held in London, 25–26 October 1991, at the Institute of Advanced Legal Studies. European Maritime Law Organization. London, 1991. 11 pp.

Fornasier, Raffaello. 'External competence of the Community in maritime transport.' *Il Diritto Marittimo* Vol. 91, 1989. pp. 31–37.

Forwood, Nicholas. *Jurisdictional limits to the application of EC competition rules to international maritime transport.* In Barry Hawk (Ed.), (1992) Annual Proceedings of the Fordham Corporate Law Institute. International Antitrust Law and Policy. Transnational Juris Publications/Kluwer. New York/Deventer, 1993, pp. 907–924.

Gabaldón García, José Luis. 'El progreso hacia una política comunitaria sobre transporte marítimo.' *Anuario de Derecho Marítimo*, Vol. 4, 1986, pp. 325 et seq.

Gilman, Sydney. *An economic analysis of European competition law and policy.* Address before the European Maritime Law Organization inaugural conference on 'EEC maritime competition law', held in London, 25–26 October 1991, at the Institute of Advanced Legal Studies. European Maritime Law Organization. London, 1991. 13 pp.

Gondra Romero, Jose María. *Las conferencias marítimas ante el derecho de la competencia.* Revista de Derecho Mercantil, N° 113, 1969, pp. 345–377.

Green, Nicholas. 'Competition and maritime trade: a critical view.' *European Transport Law*, Vol. 23, N° 5, 1988, pp. 612–628.

Green, Nicholas. 'Regulation 4056/86: competition law and maritime transport.' In '*The EEC and shipping. Maritime practice and competition law: heading for a collision? Proceedings of a conference held in London on 11 February of 1988 by the Institute of Maritime Law*'. IML/Southampton University. Southampton, England, February, 1988, pp. XVIII–XXVIII.

Green, Nicholas. 'Consortia and multi-modal transport.' In '*EEC Shipping Law. Proceedings of the 2nd Conference, held on 7–8 February 1991, at the Scandic Crown Hotel, Antwerp, organized by European Study Conferences, Ltd. in association with the EEC Section of the UIA (Union Internationale des Avocats)*'. European Study Conferences Ltd. Corby, 1991. 20 pp.

Heldring, Balt. 'The UNCTAD Code and the European Economic Community.' In: *Shipping nationalism and the future of the United States liner industry: the UNCTAD Code and Bilateralism. Proceedings of a workshop. November 1983. Center for Ocean Management Studies.* Edited by Lawrence Juda. Times Press Educational Publishing. Wakefield, Rhode Island, 1984, pp. 13–18.

Herman, Amos. *Shipping conferences.* Lloyd's of London Press Ltd. London, 1983.

Holman, Fenwick & Willan. *First fine imposed in EC maritime competition law. French/West African Shipowner's Committees case.* Corporate Briefing, Vol. 6, N° 8, July 1992, pp. 195–197.

Hernández Yzal, Santiago. 'La marina mercante española y la integración de España en el Mercado Común.' *Noticias* CEE/CISS, Vol. 2, N° 17, 1986, pp. 57–67.

Institute of Maritime Law, Southampton University. *The EEC and shipping. Maritime practice and competition law: heading for a collision? A one-day conference. London, 11 February 1988.* Institute of Maritime Law, Southampton University. Southampton, England, 1988.

Ivancie, Francis J. *Harmony in EEC/US relations. Maritime competition policy: a comparison.* Address before the European Maritime Law Organization inaugural conference on 'EEC maritime competition law', held in London, 25–26 October 1991, at the Institute of Advanced Legal Studies. European Maritime Law Organization. London, 1991. 14 pp.

Juda, Lawrence. 'The UNCTAD Liner Code. A preliminary examination of the implementation of the Code of Conduct for Liner Conferences.' *Journal of Maritime Law and Commerce*, Vol. 16, N° 2, April 1985, pp. 181–217.

Kreis, Helmut W.R. 'Maritime transport and EEC competition rules.' *European Transport Law*, Vol. 23, N° 5, 1988, pp. 562–570.

Kreis, Helmut W.R. 'European Community competition policy and international shipping.' *Fordham International Law Review* Vol. 13, 1990. pp. 411–445.

Kreis, Helmut W.R. 'Conferences and outsiders.' In: *EEC Shipping Law. Proceedings of the 2nd Conference, held on 7–8 February 1991, at the Scandic Crown Hotel, Antwerp, organized by European Study Conferences, Ltd. in association with the EEC Section of the UIA (Union Internationale des Avocats).* European Study Conferences Ltd. Corby, 1991. 12 pp.

Kreis, Helmut W.R. *The Commission's policy and practice in maritime competition law.* Address before the European Maritime Law Organization inaugural conference on 'EEC maritime competition law', held in London, 25–26 October 1991, at the Institute of Advanced Legal Studies. European Maritime Law Organization. London, 1991. 11 pp.

Kreis, Helmut W.R. and van der Woorde, Eddy. 'EC competition law and maritime transport.' *Antitrust Bulletin*, Vol. 37, N° 2, 1992, pp. 481–528.

Kuyper, P.J. 'The European Comunity and the code of conduct for liner conferences: some problems on the border-line between general international law and Community law.' *Netherlands Yearbook of International Law*, Vol. 12, 1981, pp. 73–112.

McIntosh, Anne C.B. 'Antitrust implications of liner conferences: alternatives to the regulation of liner trades with emphasis on the European approach.' *Lloyd's Maritime and Commercial Law Quarterly*, May, 1980, pp. 139–154.

Manzini, Pietro. 'Sviluppi comunitari e statunitensi in materia di disciplina della concorrenza e regolamentazione dei trasporti marittimi'. *Rivista di Diritto Europeo*, 1987, pp. 103–124.

Martínez Lage, Santiago. 'El régimen comunitario del transporte marítimo y el Real Decreto 990/1986 sobre ordenación del transporte marítimo en España.' *Gaceta Jurídica de la CEE*, N° 57, 1988, pp. 387–429.

Marx, Daniel Jr. *International shipping cartels: a study of industrial self-regulation by shipping conferences*. Princeton University Press. Princeton, New Jersey, 1953.

Morton, Nigel. 'E.E.C. competition rules and sea transport.' In 'Les transports maritimes à l'heure comunautaire. 1er Colloque. Marseille 10/11/12 Octobre 1979. Compte rendu des travaux'. *Cahiers de Documentation de la Chambre de Commerce et d'Industrie de Marseille*. Edited in cooperation with the Institut Méditerranéen des Transports Maritimes. Marseille, 1980, pp. 83–85.

—— 'Le cadre institutionnel: le projet de règlement sur les conditions d'application de règles de concurrence du Traité de Rome aux transports maritimes. Présentation.' Les transports maritimes à l'heure communautaire. 2e Colloque, Marseille 1, 2, 3 Juin 1982. Compte rendu des travaux. *Cahiers de Documentation de la Chambre de Commerce et d'Industrie de Marseille*. Marseille, 1982, pp. 131–133.

Munari, Francesco. 'Das europäische Wettweberbsrecht des Seeverkehrs.' *Rabels Zeitschrift für Ausländisches und Internationales Privatrecht* Vol. 54, N° 4, 1990. pp. 628–676.

Nascimbene, Bruno. 'Diritto di stabilimento e libera prestazione di servizi delle compagnie marittime europee.' *Il Diritto Marittimo*, 1989, pp. 39–49.

Pernice, Ingolf. 'Offene Märkte und Wettbewerbsordnung der EG im Bereich der Seeschiffahrt.' In: *Europarecht, Kartellrecht, Wirtschaftsrecht. Festschrift für Arved Deringer*. Edited by Ulrich Everling, Karl-Heinz Narjes and Jochim Sedemund. Nomos. Baden-Baden, 1993, pp. 135–159.

Pinacho Bolaño-Rivadeneira, Javier. 'España ante la ratificación del Código de Conducta para las conferencias de fletes de la UNCTAD.' *Anuario de Derecho Marítimo*, Vol. 1, 1981, pp. 369–376.

Power, Vincent. *EC shipping law*. Lloyd's of London Press. London, 1992.

Pueyo Losa, Jorge. 'La política de transportes marítimos de la Comunidad Europea. Libre prestación de servicios y libre acceso al trafico transoceánico.' *Revista de Instituciones Europeas*, Vol. 18, N° 1, Jan.–Apr. 1991, pp. 85–140.

Rabe, Dieter and Schütte, Michael. 'Die erste Verordnung des Rates zur Anwendung des EWG-Kartellrecht (Art. 85 und 86 EWGV) auf den Seeverkerhr.' *Recht der Internationales Wirtschaft*, Vol. 9, September 1988, pp. 701–705.

—— 'EEC competition rules and maritime transport.' *Lloyd's Maritime and Commercial Law Quarterly, May*, 1988, pp. 182–210.

Rabe, Hans Jürgen; Kröger, Bernd; Petersen, Karl-Friedrich, *et al.* 'Dossier: Seerecht in der Europäischen Union. Tagung in der Handelskammer Hamburg 1993. III (Ende)'. *Archiv des Volkerrechts*, Vol. 32, N° 3–4, October 1994, pp.422–479.

Rakovsky, Claude. 'Sea transport under EEC competition law.' In: Barry Hawk (Ed.), (1992) *Annual Proceedings of the Fordham Corporate Law Institute*. International Antitrust Law and Policy. Transnational Juris Publications/Kluwer. New York/Deventer, 1993, pp. 845–906.

Ruttley, Philip. 'International shipping and EEC competition law.' *European Competition Law Review*, Vol. 12, N° 1, 1991, pp. 5–18.

Scheivnar, Isaac. 'El código de conducta de las conferencias marítimas: significado y perspectivas.' *Comercio Exterior*. (Mexico), Vol. 34, N° 9, September, 1984, pp. 899–909.

Slot, Piet Jan. 'Het Europees zeevervoerbeleid.' *Tijdschrift voor Europees en Economisch Recht*, Vol. 35, N° 12, December 1987, pp. 774–795.

—— 'Shipping and Competition.' In: *Exploiting the internal market: co-operation and competition toward 1992*. Edited by P.J. Slot and M.H. van der Woude. Kluwer. Deventer, 1988, pp. 31–43.

Sproul, Gillian. 'Articles 85 and 86: First application to maritime transport.' *European Competition Law Review*, Vol. 13, N° 5, September–October 1992, pp. 215–221.

Sturmey, S.G. 'The Code of Conduct for Liner Conferences: a 1985 view.' *Maritime Policy and Management*, Vol. 13, N° 3, 1986, pp. 185–221.

—— *The Code of Conduct and the review conference*. S.G. Surmey, Publisher. Athens, 1988.

Summers Rivero, Francisco. 'Problemas actuales del transporte marítimo en los países de la C.E.E.' *Noticias* CEE/CISS, Vol. 2, N° 17, 1986, pp. 69–73.

Temple Lang, John. *Current issues in Community maritime competition law*. Address before the European Maritime Law Organization Second Conference, held in London, 23–24 October 1992, at the Institute of Advanced Legal Studies. European Maritime Law Organization. London, 1992. 34 pp.

United Nations Conference on Trade and Development. *The liner conference system. Report by the UNCTAD Secretariat*. Doc. TD/B/C.4/62/Rev.1. United Nations, New York, 1970.

—— *The regulation of liner conferences (a code of conduct for the liner conference system)*. United Nations. Doc. TD/104/Rev. 1. New York, 1972.

van der Ziel, G.J. 'Samenverkingsovereenkomsten in de lijnscheepvaart en de EG-mededingingsbepalingen.' Tijdschrift voor vervoerswetenschap, Vol. 27, N° 4, 1991, pp. 447–456.

Vermote, Lieven. 'Le Code de conduite des conférences maritimes et le compromis de Bruxelles, une analyse du contenu et de la portée du règlement CEE, N° 954/79 du Conseil des ministres des Communautés européennes.' *European Transport Law*, Vol. 21, N° 1, 1986, pp. 3–36.

Vitzthum, Wolfgang. 'Die Europäische Gemeinschaft und das internationale Seerecht.' Archiv des öffentlichen Rechts, Vol. 111/01, 1986, pp. 33–62.

Werner, Walter. 'Eine Wettbewerbsordnung für den Seeverkehr.' *Wirtschaft und Wettbewerb*, Vol. 37, N° 10, October 1987, pp. 796–808.

—— 'Die Wettbewerbsordnung der EWG für den Seeverkehr.' *Neue Juristiche Wochenschrift*, Vol. 41, N° 35, 1988, pp. 2159–2160.

Zamora Cabot, Francisco Javier. 'Un apunte sobre la incidencia en España del Código UNCTAD sobre conferencias marítimas.' *Anuario de Derecho Marítimo*, Vol. 8, 1990, pp. 245–256.

Air transport

Abbot, Kim and Thomson, David. 'De-regulating European aviation: the impact of bilateral liberalisation.' *International Journal of Industrial Organization*, Vol. 9, N° 1, March 1991, pp. 125–140.

Adkins, Bernardine. *Air Transport and EC Competition Law.* Sweet and Maxwell. London, 1994.

Albers, I. and Mulder, P.R. 'Op de scheidslijn van protectie en liberalisering.' *Sociaal-Economische Wetgeving,* Vol. 37, N° 8/9, August–September 1989, pp. 574–594.

Argyris, Nicholas. 'The EEC Rules of Competition and the Air Transport Sector.' *Common Market Law Review,* Vol. 26, N° 1, 1989, pp. 5–32.

Balfour, John M. 'Freedom to Provide Air Transport Services in the EEC.' *European Law Review,* Vol. 14, 1989, pp. 30–46.

—— *Competition and Aviation in the EEC.* Shawcross & Beaumont. London, 1992.

—— 'Airline Mergers and Acquisitions: What Controls does EEC law provide?' *Air Law,* Vol. 15, N° 5/6, 1990, pp. 237–251.

—— 'The Second EEC Air Transport Package—Substance or packaging ?' *European Business Law Review,* Vol. 1, N° 3, November 1990, pp. 66–69.

Basedow, Jürgen. 'National Authorities in European Airline Competition Law.' *European Competition Law Review,* Vol. 9, N° 3, 1988, pp. 342–353.

Bellis, Jean-François. 'Nouvelles frontières' and EEC competition law in the air transport sector: a restatement of classical jurisdictional rules.' *Swiss Review of International Competition Law,* N° 27, June 1986, pp. 51–56.

Busti, Silvio. 'La nuova disciplina comunitaria dei servizi aerei.' *Diritto Comunitario e degli Scambli Internazionali,* Vol. 32, N° 1–2, January–June 1993, pp. 187–211.

Button, Kenneth J. and Swann, Dennis. 'European Community airlines—Deregulation and its problems.' *Journal of Common Market Studies,* Vol. 27, N° 4, 1989, pp. 259–282.

Cavani, Raffaele. 'Computerized Reservation Systems for air transport: Remarks on the European Community legislation.' *Fordham International Law Journal,* Vol. 17, N° 2, 1994, pp. 441–457.

Chavan, A. 'Comments on the judgement delivered by the Court of Justice of the European Communities on April 30 th, 1986 concerning the application of the competition rules of the Treaty of Rome to air transport.' *Swiss Review of International Competition Law,* N° 27, June, 1986, pp. 57–63.

Cienfuegos Mateo, Manuel. 'L'application de la nullité de l'article 85, §2, du Traité CEE par les juridictions nationales (avec un examen particulier du transport aérien).' *Cahiers de droit européen,* N° 3/4, 1991, pp. 317–353.

Clark, Virginia. 'New frontiers in EEC air transport competition.' *Northwestern Journal of International Law and Business,* Vol. 9, 1987, pp. 455 et seq.

Close, George L. 'Article 84 EEC: the development of transport policy in the sea and air sectors.' *European Law Review,* Vol. 5, N° 3, June, 1980, pp. 188–207.

Crans, B.J.H. and Biesheuvel, M.B.W. 'Europees recht en luchtvervoer.' *Sociaal-Economische Wetgeving,* Vol 36, N° 5, May 1988, pp. 300–320.

Dagtoglou, Prodromos D. and Soames, Trevor. (Eds.) *Airline Mergers and Cooperation in the European Community.* Kluwer. Deventer-Boston, 1990.

Dagtoglou, Prodromos D.; Balfour, John M. and Stuyck, J. (Eds.). *Second Annual Conference, 9 November 1990 in Brussels. European Air Law Association.* A.N. Sakkoulas Publishers / Kluwer. Athens / Deventer, 1991.

Dagtoglou, Prodromos D.; Montag, Frank and Balfour, John M. (Eds.). 'Third Annual Conference, 15 November 1991 in Berlin. European Air Law Association.' A.N. Sakkoulas Publishers / Kluwer. Athens / Deventer, 1992.

—— 'Fourth Annual Conference in Rome [1992]. European Air Law Association.' Kluwer. Deventer, 1994.

276 *Bibliography*

Drolshammer, J. and Rauber, G. 'Die Liberalisierung des Europäischen Luftverkehrs EG-EWR-Schweiz.' *Aktuelle Juristische Praxis*, 1992, pp. 1242 et seq.

Duchene, Dennis A. 'The Third Package of liberalization in the European air transport sector: Shying away from full liberalization.' *Transportation Law Journal*, Vol. 23, N° 1, 1995, pp. 119–161.

Dussart-Lefret, C. and Federlin, C. 'Ground Handling Services and EC Competition Rules. A Commission initiative to open up ground handling markets.' *Air and Space Law*, Vol. 19, N° 2, 1994, pp. 50–61.

Dutheil de la Rochère, Jacqueline. 'Transport aérien européen, problèmes de concurrence.' *Annuaire Français de Droit International*, 1986, pp. 810 et seq.

Ebke, W. and Wenglorz, G. 'Die zweite Stufe der Liberalisieriung des Linienverkehrs in EG.' *Recht der internationalen Wirtschaft*, Vol. 36, N° 6, junio 1990, pp. 468–478.

—— —— 'Liberalizing scheduled air transport within the European Community: from the first phase to the second and beyond.' *Denver Journal of International Law and Policy*, Vol. 19, N° 3, 1991, pp. 493–527.

Erdmenger, Jürgen. *Die Anwendung des EWG-Vertrages auf Seeschiffahrt und luftfahrt. Zur Auslegung von Art. 84. Abs 2 des Vertrages.* Cram, de Gruyter & Co. Hamburg, 1962.

Estienne-Henrotte, E. 'Le transport aérien et le Traité CEE: Défi et perspectives (Journée d'études—5 décembre 1986). Les consequénces de l'arrêt "Nouvelles Frontières"'. *European Transport Law* N° 6, 1986. pp 537 et seq.

—— 'L'application des règles générales du Traité de Rome aux transports aériens.' *Editions de l'Université de Bruxelles.* Bruxelles, 1988.

Frühling, Pierre and Godfroid, Marc. 'Examen de jurisprudence: Droit aérien communautaire 1986–1992.' *Revue de Droit Commercial Belge*, Vol. 25, N° 9, September 1995, pp. 755–779.

Garland, Gloria J. 'The American deregulation experience and the use of Article 90 to expedite EEC air transport liberalisation.' *European Competition Law Review*, Vol. 7, N° 2, 1986, pp. 259–282.

Goh, Jeffrey. 'Air antitrust competition in the European Economic Community: The antitrust procedures.' *Transportation Law Journal*, Vol. 21, N° 1, 1992, pp. 91–103.

Gonzalez-Lebrero, Rodolfo A. 'La Comunidad Económica Europea y la navegación aérea.' *Derecho de los negocios*, Vol. 2, N° 12, Sept. 1991, pp. 17–28.

Kark, Andreas. 'Prospects for a liberalisation of the European air transport industry. A study of commercial air transport policy for the Community.' *European Competition Law Review*, Vol. 10, N° 2, 1989, pp. 377–406.

Kreis, Helmut W.R. and van der Woorde, Eddy. 'European air transport after 1992: Dergulation or re-regulation?.' *Antitrust Bulletin*, Vol. 37, N° 2, 1992, pp. 481–528.

Kuyper, P.J. 'Airline Fare-Fixing and Competition: An English Lord, Commission Proposals and US Parallels.' *Common Market Law Review*, Vol. 20, N° 2, August 1983, pp. 203–232.

—— (Note) 'Joined cases 209 to 213/84, Ministère public v. Lucas Asjes et al.' *Common Market Law Review*, Vol. 23, N° 3, Autumn 1986, pp. 661–681.

—— 'Legal problems of a Community transport policy with special reference to air transport.' *Legal Issues of European Integration*, N° 2, 1985, pp. 69–85.

Lange, D. and Weitbrecht, A. 'European Merger Control in the Air Transport Industry. Comments on the Delta Airline/Pan Am Decision of the European Commission.' *Zeitschrift für Luft- und Weltraumrecht*, Vol. 41, N° 1, March 1992, pp. 41–50.

Leaning, Marj P. 'Enlightened regulation of Computerized Reservations Systems requires a conscious balance between consumer protection and profitable airline marketing.' *Transportation Law Journal*, Vol. 21, N° 2, 1993, pp. 469–517.

Lenz, Carl Otto. 'Die Rechtsprechung des Gerichthofes der Europäischen Gemeinschaften zur Anwendung des EWG-Vertrages auf den Luftverkehr.' In: Jürgen F. Baur (Ed.), *Europarecht—Energierecht -Wirtschaftsrecht. Festschrift für Bodo Borner*. Carl Heymanns Verlag. Köln, 1992, pp. 277 et seq.

Lloyd's Maritime and Commercial Law Quarterly. 'Air and maritime transport and the EEC competition rules (Ministère Publique v. Asjes, Nouvelles Frontières et al.).' *Lloyd's Maritime and Commercial Law Quarterly*, 1987, pp. 14–17.

Mapelli, Enrique. 'La Comunidad Europea y el transporte aéreo. Conferencia pronunciada en Madrid el día 8 de marzo de 1993.' *Revista General de Derecho*, Valencia, Vol. 49, N° 585, June 1993, pp.6103–6112.

Masclet, Jean Claude. 'L'application des règles de concurrence du traité de Rome aux transports aériens.' In: *Recueil* Dalloz Sirey, N° 8, 23 February 1989, pp. 73–80.

Mazarella, David. 'The Integration of aviation law in the EC: teleological jurisprudence and the European Court of Justice.' *Transportation Law Journal*, Vol. 20, N° 2, 1992, pp. 353–372.

Merckx, Alfred L. 'Air fare fixing and the EEC competition rules.' *European Transport Law*, Vol. 21 N° 1, 1986. pp. 57 et seq.

Naveau, J. 'Aspects juridiques de la cooperation en transport aérien.' *European Transport Law*, Vol. 18, N° 2, 1983. pp. 218 et seq.

—— 'L'arrière plan international de l'application du Traité CEE au transport aérien européen.' *European Transport Law*, Vol. 21, N° 6, 1986, pp. 508 et seq.

Organisation for Economic Cooperation and Development. *Deregulation and Airline Competition*. OECD. Paris, 1988.

Quintana, Carlos Ignacio. 'La aplicación de las reglas de competencia del Tratado de Roma y la fijación de tarifas en los transportes aéreos.' *Revista de Instituciones Europeas*, 1988, pp. 501 et seq.

—— La aviación civil española ante el Derecho comunitario.' *Gaceta Jurídica de la CEE*, N° 68, Serie D–11, July 1989, pp. 194–227.

Rycken, Willem. 'European antitrust aspects of maritime and air transport (Part I).' *European Transport Law*, Vol. 22, N° 5, 1987, pp. 483–504.

Salzman, Alan. 'IATA, airline rate-fixing and the EEC competition rules.' *European Law Review*, 1977, pp. 409 et seq.

San Román, José Rubio and Zamora Cabot, Francisco Javier. 'Los sistemas informatizados de reservas (Computer Reservation Systems) en el contexto de las relaciones CE-EEUU.' *European Transport Law*, Vol. 27, N° 4, 1992, pp. 435–443.

Sedemund, Joachim and Montag, Frank. 'Liberalisierung des Luftverkehrs durch Europäisches Wettbewerbrecht.' *Neue Juristische Wochenschrift*, 1986, pp. 2146 et seq.

Slot, Piet Jan and Dagtoglou, Prodromos D. (Eds.). *Toward a Community Air Transport Policy*. Kluwer. Deventer-Boston, 1990.

Soames, Trevor and Ryan, Alan. 'Predatory Pricing in Air Transport.' *European Competition Law Review*, Vol. 15, N° 3, May–June 1994, pp. 151–164.

Strivens, R. and Weightman, E. 'The Air Transport Sector and the EEC Competition Rules in the light of the Ahmed Saeed Case.' *European Competition Law Review*, Vol. 10, N° 4, 1989, pp. 557–567.

Temple Lang, John. 'Air Transport in the EEC—Community Antitrust Law Aspects.' In Barry Hawk (Ed.), (1991) *Annual Proceedings of the Fordham Corporate Law Institute. EC and US Competition Law and Policy.* Transnational Juris Publications. New York, 1992, pp. 287–396.

Tosi, J.-P. 'L'actualité en droit aérien.' *European Transport Law*, Vol. 25, N° 6, 1990, pp. 816–830.

Tucci, Gianrocco. 'Regulation and 'contestability' in formulating an air transport policy for the European Communities.' *Rivista di Politica Economica* (Selected Papers. English Edition), Vol. 75, 3rd series, December 1985, pp. 219–239.

Tyrell, A. 'Evolution or revolution—A review of progress on the abolition of restriction on competition in the air transport sector.' *European Competition Law Review*, Vol. 2, N° 1, 1981, pp. 91–96.

van Bakelen, F.A. 'Het communautaire vervoerbestel zeevaart en luchtvaart.' *Ars Aequi*, May, 1989, pp. 417–427.

van Houtte, Ben. 'Relevant Markets in Air Transport.' *Common Market Law Review*, Vol. 27, N° 3, Autumn 1990, pp. 521–546.

—— 'Competition Aspects.' In H.A. Wassenbergh (Ed.), *External Aviation Relations of the European Community.* Kluwer. Deventer-Boston, 1992, pp. 21–29.

—— 'Community Competition Law in the Air Transport Sector: A Survey of the First Five Years.' *Air and Space Law*, Vol. 28, N° 2, April 1993, pp. 61–70 and N° 6, December 1993, pp. 275–287.

Vincent, M. 'Position de la Commission CEE. La politique commune du transport aérien.' *European Transport Law*, Vol. 21, N° 6, 1986. pp. 518 et seq.

Wheatcroft, S. and Lipman, G. *European Liberalisation and World Air Transport.* The Economist Intelligence Unit. London, 1990.

Zapico Landrove, Cora. 'La aplicación de las normas de competencia del Tratado CEE al transporte aéreo: Comentario de la Sentencia 'Saeed' del Tribunal de Justicia de las Comunidades Europeas de 11 de abril de 1989.' *La Ley, Suplemento Comunidades Europeas* N° 58, 31 July 1990.

Index